LEARN, TEACH... SUCCEED...

With **REA's MTEL** test prep, you'll be in a class all your own.

REA: THE LEADER IN TEACHER CERTIFICATION PREP **2nd Edition**

MTEL® GENERAL CURRICULUM (FIELD 03)

MASSACHUSETTS TESTS FOR EDUCATOR LICENSURE®

TestWare® Edition

Edited By

Audrey Friedman, Ph.D.

Research & Education Association

Visit our Educator Support Center: www.rea.com/teacher

Updates to the test and this book: www.rea.com/mtel.htm

Planet Friendly Publishing
✔ Made in the United States
✔ Printed on Recycled Paper
Text: 10% Cover: 10%
Learn more: www.greenedition.org

At REA we're committed to producing books in an Earth-friendly manner and to helping our customers make greener choices.

Manufacturing books in the United States ensures compliance with strict environmental laws and eliminates the need for international freight shipping, a major contributor to global air pollution.

And printing on recycled paper helps minimize our consumption of trees, water and fossil fuels. This book was printed on paper made with **10% post-consumer waste.** According to Environmental Defense's Paper Calculator, by using this innovative paper instead of conventional papers, we achieved the following environmental benefits:

Trees Saved: 7 • Air Emissions Eliminated: 1384 pounds
Water Saved: 1259 gallons • Solid Waste Eliminated: 408 pounds

For more information on our environmental practices, please visit us online at **www.rea.com/green**

The General Curriculum Test Objectives presented in this book were created and implemented by the Massachusetts Department of Elementary and Secondary Education and Pearson Education, Inc. For further information visit the MTEL website at *www.mtel.nesinc.com.*

Research & Education Association
61 Ethel Road West
Piscataway, New Jersey 08854
E-mail: info@rea.com

The Best Teachers' Test Preparation for the Massachusetts MTEL®
General Curriculum Test (03)
With TestWare® on CD-ROM

Printed in the United States of America

Library of Congress Control Number 20100926695

ISBN-13: 978-0-7386-0410-7
ISBN-10: 0-7386-0410-0

E10-0101

About the Editor

Dr. Audrey Friedman is a Lynch School of Education Associate Professor and Department Chair at Boston College. She received the Distinguished Faculty Award from Boston College in 2000-2001 and the Boston Higher Education Partnership Award in 2005. In 2009, Dr. Friedman was named Massachusetts Professor of the Year by the Carnegie Foundation for the Advancement of Teaching in recognition of her commitment to preparing the next generation of teachers. Dr. Friedman says that her ". . . most coveted award (2003) is the Mary Kaye Waldron Award, an honor awarded by undergraduates to faculty or an administrator 'who has worked to enhance student life at Boston College.' An elegant, crystal eagle, this symbol reminds me of just how fortunate I am that teaching is indeed an option."

Acknowledgments

We would like to thank REA's Larry B. Kling, Vice President, Editorial, for supervising development; Pam Weston, Vice President, Publishing, for setting the quality standards for production integrity and managing the publication to completion; John Paul Cording, Vice President, Technology, for coordinating the design, development, and testing of REA's TestWare®; Alice Leonard, Senior Editor, for coordinating new edition; Christine Reilley, Senior Editor, for project management and preflight editorial review; Diane Goldschmidt, Senior Editor, for post-production quality assurance; Heena Patel, software project manager, for her software testing efforts; and Christine Saul, Senior Graphic Artist, for cover design.

We gratefully acknowledge David M. Myton, Ph.D., Renay M. Scott, Ph.D., Karen Bondarchuck, M.F.A., John A. Lychner, Ph.D., Janet E. Rubin, Ph.D., Ellen R. Van't Hof, M.A., Nelson Maylone, Ph.D., and Ginny Muller, Ph.D., for providing foundational material for this book. We also thank Al Davis, M.A., M.S., for editing this book in accordance with the MTEL General Curriculum test objectives and Joan and Norman Levy for creating Practice Test 2.

We also gratefully acknowledge Kathy Caratozzolo of Caragraphics for page composition and typesetting, Julie Clark for technical and copyediting, and Stephanie Reymann for creating the Index.

About Research & Education Association

Founded in 1959, Research & Education Association is dedicated to publishing the finest and most effective educational materials—including software, study guides, and test preps—for students in middle school, high school, college, graduate school, and beyond.

REA's Test Preparation series includes books and software for all academic levels in almost all disciplines. Research & Education Association publishes test preps for students who have not yet completed high school, as well as for high school students preparing to enter college. Students from countries around the world seeking to attend college in the United States will find the assistance they need in REA's publications. For college students seeking advanced degrees, REA publishes test preps for many major graduate school admission examinations in a wide variety of disciplines, including engineering, law, and medicine. Students at every level, in every field, with every ambition can find what they are looking for among REA's publications.

REA's practice tests are always based upon the most recently administered exams and include every type of question that you can expect on the actual exams.

REA's publications and educational materials are highly regarded and continually receive an unprecedented amount of praise from professionals, instructors, librarians, parents, and students. Our authors are as diverse as the fields represented in the books we publish. They are well-known in their respective disciplines and serve on the faculties of prestigious high schools, colleges, and universities throughout the United States and Canada.

Today, REA's wide-ranging catalog is a leading resource for teachers, students, and professionals.

We invite you to visit us at *www.rea.com* to find out how "REA is making the world smarter."

Contents

MTEL General Curriculum

Introduction

Introduction

ABOUT THIS BOOK AND TestWare®

REA's *The Best Teachers' Test Preparation for the MTEL General Curriculum (03) Test* is a comprehensive guide designed to assist you in preparing to take this MTEL test. To help you to succeed in this important step toward your teaching career in Massachusetts schools, this test guide features:

- An accurate and complete overview of the *MTEL General Curriculum (03) Test*
- The information you need to know about how the exam works
- A targeted review of each subarea
- Tips and strategies for successfully completing standardized tests
- TestWare® on CD includes diagnostic tools to identify areas of strength and weakness
- Two full-length, true-to-format practice tests based on the most recently administered MTEL General Curriculum (03) Test
- Detailed explanations for each answer on the practice tests. These allow you to identify correct answers and understand not only why they are correct but also why the other answer choices are incorrect.

When creating this test prep, the authors and editors considered the most recent test administrations and professional standards. They also researched information from the

Massachusetts Department of Elementary and Secondary Education, professional journals, textbooks, and educators. The result is the best MTEL test preparation materials based on the latest information available.

ABOUT TEST SELECTION

The MTEL tests are conducted during morning and afternoon test sessions. Test sessions are four hours in length. However, the General Curriculum test is only given in the afternoon session. The afternoon session has a reporting time of 1:00 P.M. and ends at approximately 5:45 P.M. You may take both subtests or just one single subtest of the General Curriculum during the four hour session.

ABOUT THE MTEL GENERAL CURRICULUM TEST

The purpose of the MTEL General Curriculum (03) Test is to assess the knowledge and skills of prospective Massachusetts' teachers. Prospective teachers are required to take the MTEL General Curriculum Test. This test encompasses two subtests:

- The Multi-Subject subtest of language arts, history and social science, science and technology/engineering, and the integration of knowledge and understanding
- The mathematics subtest

What Does the Test Cover?

The following table lists the objectives used as the basis for the MTEL General Curriculum Test and the approximate number of questions in both subtests. A thorough review of all the specific skills is the focus of this book.

Test Overview Chart:

Multi-Subject Subtest

Subareas	Approximate Number of Multiple-Choice Items	Range of Objectives	Percent of Subtest	Number of Open-Response Items
Language Arts	18–20	01–05	30%	
History and Social Science	17–19	06–09	30%	
Science and Technology/ Engineering	17–19	10–14	30%	
Integration of Knowledge and Understanding		15	10%	1
Total	55			1

Mathematics Subtest

Subareas	Approximate Number of Multiple-Choice Items	Range of Objectives	Percent of Subtest	Number of Open-Response Items
Numbers and Operations	19–21	16–19	41%	
Functions and Algebra	10–12	20–22	22%	
Geometry and Measurement	8–10	23–24	18%	
Statistics and Probability	4–6	25–26	9%	
Integration of Knowledge and Understanding		27		1
Total	45			1

How Is the MTEL General Curriculum Test Scored?

Multiple-Choice Questions. Scoring of the multiple-choice questions is based strictly on the number of test questions answered correctly. You do not lose any additional points for wrong answers. Each multiple-choice question counts the same toward the total score.

Open-Response Questions

Open-response questions are scored holistically by two or more qualified educators. Scorers receive training in scoring procedures and are monitored for accuracy and consistency. Scorers are typically teachers, administrators, arts and science faculty, teacher education faculty, and other content specialists.

Scorers are trained to provide an overall judgment, not to indicate specific errors. A score is assigned based on a scale of various levels of performance from weak to strong. If a response is blank, unrelated to the assignment, illegible, or in a language other than the target language, no points will be given for it.

When Will I Receive My Score Report, and What Will It Look Like?

Reporting of Scores. Your scores will be mailed to you on the score date published at *www.mtel.nesinc.com/MA13_testdates.asp.*

Unofficial test scores are posted on the Internet at 5:00 P.M. Eastern Time on the score report dates listed on *http://www.mtel.nesinc.com/MA13_testdates.asp*. For each test date, the unofficial scores are kept on the Internet for approximately two weeks. You may only view these scores once during the posting period—for security reasons.

Can I Retake the Test?

Retaking a Test. If you wish to retake a test, you may do so at a subsequent test administration. Please consult the MTEL website at **www.mtel.nesinc.com** for information about test registration. The MTEL website also includes information regarding test retakes and score reports.

Who Administers the Test?

The MTEL is administered by the Massachusetts Department of Elementary and Secondary Education.

When and Where Is the Test Given? How Long Will It Take?

The MTEL is administered five times a year at eight locations across the state, as detailed in the MTEL Registration Bulletin. Additionally, on two of the eight test days, the MTEL is offered at seven out-of-state locations, provided that a minimum number of candidates register per area. To receive information on upcoming test dates and locations, you may contact the test administrator at:

Massachusetts Tests for Educator Licensure
Evaluation Systems
Pearson
P.O. Box 660
Amherst, MA 01004-9013
Telephone: 413-256-2892 or (866) 565-4894
Fax: 413-256-7077
Website: *www.mtel.nesinc.com*

The tests are scheduled to be completed within a maximum of four hours. Note that the MTEL General Curriculum is available on all test dates but is given only during the afternoon sessions.

HOW TO USE THIS BOOK AND TestWare®

When Should I Start Studying?

It is never too early to start studying for the MTEL General Curriculum Test. The earlier you begin, the more time you will have to sharpen your skills. Do not procrastinate! Cramming is not an effective way to study because it does not allow you the time you need to think about the content, review the content required in the objectives, and take the practice tests.

What Should I Study First?

We strongly recommend that you begin your preparation with the TestWare® tests. The software provides the added benefits of instant, accurate scoring and enforced time conditions.

What Do the Review Sections Cover?

The targeted review in this book is designed to help you sharpen the skills you need to approach the MTEL General Curriculum Test, as well as provide strategies for attacking the questions.

Each teaching area included in the MTEL General Curriculum Test is examined in a separate chapter. The skills required for all areas are extensively discussed to optimize your understanding of what the examination covers.

Your schooling has taught you most of the information you need to answer the questions on the test. The education classes you took should have provided you with the know-how to make important decisions about situations you will face as a teacher. The review sections in this book are designed to help you fit the information you have acquired into the objectives specified on the MTEL. Going over your class notes and textbooks together with the reviews provided here will give you an excellent springboard for passing the examination.

STUDYING FOR THE MTEL GENERAL CURRICULUM TEST

Choose the time and place for studying that works best for you. Some people set aside a certain number of hours every morning to study, while others prefer to study at night before going to sleep. Other people study off and on during the day—for instance, while waiting for a bus or during a lunch break. Only you can determine when and where your study time will be most effective. Be consistent and use your time efficiently. Work out a study routine and stick to it.

When you take the practice tests, simulate the conditions of the actual test as closely as possible. Turn off your television and radio, and sit down at a table in a quiet room, free from distraction. On completing a practice test, score it and thoroughly review the explanations to the questions you answered incorrectly; however, do not review too much at any one time. Concentrate on one problem area at a time by reviewing the question and explanation, and by studying the review in this guide until you are confident that you have mastered the material.

Keep track of your scores so you can gauge your progress and discover general weaknesses in particular sections. Give extra attention to the reviews that cover your areas of difficulty, so you can build your skills in those areas. Many have found the use of study or note cards very helpful for this review.

How Can I Use My Study Time Efficiently?

The following study schedule allows for thorough preparation for the MTEL General Curriculum Test. The course of study presented here is seven weeks, but you can condense or expand the timeline to suit your personal schedule. It is vital that you adhere to a structured plan and set aside ample time each day to study. The more time you devote to studying, the more prepared and confident you will be on the day of the test.

Study Schedule

Week	Activity
1	After having read this first chapter to understand the format and content of this exam, take the first practice test on the CD. It covers both subtests. The scores will indicate your strengths and weaknesses. Make sure you simulate real exam conditions when you take the tests. Afterward, score them and review the explanations, especially for questions you answered incorrectly. Use index cards to track the information about which you need to learn more.
2	Review the explanations for the questions you missed, and review the appropriate chapter sections. Useful study techniques include highlighting key terms and information, taking notes as you review each section, and putting new terms and information on your index cards to help retain the information.
3 & 4	Reread all your index cards, refresh your understanding of the objectives included in the exam; study the chapters in this book, especially those that cover the areas in which you feel weak; review your college textbooks, and read over notes you took in your college classes. This is also the time to consider any other supplementary materials that your counselor or the Massachusetts Department of Elementary and Secondary Education suggests. Review the department's Website at *http://www.mtel.nesinc.com*. Make additional notes as needed.
5	Begin to condense your notes and findings. A structured list of important facts and concepts, based on your index cards and the MTEL General Curriculum objectives, will help you thoroughly review for the test. Review the answers and explanations for any questions you missed.
6	Have someone quiz you using the index cards you have amassed. Take the second practice test on the CD, adhering to the time limits and simulated test day conditions.
7	Using all your study materials, review areas of weakness revealed by your score on the second set of practice tests. Then retake sections of the practice tests that are printed in this book, as needed.

TEST-TAKING TIPS

Although you may not be familiar with tests like the MTEL, this book will acquaint you with this type of exam and help alleviate your test-taking anxieties. By following the seven suggestions listed here, you can become more relaxed about taking the MTEL, as well as other tests.

Tip 1. Become comfortable with the format of the MTEL. When you are practicing, stay calm and pace yourself. After simulating the test only once, you will boost your chances of doing well, and you will be able to sit down for the actual MTEL with much more confidence.

Tip 2. Read all the possible answers. Just because you think you have found the correct response, do not automatically assume that it is the best answer. Read through each choice to be sure that you are not making a mistake by jumping to conclusions.

Tip 3. Use the process of elimination. Go through each answer to a question and eliminate as many of the answer choices as possible. If you can eliminate two answer choices, you have given yourself a better chance of getting the item correct, because only two choices are left from which to make your guess. Do not leave an answer blank. It is better to guess than not to answer a question on the MTEL test because there is no additional penalty for wrong answers.

Tip 4. Place a question mark in your answer booklet next to the answers you guessed, and then recheck them later if you have time.

Tip 5. Work quickly and steadily. You will have four hours to complete the test, so the amount of time you spend will depend upon whether you take both subtests in one test session. Taking the practice tests in this book or on the CD will help you learn to budget your precious time.

Tip 6. Learn the directions and format of the test. This will not only save time but also will help you avoid anxiety (and the mistakes caused by being anxious).

Tip 7. When taking the multiple-choice portion of the test, be sure that the answer oval you fill in corresponds to the number of the question in the test booklet. The multiple-choice test is graded by machine, and marking one wrong answer can throw off your answer key and your score. Be extremely careful.

THE DAY OF THE TEST

Before the Test

On the morning of the test, be sure to dress comfortably so you are not distracted by being too hot or too cold while taking the test. Plan to arrive at the test center early. This will allow you to collect your thoughts and relax before the test and will also spare you the anguish that comes with being late. You should check your MTEL Registration Bulletin to find out what time to arrive at the center.

What to Bring

Before you leave for the test center, make sure that you have your admission ticket. Your admission ticket lists your test selection, test site, test date, and reporting time. See the Test Selection *http://www.mtel.nesinc.com/MA13_whattobring.asp.*

You must also bring two pieces of personal identification. One must be a current, government-issued identification, in the name in which you registered, bearing your photograph and signature, and one additional piece of identification (with or without a photograph). If the name on your identification differs from the name in which you are registered, you must bring official verification of the change (e.g., marriage certificate, court order). Examples of acceptable government-issued documents would be: a driver's license, military identification; State ID; passport, or Resident Alien Card (often called a Green Card).

You must bring several sharpened No. 2 pencils with erasers, because none will be provided at the test center. If you like, you can wear a watch to the test center. However, you cannot wear one that makes noise, because it might disturb the other test takers. Dictionaries, textbooks, notebooks, calculators, cell phones, beepers, PDAs, scratch paper, listening and recording devices, briefcases, or packages are not permitted. Drinking, smoking, and eating during the test are prohibited. You may not bring any visitors, including relatives, children, and friends.

You may bring a water bottle into the testing room, as long as it is clear without a label but with a tight lid. During testing, you will have to store your bottle under your seat.

Security Measures

As part of the identity verification process, your thumbprint will be taken at the test site. Thumbprints will be used only for the purpose of identity verification. If you do not provide a thumbprint, you will not be permitted to take the test and you will not receive a refund or a credit for the fee paid.

Enhanced security measures, including additional security screenings, may be required by test site facilities. If an additional screening is conducted, only screened persons will be admitted to the test site. If you do not proceed through the security screening, you will not be allowed to test and you will not receive a refund or credit of any kind.

Late Arrival Policy

If you are late for a test session, you may not be admitted. If you are permitted to enter, you will not be given any additional time for the test session. You will be required to sign a statement acknowledging this.

If you arrive late and are not admitted, you will be considered absent and will not receive a refund or credit of any kind. You will need to register and pay again to test at a future administration.

Absentee Policy

If you are absent, you will not receive a refund or credit of any kind. You will need to register and pay again to test at a future administration.

A day of so before your scheduled test, be sure and check the MTEL website for any changes to the Test Site Rules. *http://www.mtel.nesinc.com/MA13_siterules.asp.*

During the Test

The MTEL General Curriculum Test is given in one sitting, with no breaks. However, during testing, you may take restroom breaks. Any time that you take for restroom breaks is considered part of the available testing time. Procedures will be followed to maintain test security. Once you enter the test center, follow all the rules and instructions given by the test supervisor. If you do not, you risk being dismissed from the test and having your score canceled.

When all the materials have been distributed, the test instructor will give you directions for completing the informational portion of your answer sheet. Fill out the sheet carefully, because the information you provide will be printed on your score report.

Once the test begins, mark only one answer per question, completely erase unwanted answers and marks, and fill in answers darkly and neatly.

AFTER THE TEST

When you finish your test, hand in your materials and you will be dismissed. Then, go home and relax—you deserve it!

MTEL General Curriculum

Review for Multi-Subject Subtest

CHAPTER

Language Arts

This chapter addresses the following: the history and structure of the English language; genres and selected literature from classical and contemporary periods in American literature; literary genres, elements, and techniques; various aspects of children's literature include genres, literary elements, and literary techniques; and the writing process and formal elements of writing and composition.

COMPETENCY 0001

Understand the history and structure of the English language.

History of the English Language: Major Developments

Speech developed between 100,000 and 20,000 BCE[1]. By the time period of 5000–3000 BCE, there was one common language, which we now call Proto-Indo-European (PIE). After many migrations, by 1000 BCE, a number of distinct Indo-European languages formed. After more migration and increased trading with Africa and Asia, there emerged one branch of the PIE tree by 0 CE: the Germanic language. Several characteristics differentiated Germanic language from other branches that broke away from Proto-Indo-European. The Germanic language placed accent or stress on the first syllable of a word (called Grimm's Law), inflected verbs only in the past and present tenses, and used the dental suffix "-ed" to form the past tense.

[1] The terms "Before Common Era (BCE)" and "Common Era (CE)" are being used in place of the traditional "Before Christ (BC) and Anno Domini (AD) to identify historical periods. The new terms are more inclusive and eliminate religious references.

After 0 CE, the Jutes, Saxons, and Angles, mercenaries that came from Denmark and what is now northern continental Germany brought with them their own dialects which fell within the Germanic branch of the Indo-European language family. Although writing was not common among these groups, the language had a Runic alphabet, called Futhroc.

By 600 CE the Germanic language began to differ somewhat from the continental German language because dialects had been intermingling for centuries in Briton away from the continent, therefore forming a new type of language. Additionally, Briton was Christianized around 600 CE and the missionaries brought the Latin alphabet with them. This new language is what scholars today consider to be Old English.

Wars led to changes in language. Viking invasions occurred around 800 CE, and the Danes invaded in the early 11th century. Old English was not very standardized and spellings were inconsistent (Example: "shield" could be spelled as "scyld," "scild," or "scield"). Although different dialects of Old English had been gaining strength, location and prominence caused the West Saxon dialect to become the dominant dialect evolving into what we today call Middle English.

There is much debate about when Middle English usage actually began, but generally scholars refer to Middle English as the language spoken after the Norman Conquest until the development of English as a full literary language during the sixteenth century. In 1066 CE, William the Conqueror brought troops from Normandy and succeeded in becoming the king of England (while also remaining the king of France). Thus for years, Norman French rulers dominated all spheres of society, including education, government, law, and the church. Latin and French became the languages of power, and English was left for the poor majority. There were many loanwords taken from French and Latin at this time, as seen in Geoffrey Chaucer's *Canterbury Tales*, which was written in the late 1330s in Middle English.

At the end of the 15th century, William Caxton brought standardization to English with the introduction of the printing press. This began the period we call Early Modern English (1500-1650 CE). During this time the English language changed tremendously. First there was a phonetic shift in the way that long vowels were pronounced in English. This was called the Great Vowel Shift. The language also became more standardized in the use of a more regular word order of subject-verb-object. Furthermore, greater trade with Asia Minor and the Middle East sparked an infusion of new vocabulary and the Renaissance in England returned to classical learning and the translation of many of the classic Latin texts into English. Shakespeare wrote during the late 1500s and early 1600s in Early Modern English, and in 1611 CE the King James Bible was written and was widely read. The *Bible* was still most often the only literature that the common people read, but now that the printing press had been introduced, many more people had access to books and therefore language.

By the 1700s, the English language was standardized and had become widely used. In this time of British Imperialism, English spread around the globe to places such as Australia, India, and South Africa through colonialism. There was a great deal of linguistic borrowing from languages around the world, and in the 19th and 20th centuries, the Scientific and Industrial Revolutions brought about the creation of technical vocabulary.

During the 18th–20th centuries, dictionaries and grammars gained much popularity with the growing belief that the English language had somehow been corrupted. Reformers called for a purer form of the language and generally fell into one of two groups: descriptivist, who wanted to describe language as it existed, and prescriptivist, who wanted to prescribe how language ought to be. One early work that was extremely popular was Samuel Johnson's *The Dictionary of the English Language.* The first writer to include quotations from other noteworthy authors to illustrate definitions, he took nine years to write his famous dictionary, which became the foundation of all subsequent dictionaries.

Linguists have been interested in the development of American English for centuries. Since the settlement of Jamestown in 1607, the English language changed drastically from its British origins, so much so that many scholars of the seventeenth century thought American and British English would diverge and eventually become two totally separate languages. Although the languages have not yet become totally separate, there is much variation between not only American/British English but also between types of English spoken within the United States. Scholars have also studied regional dialects and social and racial variations in language. Dictionaries such as DARE (Dictionary of American Regional English) are becoming more common.

Today as we study the history of language development and the current changes that the English language is facing, it is important to realize that the language is in a state of flux and always will be, no matter how much people try to impede its changes. Whether one views this state of flux as progress or as regression, language change is nonetheless a natural part of life and of history.

Major Linguistic Origins of the English Language

Most words in contemporary English language emerged from or are rooted in Latin, Greek, Anglo-Saxon, and Celtic languages. The following chart presents common roots, their language origin, and examples of contemporary words.

LATIN Roots, Suffixes, and Prefixes: Meaning in English, and Examples in the English Language

Root	Meaning in English	Examples in the English Language
ab, a, abs	away	abnormal, abrasion, abstract, aversion
ac, ak, acu	sharp or pointed	acid, acupuncture, acute
amic, imic	friend	amicable, inimical
ampl	ample	amplification
bell(i)	war	antebellum, bellicose, belligerent
ben	good, well	benefit, benignity
bi	two	binoculars, bigamy, biscotti
cap, cip, capt, cept	hold, take	capture, captive, recipient
capit, cipit	head	capital, chief, chef, decapitate
carn	flesh	carnival, carnivore
cid, caes, cis	cut	caesura, incisor
civ	citizen	civility
cogn	know	cognitive, cognizant, recognize
corpor	body	corporation, corpse
damn, demn	loss or harm	condemn, damnation
de	from, away from, removing	delete, demented
dent	tooth	dental, dentures
dexter	right	dexterity
dict	say, speak	dictation
duc, duct	lead	abduction, conductor, introduce
dulc	sweet	dulcet, dulcimer
dur	hard	durable, duration, duress, endure, obdurate

Root	Meaning in English	Examples in the English Language
emul	striving to equal, rivaling	emulation
equ, iqu	even, level	equal
ex, e, ef	from, out of	exclude, extrude, extend, efferent
exter, extra	outer	exterior
fac, fic, fact, fect	make	defect, factory, manufacture
fall, fell, fals	deceive	falsity, infallible
fend, fens	protect	defend, offense
fer	carry	reference, transfer
feroc	fierce	ferocity
germin	sprout	germination
glob	sphere	global, globule
grad, gred, gress	walk, step, go	grade, regress
grand	grand	grandiloquous
grav	heavy	gravity
hab, hib, habit, hibit	have	habit, prohibition
hibern	wintry	hibernation
ign	fire	igneous, ignition
in (1), **im**	in, on	invite, incur, intend
in (2), **il**, **im**, **ir**	in, un- (negation)	**il**licit, **im**possible, **in**imical, **ir**rational
infra	under	infrastructure
inter	among, between	intermission, intercollegiate, intercourse
intra	within	intracollegiate
jac, ject	cast, throw	eject, interject, ejaculate, trajectory
jung, junct	join	conjunction, juncture
jus, jur, judic	law, justice	justice, jury, judge
juxta	beside, near	juxtaposition
lacer	tear	laceration
lacrim	cry, tears	lacrimal, lacrimous
laud, laus	praise	laud

→

Root	Meaning in English	Examples in the English Language
liber	free	liberation
liter	letter	alliteration, illiterate, literacy, literal, obliterate
loqu, **locut**	speak	allocution, eloquent
luc	bright, light	Lucifer (bearer of light)
magn	great, large	magnanimous, magnificent
mal	bad, wretched, evil	malicious, malign, malfeasance, malodorous
melior	better	amelioration
mill	thousand	millennium, million
min	less, smaller	minority, minuscule
mitt, **miss**	send	intermittent, transmission
moll	soft	emollient, mollify
mort	death	immortal, mortality
mut	change	mutation
narr	tell	narrative
nasc, **nat**	born	nascent, native
nihil	nothing	annihilation
noct	night	nocturnal
nomin	name	nomination
non	not	nonentity
nunci	announce	pronunciation
nupti	pertaining to marriage	nuptial
ob,	against	obstinate, ostentatious, obstreperous
ocul	eye	ocular
omni	all	omnipotence
oner	burden	onerous, onus
ossi	bone	ossification
ov	egg	ovary, ovule

Root	Meaning in English	Examples in the English Language
quadr	four	quadrangle, quadrillion
quasi	as if	quasi-reflective
quer, quisit	search, seek	inquisition, query, question, quest
quint	fifth	quintile
quot	how many, how great	quota, quotient
radic	root	eradicate, radical
ram	branch	ramification
ranc	rancidness, grudge, bitterness	rancid, rancor
re, red	again, back	recede
retro	backward, behind	retrograde, retrospective
rid, ris	laugh	derision, ridicule
rog	ask	interrogation
sacr, secr	sacred	consecrate, sacrament
sagac	wise	sagacity
salv	save	salvation
sanct	holy	sanctify, sanctuary
sanguin	blood	sanguine
sci	know	prescient, science
sec, sect, seg	cut	secant, section, segment
sequ, secut	follow	consecutive, sequence
sex, se	six	semester, sexangle, sexennium
sicc	dry	desiccation
sinistr	left	minstrel
sol	sun	solar
solv, solut	solvent	solution, solvency
somn	sleep	insomnia
tac, tic	be silent	reticent, tacit
tang, ting, tact,	touch	contact, tangent
tempor	time	temporary, temporal

Root	Meaning in English	Examples in the English Language
ten, tin, tent	hold	continent, tenacious
tend, tens	stretch	extend, extension
termin	end	determine, termination
terr	dry land	terrace, terrain, terracotta
tex, text	weave	texture
trah, tract	pull	subtrahend, tractor
trem	tremble	tremor
uber	over	exuberant
ultra	beyond	ultrasonic
un, uni	one	unary, union
und	wave	undulate
uxor	wife	uxoricide
vac	empty	vacancy, vacation, vacuum, vacuole
vad, vas	go	evade, pervasive
vell, vuls	pull	convulsion
ven, vent	come	advent, convention
vend	sell	vendor, vending
vener	respectful	veneration, venerable
ver	true	verify, verity
verb	word	verbal, verbatim, verbosity
vert, vers	turn	convert, inversion, invert, vertical
vesper	evening, western	vespers
vet	forbid	veto
veter	old	inveterate, veteran
vi	way	deviate, obvious, via
vid, vis	see	video, vision
vinc, vict	conquer	invincible, victory
viscer	organs of the body cavity	visceral
vit	life	vital

Root	Meaning in English	Examples in the English Language
viv	live	revive, survive, vivid
voc	voice	vocal, vocation, provocative
volv, volut	roll	convolution, revolve
vor, vorac	swallow	devour, voracious
vulner	wound	vulnerable

GREEK Roots, Suffixes, and Prefixes: Meaning in English, and Examples in the English Language

Root	Meaning in English	Examples in the English Language
a, an	not, without	atypical, ahistorical
aer, aero	air, atmosphere	aeronautics, aerosol
aesth	feeling, sensation	aesthetics
amphi	around, both, on both sides	amphibian, amphitheatre, amphibious
ana	again, against, back	anomaly, anaphylaxis
ant, anti	against, opposite, preventive	antibiotic, antipodes
archaeo, archeo	ancient	archaeology or archeology, archaic
arthr, arthro	joint	arthritis, arthropod
astr, astro	star, star-shaped	astronomy
aut, auto	self; directed from within	automobile, autonomy
baro	weight, pressure	barometer, barograph
basi	at the bottom	basic, basis
bibl	book	bibliography,
bi(o)	life	biology, biography
blast	embryo, bud, cell with nucleus	blast
botan-	plant	botany
brachi(o)	arm	brachial artery, brachiosaurus
bronch	windpipe	bronchitis

Root	Meaning in English	Examples in the English Language
dactyl	finger	dactylology, pterodactyl
deca, dec	ten	decade
delta	triangular	deltoid
dendr, dendro	resembling a tree	dendrite
derm	skin	dermatitis
di, dy, dipl	two	dicot
dog, dox	opinion, teaching	dogmatic, orthodox
dys	badly, ill	dysentery
eco	house	ecology, economics, ecumenism
ecto	outside	ectoderm
ego	self, I (first person)	egocentric
eme	vomit	emetic
en, em	in	emphasis
endo	inside	endocrine, endothermic
epi, ep	upon	epicenter, epoch
epistem	knowledge or science	epistemic
erythr(o)	red	erythrocyte
eso	within	esoteric
ethn	people, race, tribe, nation	ethnic, ethnicity
etym(o)	true	etymology
eu	well	euphoria
galact	milk	galactic
gastr	stomach	gastric, gastroenterologist
ge(o)	earth	geology
graph	draw, write	graphic, graphology, autograph
haem(o)	blood	hemophilia
hapl(o)	simple	haploid
heli(o)	sun	helium, heliotrope
hemi	half	hemisphere

Root	Meaning in English	Examples in the English Language
hept	seven	heptagon, heptathlon
heter(o)	different, other	heterogeneous
heur	find	heuristic
homeo	like	homeostasis
hydr	wet	hydrolysis
hyp(o)	under	hypothermia
ichth	fish	ichthyology
ide(o)	idea	ideology, ideologue
idi(o)	personal	idiosyncrasy
is(o)	equal, the same	isomers, isometric
kil(o)	thousand	kilogram, kilometer, kilobyte
kine	movement, motion	telekinesis, kinetic energy, kinesthetic
klept	steal	kleptomania
kudo	glory	kudos
leuc(o), leuk(o)	white	leucocyte
lip(o)	fat	lipid, liposuction
macro	long, large	macron, macroeconomics
meg	great, large	megaphone
melan	black, dark	Melanesia, melanoma
mening	membrane	meningitis
mes	middle	mesolithic, Mesozoic
meter, metr	measure	metric, thermometer
meta	above, among, beyond	metaphysics
micr(o)	small	microphone, microscope
mis	hate	misogyny, misanthrope
mne	memory	mnemonic
mon(o)	one	monolith, monotone, monism
morph	form, shape	morpheme, anthropomorphic, morphology
palae, pale	ancient, old	paleontology

→

Root	Meaning in English	Examples in the English Language
par(a)	beside, near	parallel, parameter
ped	child	pediatric
penia	deficiency	leucopenia
pent	five	pentagon
peri	around	perimeter, periscope
phag	eat	sarcophagus
phalang	close formation of troops	phalange
pher	bear, carry	pheromone
philia	love, friendship	philanthropy
phob(ia)	fear	hydrophobia
phon(o)	sound	microphone, phonograph
phyll	leaf	chlorophyll
platy	flat, broad	platypus
pleth	full	plethora
plex	interwoven	complex
pneu	air, lung	pneumatic
pod-	foot	podiatry, tripod
pol	pole	dipole
polem	war	polemic
poly	many	polygon
pro	before, in front of	proponent
pseud(o)	false	pseudonym
pter	wing, fern	helicopter
pyr(o)	heat, fire	pyromaniac, pyrotechnics
rhe-	flow	rheostat
rhin-	nose, snout	rhinoplasty
rhiz-	root	rhizome
rhomb-	spinning	rhombus
tax-	arrangement, order	taxonomy

Root	Meaning in English	Examples in the English Language
techn-	technique	technology
tel-	far, end	telephone, telescope, telegram
teleo-	complete	teleology
tetr-	four	tetrahedron
than	death	euthanasia
the(o),	god	theology
therm	heat	thermometer
tri	three	triad, tripod
trop	turning	tropic
troph	feed, grow	autotroph, heterotroph
tympan	drum	tympanic
xanth	yellow	xanthophyll
xen	foreign	xenophobia
xer	dry	xerography
xyl	wood	xylophone
zo	animal, living being	protozoa, zoo, zoology
zyg	yoke	heterozygous, zygote
zym	ferment	enzyme

ANGLO-SAXON Suffixes and Prefixes: Meaning in English, and Examples in the English Language

	Meaning in English	Examples in the English Language
-dom	condition of	boredom, freedom
-ed	past tense	hopped, jumped, skipped
-en	made of or to make	wooden, tighten
-er, -or	person connected with or comparative	crooner, smarter, suitor
-ery	related to, quality, place where	Imagery, refinery, pottery

	Meaning in English	Examples in the English Language
-est	superlative	kindest, mildest
-fore-	before, earlier	foreshadow, foreground
-ful	full of	beautiful, fruitful
-hood	state of or condition of	boyhood, neighborhood
-ion, -ation, -sion, -tion	act or state of	action, determination, apprehension, intention
-ing	action or process	crying, singing
-ish	relating to or characteristic of	childish, fiendish
-less	without	careless, motionless
-ly	characteristic of	lovely, genuinely
mid-	middle	midway, midland
-ness	state or condition of	kindness, goodness
over-	too much, above	overzealous, overhead
-s, -es	plural, more than one	hats, boxes, sundries
-ship	condition of or skill	friendship, kinship
-some	characterized by a quality	winsome, handsome
un-	not, opposite	unlock, undo
under-	too little, below	underground, underfed
-y	characterized by/like	cloudy, fishy

Fundamental Language Structures

Linguistics

Linguistics is the science or study concerned with developing models of linguistic knowledge. The major core of theoretical linguistics includes phonology, morphology, syntax, and semantics. Phonetics, psycholinguistics, and sociolinguistics are usually excluded from the core components.

Linguistic Terms:

- *base word*: stand alone linguistic unit that cannot be deconstructed or broken down into smaller words, Example: *dog, house*
- *compound word*: two or more base words connected to form a new word, Example: *doghouse*

- *contraction*: shortened form of two words in which one or more letters have been deleted and replaced by an apostrophe. Example: *It's* = *It is*

- *etymology*: history or origin of a word

- *grapheme*: letter or letters that constitute a phoneme

- *heteronyms*: words that are spelled the same but differ in pronunciation and meaning

- *root word*: word from which another word is developed. Example: *symbol* is a root word for *symbolism, symbolize, symbolic, symbolical, symbolist, symbolistical, symbolizer, symbology, symbologist, symbolically, symbolicalness, symbolics*

- *syllabication*: the breaking down of words into each uninterrupted unit of spoken language

Morphology is the identification, analysis, and description of the structure of words.

- A *morpheme* is the smallest structural unit with meaning.

- A *lexeme* is the different forms a phoneme can take; *sit, sat, sitting* are all forms of the same lexeme.

Types of Morphemes

- *Free Morphemes* are units that stand alone like *ditch* and *dog* or can appear with other lexemes like *dog house*.

- *Bound Morphemes* appear with other morphemes to form a lexeme. These are usually suffixes and prefixes. Example: "un," "able," "non." Example: *unhappy*.

- *Derivational Morphemes* add to a word to create another word. Example: Add "ment" to *state* to create *statement*. These morphemes carry semantic information.

- *Inflectional Morphemes* change the function of a word, such as in number, tense, etc. creating a new word. Example: Add "s" to *cat* to create the plural, *cats* or "ed" to *hint* to create the past tense *hinted*. Inflectional morphemes carry grammatical information.

- *Allomorphs* are variants of the same morpheme. Example: the sound denoting the past tense can be "*t*," "*d*," or "*td*."

Phonology (from the Greek *phōnō* "voice, sound" and *lógos*, "word, speech, subject of discussion") is the systematic use of sound to encode meaning in any spoken human language.

- A *phone* is a speech sound.
- A *phoneme* is the smallest linguistically distinctive unit of sound. Example: /d/ sound in *d*ig and *d*rill. Phonemes have no semantic content.
- An *allophone* is one of several similar speech sounds that belong to the same phoneme. Example: *night rate* with a space or *nitrate* without a space.

Phonetics is the science of speech sounds. It deals extensively with the minute differences in sounds and the symbols used to represent these sounds. Phonetics is concerned with the physical apparatus involved in actually making the sound: the control and flow of breath, placement of the lips, tongue, and teeth, etc.

Phonics is a term that describes the part of phonetics applied to the teaching of reading. Phonics is concerned with sounds of word elements only to the extent that knowing these sounds aids in word recognition and subsequently reading. Phonics is also a method of teaching beginners to read using the phonetics of letters, groups of word, and syllables.

Phonics Patterns: Vowels

- *Short vowels* are the five single letter vowels, *a*, *e*, *i*, *o*, and, *u* when they produce the sounds /a/ as in *cat*, /e/ as in *bet*, /i/ as in *sit*, /o/ as in *hot*, and /u/ as in *cup*. The term "short vowel" does not really mean that these vowels are pronounced for a particularly short period of time, but they are not diphthongs like the long vowels.
- *Long vowels* are synonymous with the names of the single letter vowels, such as /a/ in *baby*, /e/ in *meter*, /i/ in *tiny*, /o/ in *broken*, and /u/ in *humor*. The way that educators use the term "long vowels" differs from the way in which linguists use this term. In classrooms, long vowel sounds are taught as being "the same as the names of the letters."

- *Schwa,* a type of reduced vowel, is the third sound that most of the single vowel spellings can produce. The *schwa* is an indistinct sound of a vowel in an unstressed syllable, represented by the linguistic symbol ə. /ə/ is the sound made by the *o* in *lesson*. Schwa is a vowel pattern that is not always taught to elementary school students because it is difficult to understand. However, some educators make the argument that schwa should be included in primary reading programs because of its importance in reading English words.

- *Barred i vowel* is the sound that /i/ makes in the word *medicine*. It is represented by /ɨ/.

- *Closed syllables* are syllables in which a single vowel letter is followed by a consonant. In the word *button*, both syllables are closed syllables because they contain single vowels followed by consonants. Therefore, the letter *u* represents the short sound /u/. (The *o* in the second syllable makes the /ə/ sound because it is an unstressed syllable.)

- *Open syllables* are syllables in which a vowel appears at the end of the syllable. The vowel will say its long sound. In the word *basin*, *ba* is an open syllable and therefore says /ba/.

- *Diphthongs* are linguistic elements that fuse two adjacent vowel sounds. English has four common diphthongs. The commonly recognized diphthongs are /au/, and /oy/. Three long vowels are also considered to be diphthongs, /aw/, /ou/ and /ew/, which partly accounts for the reason they are considered "long."

- *R-controlled vowels* occur when an *r* follows a vowel, modifying that vowel's sound, for example, *a* followed by *r* as in *arms* has neither the short sound of *a* as in *apple* or the long sound of *a* as in *ale*.

- *Vowel digraphs* are those spelling patterns wherein two letters are used to represent the vowel sound. The *ai* in *sail* is a vowel digraph. Because the first letter in a vowel digraph sometimes says its long vowel sound, as in *sail.* Other digraphs include /ea/, /oa/, /ay/, and /ee/.

- *Consonant-E* spellings are those wherein a single vowel letter, followed by a consonant and the letter *e* makes the long vowel sound. Examples of this include *bake*, *theme*, *hike*, *cone*, and *cute*. (The *ee* spelling, as in *meet* is sometimes considered part of this pattern.)

Phonics Patterns: Consonants

- *Consonant digraphs* are those spellings wherein two letters are used to represent a consonant phoneme. The most common consonant digraphs are *ch-*, *ph-*, *sh-*, *th-*, *wh-*, *-ch, -ck, -sh, -tch,* and *-th*. Letter combinations like *wr* for /r/ and *kn* for /n/ are also consonant digraphs, although these are sometimes considered patterns with "silent letters."

Semantics

Semantics is the study or science of meaning in language. Semantic information addresses meaning in a variety of ways.

Vocabulary

Understanding vocabulary on specific, functional, and conceptual levels reflects an ability to understand semantic information.

- *Specific* understanding refers to the literal definition of the word. Example: I *run* twenty miles every day; in this sentence "run" is a verb that means "to move swiftly so that both feet leave the ground."
- *Functional* understanding refers to the ability to use a word in writing and in speech.
- *Conceptual* understanding refers to the ability to understand the word in a variety of contexts and syntactical forms. Example: There was a *run* on the bank. He knows how to *run* a campaign. I have a *run* in my stockings. The river *runs* through the canyon. He *runs* the printing press. The *run* of fabric is damaged. There are almost 100 ways the word *run* can be used.
- *Polysemy* is when one word has many meanings. *Run* is such a word.

Semantic information includes not only understanding the mean of a word but other meanings that relate to the word.

- *Antonym* is a word that means the opposite of a word. Example: Possible antonyms for the word *hot* include *cold, frigid, icy,* and *freezing.*

- *Synonym* is a word that means the same or almost the same as another word. Example: Possible synonyms for the word *hot* including *burning, boiling, ardent, feverish, scorching,* and *torrid.*

- *Homonyms* or *homophones* are words that sound alike but have different meanings. Example: *there, there,* and *they're.* Sometimes, homonyms can also be spelled the same. Example: *bark* of a dog and *bark* of a tree.

Semantic Shifts are ways meaning changes.

- *Amelioration* is when a word's original meaning becomes improved or enhanced. Example: The word *sophisticated* derives from the Old French word *sophistrie*, which originally meant contaminated or unnatural or the more current word *sophistry*, which still means specious of fallacious reasoning. The current meaning of *sophisticated* means cosmopolitan, classy or discriminating, demonstrating that the meaning has improved or been enhanced.

- *Deterioration* or *pejoration* is when a word's original meaning is diminished or lessened. Example: The meaning of the word *villain,* changed from being an inhabitant of a village to meaning a scoundrel.

- *Expansion* of a word means that the range of the word's meaning increases over time. Example: The word *arrive* derives from Latin *arrivare*, which originally comes from ad *ripam*, which means at the shore. Currently *arrive* means to reach a destination, achieve success or take place.

- *Restriction* is the opposite of expansion as the range of the word's meaning diminishes. Example: The word *meat* comes from the Middle English *mete*, which generally meant food. Now *meat* means edible flesh.

Metaphorical Changes

- Word meanings can change metaphorically. Example: *Light* can be a metaphor for *hope, heaven, truth,* or *understanding.*

- A euphemism is the substitution of a more agreeable word for one that is offensive. Example: *a reduction in force (RIF)* is a euphemism for being fired, let go, or laid off; *termination* can be a euphemism for murder; *ethnic cleansing* is a euphemism for genocide.

Syntax and Syntactical Features

Syntax is the study of the principles and rules for constructing sentences in natural language. Syntax also refers directly to the rules and principles that govern the sentence structure of any individual language. There are several theories that address the study of syntax.

Generative Grammar assumes that language is a structure of the human mind and that there are rules that can be used to produce or create any sentence. Pioneered by Noam Chomsky, this kind of grammar focuses on the form of a sentence rather than how it functions as communication. Chomsky's view is that all language has certain structures in common. Example: Lewis Carroll's "The Jabberwocky" presents an array of inane and made-up words, but because of syntax and rules of generative grammar, the reader is able to identify the purpose of the words, even though the reader does not know the meaning of the words. "Twas brillig, and the slithy toves. Did gyre and gimble in the wabe; All mimsy were the borogoves, And the mome raths outgrabe." Although the reader does not know the meaning of "*brillig, slity, toves, gimble, wabe*," etc., the reader does have a sense of the function of each word in the phrases and sentences and can answer questions based on this understanding. Example: What did the "slithy toves" do? They "Did gyre and gimble in the wabe."

Parts of Speech and Sentence Structures

Syntactic Terms are generally called *parts of the speech*. The following list, although not exhaustive, provides the most common parts of speech, their definitions, and examples.

Adjectives are words that modify a person, place, thing, or idea. Adjectives are generally used in four different ways:

- *Attributive* adjectives modify or are attributed to the noun they modify. Example: *angry* mob
- *Predicative* adjectives are linked by a linking mechanism to the noun or pronoun they modify. Example: The children are *quiet.* Also called subject complement.

- *Absolute* adjectives typically modify either the subject or whatever noun or pronoun they are closest to. Example: *Angry* about losing the game, the boy trudged home.
- **Substantive** adjectives act almost as nouns. Example: "The *meek* shall inherit the Earth."

Adverbs are words that modify any part of speech (sentence, clause, phrase, verb, or adjective) except for a noun.

- Adverbs of manner answer the question "How?" by modifying verbs or adjectives.

  These often either begin with the prefix *a-* (Example: *afloat*) or end in the suffixes *-ly* (Example: *suddenly*) and *-wise* (Example: *clockwise*). Example: *surprisingly* simple

- Comparative and superlative adverbs indicate the degree to which something occurs or is true. Example: He studies *harder* than his peers.
- Conjunctive adverbs can be used to join two clauses together. Example: She has bruised her foot; *consequently* she won't be able to race today.

An **appositive** is a noun or phrase that renames or clarifies the noun next to it. It must always be separated from the rest of the sentence by commas. Example: Chess, *the ancient game of strategy*, is one of the world's most popular games.

An **article** is a word that precedes a noun to indicate the type of reference or meaning made by the noun. An article often offers specific information about range or volume. There are three types of articles:

- A *definite article* is used before either a singular or plural noun to refer to specific members of the group represented by the noun. Example: *The* zamboni resurfaced the ice rink.
- An *indefinite article* (*a* or *an*) is used before a singular noun that refers to any member of the group referenced by the noun. Example: *a* haunted house
- A *zero article* is the absence of an article in contrast to the presence of one. Example: Do you like fondue?

An **auxiliary verb** is a verb preceding a main verb for some kind of added emphasis. Auxilliary verbs impact language in five ways:

- *Passive voice* occurs when the auxiliary verb *be* is used with a past participle to indicate that some event happened but not who or what caused the event. Example: A politician's apology: It is unfortunate that people *were* hurt.
- *Progressive aspect* is formed when the auxiliary verb *am* is used with a present participle to indicate that the speaker is engaging in a specified action at the exact moment of speaking. Example: I *am* packing my bags and leaving town!
- *Perfect aspect* occurs when the auxiliary verb *have* is used with a past participle to indicate that an event in the past is still happening or has some connection to the present. Example: Brianna *has* lapsed in her study habits.
- *Modal verbs* can never be used as main verbs and must always function as an auxiliary verb. They express the speaker's opinion. There are ten modal verbs: *can, could, may, might, ought, shall, should, will, would,* and *must.* Example: We *shall* overcome.
- *Dummy auxiliary* refers to the insertion of *do* into a sentence to make it a question, or negation or to add emphasis. Example: *Do* you understand? You *do* not understand. You *do* understand.

A **clause** is a group of words that includes a subject and a predicate. A subset of clauses, dependent clauses, cannot function alone and must be part of a larger sentence. There are three types of dependent clauses:

- *Noun clauses* are those in which a noun is replaced with a dependent clause. Example: *What happened* isn't important.
- *Adjective clauses* are dependent clauses that modify a noun. Example: The squirrel *I observed* stashed nuts.
- *Adverb clauses* are dependent clauses that modify the entire main clause. Example: *When the crumpets arrive*, tea will be served.

Comparative refers to an adjective or adverb that modifies by making a statement about quantity, quality, degree, or grade. The comparative is used with a subordinating conjunction like *than* or *as . . . as*. Example: *As rough as* sandpaper.

- *Null comparative* occurs when no subordinating conjunction is used, so it is unclear to what standard the subject is being compared. Example: Sun Shine Sunscreen works *better*!

A **complement** is a word, phrase, or clause that is needed in the predicate of a particular sentence to complete its meaning. Example: The zoo is *carefully maintained.*

A **compound adjective** is a noun modifier created by combining two separate adjectives into one. The adjectives are separated by a hyphen, and there is no hyphen between the compound adjective and the noun. Example: A *well-maintained* bridge.

A **compound noun** is a noun formed by the combination of two nouns. Example: *doghouse.* There are four types of compound nouns:

- *Endocentric*, in which the first portion denotes a specific type of the word represented by the second portion. Example: *backboard*
- *Exocentric*, in which the words together describe an unexpressed idea. Example: *bittersweet*
- *Copulative*, in which the words together describe a new idea. Example: *rundown*
- *Oppositional*, in which each element describes a different aspect of the same subject. Example: *meatlover*

Conjugation is the creation of derived forms of a verb, adjective, or noun based on person, number, tense, gender (in some languages), and other factors. Example:

I *scream.*

You (singular) *scream.*

She, he or it *screams*.

We *scream*.

You (plural) *scream*.

They *scream*.

A **conjunction** is a word that connects two words, phrases, or clauses. There are three types of conjunctions:

- *Coordinating conjunctions* join two words or phrases of equal significance. They include *for, and, nor, but, or, yet,* and *so.* Example: Christy and Colleen *are* roommates.
- *Correlative conjunctions* are two words that work to coordinate two words or phrases. Example: *Both* Christy *and* Colleen hope to be doctors.
- *Subordinating conjunctions* introduce and connect a dependent clause. They include *after, although, if, unless, so that, therefore,* and *because.* Example: You cannot have dessert *unless* you eat all of your dinner.

Dangling modifier refers to a mistake made by an author who places a modifier in a sentence so that it seems to modify a different word than intended. Example: I saw the electronics store *walking through the mall.*

Declension is a change in a noun, pronoun, or adjective reflecting number, gender, or case. It is far more prevalent in European languages than in English; English words only decline to indicate number as singular or plural. Example: I had to return my old library *books* before I could check out a new *book*.

An **expletive** is a word that is considered to be filler or padding in a sentence. They are often necessary grammatically, but contribute nothing to the meaning of a sentence. Example: It is *so* sunny outside!

Function words are those words that mean very little by themselves but which structure a sentence or express relationships of words within a sentence. Appositions, articles, auxiliary verbs, conjunctions, expletives, interjections, and pronouns are examples of function words. Function words are the opposite of content words like nouns, verbs, adjectives, and adverbs. Example: *The* apple pie *and* brownies are delicious!

Gender is the system used in many languages besides English, particularly Indo-European languages, in which words are assigned male, female, and sometimes neuter genders. Adverbs or adjectives are inflected differently to accommodate the gender of a specific noun in a sentence.

A **gerund** is a form of a verb ending with the suffix *-ing*. The gerund often looks exactly like the present participle of the verb, but it functions as a noun in a sentence. Gerunds can be subjects, direct objects, and objects of prepositions. Example: The girls love *shopping* in the city.

The **infinitive** is the most basic form of a verb. In English, this can be with or without the particle *to*. Example: *find* and *to find.*

Measure words, also known as numeral classifiers, are words that are used with a number to express the count of an item.

- Some measure words are fully independent grammatical particles. These types of words are rare in English and more common in Asian languages. Example: The cowboy rounded up eighty *head* of cattle.
- Most English measure words are actually units of measurement. Example: three *loaves* of French bread

A **noun** is a part of speech that names a person, place, thing, or idea. Nouns can exist in the subject and predicate of a sentence or in a prepositional phrase. There are many more specific distinctions between nouns:

- *Proper nouns* are nouns that represent words that are specific entities. They are often capitalized. They differ from *common nouns*, which refer to an entire group of similar things. Example: *Bermuda, John, United States of America*
- *Uncountable nouns* are nouns, which cannot be quantified, unlike countable nouns. Example: *laundry*
- *Collective nouns* refer to groups, even when singular. Example: The *board* of the company voted to sell shares of controlling stock.

An **object** is a noun in the predicate of a sentence that relates to the action of the verb. There are three types of objects:

- *Direct objects* are the immediate recipients of the action of the verb. Example: I washed the *towel.*
- An *indirect object* is a secondary recipient of a verb's action. Example: She showed *me* her new dress.

- A *prepositional object* is an object at the end of a prepositional phrase. Example: We put the pan in the *oven*.

A **part of speech** is a classification of words determined by their function within a sentence. Example: *nouns, pronouns, adjectives, verbs, adverbs, prepositions, conjunctions,* and *interjections*. Most of the terms defined in this list are parts of speech.

A **participle** is a form of a verb that functions independently as an adjective. Participles can end in *-ing* (present participles). *Blowing* in her face, the wind felt *refreshing*. Participle can also assume the past tense of the verb. Example: We ate *baked* beans.

A **particle** is a catch-all phrase for words that do not fit within traditional grammatical classifications. Example: *not* and *to* (as in the infinitive of a verb, not as a preposition).

Person is a language's way of referencing participants in an event described in a sentence through personal pronouns. In English, there are three persons:

- *First person* refers to the speaker. Example: *I, we*
- *Second person* refers to the listener. Example: *you*
- *Third person* refers to another party. Example: *he, she, it, they*

A **phrase** is a group of words that function as a unit in a sentence. There are several possible types of phrases:

- Adjective phrase begins with an adjective. Example: *speedy rabbit.*
- *Adverbial phrase* begins with an adverb. Example: *truly unexpectedly*
- *Noun phrase* begins with a noun. Example: *Queen of hearts*
- *Prepositional phrase* is composed of a preposition and an object. Example: *to the circus*
- *Verb phrase* begins with a verb. Example: *Expect the worst.*

A **phrasal verb** is the joining of a verb with a preposition, adverb, or both so that they form a complete unit within the sentence. Example: *Swim underwater, clean up.*

Plural is a form of a noun referencing either zero or more than one of the items in the group known by that noun. Example: The recipe calls for two *cups* of sugar but no *eggs*.

The **predicate**, also known as verb phrase is the major part of any sentence containing the verb. It modifies the other main part of the sentence, the subject. It must include a verb, but it can also include various other parts of speech like adjectives, adverbs, and others. Example: She *napped in the blue chair.*

A **predicative** is a part of the predicate of a sentence that gives additional information after the verb. There are two types of predicative:

- *Adjectival predicative* occurs when an adjective follows the verb. Example: Dana looks *glamorous*.
- *Nominal predicative* occurs when a noun or pronoun follows the verb. Example: Carly lost her *phone*.

A **preposition** is the first element of a prepositional phrase. Prepositions include *to, of, from, under, above, around, through, with, in*, and many other words. These words indicate the relationship between the other parts of the sentence and the prepositional object. Prepositions can modify verbs and nouns and complement verbs, nouns, adjectives, and other prepositions. Example: Let's ban Max *from* our room.

A **personal pronoun** is a generic substitute for animate proper or common nouns. The three most common types of personal pronouns are:

- *First-person pronouns* refer to the speaker. Example: *I, we*
- *Second-person pronouns* refer to the listener. Example: *you*
- *Third-person pronouns* refer to another party. Example: *he, she, they*

A **pronoun** is a generic substitute for any noun. In addition to personal pronouns, the category of pronouns also includes substitutes for inanimate objects. Example: *You* have to explain *it* to *them* when *you* arrive.

A **sentence** is one or more words organized according to set grammatical rules to express an intended meaning. Sentences can vary in purpose as well. They can question, state, command, negate, or exclaim. There are four types of sentences:

- *Simple sentences* have one independent clause. Example: *Natalie is reading.*
- *Compound sentences* have multiple independent clauses. Example: *Natalie is reading, and Max is bored.*
- *Complex sentences* have at least one independent clause with a dependent clause. Example: *Cassie is a student who wants to be a nurse.*
- *Compound-complex sentences* have multiple independent clauses and at least one dependent clause. Example: *Cassie is a student who wants to be a nurse, and she is getting her degree soon.*

Singular is a form of noun referencing exactly one item. Example: A *duck* likes to swim.

The **subject** is one of the two parts of every sentence. It is a noun phrase that defines the object or topic to be modified by the sentence's predicate. Example: *Nikki* went to El Salvador.

Superlative is the form of an adverb or adjective, which expresses that the modified object possesses the quality to the greatest degree of all the objects in question. Example: Chris has the *happiest* smile of all our friends.

Tense indicates the time at which an action expressed by a verb occurs. English has multiples tenses:

- *Present simple* often expresses habit or routine. Example: I *study.*
- *Present continuous* expresses action occurring at the moment of speech. Example: I *am studying.*
- *Present perfect* indicates an action that has occurred at some, often vague, point in the past. Example: I *have studied.*
- *Preterite* indicates that an action took place and has ceased to take place. Example: I *studied.*
- *Imperfect* indicates a habitual action has ended. Example: I *used to study.*
- *Past continuous* indicates an action that was taking place in the past at the time of a more specific action. Example: I *was studying*.

- *Conditional* indicates a requirement or condition. Example: I *would study*.
- *Future indicates* an action is going to occur. Example: I *will go*.
- *Pluperfect*, also known as past perfect, indicates that an action ended before another began. Example: I *had studied*.

A **verb** is a part of speech that indicates action, occurrence, or state. It can vary with number, gender (in languages besides English), persona, and tense. There are three kinds of verbs:

- *Intransitive verbs* only have a subject. Example: He *laughs*.
- *Transitive verbs* have a subject and a direct object. Example: She *pets* the puppy.
- *Ditransitive verbs* have a subject, direct object, and indirect object. Example: I *showed* her my dance.

English Grammar and Language Conventions in Oral and Written Contexts

English Grammar has numerous definitions. Grammar is

- the study of how words and their component parts combine to form sentences.
- the study of structural relationships in language or in a language, sometimes including pronunciation, meaning, and linguistic history.
- the system of inflections, syntax, and word formation of a language.
- the system of rules implicit in a language, viewed as a mechanism for generating all sentences possible in that language.
- writing or speech judged with regard to such a set of rules. (*The American Heritage Dictionary*)

In this section, sentence types and structures, the most common English grammar and language conventions, and general punctuation rules are defined and illustrated. For a complete list of parts of speech and other language conventions, see Chapter 2.

Sentences

A *sentence* is commonly defined as "a complete unit of thought." Normally, a sentence expresses a relationship, conveys a command, poses a question, or describes someone or something. A sentence begins with a capital letter and ends with a period, question mark, or exclamation point. The basic parts of a sentence are the subject and the verb. The subject is usually a noun—a word that names a person, place, thing, or pronoun. The predicate (or verb) usually follows the subject and identifies an action or a state of being.

> Example: The wind blows. "The wind" is the complete subject and "wind" is the simple subject of the sentence. The predicate of the sentence is "blows," which tells what the wind does or how the wind acts.

There are four different kinds of sentences: *declarative, interrogative, exclamatory,* and *imperative.*

- A **declarative sentence** states, declares, describes, or defines. A declarative sentence ends with a period **(.)**.

  Example: *Hannah likes ice cream.* (This sentence states a simple fact about Hannah.)

- An **interrogative sentence** asks a question. An interrogative sentence ends with a question mark **(?)**.

  Example: *What does Hannah like to eat?* (This sentence asks what Hannah likes to eat.)

- An **exclamatory sentence** exclaims or shows excitement. An exclamatory sentence ends with an exclamation point **(!)**.

  Example: *Hannah absolutely loves ice cream!* (This sentence emphasizes the fact that Hannah truly loves ice cream and that she is excited about eating it.)

- An **imperative sentence** poses a command. A verb often begins an imperative sentence. An imperative sentence can end with a period **(.)** or an exclamation point **(!)**.

  Example: *Please step up to the plate.* (Someone is being commanded to step up to the plate.)

  Eat your ice cream right now! (Hannah is being commanded or ordered to eat ice cream at this very minute.)

I want Hannah to eat her ice cream! (I am commanding that Hannah eat her ice cream.)

Sentence Variety

There are four different varieties of sentence structures: *simple, compound, complex,* and *compound-complex.*

- **Simple Sentence**: A sentence that has one subject and one predicate. Another term for a simple sentence is an *independent clause*, "independent" because it can stand alone and make sense.

  Example: *Mary sells seashells by the seashore.* "Mary" is the subject; "sells seashells by the seashore" is the predicate.

- **Compound Sentence**: Two simple sentences or *independent clauses* that are joined by a conjunction. Conjunctions include *and, but, or, nor, for, yet*, and *so*.

  Example: *Agatha peeled the vegetables and Joshua barbecued the hamburgers*. The two individual sentences or *independent clauses* in this compound sentence are "Agatha peeled the vegetables" and "Joshua barbecued the hamburgers." The conjunction "and" joins the two simple sentences together.

- **Complex Sentence:** A complex sentence has an independent clause joined by one or more *dependent clauses*. A clause is "dependent" because it cannot stand alone, and depends on the independent clause to complete its meaning. A complex sentence always has a subordinating conjunction such as *because, since, after, although,* or *when* or a relative pronoun such as *that, who,* or *which*.

  Example: *Sam is studying all night because he must pass the exam in order to graduate.* "Sam is studying all night" is the independent clause and "because he must pass the exam in order to graduate" is the dependent clause.

  Example: *Jenny is the girl who won the contest.* "Jenny is the girl" is the independent clause and "who won the contest" is the relative clause because it relates specific information (who won the contest) to the girl in the sentence.

- **Compound-Complex Sentence**: A compound-complex sentence has both a compound sentence (*two independent clauses* joined by a coordination conjunction) and a dependent clause joined to the compound sentence by a subordinating or a relative pronoun.

Example: *Ben brought his sister to soccer practice and his brother bought groceries, after their parents told them to assume more responsibilities around the house.* "Ben brought his sister to soccer practice" and "his brother bought groceries" are independent clauses joined by "and." The dependent clause "after their parents told them to assume more responsibilities around the house" is connected to the compound sentence by "after."

Fragments and Run-ons

Fragments and run-ons are among the most common types of sentence errors students make in their writing. A *sentence fragment* is

1. a phrase that is missing either a subject or verb (predicate) and therefore does not form a complete thought.

   Example: *The girl with the pink hair* (What about her?)

   ran across the street (Who ran across the street?)

2. a subordinate clause that has a subject and verb but does not form a complete thought.

   Example: *After he finished writing the report* (What did he do after….)

   If I were you (What would you do?)

   Because she was afraid to fail (What happened?)

   For example, lions and tigers (What are these examples of?)

Run-on Sentences

Run-on sentences consist of at least two complete sentences that are not joined correctly using a coordinating conjunction (*and, or, but, nor, for, so, yet*). If you do not use one of these words, you must either separate the run-on into two separate, complete sentences or connect them with a semicolon (;). Connecting two complete sentences with a comma is also incorrect; this is called a *comma splice*.

Example: *I missed my bus I had to walk.* (run-on)

I missed my bus, I had to walk. (comma splice)

Correct Forms: I missed my bus, so I had to walk.

I had to walk because I missed my bus.

I missed my bus; I had to walk.

Subject-Verb Agreement

Another very common error students make when writing is incorrect subject-verb agreement. In a sentence, the subject must agree with the verb. This means that a singular subject takes a singular verb, and a plural subject takes a plural verb. This is called ***subject-verb agreement.*** This grammatical structure is especially difficult for English language learners because some rules of English grammar simply do not make sense. The following are basic definitions and rules that govern correct subject-verb agreement.

A subject of a sentence can be *singular* or *plural*.

Example: The *girl* cries. (There is one subject, "The *girl*," which makes the subject *singular*. The verb "cries" is the singular form of the verb "to cry." Because the subject "girl" is a *singular subject* it must work with a *singular* form of the verb "cries" in order to have *subject-verb agreement*.)

Sarah cries. (There is one subject, "*Sarah*," which makes the subject *singular*.)

The *girls* cry. (There is more than one girl "*girls*" so the subject is *plural*.)

Sarah and *Sally* cry. (There are two subjects "*Sarah and Sally*," which makes the subject *plural*.)

That a *singular verb* usually ends in "s" is somewhat ironic because "s" is added to a subject to make it plural. An easy way to remember that a singular verb ends in "s" is to remember: "s is for singular."

General Rules for Subject-Verb Agreement

1. When the subject of a sentence is composed of two or more nouns or pronouns connected by *and*, use a plural verb.

   Example: *James and Carrie love to walk.* ("James *and* Carrie" form a plural subject so they take a plural verb *love*.)

2. When two or more singular nouns or pronouns are connected by *or* or *nor*, use a singular verb.

   Example: *Running or jumping requires energy.* (The use of *or* makes the subject singular and therefore, takes a singular verb.)

3. When a compound subject contains both a singular and a plural noun or pronoun joined by *or* or *nor*, the verb should agree with the part of the subject that is closest to the verb.

   Example: *Neither the girls nor he likes to work.* (In this sentence, the verb *likes* is singular because it is closest to the pronoun *he* which is singular.)

   Example: *Neither he nor the girls like to work.* (In this sentence, the verb *like* is plural because it is closest to the noun *girls* which is plural.)

4. The words *each*, *each one*, *either*, *neither*, *everyone*, *everybody*, *anybody*, *anyone*, *nobody*, *somebody*, *someone*, and *no one* are singular and require a singular verb.

   Example: *Everyone likes brownies.*

5. Nouns such as *scissors*, *tweezers*, *trousers*, *shoes*, and *shears* require plural verbs because they come in pairs.

   Example: *Sharp scissors cut easily.*

6. Nouns such as *civics*, *mathematics*, *dollars* (when talking about money as a whole), *measles*, and *news* require singular verbs.

   Example: *The nightly news shows bias towards the new governor.*

7. When a phrase separates a subject and a verb, the verb agrees with the subject not the noun or pronoun in the phrase.

   Example: *Jenny, along with her sisters, visits the beach every summer.* (The subject is "Jenny" so it takes a singular verb.)

Example: *Her sisters, along with Jenny, visit the beach every summer.* (The subject is "sisters" so it takes a plural verb.)

8. Expressions such as *with*, *together with*, *including*, *accompanied by*, *in addition to*, or *as well* do not change the number of the subject. If the subject is singular, the verb is too.

   Example: *Sam in addition to Joey likes carrots.*

9. Collective nouns are words that imply more than one person but that are considered singular and take a singular verb, such as: *group*, *team*, *committee*, *class*, and *family*.

   Example: *The family visits the beach every summer.*

10. The contraction for *does not—doesn't*—is generally used with a singular subject. The only exception to this rule is when pronouns *I* and *you* are the subjects of a sentence. Even though these pronouns may represent only one person, each takes the plural form of the contraction for *do not* which is *don't*.

    Example: *He doesn't understand the rules.*

    I don't understand the rules.

General Rules of Punctuation

Punctuation is the use of standard marks and signs in writing and printing to separate words into sentences, clauses, and phrases in order to clarify meaning. There are fourteen kinds of punctuation that serve different purposes.

The apostrophe (') is used to indicate the omission of a letter or letters from a word, to show possession, or to indicate the plurals of numbers, letters, and abbreviations.

Example: He *doesn't* wish to attend the dance. This matter is of *internat'l* importance.

John's dog has rabies.

Twenty-five phone numbers had *6's* in them.

The **period(.)**, **question mark(?)**, and **exclamation point(!)** are used to end sentences. See above.

A **period (.)** is also used at the end of an abbreviation.

Example: *Dr.* Frankenstein was a cruel dude.

The **comma(,)**, **semicolon (;)**, and **colon (:)** are marks used to create a pause in a series.

A **comma (,)** separates items in a series.

Example: *Adam loves broccoli, asparagus, and squash.*

A **comma** is used after a salutation and closing in a letter.

Example: *Dear John,*

Yours truly,

A **comma** is used to separate two independent clauses and appears before the conjunction.

Example: *John likes broccoli, but Ted prefers carrots.*

A **comma** is used to separate an introductory phrase or clause from the rest of the sentence.

Example: *After you complete your composition, please check it for punctuation errors.*

Use **commas**—one before and one after—to set off any group of words that can be taken out of the sentence without changing the meaning of the sentence as in appositives, parts of dates, places, and interrupters.

Example: *Dr. Smith, one of my physicians, was in Europe.* (appositive)

I was born June 11, 1950. (date)

My hometown is Attleboro, Massachusetts. (place)

Commas, for example, have many uses. (interrupter)

A **semicolon(;)** is used to separate two independent clauses.

Example: *The day grew long; he grew weary.*

A **colon (:)** is used after a word that introduces a quotation, an explanation, an example, a series, or after the salutation in a business letter.

Example: *Most researchers observe: "Punctuation is easy to correct."*

This is the best way to boil lobster: fill a large pot with water up to the two-inch mark, ...

The following are examples of fruits: apples, peaches, and pears.

Dear Madam:

A colon is also used to separate the hour and minute in time.

Example: *3:45 am*

The **dash (–)** and **hyphen (-)** have several uses.

A **dash (–)** used to connect a range of numbers or a compound adjective.

Example: *1910–1945*

Boston–Providence line

A **hyphen (-)** is used between the parts of a compound word, name, or the syllables of a word that falls at the end of a text.

Example: *Sally Winston-Carver*

back-to-back

Johnny kindly brought Mrs. Smith the muffins his mother baked.

Parentheses (( )), brackets ([ ]), and **braces ({ })** are used to contain words or phrases that further explain or form a group.

Parentheses (( )) are used to contain further thoughts or qualifying remarks. Generally, commas can replace parentheses without changing the meaning.

Example: *Jessie and Danesha (who were also in the wedding) flew in from Florida.*

Brackets ([ ])are used to contain technical information.

Example: *[See www.ask.com for additional information.]*

Braces ({ }) are used to contain at least two lines of text or to group information in a unit. Braces are rarely used in writing but more often in computer language to indicate that all the information belongs in one line or command.

Quotation marks (" ") are used to set off a word, phrase, sentence, or sentences that are being directly quoted.

Example: *Mom hollered, "Turn off that radio!"*

"Wow!" she observed. "Can you believe that he left her at the altar?"

It is important to keep in mind that different style manuals (APA, MLA, etc.) have different rules for citing information, especially with respect to quotations.

Capitalization Rules

1. Capitalize the first word of a sentence.

   Example: *He* lumbered toward the pool.

2. Capitalize the pronoun *I*.

   Example: The teacher and *I* will attend the debate.

3. Capitalize people's names and titles used with people's names.

   Example: Former *Prime Minister Winston Churchill* attended the ceremony.

4. Capitalize such words as *mother, father, mom, dad, aunt, uncle, grandmother,* and *grandfather* only when they are used as a name.

   Example: I went fishing with *Grampa.*

5. Capitalize titles of high importance, even without the person's name.

   Example: The *President of the United States*; the *Pope*

6. Capitalize the names of geographical places, such as cities, states, countries, rivers, parks, roads, mountains, etc.

   Example: Joshua toured the *Vatican, Greece,* and *Crete.*

7. Capitalize the names of languages, races, nationalities, religions, and related adjectives.

   Example: Darnell studied *Mandarin* and lived with a *Chinese* family.

8. Capitalize days of the week, months, and holidays but NOT seasons.

   Example: The first day of spring is *Sunday, March 20.*

9. Capitalize the names of organizations and institutions (such as schools, universities, churches, hospitals, clubs, businesses) and their abbreviations; historical events and documents; and ships, trains, airplanes, and automobiles.

   Example: *United Nations, U.N., Empire State Building, Mt. Everest, Declaration of Independence, Boston College, Anaheim Chamber of Commerce, U.S.A., Starship Enterprise*

10. Capitalize titles of literary works, songs, movies, chapters, textbooks, works of art, titles of specific courses, etc.

    Example: *The Tragedy of King Lear*, *Of Mice and Men, Apocalypse Now, Adventures in British Literature,* "To a Skylark," *Life Magazine*, "Madman Across the Water," Chemistry 101.

11. Capitalize sections of the country.

    Example: *Massachusetts* is a *Northeastern* state that is north of *Connecticut* and *Rhode Island.*

COMPETENCY 0002

Understand American literature and selected literature from classical and contemporary periods.

This major body of literature is organized into specific literary periods. In most cases, a brief historical background is provided in order to contextualize the period and provide the reader with a sense of the political, social, economic, religious, and cultural elements that influenced literary movements and particular works of the period. Following the historical background is a description of the literary elements pervasive in the literature of the period. In some instances, specific literary devices truly unique to the period are described and illustrated. Finally, a list of the major writers and works of the period are presented in alphabetical order. At the end of all sections is a series of timelines that not only help the reader visualize relationships between and among the various bodies of literature, but also the immensity of the category of literature and language itself.

Pre-Colonial and Early Native American Literature

Historical Background

Approximately a century before the first permanent settlement in Jamestown, Virginia (1607), Native Americans had already encountered European explorers such as Columbus in the West Indies, Balboa on the Pacific Coast of North America, Vasquez and Coronado in the Southwest, and later, Menendez in St. Augustine, Florida. While no authentic, fixed, or continuous written record of Native American literature exists, artifacts such as pictures painted on wood or stone have provided researchers with songs, myths, and legends derived from the Native American oral language tradition.

Literary Elements

Poetic and symbolic, this literature, viewed primarily as *folklore,* describes the beauty, power, and awe of nature. Most prevalent in this literature are *myths*, stories passed down from generation to generation that explain natural phenomena and significant cultural and religious rituals. Examples of these myths include *The Walum Olum* of the Delaware tribe and *The Navajo Origin Legend* and the "Night Chant" of the Navajo tribe, which detail tribal origins and are recounted during special ceremonies and religious celebrations.

Colonial Literature (1607–1763)

Historical Background

The Colonial Period in American Literature began with the first permanent settlement in Jamestown, Virginia, in 1607. Settlement in America began after a group of London merchants received a license from England to colonize "Virginia," a name that referred to the entire eastern seaboard claimed by England. Although the first charter addressed the obligation of the settlers to civilize the native inhabitants, whom they called savages and infidels, their primary motive was to dig, mine, and search for gold, silver, and copper.

Puritan Settlers of New England came to North America primarily to establish a Calvinistic brand of Protestantism. Puritans believed they were "chosen people." Both the Puritans and Plymouth Pilgrims were dissatisfied with the English church; the Puritans, however, insisted that their movement was non-separatist (one of reform), while the Pilgrims broke from the Church of England. A critical event in colonial history is the Salem Witch Trials, where twenty women and men were executed by hanging or pressing for witchcraft. Cotton Mather, son of Increase Mather and grandson of Richard Mather, campaigned tirelessly to convince New England that witchcraft was a real and present danger affecting the well-being of the community.

Literary Elements

The English Puritans, being the most literate, best-educated, and most committed to intellectualism, had the greatest impact on colonial literature. The Leaders of Massachusetts Bay Colony founded Harvard College in 1636 (modeled after Cambridge University in England), and set up the first printing press at Harvard in 1639. Two themes dominated the literature: religion and politics. Puritan literature focused primarily on the defense or explanation of religious beliefs. The Puritan version of Protestantism emphasized the exclusive authority of the *Bible* in matters of faith and on the contractual nature of God's election of saints. Puritan preachers' sermons comprised the first substantial literary genre in the English-speaking New World. The rhetoric was plain, emphasizing logic and clarity. Puritans used allegories; for example, each Indian attack or natural event had a spiritual significance. This symbolic nature of the world would continue to influence the American literary tradition long after the Puritans died.

Every Puritan wrote a diary, often didactic, to be handed down to sons and daughters. Puritan elegies lamented the loss of a deceased loved one. Puritans also composed meditations about the end of events, and because they felt they knew history's destination, they expressed apocalyptic expectations using Biblical imagery.

Major Writers and Works

William Bradford (1590–1657), governor of his settlement, became the best source of information about the Pilgrims and early colonization of New England. He wrote the *History of Plymouth Plantation* and *The Mayflower Compact.*

Jonathan Edwards (1703–1758), the last of the great Calvinistic clergymen and an American theologian, studied at Yale. He describes spiritual development and the idea that God in his infinite power is able to cast wicked men into hell. He is well-known for his sermon "Sinners in the Hands of an Angry God," an influential text that describes man's corruption and God's justice.

John Smith (1580–1631), a leader of the Virginia Colony at Jamestown, was condemned to death by Chesapeake King Powhatan and was rescued by Powhatan's daughter, Pocahontas. The story is a romantic parable characterizing the inevitability of white triumph over Indian opposition. Smith's account of Virginia in 1608 was the first book written in English in America; his *Description of New England* followed.

John Winthrop (1588–1649) served as Deputy Governor of Massachusetts Bay Colony. He believed that God had sent his people to the New World and that all of Europe were watching to see if they would succeed or fail. He is most well-known for his sermon "A Model of Christian Charity."

Revolutionary Literature (1764–1789)

Historical Background

From 1760 on, literary and cultural aspirations were linked to revolutionary politics. The British had spent a lot of money defending the colonies against attacks by the French and Native Americans (French and Indian War, 1754–1763), as their mission was religious conversion and territorial expansion. Both New England and New France wanted to expand their colonies and trading outposts. The Protestant colonists in New England also feared the French Catholic and papal influence. To fund the war, the British decided to shift the financial burden of high taxes to the colonists. The Stamp Act, in 1765, taxed all legal documents and newspapers, and was met with great uproar in the colonies. It was repealed a year later in 1766. The Boston Tea Party in 1773 was an act of revolt against the British and their tax on tea. The American Revolution began a year after the writing of the *Declaration of Independence*, in 1777, and the British eventually surrendered in 1781. In 1787, the members of the Constitutional Convention ratified the *Constitution of the United States of America*. The First Ten Amendments of the Constitution are the *Bill of Rights*.

Literary Elements

Benjamin Franklin was considered the colonies' first citizen, the man who personified the peculiar genius of America. Franklin wrote the "Dogood Papers" with common sense, humor, and freethinking irreverence. He dismantled the Puritan elegy, reducing it to formulas and hackneyed similes. Franklin's rise to international prominence signaled the end of the dominance of Puritan ideology. Franklin's *Autobiography*, similar to the Puritan diaries in its design and structure, offers his life as a representative model of trial, pilgrimage, and success intended to teach and instruct others. The difference, however, is that Franklin's journey is purely secular, in which *reason* is the primary guide, and heaven has become a vague metaphor for the unknowable and peripheral beyond. Franklin's self-portrait shows beginnings of the American myth/story: a poor boy finds his way to wealth, the chartered servant earns his freedom, the colonial subject takes up the cause of national independence. Poetry served nationalism.

Major Writers and Works

John (1735–1826) and Abigail Adams' (1744–1818) letters in correspondence between Boston and Philadelphia serve as primary sources that document the dangerous period in history during the Revolution.

Benjamin Franklin (1706–1790) bought the unprofitable *Pennsylvania Gazette* and made it a widely read weekly periodical in America. He also authored *Poor Richard's Almanack,* which contained rash weather predictions and brief sayings that urged virtue and good business practices. He founded the debate club, which later turned into the University of Pennsylvania and the first lending library. He helped draft the *Declaration of Independence*, and negotiated an alliance with France during the Revolution. He signed the peace treaty in 1783 and helped write and signed the *Constitution* in 1787. His last public act was to petition Congress for the abolishment of slavery.

Alexander Hamilton (1757–1804) was the author of the majority of the series of eighty-five essays collected as *The Federalist Papers*, in order to secure the ratification of the *Constitution*.

Patrick Henry (1736–1799), a great orator of the Revolution, is remembered for two speeches: one to the Virginia Legislature about the Stamp Act and the other, his Speech to the Virginia House of Burgesses, where he cried, "Give me Liberty or give me Death."

Thomas Jefferson (1743–1826), the third President of the United States, was the first American champion of the people who authored almost all of the *Declaration of American Independence* and *the Statute of Virginia for Religious Freedom.* He founded the University of Virginia in 1819. *Notes on the State of Virginia* is a historic source of information on the region of Virginia.

Thomas Paine (1737–1809), author of *Common Sense*, appealed for complete political independence. His rhetorical power was his mastery of plain style.

George Washington (1732–1799) wrote letters, diaries, and other pieces, which have been collected in thirty-seven volumes. Washington's *Farewell Address* is considered to be his best work, written with the help of Alexander Hamilton and James Madison. It explains his reasons for leaving the presidency.

Gustavus Vassa (1745–1797), or Olaudah Equiano, was taken from Africa and enslaved as a child. He later earned his freedom and became a leading figure in 18th century abolition movement. *The Interesting Narrative of the Life of Olaudah Equiano, or Gustavus Vassa the African* (1789) is an abolitionist autobiography.

Phillis Wheatley (1753–1784), an African-born black woman, was captured at the age of eight and sold to John Wheatley, a Boston merchant. Attractive and intelligent, she was encouraged to learn by her owner. She began writing poetry at the age of thirteen and wrote *Her Poems on Various Subjects* when she was twenty.

Romantic Literature (1790–1865)
(Also known as the American Renaissance)

Historical Background

America expanded its boundaries significantly in the time between independence and the Civil War. Jefferson purchased the Louisiana Territory from France in 1803 and doubled the nation's size. War and effective diplomacy added the areas of Texas, California, and Oregon. By 1860 twenty new states had entered the Union, adding to the thirteen original states. America began moving westward (Manifest Destiny).

Flatboats, keelboats, and packet boats sailed the rivers of the East, South, and Midwest. Steamboats, which permitted upstream travel, allowed for inland navigation canals (like the Erie Canal). The railroad guided and shaped much of economic development, allowing the nation to meet the needs of its vast expansion. Cycles of economic boom and bust occurred as debates over currency continued. Financial panic swept through nation's banks, wiping out many large and small investors. John Adams and Thomas Jefferson both died on July 4, 1826, the fiftieth anniversary of the *Declaration of the Independence*.

The War of 1812 with Britain, fought on land and sea, inspired the writing of the "Star Spangled Banner" by Francis Scott Key. There were also three major orators whose speeches dominated the political climate between War of 1812 and the Civil War. Henry Clay (1777–1852), a lawyer and statesman, advocated conciliatory measures such as the Missouri Compromise and regulating slavery in Western territories. He also made public attacks on Abolitionism. John C. Calhoun (1782–1850) was an ardent supporter of slavery and states rights. Daniel Webster (1782–1852), a supporter of nationalism, advocated conciliatory measures like Henry Clay, in opposition to Calhoun.

Literary Elements

This period saw the emergence of Early American folktales and a distinctly American style of writing. The south revered learning and aspired to a literary culture. The College of William and Mary in Virginia, the nation's second oldest college, established the nation's intellectual leadership in the eighteenth and early nineteenth century. However, the South became increasingly dependent upon slavery, and Southern writers were driven to propagandize in defense of slavery or to write escapist fantasies. The South produced a lot of romance fictions and chivalric melodramas. An indigenous southern genre was the plantation novel, which pictured slavery as white benevolence and black loyalty. Despite major works of Southern literature, New England was still the center of American literature, as represented by major writers of this period: Thoreau, Emerson, Hawthorne, and Melville.

During this period a belief in Transcendentalism emerged. Another movement, Romanticism, a reaction against the Age of Reason, began in late 18th century and stormed across the first half of 19th century. Romanticism involved subordination of rationality to emotion and intuition, found value and interest in the individual, and considered nature, which offered harmony, joy, and spiritual refreshment. A theme of literary independence emerged as Emerson wanted a complete break with Old World Literary traditions and Poe and Hawthorne developed the short story into a distinctive American genre. And finally, Whitman wrote entirely on American topics, from an entirely American point of view.

The Fireside poets were called this because American families in the harsh and enduring New England winters read their works. Poets in this genre included James Russell Lowell, Oliver Wendell Holmes, Henry Wadsworth Longfellow, and John Greenleaf Whittier.

Major Writers and Works

James Fenimore Cooper (1789–1851), born in his father's frontier town of Cooperstown, New York, wrote *The Last of the Mohicans*, which depicts Natty (called Hawkeye), a young scout during the French and Indian War and many chases and battles between white men and two Indians, Chingachgook and Uncas, who are the last of the Mohicans. He also wrote *The Pioneers*, part of the Leatherstocking series, which features Natty Bumppo, a middle-aged frontiersman.

Ralph Waldo Emerson (1803–1882) wrote about hard work, the intellectual spirit of Americans, and the importance of learning about nature firsthand, rather than through books. He encouraged readers to trust themselves and not the opinions of others. *Nature* (1836) his first and one of his best books is considered a central piece on Transcendentalism. Emerson also wrote volumes of poetry.

Nathaniel Hawthorne (1804–1864) wrote *The Scarlet Letter*, a book about Puritan New England society whose members left England to establish religious freedom. The society's Puritanical ways ruin the life of Hester Prynne, who has a child with a minister but out of wedlock. Her child, Pearl, is condemned as she is considered the child of Satan. Hawthorne also wrote *The House of the Seven Gables.*

Herman Melville (1819–1891) left Nantucket in the whaler "Acushnet" in 1841 and deserted ship in the Marquesas Islands. Hawthorne and Melville, neighbors in Lenox, Mass., combined symbolism and romance. Hawthorne's obsession with the power of sin affected Melville's work *Moby Dick*, in which Captain Ahab tries to capture a great white whale that has taken his leg. At last the whale triumphs and crashes into the ship and sinks it, and Ahab is killed in the act of harpooning the whale. Melville's commentary on the gruesome and harsh life of a whaler in Nantucket is also depicted in *Billy Budd*, an allegory of how forces of evil triumph over innocence and beauty.

The poet Edgar Allan Poe (1809–1849) wrote works that include "The Raven," "To Helen," "Annabelle Lee," "The Tell-Tale Heart," "The Cask of Amontillado," and "The Fall of the House of Usher." Poe was unyielding in his aesthetic commitment and was idolized on account of his poverty and early death. Known for his gothic, psychologically thrilling tales, he believed that beauty was akin to truth and considered writing a religious and moral obligation. Many of his poems idolized the death of women and dead female bodies observing that there were always elements of strangeness in beauty.

Henry David Thoreau (1817–1862) wrote about nature in *On Walden Pond* and civil disobedience in "On the Duty of Civil Disobedience." The second greatest of the Transcendentalists, Thoreau lived a hermetic life on Walden Pond to test his Transcendental philosophy of individualism, self-reliance, and spiritual growth.

Walt Whitman (1819–1892) wrote *Leaves of Grass*. Whitman was original and rejected the traditional elements of verse-meter, rhyme, and conventional poetic diction. His subject matter centered on democracy and the individual common man. He is also famous for writing the famous elegy for Lincoln, "O Captain! My Captain!"

Civil War Literature (1861–1865)

Historical Background

During this time, Thoreau wrote vicious abolitionist polemics, like "Slavery in Massachusetts," in which he protested the return of two escaped slaves to their southern masters under the Fugitive Slave Law, passed as part of the Compromise of 1850. Later, Thoreau met John Brown and concluded that he had found a man whose righteousness lifted him above the debased level of antebellum politics. Brown later attacked a federal arsenal at Harper's Ferry, Virginia, trying to provoke slave insurrection across the South. Although later hanged, Brown was a hero in the eyes of Thoreau and Emerson; thus Transcendentalism became connected with the abolitionist movement.

Territorial expansion repeatedly raised the question of slavery's extension beyond the South, resulting in the Missouri Compromise. Differences between the North and the South heightened sectional tensions and were exacerbated by newspapers, books, and pamphlets expressing antislavery sentiment (ex. *Uncle Tom's Cabin*). A number of black abolitionists emerged: Harriet Tubman made many dangerous trips to the South to help slaves escape; and Sojourner Truth, an orator and organizer, led campaigns for abolition and women's rights.

Literary Elements

Significant literary themes focused on abolition and polemics between advocates of slavery and abolitionists. Much of Whitman's writing was influenced by his experience in the Civil War as a field medic. The writing of this period precipitated tensions in the country. Writing in this period is obviously looked at in the context of new (or old) historicism rather than formalism.

Major Writers and Works

Frederick Douglass (1818–1895), in his *Narrative of the Life of Frederick Douglass*, wrote about slavery and masters' desires to keep their slaves ignorant. Knowledge was denied to slaves, as it would only bring discontent. Douglass's desire for freedom heightened as he learned to read. He noted that democracy and Christianity, although deformed by slavery, were worthy of allegiance.

Abraham Lincoln (1809–1865), a great statesman, in spite of his lack of formal education, was a master of direct and tactful expression. An accomplished lawyer in Illinois, Lincoln persevered to become a Republican President in 1860, and his election triggered the Civil War. Lincoln is most famous for *The Gettysburg Address,* a classic of oratory. His less famous second inaugural address was a blueprint for the reconciliation of the nation ("With malice toward none, with charity for all…), and his letter to Mrs. Bixby consoling her for the loss of her five sons in the war was a masterpiece of sympathy and compassion. Earlier speeches contained rough frontier humor and idioms of the common man, but his oratory style became known as directly to the point and appropriate for the occasion.

Harriet Beecher Stowe (1811–1896) wrote *Uncle Tom's Cabin*, a story of slave life written by a New England woman whose knowledge of the subject was limited to observations during her brief visit in Kentucky. She wrote the book to arouse antislavery sentiment and was so successful that Lincoln called her "the little woman who caused the Great War." Its notable characters include honest, black Uncle Tom, the mischievous slave girl Topsy, little angelic Eva, and the cruel slave driver Simon Legree. The novel introduced a new era by presenting a realistic picture of contemporary life, rather than romantic adventures of the past.

Susan B. Anthony (1820–1906), who became an agent for William Lloyd Garrison's American Anti-Slavery Society of New York State, promoted women's rights and although originally friends with Frederick Douglass, she disagreed with his contention that only males should have the right to vote.

Sectional Independence and Local Color Literature (1865–1930)

Historical Background

During this period, millions of immigrants moved westward. From Mississippi to the Pacific, new states were admitted; territories were annexed and subdued in expansion of white settlement. The first transcontinental railroad system was established. Reconstruction after the Civil War was distinctly different between the North and the South. The South was impoverished for years afterwards, while the North remained virtually untouched. By 1900 America became a leading economic power because of northern industry. Names like Rockefeller, Morgan, Gould, Carnegie, and Hill represented achievement of a culture obsessed with success and the American dream.

Literary Elements

This literary era marked the transition between the 19th and 20th century. This period included the Gilded Age (1873), which influenced literature and life in general. New England lost its monopoly on America's literary output. Themes included conformity, self-discipline, and dreams of material comfort. There were moral tales and tales of rags to riches. The voice of the common people was heard from across the country initially in folk stories like "Johnny Appleseed," the "Hatfields and McCoys," "Paul Bunyan," and "Pecos Bill," then in humorists like Lincoln and Twain. Readers became conscious of regional differences: romance of the Far West, rusticity of the Middle West, and glamour of the Deep South. Literary works included poetry, elegy, puns, allegory, and satire.

Major Writers and Works

Willa Cather (1873–1947) wrote about life on the Nebraska prairie and the immigrant farmers of the West, with whom she lived from age nine until she graduated from University of Nebraska. *O Pioneers!* describes the life of a Swedish immigrant who keeps her family together after the death of their father. “Paul’s Case” is of Cather’s most moving short stories about a troubled, bright, young, gay man who eventually kills himself by being hit by a train. Kate Chopin (1850–1904) was raised in St. Louis and moved to New Orleans with her Creole husband. After he died she moved back to St. Louis to support herself and her children. *Bayou Folk* and *A Night in Acadia* are a series of sketches based on the Creole people and customs, which she observed during her marriage. *The Awakening,* an erotic and sympathetic exploration of female desire, takes her theme of passion dominating civility to extreme.

Samuel Langhorne Clemens, “Mark Twain” (1835–1910) wrote about local color and the particularities of the region in which he lived, life along the Mississippi. Twain preserved important elements of speech, like the dialect of the region. Considered a “great American humorist,” he used vernacular, exaggeration, and deadpan narration to create humor. Self-educated, he wanted to become a Mississippi steamboat pilot, which shows just how entrenched he was in Southern culture. Inspired by the tall tales and frontier humor that came out of the Old Southwest, for example “Paul Bunyan” and “Babe the Blue Ox,” his literature is based on his early experiences along the Mississippi. Such works include “The Celebrated Jumping Frog of Calaveras County,” a short story that relates the accomplishments of a frog named Dan’l Webster. The story brought Mark Twain immediate fame. *The Adventures of Tom Sawyer* depicts the carefree, primitive life Clemens had lived before his father died and he was forced to work at age twelve. Notable characters are Aunt Polly and Huck Finn. Tom is boyishly imaginative but more civilized then Huck. *The Adventures of Huckleberry Finn,* a sequel to *Tom Sawyer*, tells how a “half-civilized” Huck drifts down the river on a raft with a runaway slave named Jim, who is eventually freed by Tom. The text is very controversial and has been considered racist by some critics. Other works include: *Life on the Mississippi* (a memoir), *The Prince and the Pauper,* and *A Connecticut Yankee in King Arthur’s Court.*

Emily Dickinson (1830–1886) obviously out of place in this era, wrote minimally about the Civil War (if at all), traveled out of the state of Massachusetts *once*, never married, and spent most of her life in her home in Amherst. Dickinson left over seventeen hundred poems upon her death, which her sister Lavinia collected and published: “I heard a Fly buzz – when I died –,” “I felt a Funeral, in my Brain,” “My Life had stood, a Loaded Gun,” and “What Soft – Cherubic Creatures.” Her poetry displayed an extremely effective use of slant rhyme and the tones of her poetry ranged from mild whimsy to impassioned delight to paralyzed despair and terror. Her poetry also included satire, celebration, elegies, riddle poems, puns, and allegory. Dickinson wrote about abstractions as if they were familiar physical objects.

Bret Harte (1836–1902) is remembered as the man who made the West a favorite realm of fiction. As a young man he went to California and had a brief experience as a miner, he then became a San Francisco journalist. Harte wrote about what he called "the old west." "The Luck of Roaring Camp" appeared in the *Overland Monthly*, the first literary presentation of a colorful section of the country (the West). *The Outcasts of Poker Flat* followed the same formula of nobility coming out in desperate characters who possess hearts of gold.

The Age of Realism and Realist Literature (1890–1920)

Literary Elements

Several factors stimulated the rise of Realist literature. Scientific interest and the emergence of a strong social consciousness influenced the writing of this period. Realism avoided the false beauty of former writing, going to extremes to point out the cruel and ugly side of real life.What also emerged at this time were Humanism and New Humanism.

Humanism advised self-restraint as the highest ethical principle and the highest freedom, eliminating the need for external compulsion. Naturalism focused on man's subjection to natural law, while humanism distinguished between man and nature, emphasizing ethical concepts and freedom of the will as being peculiar to man.

Major Writers and Works

Henry James (1843–1916) was most noted for contrasting American and European cultures. *Daisy Miller,* his most popular novel, tells how a charming American girl offends her European friends and an American gentleman of European training by her innocent familiarity with a young Italian. The style is simple and direct, unlike his later works.

William James (1842–1910), Henry's brother, developed his thinking in and between the disciplines of philosophy, physiology and psychology. William had a clear and forceful style of writing in complete opposition to his brother. Distinguished by pragmatic thinking, he rejected what was traditionally American and emphasized practicality as a criterion of truth. His works explore topics such as conversion, the sick soul, and blind faith.

Edith Wharton (1862–1937) lived in cosmopolitan circles, which supplied the setting for most of her work. Her major theme, the destructive effects of social conventions, is observed in *The House of Mirth*. *Ethan Frome* recounts the struggle of an individual against convention.

Naturalist Literature

Literary Elements

During the late 18th century, the literature reflected intense realism. Emphasizing man's subjection to the laws of nature, particularly natural selection, man is represented as lacking in free will and controlled by his passions and environment. Seen as an animal struggling against nature in an impersonal, amoral universe, the literature omits moral considerations and stresses unpleasant phases of life.

Major Writers and Works

Stephen Crane (1871–1900) is considered the first Naturalist. *The Red Badge of Courage* is a realistic psychological novel of a Civil War soldier. Obviously not in the Civil War himself, Crane drew from Tolstoy and stories of Civil War veterans to create a very convincing depiction of a young soldier's first experiences in battle.

Charlotte Perkins Gilman (1860–1935) incorporated a Darwinist perspective to different ends. She demanded complete emancipation of women, not only in particular reforms in education, voting laws, and wages but also in the redefinition of institutions of marriage and motherhood, which she believed led to oppression. *The Yellow Wallpaper,* a popular work in today's literary canon, is the study of a woman driven out of her mind by the isolation imposed by her husband.

Jack London (1876–1916), essentially self-educated, read many adventure stories as a child. He became a tramp at eighteen and traveled around the United States and Canada. The experience taught him that wealth is important, and intellectual and physical strength was needed to acquire it. He sought gold in the Klondike, where he did not find gold but rather material for his stories. London pushed Naturalism to its limits. *Call of the Wild* describes a tame dog, Buck, who is forced to revert to his original primitive state. The short story *To Build a Fire* reflects survival of the fittest. London's protagonists often reflect Nietzsche's concept of a superman.

The Modern Period (1914–1945)

Historical Background

This period was a time of overwhelming technological changes as well as two devastating world wars. There was immense grief over the loss of the past and fear of eroding traditions. This became evident in the work of the muckrakers, a term coined by Roosevelt to describe writers who mission focused on exposing corruption in politics and business. Several leading periodicals of the time lent their pages to the muckrakers, among them *McClure's, Collier's,* and *Cosmopolitan*.

Literary Elements

Literature reflected the dominant mood of this period, which was alienation and disconnection. Writing was highly experimental as authors made extensive use of fragments, stream of consciousness, and interior dialogue in efforts to create a unique style. A kind of regionalism reemerged emphasizing the belief that history is socially constructed paving way for multicultural literature. Literature moved beyond the notion that a writer writes for everyone. Instead, certain writers wrote from a particular social, cultural, and ethnic perspective, about social, cultural, and ethnic topics, and for a particular social, cultural, and ethnic audience.

Major Writers and Works

William Faulkner (1897–1962) wrote novels and short stories that dealt with the steady decline of aristocratic families in the fictional Southern town of Jefferson, modeled after his own town of Oxford, Mississippi. Faulkner is noted for his convincing portrayal of abnormal minds and for his richly descriptive style with its affected and puzzling adjectives and metaphors. The most original writer of his time in terms of the subject of his literature: heritage, Southern memory, reality, and myth. His works include *As I Lay Dying* and *The Sound and the Fury* (his masterpiece).

F. Scott Fitzgerald (1896–1940) chronicled the manners, moods, and culture of his time, the "Roaring Twenties." *The Great Gatsby* is an ironic and tragic treatment of the American success myth.

Ernest Hemingway (1899–1961) joined a volunteer ambulance unit in France then transferred to the Italian infantry until the close of World War I. He finally settled in Paris as a member of the expatriate group. He became a leading spokesman for the "lost generation," expressing feelings of war-wounded people disillusioned by the loss of faith and hope. Demonstrating a stoic writing style, Hemingway did not emphasize emotions, only bare happenings reported with understatement and dialogue. His style was concise, direct, spare, objective, precise, and rhythmic. His works include *The Sun Also Rises*, *A Farewell to Arms*, *For Whom the Bell Tolls,* and *The Old Man and the Sea*, a parable of man against nature, for which he won the Pulitzer Prize. He won the Nobel Prize for Literature in 1954.

John Steinbeck (1902–1968) combined naturalism and symbolism to express outrage and compassion for the plight of the farmers displaced by the Depression and the Dustbowl. His writing reflected a belief in the need for social justice, and hope that people can learn from the suffering of others. *Grapes of Wrath, Of Mice and Men, The Red Pony*, and *The Pearl* are among his most well-known works.

Upton Sinclair (1878–1968) is most famous for his work *The Jungle*, written about the corruption and disgusting practices of the meatpacking industry in the early 20th century. Sinclair's work depicts poverty, horrendous living conditions, and hopelessness.

Major 20th Century Poets

T.S. Eliot and Ezra Pound were the two most influential poets and critics of their era. Their work dictated the tone, direction, and subject matter for a generation of poets. T. S. Eliot (1888–1965) wrote about questions that addressed our place in the universe and humankind's ability to love and communicate with others as reflected in *The Love Song of J. Alfred Prufrock.* His longest work *The Waste Land* critiqued the failure of Western civilization as illustrated by World War I. Ezra Pound (1885–1972) used ordinary language, free verse, and concentrated word pictures, a technique used by Japanese and Chinese poets to create extraordinary imagery. This movement, called Imagism, emphasized clarity, precision, and concise word choice. His later work, for nearly fifty years, focused on the encyclopedic epic poem he entitled *The Cantos*. Accused in 1945 of treason for spreading Fascist propaganda on the radio, Pound was acquitted but spent a decade in a mental institution.

e. e. cummings (Edward Estlin Cummings) (1894–1962) played around with form, punctuation, spelling, font, grammar, imagery, rhythm, and syntax. His works include *The Enormous Room* (1922), *Tulips and Chimneys* (1923), and *XLI Poems* (1925).

Robert Frost (1874–1963) is considered America's best-known and among its most beloved poets. He wrote in tradition verse forms and the plain speech of rural New

Englanders. His poetry often explored the conflict between nature and industrialization. Among his works are "Death of the Hired Man," "Birches," "Stopping by the Woods on a Snowy Evening," "The Road Not Taken," "Out! Out!," and "Mending Wall."

Carl Sandburg (1878–1967), one of Chicago's poets, described everyday Americans in a positive tone, with simple, easy to understand words and free verse. He is most well-known for his *Chicago Poems*.

William Carlos Williams (1883–1963) wrote poetry and prose that drew on his experience as a physician and his observations of the working class women whose babies he delivered. Like Whitman, Williams incorporated American speech, expression, local culture and ethnicity, and rhythm into his poetry. His most often studied works include "The Young Housewife," "The Red Wheelbarrow," and "This Is Just to Say."

Harlem Renaissance Literature (1915–1929)

Literary Elements

The dominant mood of this period was alienation and disconnection. Writing was highly experimental with the use of fragments, stream of consciousness, and interior dialogue. African American writers sought to create a unique style, and the Harlem Renaissance was a catalyst. The Harlem Renaissance was a black cultural movement that emerged in Harlem during the 20s during which literature, music, and art flourished. There was an outpouring of black prose and poetry. During this literary period, African American writers asked questions like: "Is there, in fact or theory, "Afro-American art?" "Are black literary norms the same as white literary norms?" "What is different and what should be held in common?"

Major Writers and Works

Countee Cullen (1903–1946) was considered the "black Keats" for his youth, skill as a poet, and use of traditional forms.

Langston Hughes (1902–1967) is considered the most successful black writer in America; among his works are poems, plays, novels, songs, and movie scripts. He is most famous for his poetry, which is marked by a powerful commitment to a separate and distinctive black identity, and a sense of the shared presence of African Americans. His poetry aims at imaginatively empathizing with the black "low-down folks." Some of his most popular poems: *Harlem, Montage of a Dream Deferred, Ask Your Mama*; the idea of a "dream deferred" continues to resonate today.

Zora Neale Hurston (1891–1960) observed through her research that women were denied access to the pulpit and the porch, the privileged sites of storytelling, and the chance of self-definition. Her aim was to revise and adapt vernacular forms to give a voice to women, creating a democratic oral culture. Her masterpiece, *Their Eyes Were Watching God,* follows Janie Crawford, an African American woman trying to win the right to speak about living for herself. She resists the demeaning definitions of society that encompass her first two failed marriages and finally she marries Tea Cake, who gives her the chance to speak herself into being.

Claude McKay (1889–1948) wrote poetry that evoked the heritage of his native Jamaica. McKay's "If We Must Die" won critical acclaim, as he was the first black poet to write in the form of an Elizabethan sonnet; it also established him as a militant. His poem, which conforms to the "white/English" sonnet structure, is a statement of irony. McKay uses the poetic form of his oppressors as a call to war. He advocated violent resistance to violence.

American Literature from the 20th Century to the Present

Historical Background

During this period a media-saturated culture has emerged where people observe life as media presents it rather than experiencing life directly. This influence insists that values are not permanent but only "local" or "historical" and media culture interprets these values. This period is marked by post-World War II prosperity, social protest against the Vietnam Conflict, The Civil Rights Movement, the rise of Black militancy, and the beginning of a new century and new millennium.

Literary Elements

The literature of this period represents a blurring of the lines of reality with a mix of fantasy and nonfiction. Heroes and anti-heroes are generally absent from the literature, and writing is concerned with the individual in isolation, and is detached, unemotional, and generally humorless. Ethnic and women writers also emerge during this period.

Major Writers and Works

Conrad Aiken (1889–1973), poet, essayist, novelist, and critic, was one of America's major figures in American literary modernism. His most powerful story "Silent Snow, Secret Snow," depicts a young man who falls deeper and deeper into an almost autistic world, as if cut off from society by silence and snow.

Ray Bradbury (b. 1920) is a prolific science fiction writer. Best known for novels such as *Fahrenheit 451*, set in a totalitarian government, in which a man whose job is to burn books begins to pilfer books and when discovered must run for his life; and *The Martian Chronicles*, a futuristic story about colonizing Mars.

Shirley Jackson (1916–1965) received critical acclaim for her short stories especially "The Lottery," which presented the disconcerting side of a Midwestern, small farming town. Her intent was to shock a nation that was becoming desensitized to brutality and violence.

Arthur Miller (1915–2005) is regarded as one of the most famous contemporary playwrights. *Death of a Salesman* relates the story of a typical and ordinary American, Willy Loman, whose choices and their consequences lead to the destruction of the American dream. He treats himself as an economic unit/social commodity and kills himself so his family can have the insurance money. Another famous play, *The Crucible,* is based on the actual events of the Salem Witch Trials (1692–1693) but was also written in response to the McCarthy Hearings in the early 1950s, during which he refused to appear before the House of Representatives' Committee on Un-American Activities spearheaded by Senator Joseph McCarthy.

J. D. Salinger (1919–2010) fought in World War II. His experiences during the war affected him emotionally, resulting in a serious nervous condition. His last interview was conducted in 1980 and he never allowed his famous novel *The Catcher in the Rye* to be made into a movie. *The Catcher in the Rye*'s Holden Caulfield became the symbol for a generation of disaffected youth.

James Thurber (1894–1961) is most well-known for witty short stories and lumpy cartoons, which appeared in *The New Yorker*. "The Secret Life of Walter Mitty," the tale of a henpecked husband who escapes into heroic daydreams is one of his best. Thurber's absurdist cartoons featured men, women, dogs, and other strange animals.

Kurt Vonnegut (1922–2007), satirical novelist, was a soldier and prisoner during World War II. This experience influenced his novel *Slaughterhouse Five* (1969), which depicts a soldier during WWII who experiences time travel. Although Vonnegut's work is often considered science fiction, Vonnegut used this genre to write black comedy. A humanist, Vonnegut believed in the value and dignity of all humans.

Contemporary Multicultural Literature

African American Literature

Maya Angelou (b. 1928) writes novels that are part autobiography, part picaresque fiction, and part social history. The central characters in her texts are strong black woman. *I Know Why the Caged Bird Sings* tells of her grandmother's religious influences and her mother's blues tradition. She meets other exemplary women, one who teaches her to speak again after a rape has struck her dumb.

James Baldwin (1924–1987) wrote autobiographical novels about his experiences growing up in Harlem. Baldwin became a preacher like his father, but felt that writing would better detail the struggles of growing up poor in a racist society. *Go Tell It on the Mountain* (1953) is an autobiographical work about growing up in Harlem. Baldwin was a critical force in the Civil Rights Movement, writing about black identity and racial struggle in *The Fire Next Time* (1963).

Gwendolyn Brooks (1917–2000) was the first Black female poet to win the Pulitzer Prize for her poem *We Real Cool* (1959). Her work in the 1970s *Riot* and *Family Pictures* focused on racial harmony, but her later works *Beckonings* (1975) and *To Disembark* (1980), demonstrated disappointment due to conflict between members of the civil rights and black militant groups.

Ralph Ellison (1913-1994) is most well-known for the *Invisible Man (*1953), whose theme demonstrates that society willfully ignores blacks, and his collection of poems about critical social and political essays, *Shadow and Act* (1964).

Toni Morrison (b. 1931) is the first Black woman to receive the Nobel Prize for Literature (1993). Morrison's novels, which include *Sula, Beloved, The Bluest Eye,* and *Song of Solomon*, combine fantasy, ghosts, and what she calls "rememory" or the recurrence of past events to elaborate the horrors of slavery and the struggles of African Americans after being freed.

Alice Walker (b. 1944) wrote *The Color Purple* (1982), which won her the Pulitzer Prize. Her novels focus on poor oppressed black women in early 1900s. One of her most widely read short stories "Everyday Use," which appears in a collection of short stories *In Love and Trouble: Stories of Black Women* (1973), tells the story of two daughters' conflicting ideas about identity and heritage.

Richard Wright (1908–1960) was one of the first black writers to attain both fame and fortune. *Black Boy* (1945) is an autobiography that recounts his childhood, growing up poor in racist Mississippi, and his struggle for individualism. *American Hunger* (published in 1977 after his death) tells of his disillusionments with the Communist Party. Wright also wrote more than 4,000 haiku.

Asian-American Literature

Amy Tan (b. 1952) wrote *The Kitchen God's Wife* in which she chronicles the harrowing early life of her mother, Daisy who escaped the turmoil of the Chinese Civil War and the 1949 Communist takeover, to come to America. Her most famous book *The Joy Luck Club* depicts the lives of four Chinese American immigrant families who start the "Joy Luck Club," playing the Chinese game of Mahjong for money.

Jewish American Literature

Saul Bellow (1915–2005) was a Canadian-born novelist who received the Nobel Prize for Literature for his works *Herzog* (1965) and *Seize the Day* (1956). Bellow primarily wrote about urban Jews struggling to find spirituality and comfort in a racist and alienating society.

Bernard Malamud (1914–1986) was a master of parables and myths. His best work *The Natural* is based on ballplayer Eddie Waitkus who tries to make a comeback after being shot by an insane serial killer.

Elie Wiesel (b. 1928) is a Holocaust survivor who has authored almost 40 works that address Judaism, the Holocaust, racism, hatred, and genocide. He was awarded the Nobel Peace Prize and the Congressional Gold Medal. *Night*, read widely in high schools across the nation, is a memoir that depicts Wiesel's struggle and guilt of having been the only one in his family to survive the Holocaust.

Latino-American Literature

Julia Alvarez (b. 1950) was born in New York City, returned to her native Dominican Republic during the Trujillo dictatorship in the early 50s. She returned to the U.S. in 1960. *How the Garcia Girls Lost Their Accents* describes the difficulties of learning American (conversational) English and being called a "spic" at school. The text is told in reverse chronological order and narrated from shifting perspectives, beginning with her four sisters' adult lives and moving to their childhood.

Sandra Cisneros (b. 1954) is a Mexican American (Chicano) writer born in Chicago. Her family constantly moved between Mexico and the U. S., giving her the sense that she never belonged to either culture. Her stories reveal the misogyny present in both these cultures. *The House on Mango Street* (1984) told in a series of vignettes is a novel about a young girl, Esperanza, growing up in the Latino section of Chicago and coming into her own.

Native American Literature

Louise Erdrich (b. 1954)[2] is a member of the Turtle Mountain Band of Chippewa. She was very close with her extended family, which had a tradition of storytelling. Her collection of short stories *Love Medicine* features characters and speakers from four Anishinaabe families that are represented in non-hierarchical terms by employing speakers of various ages and stations within the community.

N. Scott Momaday[3] (b. 1934) is a Kiowa Native American who grew up on the reservations and pueblos of the Southwest, far from centers of learning and letters. In 1969 he won the Pulitzer Prize for Fiction for *House Made of Dawn*, a semi-autobiographical account of his life at Jemez Pueblo. His main character Abel returns to his New Mexico reservation after fighting in World War II and struggles in readapt to what was once his home.

Literary Theory and Criticism

This section addresses **Literary Theory and Criticism** and describes the emergence of literary criticism as a form and theories of literary criticism, describing elements that differentiate the various forms of criticism, authors aligned or identified with a particular theory of criticism, and illustrative examples of the application of a particular form of critique.

[2] http://voices.cla.umn.edu/vg/Bios/entries/erdrich_louise.html
[3] http://www.achievement.org/autodoc/page/mom0pro-1

In a strict sense, a **literary theorist** is one who studies the nature of literature and ways to analyze literature in a systematic way. Aristotle and Plato are credited for establishing the parameters of literary critical study in their search for truth. Plato banned poetry from the ideal republic because it was three times removed from truth, imitated imitation, and appealed to our lower nature. Aristotle, on the other hand, viewed poetry as productive art but with an embedded moral purpose. Later, Plotinus (an Egyptian philosopher) held literature as a direct expression of eternal essences and a vehicle for providing access to higher spiritual realms and to the divine. Augustine traced connections appropriate connections between literal and figurative language in the reading of scripture. During the Middle Ages, St. Thomas Aquinas and Alighieri Dante (*Dante's Inferno*, in which you probably believe you are living as you read this section) used allegory not only at literal levels, but also moral, anagogical, or mystical levels. These theorists emphasized beauty, order, and harmony of God's creation. Literature, therefore, was one part of an ordered hierarchy of knowledge leading to the divine, its climax being theology.

During the Renaissance criticism assumed more humanistic and secular view, reviving classical learning, reexamining the notions of imitations, the didactic role of literature, classification of genres, and vernacular as medium of poetic expression and reassessment of classical heritage. During the 18th Century, theorist such as Dr. Samuel Johnson, Alexander Pope, and John Dryden analyzed literature according to the classical virtues rationality, moderation, balance, decorum harmony of form and content), and dramatic unities of time and place and action. Dr. Samuel Johnson, a poet, critic, biographer, and political essayist, became a national sensation after writing *The Dictionary of the English Language.* The first writer to include quotations from other noteworthy authors to illustrate definitions, he took nine years to write his famous dictionary, which became the foundation of all subsequent dictionaries. This century also valued imagination as a higher and more comprehensive faculty than reason. By the mid-19th century, theorists described life, particularly setting, with objectivity, detail, and rich example. Another word for realism is verisimilitude, which reflects the author's attempt to present the setting or subject with such convincing detail that the reader easily visualizes the content. Poe was noted for his realistic and convincing depiction of the *House of Usher*. More contemporary authors such as Cisneros, use description, vernacular, and vignettes to create accurate description in *House of Mango Street*. By the late 19th century, naturalism took hold, developing characterization using a more scientific approach. More pessimistic and unromantic, naturalists presented humankind as products of heredity, instinct, and environment.

Classical Literary Criticism

Contemporary theorists, who would likely be studied by English majors, would use the following kinds of theory or rules to analyze literature. Each form of literary criticism is briefly explained.

Formalism

Formalism, still commonly called New Criticism, emphasizes the unity of all parts to create a whole. A formalist analysis considers how all the elements, literary and syntactical, fit together to provide understanding and how understanding the whole gives relevance to the comprising elements. In formalism content is NOT separated from form, but rather inextricably linked to create meaning. All the parts of a poem are related to each other and to the poem as an organic whole. A formalist reading is a close reading or explication of a text in which the reader performs a detailed and subtle analysis of the complexities and ambiguities of the components or elements within a work. Analysis attends to the meanings and interactions of words, figures of speech, symbols, complexity, and coherence, regardless of literary genre. Formalists ask questions such as: What is the motif, what does it mean, and how does it fit into the overall meaning of the poem? What word patterns emerge and how do these patterns function in the text? What are the symbols and imagery and how do they function in the text to create an overall meaning? For example, a poet might use the word "blue" in a text. Consulting a traditional and a historical dictionary would certainly uncover numerous definition of the word "blue," but formalists would argue that the reader can only know the correct definition when she understands how the word fits into the larger whole or scheme of the poem.

Historicism

Historicism, also called Genetic Criticism, views literary texts as integrally informed by the historical milieu. Historicists believe that each past age possesses unique events, assumptions, values, and beliefs, and only someone who is an expert in the particular period during which the text was written can truly understand these events, assumptions, values, and beliefs. Historicism deals with the facts, the historical facts. Literature must be read and interpreted within broader context that is grounded in the life, times, beliefs, class, privilege, and values of the author. A reader might best approach a novel by Charles Dickens through a historicist lens as these texts truly reflect the social, political, and economic contexts of the time. Richard Wright's *Black Boy* and *American Hunger* would also benefit from this form of critique because they are autobiographical memoirs.

New Historicism or Cultural Criticism

New Historicism regards text as discourse situated within complex cultural, religious, political, economic, and aesthetic discourses, which shape the literature and are shaped by the literature. New Historicists assert that history itself is a text, an interpretation that has no single history or any kind of unity or homogeneity to history/culture. Much like Historicists, New Historicists believe that readers must interrogate and identify the historical causes of the text but also contend that readers must examine the historical effects or consequences as well. The reader could used cultural critique to contextualize and understand Morrison's *Beloved* or Miller's *The Crucible*, as these works integrate historical elements but also represent the contradictory, competing, and dissonant forces of the time.

Reader Response Criticism

Reader Response Criticism asserts that just as texts have authors, they also have audiences. Reading therefore is not interpretation, but a transaction between a reader and the text. The reader (audience) interprets texts based on his/her personal experiences, values, beliefs, and emotions; the reader reads text to gain insight into his/her own life. In *Literature as Exploration* (1938), Louise Rosenblatt explained that readers transact with text for different purposes. She developed a continuum that represented reader responses ranging from the efferent to the aesthetic stances. Embedded within an efferent stance is the purpose of taking away information from the text. An aesthetic stance addresses the purpose of experiencing the text. When one reads literature, one interacts with literature as event, and this interaction explore responses that reflect particular emotions, attitudes, beliefs, and interests. The text has meaning because the reader makes meaning from the text by bringing personal experiences, morals, social codes, and views of the world to reading the text. The range of reader responses will vary because each reader is unique. This lens is employed in teaching text particularly in elementary and middle school grades because it makes the reader and the reader's history more relevant to the text, but engagement with the text depends on the degree of the reader's personal interaction or transaction with the text, thus potentially limiting the overall experience and interpretation of the text.

Mimetic Criticism

Reality serves as the context for Mimetic Criticism. That literature is a reflection of reality was basically unchallenged until the mid 18th century. Mimetic critics believe that great literature mimics reality. The reader constructs meaning within a larger framework or reality. As a result, Marxism, Feminism, and Psychological Critique fall within the broader category of Mimetic Criticism because each provides a larger framework of reality to inform interpretation. A Marxist looks at literature through the lens of power and economics, posing questions like "Who has power? Who has money? Who has social capital? Telling stories is a purposeful and political act that has different consequences given the storyteller; interpreting a text means identifying how issues of power, class, and ideology impact the text. Marxist critique works especially well with Orwell's *Animal Farm*, which establish clearly the relationships of power between characters, classes, and political bureaucracies.

Feminists look at the cultural and economic limitations on women in a patriarchal society that has prevented women from realizing their potential and acquiring power. This kind of criticism focuses on the relationships between genders and examines the patterns of thought, behavior, values, and power relations between sexes.

Psychological Criticism argues that characters that are believable are those that are most realistic. Psychological criticism derives from the work of Freud and particularly Jung. According to Jung, man is on an individual quest towards self-realization. Freud saw the individual as deeply dependent on society and anxious to conform to it, while Jung saw society as little more than a number of individuals of similar nature. Jung asserted that myths contain messages that speak to individuals in the same way. These myths contain archetypes, which have a fixed meaning. Among these are heroes, the self, the shadow, the villain, the serpent, the lion, the trickster, the magician, the fool, the sage, the child, gold, coal, and so on. Each of these archetypes serves as a powerful symbol. Jung also noted that these archetypes pervade all philosophies, ideologies, mythologies, literatures, and belief systems and are therefore common to all individuals.

Intertextual Criticism

Keesey summarizes the tenets of Intertextual Criticism in the statement: "Poems do not imitate life; they imitate other poems" (279). In other words, understanding the literary conventions and linguistic constructions inherent in all literature enables us to interpret text; interpreting text is by analogy. Northrop Frye identifies four principles that govern intertextual criticism: convention, genre, archetype, and the combination of the three. Literary conventions are literary devices that serve as a common language, which is used to discuss literature: plot, characterization, flashback, foreshadowing, etc. Genres are the distinct forms of literature: poetry, essay, short story, and so on. Archetypes include the Jungian definition but also other symbols that appear throughout different genres of literature. Understanding *Beowulf*, the *Iliad,* or the *Odyssey* can help us understand more contemporary epics.

Structuralism

Structuralism is the study of signs or symbols. Structuralism assumes that meaning occurs through difference. A technique of structural analysis is identifying binary oppositions. Examples of binary oppositions include hot/cold, old/new, and regression/progression. These oppositions can be used to construct meaning. For example identifying the binary opposition in "Out! Out!" by Frost, reveals the pattern of nature vs. technology, which helps the reader identify one of the major themes of the poem.

Post-structural Criticism

Post-structural Criticism assumes that the most effective way to interpret a text is to deconstruct it and suggest that there is no way of knowing what the "meaning" of a story is. Like the formalists, post-structuralists and deconstructionists use literary devices, conventions, and other formalist tools but use them to break down or deconstruct the text rather than derive a coherent and unifying whole. This view of criticism asserts that a text has no one single interpretation but many meanings because literature is political, cultural, and social. Achebe's *Things Fall Apart* clearly delineates how meaning is cultural, political, social, and gender-related.

COMPETENCY 0003

Understand literary genres, elements, and techniques.

Characteristics of Various Genres and Types of Literature

This section differentiates among the four major genres of literature, and defines specific forms within each genre also identifying literary terms unique to each genre and form. Included in this section is a fairly thorough and inclusive list of literary devices and terms with which all English educators should be familiar.

Genres and Characteristics

Fiction

Fiction is any text that is invented or imagined, usually in the form of prose narrative. Fiction may be based on personal events or experiences, but the characters in the story are invented. Even if a story is set in an actual place and involves a recognizable character, the story is still fictitious.

Elements of Fiction

Character

Character refers to the person in a work of fiction. There are two general types of characters: the *protagonist*, the character, usually a hero, that is central to the story with all major events in the story having some importance to this character, for example, Harry Potter; and the *antagonist*, the character who opposes the main character, in either an openly cruel or subtle way, for example, Lord Voldemort or Cruella de Vil.

Characterization

Characterization is the process and information the author provide to the reader about the characters. The author develops characterization in the following ways:

- by describing the character's physical, emotional, and social characteristics
- by explaining what the character thinks, feels, or dreams (psychologically introspective) Two examples are: Holden Caulfield in *Catcher in the Rye* is a first-person psychologically introspective character. Jane Austen is the master of creating a psychologically introspective, objective (albeit loosely) third person narrator.
- by divulging what the character does or does not do or the actions or decisions the character makes (ethics) by describing what other characters in the story say about the character (dialogue) and how they react to the character's behavior (external evidence)

Characters may be *round* or *flat*.

- *Round* characters are fully developed, acting according to complex and believable patterns of emotion, motivation, and behavior. Nora Helmer, in Ibsen's *A Doll House* is a round character.
- *Flat* characters are one-dimensional, predictable, and uncomplicated. Lennie in *Of Mice and Men* is a flat character.

Characters may also *dynamic* or *static*.

- *Dynamic* characters develop and grow in response to events or motives.

- *Static* characters remain the same throughout the course of the narrative, untouched by events or the people the encounter.

Plot

Plot is the sequence of events in a story or a play, a series of events planned by the author that has a beginning, middle, and end. The five essential parts of a plot are:

- *Introduction:* the beginning of the story, in which the author introduces the characters and the setting.
- *Rising Action:* the part of the story in which the conflict is revealed, in essence a "leading up" to the climax. They are all the events between the introduction and the climax.
- *Climax:* usually most interesting and revealing part of a story, a turning point, which begs the question of whether or not the conflict will be resolved.
- *Falling Action:* the point at which the events and complications that occur in the rising action and climax resolve themselves. At this point the reader now knows whether or not the conflict has been resolved.
- *Denouement:* the final outcome or untangling of events in a story.

Setting

Setting is the time, context, and location in which a story takes place. A reader should consider several types of setting when analyzing a work of fiction.

- *Place:* geographical location, where the action of the story occurs.
- *Social Conditions:* daily life, speech, dress, mannerisms, customs. The social conditions/customs of a novel like *Jane Eyre* will obviously be very different from a William Burroughs novel like *Naked Lunch* (a modern author who talks openly of drug addiction).
- *Time:* when the story is taking place—chronologically, the historical time period, the time of year, and the time of day.
- *Weather:* what the weather in the story is like, noting things like rain, the color of the sky, and natural phenomena like mountains and brooks.

- *Mood or atmosphere:* is the story cheerful or frightening, for example, the beginning of *Anna Karenina* established a less cheery, somewhat troubling but somewhat matter-of-fact mood: "Every family is dysfunctional."

Theme

The *theme* of a fictional text is its controlling idea or insight. It is the underlying meaning or central idea of the work and essentially what the author is trying to tell the reader. For example, one theme in the *Great Gatsby* is that one cannot relive the past, as Daisy Buchanan became an "unattainable object" for Jay Gatsby.

Different Types of Fiction

A **novel** is a fictional narrative in prose, usually longer than a short story. The author is not restricted by historical facts but is free to create fictional personalities in a fictional world.

Example: *Lord of the Flies* by William Golding

A **short story** is narrative prose fiction that is shorter than a novel. Short stories often vary in length with some no longer than a few hundred words and some are over fifty thousand words. "The Lottery" by Shirley Jackson is an example of a short story. An extended short story, such as "First Contact" by Murray Leinster, is referred to as a *novelette*. And when the story is longer, as in "The Metamorphosis" by Franz Kafka, it is called a *novella*. Unlike in a novel, the literary elements of plot, setting, and character are compressed in a short story.

Types of Fictional Narratives

Allegory is a form of extended metaphor, in which objects, persons, and actions in a narrative are equated with meanings that lie outside the narrative itself. The underlying meaning has moral, social, religious, or political significance, and characters are often personifications of abstract ideas like charity, greed, or envy. An allegory has both literal and symbolic meanings. Nathaniel Hawthorne's *Young Goodman Brown* is an allegory that describes what happens when one abandons one's faith and becomes associated with the devil.

Fable is a brief story or poem that is told to present a moral or practical lesson. The characters in fables are often animals that speak or act like humans. *Aesop's Fables*, told by Aesop, a slave in ancient Greece, used animals to tell stories about important virtues.

Folk Legend is a traditional narrative or collection of narratives, supposedly historically factual but usually a mixture of both fact and fiction, which has its origins in oral storytelling. The story of Pecos Bill, who apparently was raised out West by wolves, is an infamous tall tale created during Westward Expansion in the United States. He was a legendary cowboy, and akin to other folk figures like Paul Bunyan.

Myth is a traditional or legendary story that usually concerns some being, hero, or event without a determinable basis of fact or a natural explanation. Myths are often created to explain what humankind cannot understand, such as the actions of deities or demigods, practices, rites, or phenomena of nature. For example, the Greek myth of the Labors of Hercules describes how he ventures to the land of the dead and proves himself by accomplishing inhuman feats, eventually becoming a "complete god."

Romance is fictional prose narrative about improbable events involving characters that are different from ordinary people. King Arthur on a quest for a magic sword (Excalibur) aided by characters like fairies or trolls is an example of Romance. Oftentimes, Gothic and Romantic literature is mixed. For example, *The Castle of Otranto* takes place in a Gothic castle, but its hero, Theodore, a peasant, has "knightly blood," and ends up taking the throne. *Don Quixote* by Miguel de Cervantes is also an example of Romance.

Modern Fantasy is a kind of fiction where the author creates a magical world where anything is possible. Fantasy may include magical beings, talking animals, and gods and goddesses. The *Harry Potter* series by J.K. Rowling is a perfect example of a fantasy.

Science Fiction is a type of futuristic or high fantasy, which explores scientific fact and often poses ethical questions about current scientific trends and predictions. The author often focuses on exploring an unknown world that has been affected by "extrapolations" of current technological advancement. The Harry Potter series falls into the realm of science fiction.

Modern Realistic Fiction presents a problem to be examined through prose narrative. An example is *The Chocolate War* by Robert Cormier.

Historical Fiction is a story that takes the reader back to a particular time period and describes the life of a person who lived during that period. Good historical fiction is as true as possible to the time period being represented. The main character may (and often does) interact with actual historical characters, but usually the main character is not based on a real person. A historical artifact or person that appears out of place in a historical fiction is called an *anachronism*.

Mystery Fiction is a novel in which a crime has been committed. The reader and protagonist have to figure out the perpetrator. Mystery fiction is noted for intense suspense, intrigue, and mysteriousness. Agatha Christie's *Miss Marple* and *Hercule Poirot* depict mystery novel protagonists who have to figure out crimes. More recent, Dan Brown's *Da Vinci Code,* follows symbologist Robert Langdon in his efforts to uncover a Biblical "secret" that Jesus was married and fathered a child with Mary Magdalene.

Nonfiction

Autobiography and biography are the most common forms of nonfiction, but periodicals and scientific papers also fall under this heading. *Nonfiction* is any prose narrative that recounts events or stories as they actually happened or that possesses factual information.

Different Types of Nonfiction

Autobiography is a person's account of his or her own life, for example, *The Story of My Life* by Helen Keller.

A *biography* is a book someone else has written about (usually) a famous historical figure. A good example is Doris Kearns Goodwin's *No Ordinary Time* about Franklin and Eleanor Roosevelt.

An *essay* is usually a short piece of nonfiction writing, which is often written from an author's personal point of view. Essays may include literary criticism, political manifestos, scholarly arguments, and everyday observations, recollections, and reflections of the author. The definition of an essay is vague, overlapping with those of an article and a short story. Almost all modern essays are written in prose, but some are written in verse.

Informational Books and *Articles* are books and shorter texts about topics of particular interest, such as Jared Diamond's *Guns, Germs, and Steel*, which traces the anthropological reasons for why the western world rose to its modern status.

A *memoir* is a form of autobiography that is objective and anecdotal. *Newspaper Accounts* are supposedly unbiased objective writing that tells exactly how an event happened. Newspaper articles are written in an "upside down pyramid" format in which the most important details are provided at the beginning and lesser details are explained in the rest of the article.

Drama

Drama is a story that is acted out, usually on a stage, where actors and actresses take parts of specific characters. Dramas are usually either tragedies in which the protagonist meets a disastrous end or comedies, in which a humorous plan ends happily[4].

Genres of Drama

Serious Drama or *Tragedy* explores the notion that life is finite and deals with serious subjects and characters who are confronted with their own mortality. Many tragic plots revolve around a crisis over succession of a throne as in *Antigone* and subsequent breaking of familial and societal ties. Murder and death occur frequently in tragedy and usually result from a transgression of sacred principles or morals as in *Oedipus Rex.* Tragic characters like Oedipus act alone and take responsibility for their actions. The audience usually empathizes with tragic characters, identifying with their suffering, experiences, and catharses. Arthur Miller's *Death of a Salesman* is a modern tragic play.

Comic Drama or *Comedy* celebrates the continuation of life and the success of generations through love and rebirth. Comic plots usually involve an outrageous idea or fantastic scheme that disrupts normal workings of the community and leads to chaos. Comedy often examines characters from a particular social class and comic characters tend to reflect human weakness. Comedy usually occurs in the realm of ludicrous and ends with a reconciliation or happy resolution, such as an engagement or marriage.

Farce is a form of drama designed to create laughter, emphasizing clowning and slapstick humor. Farce

- contains exaggerated physical action by stereotypical characters.
- exaggerates characters so intensely that they are highly unlikely to be found in the real world.

[4] http://library.thinkquest.org/23846/library/terms/index.html

- incorporates absurd situations, improbable events, and unexpected experiences.
- includes complex plots with character and dialogue less important to plot and situation.
- writers include Aristophanes (*The Clouds*) and Plautus (*Miles Gloriosus*), Greek masters of the farce. Monty Python and the Marx Brothers are modern examples of farce.

Melodrama[5] has its origins in music as it incorporated music to increase emotions or to signify characters with signature music. Such works

- reflected interest in morality and virtue.
- were set in the medieval world, with castles, dungeons, and torture chambers.
- simplified the moral universe with good and evil embodied in stock characters.
- occurred in an episodic form: villain poses a threat, and the hero or heroine escapes with a happy ending.
- used many special effects: fires, explosions, drowning, and earthquakes.

Tragicomedy is drama that mixes the elements and styles of tragedy and comedy. In the Jacobean era of Great Britain these plays had romantic and exciting plots in which disaster persisted throughout the play, eventually reaching a happy conclusion. An example of such a play is Shakespeare's *The Winter Tale.* Modern drama explores existential themes that describe human activities that have no fixed meaning, are always in flux, uncertain, and ambiguous. Loneliness and alienation are significant themes in modern tragicomedy. More modern tragicomedy writers are Samuel Beckett (*Endgame* (a play), "Molloy," and "Malone Dies" (both are novels) and Anton Chekhov (*Three Sisters)*[6]

Poetry

Poetry is language arranged in lines, with a regular rhythm and definitive rhyme scheme. Nontraditional poetry or *free verse* does away with regular rhythm and rhyme,

---

[5] http://novaonline.nv.cc.va.us/eli/spd130et/melodrama.htm

[6] *www.**drama**.uwate.rloo.ca/**Genre**-2005.ppt*

though it is still usually written in lines. The sounds of words and the strong feelings evoked by images distinguish poetry from other forms of literature.

Genres of Poetry

Concrete Poetry, also often referred to as visual poetry, relies on the typographical arrangement of words to convey the meaning of the poem, along with other conventional elements of a poem, such as rhythm, meter, and word choice.[7] A simple example is

I
Like
Triangles

Dramatic Poetry is written in either a monologue or a dialogue and in the voice of a character assumed by the poet. Famous dramatic monologues include Alfred Lord Tennyson's "Ulysses" and Robert Browning's "My Last Duchess."

The *Epic Poem* is a long narrative poem, often extending to several books with sections of several hundred lines. The poem usually focuses on a significant and serious subject. Homer's *Odyssey* is an example of an early and historic epic poem.

Lyric Poetry was originally songs performed in Ancient Greece accompanied by a small harp-like instrument called a *lyre*. The current definition of lyric poetry is a poem presented in the voice of a single speaker. The speaker's *voice* is frequently different from that of the actual author's, so readers should remember that the author often invents a fictional character in the poem to speak. The majority of poems that we read nowadays in English classes are lyric poems.

There are several types of lyric poetry.

- *Ballad* is a type of quatrain, or stanza of four lines. The ballad stanza's lines are in iambic tetrameter, alternating with a rhyming abcb (lines 1 and 3 are unrhymed), less commonly, abab, for example, Coleridge's *Rime of the Ancient Mariner.*
- *Blank Verse* is unrhymed (blank) iambic pentameter, found in Shakespeare's plays.

[7] http://members.optushome.com.au/kazoom/poetry/concrete.html

- *Couplet* is two lines of verse, usually coupled by rhyme. Chaucer was the first poet to use this form in the "General Prologue" to *The Canterbury Tales.* Pope uses a couplet in "An Essay on Man": *Why has not Man a microscopic eye?/ For this plain reason, Man is not a Fly.*

- *Heroic Couplet* is two consecutive lines of rhyming poetry that are written in iambic pentameter and that contain a complete thought. In a heroic couplet, there is usually one pause at the end of the first line, and another heavier pause at the end of the second line.[8] Example: In John Keats's *Endymion*: "*A thing of beauty is a joy forever;/ Its loveliness increases, it will never/ Pass into nothingness; but still will keep/ A bower quiet for us, and a sleep…*

- An *elegy* is a poem that laments the loss of someone who has died "To An Athlete Dying Young."

- *Limerick* is a five-line stanza that comes from an old custom at parties where each person was required to sing an extemporaneous nonsense verse, which was followed by a chorus with the words "Will you come up to Limerick." The master of the limerick was Edward Lear (1812–1888), who wrote: "There Was an Old Man with a Beard." The first and fifth lines of the limerick must end with the same word, which is usually a place name. Lear, however, deviates from this convention.

- The *Sonnet* traditionally is a poem of fourteen iambic pentameter lines linked together by a rhyme scheme. This is one of the oldest verse forms in English. The sonnet originated in Italy, and was introduced into England by Sir Thomas Wyatt in "Whoso List to Hunt." The three basic types of sonnet are the Italian or Petrarchan sonnet, the English or Shakespearean sonnet, and the Spenserian sonnet. The Italian sonnet has an octave, consisting of eight lines, and a "turn" in the poem called a sestet, a series of six lines. Spenserian stanza has nine lines, in which the first eight are iambic pentameter and the last is an iambic hexameter (called an alexandrine, defined in the meter section); the lines rhyme *ababbcbcc.*

[8] http://library.thinkquest.org/23846/library/terms/index.html

Criteria for Evaluating Poetic Works

This section provides a few guidelines to consider when a reader analyzes, interprets, explicates or reads a poem closely.

Pattern of the Sound and Rhythm

- *Free verse* has neither regular rhyme nor regular meter.

The Visible Shape or Structure

- *Line structure*, especially in concrete poetry

Rhyme in Poetry

- *End rhymes*—rhymes appear at the end of a line.
- *Feminine rhymes*—rhymes consist of a stressed syllable followed by an unstressed syllable (*flying, crying*)
- *Internal rhyme*—rhymes whose internal syllables sound the same, such as *when/men*
- *Masculine rhymes*—rhymes consist of single stressed syllable (*bly, fly*)
- *Perfect rhyme*—if correspondence of rhyme sounds is exact

Imperfect Rhyme in Poetry

- *Off-rhyme*, or half rhyme, near rhyme, or slant rhyme, differs from perfect rhyme in changing the vowel sound and or concluding consonants in a sound (Example: *gone/alone*)
- *Vowel rhyme*: the rhyme words only have their vowel sounds in common (Example: *boughs/towns*)
- *Similar consonants*: (Example: *trod/trade*)

Literary Devices

Alliteration: The repetition of initial sounds in neighboring words

Example: Repetition of "p" sound in P*eter Piper picked a peck of pickled peppers*

Allusion: A reference to a person, event, or place, real or fictitious, or to a work of art. May be drawn from history, geography, literature, or religion.

Example: In Mary Shelley's *Frankenstein* the creature reads *Paradise Lost* by John Milton.

Analogy: A rather fully developed comparison between two things or ideas that are basically unlike each other although they share something in common. Frequently, something unfamiliar or complex will be described in terms of something familiar or simple.

Example: In Longfellow's "The Arrow and the Song," he analogizes, kindness : friend :: arrow : tree.

Apostrophe: When an absent or deceased person, abstract concept, or important or inanimate object is directly addressed.

Example: "Oh water, giver of life!" In Ovid's *Metamorphoses*, Pyramus and Thisbe address the wall that separates them in this way: "You envious barrier."

Archetype: A character, symbol, plot, or theme that recurs often enough in literary works to have universal significance. Archetypes appeal to readers on a fundamental level, as dreams and myths do. Don Quixote and Odysseus are archetypes of characters on a great quest.

Assonance: Repetition of vowel sounds

Example: repeating "ea" sound in "cheap leap"

Blank Verse: Unrhymed poetry in iambic pentameter, lines of five feet, with each foot having an unstressed syllable followed by a stressed one. Blank verse reflects the natural rhythms of the English language.

Example: Milton uses blank verse to describe Satan's banishment from Heaven in *Paradise Lost*.

Nine times the space that measure day and night
To mortal men he, with his horrid crew,
Lay vanquished, rolling in their fiery gulf,
Confounded though immortal. But his doom
Reserved him to more wrath; for now the thought
Both of lost happiness and lasting pain

Torments him: round he throws his baleful eyes,
That witnessed huge affliction and dismay,
Mixed with obdurate pride and steadfast hate.

Connotation: The emotional or cultural associations surrounding a word, as opposed to its strict, literal dictionary meaning

Example: *In Romeo and Juliet*, Romeo associates Juliet with the sun. A steed conjures up associations of a noble and powerful horse; yet a hack conjures up associations of a workhorse. Both are horses.

Consonance: The repetition of consonant sounds

Example: repeating the "s" sound in "someone sees something."

Denotation: The strict dictionary meaning of a word, presented objectively, without emotional associations.

Example: A horse is a large hoofed mammal *(Equus caballus)* having a shorthaired coat, a long mane, and a long tail, domesticated since ancient times, used for riding and for drawing or carrying loads.

Epigram: A short, witty saying, often ending with a clever twist

Example: *The heart that is distant creates its own solitude. (T'oa Ch'in from "I Built my Cottage . . . ."* or *"Thy praise or dispraise is to me alike;/ One doth not stroke me, nor the other strike.* Ben Jonson's *Epigrams*.

Euphemism: A commonly used term or phrase used to express an idea without bluntly declaring that idea. Example: He kicked the bucket." instead of "He died."

Foreshadowing: The use of hints or clues to suggest what will happen later in literature

Example: In *Of Mice and Men*, Carlson's shooting Candy's dog is a foreshadowing of George's shooting Lennie.

Free Verse: Verse that has no fixed pattern of rhyme, rhythm, or line length. Although "free" from the demands of regular rhythm and rhyme, free verse achieves its effects with sound devices and subtle patterns of rhythm.

Example: Crane's "*There Was Crimson Clash of War.*" *There was crimson clash of war./ Lands turned black and bare;/ Women wept;/ Babes ran, wondering.*

Hyperbole: An exaggeration or overstatement

Example: I'm so hungry I could eat a horse.

Imagery: Language that evokes one or all of the five senses: seeing, hearing, tasting, smelling, or touching. These sensory details provide vividness by arousing a complex of emotional associations.

Example: In James Masao Mitsui's *"When Father Came Home for Lunch."*

Mother adds fried onions, a fried egg
and potatoes to his main bowl.
He adds catsup, shoyu
and mixes it with the white radish,
He works around to the mustard-caked bowl
before each mouth of rice,
sauce hanging from his moustache.
Hot coffee, heavy with sugar & cream,
steams from a china mug.
Half-an-hour of noisy manners
and he's gone, back to work
in oily bib overalls,
I can still smell sweat
soaking his long-sleeved workshirt.

Inference: A reasonable conclusion about characters or events based on the limited information provided by an author. The following excerpt from *David Copperfield* leads Davy to believe that his mother and this gentleman are romantically involved:

> "I never saw such a beautiful color on my mother's face before. She gently chide me for being rude; and, keeping me close to her shawl, turned to thank the gentleman for taking so much trouble as to bring her home. She put out her hand to him, as she spoke, and as he met it with his own, she glanced, I thought, at me."

Irony: A discrepancy between what is said and what is meant. There are three different kinds of irony:

Verbal Irony: When an author says one thing and means another.

Example: A man who says, "Lovely day for a stroll," when there is a blizzard outside.

Dramatic Irony: When an audience perceives something that a character in the play/literature does not know.

Example: In *Macbeth*, the audience knows that the movement of Birnham Wood is soldiers holding tree branches; Macbeth thinks that the woods *are* indeed moving.

Situational Irony: A discrepancy between the expected result and actual result

Example: You buy a special pair of earrings for yourself as a birthday gift, only to learn that your friend gives you the same pair as a birthday present.

Malapropism: The act of misusing a word often in a humorous manner, usually because the words sound the same.

Example: Using *incinerating* instead of *insinuating* in the question: What are you incinerating?

Metaphor: The comparison of two things without using *like* or *as*

Example: In the wrestling ring, he was a lion.

Mood: The general atmosphere or prevailing emotion of a work, as created by the choice of words, setting, images, and details. Crane uses imagery to create a mood that turns from peaceful to foreboding, sleep to eagerness in *The Red Badge of Courage:*

"The cold passed reluctantly from the earth, and the retiring fogs revealed an army stretched out on the hills, resting. As the landscape changed from brown to green, the army awakened, and began to tremble with eagerness at the noise of rumor. It cast its eyes upon the roads, which were growing from long troughs of liquid mud to proper thoroughfare. A river, amber tinted in the shadow of its banks, purled at the army's feet; and at night, when the stream had become of a sorrowful blackness, one could see across it the red, eyelike gleam of hostile campfires set in the low brows of distant hills."

Onomatopoeia: A word that imitates the sound it represents

Example: *buzz* for the sound that bees make

Oxymoron: Putting two contradictory words together

Example: "wise fool"

Paradox: A statement, character, or situation that appears to be contradictory but that is nonetheless true

Example: In Rumi's "The Soul of Goodness in Things Evil": *'Tis the love of right/Lures men to wrong.'*

Parallelism: The use of phrases, clauses, or sentences that are similar or complementary in structure or in meaning

Example: I enjoy cooking, eating, and reading.

Parody: A form of satire that is a humorous imitation of the style, characters, or subject matter of serious writing designed to ridicule a work or to point up or exaggerate its characteristics.

Example: *Austin Powers* is a parody of James Bond.

Personification: Giving human qualities to animals or objects

Example: The fire danced in the dark night.

Point of View: The vantage point from which an author presents the actions and characters in a story. The story may be related by a character (first-person point of view) or by a narrator who does not participate in the action (third-person). Further, the third-person narrator may be *omniscient*, able to see into the minds of all characters; *limited*, confined to a single character's perceptions; or *objective*, describing only what can be seen. Most events, pictures, and stories can be presented from more than one perspective, or point of view. Because every story can be told from a number of perspectives, an author must decide on a particular point of view from which to present the narrative and choose a narrator who shapes how the reader perceives characters, actions, settings, and events.

Rhythm: The arrangement of stressed and unstressed syllables in speech or writing. Rhythm, or meter, may be regular, or it may vary within a line or work. The four most common meters are iamb, trochee, anapest, and dactyl. In daily conversation, certain words and syllables receive more emphasis than others. Like ordinary speech, poetry has patterns of accented and unaccented syllables that form a beat, or rhythm. Although poems may or may not use rhyme, all poetry—even free verse, to some extent—has rhythm that is regular or irregular.

Feet and Meter

An identifiable pattern of stressed and unstressed sounds in poetry is called *meter*. To determine the meter or rhythm of a poetic passage, mark the stressed syllables and unstressed syllables. In addition, each line can be divided into smaller units, each with an accented syllable and one or more unaccented syllables. Such units of measure, called *feet*, are divided by a slash. Determining the metrical pattern in poetry is called *scansion*.

The number of feet within a line of poetry may range from one to eight. The following terms are used to represent the number of feet that occupy a line of poetry. *Pentameter*, *tetrameter*, and *trimester* are probably the most common line lengths in English verse.

A single *foot* in poetry is often the combination of just two syllables, an iamb and a trochee. If the foot is anapestic or dactylic, then it will have three syllables.

Satire: A technique that exposes human weakness or social evils. Satire may use exaggeration, wit, irony, or humor to make its point. The satirist may adopt a tone ranging from good-natured humor to biting ridicule or scorn. Satire can entertain, instruct, or reform or bring about action.

Example: In "A Modest Proposal," Jonathan Swift satirizes Irish aristocrats for their handling of the Irish potato famine, by suggesting that the starving eat babies.

Simile: The comparison of two unlike things using *like* or *as*.

Example: He eats like a pig.

Style: An author's choice of structure, selection and arrangement of words, tone, and degree of reliance on sound effects, imagery, and figurative language.

Example: William Faulkner's use of foreshadowing, flashbacks, symbolism, narration and characterization as well as his immensely long sentences in *The Sound and the Fury* creates an unusual writing style.

Symbolism: The use of an object or action that means something more than its literal meaning, representing things by means of symbols or attributing symbolic meanings or significance to objects, events, or relationships.

Example: The hammer and sickle was once a symbol of Soviet communism.

Theme: The underlying meaning of a literary work. A theme can be stated or implied. Theme differs from the subject of a literary work in that it usually makes an observation about the subject. Some literary works have no theme, others have more than one.

Example: The theme of William Blake's "A Poison Tree" is about anger, not a tree.

Tone: The attitude a writer takes toward a subject, character or audience, such as serious, humorous, sarcastic, ironic, pessimistic, formal, critical, objective, and playful. Although tone and mood are related, they should not be confused. Mood is the overall effect that a work has on the reader, while tone involves the voice and attitude of the writer.

Voice: The author's style or the quality that makes his or her writing unique, and which conveys the author's attitude, personality, and character.

COMPETENCY 0004

Understand literature for children, including genres, literary elements, and literary techniques.

Children's and Young Adult Literature serve as extraordinary vehicles for not only teaching reading and comprehension but also for teaching literary devices, criticism, genres, and forms or types of literature. Donna Norton's *Through the Eyes of a Child: An Introduction to Children's Literature*, *7th Edition*, is probably one of the best texts in print that addresses reading, selecting, evaluating, and teaching children's and young adult literature. High interest, easy reading (low readability) children's and young adult literature can provide valuable texts to engage nonreaders in exploring literature and improving reading fluency, stamina, and comprehension. Picture books and wordless books, especially can offer non-native English speakers and struggling readers a common focal point for identifying sequence, developing vocabulary, explaining and illustrating concepts and ideas, and deriving meaning. Alphabet books like *Animalia* present exquisite illustrations of animals, idea, and objects, that represent the letter accompanied by alliterative phrases composed of challenging vocabulary. Other picture books like *The Middle Passage* depict the profoundly emotional, forced journey of African slaves to the New World and serve as a gripping pre-reading activity that contextualizes difficult content in a way that is accessible to all students. The following section describes the most common types (sometimes called genres) of children's and young adult literature and provides specific examples of quality selections of each genre by title and author.

Types of Literature

Picture Books: Nodelman (1990) defines picture books as books that "communicate information or tell stories through a series of many pictures combined with relatively slight texts or no texts at all" (VII). Pictures books help students learn sequence, characterization, story line, and vocabulary. Picture books include:

Alphabet Books: Books that present the letters of the alphabet using rich details, innovativeness, and numerous objects.

- *Animalia* by Graeme Base
- *Bestiary: An Illuminated Alphabet of Medieval Beasts* by Jonathan Hunt
- *Ashanti to Zulu* by Margaret Musgrove
- *A Walk in the Rainforest* by Kristin Joy Pratt

Concept Books: Books that help readers learn concepts such as colors, shapes, trains, planes, night, and day.

- *The Grouchy Ladybug* by Eric Carle
- *Circles, Triangles, and Squares, Of Colors and Things*, and *Shapes, Shapes, Shapes* by Tana Hoban
- *Changes, Changes* by Pat Hutchins

Counting Books: Books that usually show one large number, the word for the number, and a representation of the number using objects.

- *Anno's Counting Book* by Mitsumasa Anno
- *Moja Means One: Swahili Counting Book* by Muriel Feelings
- *Count Your Way through Italy* by Jim Haskins
- *Eating Fractions* by Bruce McMilan
- *The History of Counting* by Denise Schmandt-Besserat

Easy-to-Read Books: Books designed for beginning readers and young children. These books, which can appear as Big Books, often reinforce phonics and linguistic patterns. Dr. Seuss books appeal to any age and often address sophisticated concepts.

- *Oscar Otter* by Nathaniel Benchley
- *My Brother* by Betsy Byars
- *Sammy the Seal* by Syd Hoff
- *Frog and Toad* series by Arnold Lobel
- *The Butter Battle, Oh, the Places You'll Go,* and *A Cat in the Hat* by Dr. Seuss

Mother Goose Books: Books of rhymes and rhythms that tell stories about imaginative characters.

- *Miss Mary Mac and Other Children's Street Rhymes* by Joanna Cole and Stephanie Calmenson
- *The Neighborhood Mother Goose* by Nina Crews
- *The Glorious Mother Goose* by Cooper Edens
- *Gregory Griggs and Other Nursery Rhyme People* by Arnold Lobel

Wordless Books: Books that present a story using only pictures. Collections of art-work also serve as foci for writing, learning new vocabulary, understanding satire, parody, and imagery.

- *Anno's Journey* by Mitsumasa Anno
- *Banksy, Banksy Graffiti,* and *Wall and Piece* by Banksy
- *Do You Want to Be My Friend?* by Eric Carle
- *Pancakes for Breakfast* and *The Hunter and the Animals* by Tomi dePaola
- *The Middle Passage* by Tom Feelings
- *Changes, Changes* by Pat Hutchins
- *A Boy, a Dog, a Frog, and a Friend* and *Frog Goes to Dinner* by Mercer Mayer
- *Circus, Clouds, Noah's Ark, People*, and *Rain* by Peter Spier
- *The Mysteries of Harris Burdick* by Chris VanAllsburg
- *Flotsam, Free Fall, Sector 7, The Three Pigs, Tuesday*, and *Hurricane* by David Wiesner

Traditional Children's Literature includes forms that have emerged from the oral tradition of storytelling. The oral tradition is indigenous to every culture, race, class, and ethnicity. Traditional children's literature selections serve as excellent models for writing in a particular genre form, especially for middle and high school students. These texts also offer simple but engaging texts to teach theme, characterization, plot, and problem-solution, can help students access prior knowledge, or serve as "hooks" into more difficult texts that share similar themes and purposes.

Fables: Tales whose main characters are animals that talk and act human. Tales usually teach a lesson or end with a moral.

- *Aesop's Fables* by Aesop
- *Ackamarackus: Julius Lester's Sumptuously Silly Fantastically Funny Fables* by Julius Lester
- *Squids Will Be Squids: Fresh Morals, Beastly Fables* by Jon Scieszka and Lane Smith

Folktales: Fictional narratives that tell about important characters, events, and beliefs and reflect the rich culture, setting, history, and ethnicity of the storyteller. Oftentimes, the main characters in folktales are animals that possess intelligence and wit. Human characters are often superheroes and heroines who demonstrate unusual abilities. Folktales may also tell stories that explain how or why a particular event happened or why an animal or character came to exist. Different types of folktales include cumulative, realistic, humorous, beast, magic, and pourquoi tales (Norton 209–211).

- *Why Mosquitoes Buzz in People's Ears* by Verna Ardeman
- *The Magic Gourd* by Baba Wague Diakite
- *More Tales of Uncle Remus: Further Adventures of Brer Rabbit* retold by Julius Lester
- *Nelson Mandela's Favorite Folktales* by Nelson Mandela
- *The Spring of Butterflies and Other Folktales of China's Minority Peoples* by Neil Philip, Ed.

Legends: Narratives and poems that border on myths, folktales, and history (Cavendish 9). Legends provide important information about the cultures, beliefs, and societies that created them. Legends not only provide students a different way of thinking about the world and others but also expose students to literary devices of theme, figurative language, characterization, and conflict.

- *Beowulf*, anonymous
- *The Iliad* and *The Odyssey* by Homer
- *Sir Gawain and the Green Knigh*t by Michael Morpurgo
- *The Legend of Sleepy Hollow* by Washington Irving
- *The Merry Adventures of Robin Hood* by Howard Pyle
- *The Once and Future King* by T. H. White

Myths: Fictional narratives that are considered to be true in the culture depicted in the myth. Myths may explain the origin of an important event, person, concept, or natural phenomenon. Humans, animals, and deities are usually the main characters in myths. Myths are an essential part of early high school curriculum as their characters and themes form the basis for later works and describe gods, events, and phenomena that are alluded to in all genres of study.

- *Cupid and Psyche* by Edith Barth
- *A Book of Myths* by Thomas Bullfinch
- *The Golden God Apollo* by Doris Gates
- *In the Beginning Creation Stories from Around the World* by Virginia Hamilton
- *The Adventures of Odysseus* by Neil Philip

Fantasy is considered among the most valuable forms of children's literature because it allows the reader to enter an imaginative world, expands curiosity, and "opens the mind to new possibilities" (Norton 272). Excellent examples of fantasy suspend disbelief, create characters that are believable, develop a magical setting, and pose universal themes, thus establishing characters that reader believes are real, worlds that the reader believes could exist, and events that the reader believes could happen. Reading fantasy exposes the reader to rich description, vivid imagery, higher level vocabulary, intricate plots, various points of view, and differing methods of characterization.

Traditional Fantasy includes:

literary folktales or fairytales that capitalize on the "Once upon a time . . ." story frame

- *The Tinderbox Box* and "The Wild Swans" by Hans Christian Andersen

religious and ethical allegory that address religious themes and moral quests

- *Chronicles of Narnia* by C. S. Lewis
- *At the Back of the North Wind* by George MacDonald

mythical quests and conflicts that address conflicts between good and evil or adventures of characters seeking precious objects or power

- *Eragon* by Christopher Paolini

- *The Seeing Stone* by Kevin Crossley-Holland
- *The Golden Compass* by Philip Pullman
- *The Hobbit, The Lord of the Rings*, and *The Fellowship of the Ring* by J. R. R. Tolkien
- *The Black Cauldron* by Lloyd Alexander
- The *Harry Potter* series by J. K. Rowling

Modern Fantasy includes:

articulate animals, stories in which animals solve problems or get into mischief;

- *The Tale of Peter Rabbit* by Beatrix Potter
- *Charlotte's Web* by E. B. White
- *Rikki-Tikki-Tavi* by Rudyard Kipling
- *The Wind in the Willows* by Robert Lawson

toy stories, where the story is told from the point of view of the toy or doll;

- *The Velveteen Rabbit* by Margery Williams
- *Winnie-the Pooh* by A. A. Milne
- *Pinocchio* by Carlo Collodi

preposterous characters and situations, stories in which characters find themselves in absurd or humorous situations and where language plays with words, parody, and satire;

- *James and the Giant Peach, Charlie and the Chocolate Factory,* and *The BFG* by Roald Dahl
- *Rootabaga Stories* by Carl Sandburg

bizarre worlds, stories that include unusual settings, elusive characters, and strange events;

- *Alice's Adventures in Wonderland* by Lewis Carroll

- *Peter Pan* by James Barrie

little people, stories in which people like the reader solve problems and go on adventures;

- *The Borrowers* by Mary Norton
- *The Hobbits* by J. R. R. Tolkien

spirits and ghosts, stories in which characters take on frightening spirits or ally with friendly creatures;

- *The Boggart* by Susan Cooper
- *The Bartimaeus Trilogy* by Jonathan Stroud
- *The Children of Green Knowe* by Lucy Boston

time warps, stories in which characters travel to the future or back in time;

- *The Devil's Arithmetic* by Jane Yolen
- *The Time Machin*e by H. G. Wells

science fiction, stories that incorporate futuristic technology, scientific advancements, and space travel. This type of literature might also address dystopias.

- *Frankenstein* by Mary Shelley
- *Dr. Jekyll and Mr. Hyde* by Robert Louis Stevenson
- *Twenty Thousand Leagues Under the Sea* by Jules Verne
- *A Wrinkle in Time by* Madeleine L'Engle
- *The Giver* by Lois Lowry

Contemporary Realistic Fiction incorporates characters, themes, plots, settings, and conflicts that replicate real-life people, events, problems, and situations in honest and authentic ways. This form of literature offers readers characters that share similar social and emotional problems, thus helping readers feel that they are not alone or unique in their struggles. Realistic fiction often provides characters that serve as models for solving "challenging moral cognitive dilemmas" (Friedman and Cataldo 7).

Critical elements of contemporary realistic fiction include:

- *conflicts* that children and young adults encounter with peers, adults, authority, and external forces;
    - *The One-Eyed Cat* by Paula Fox
    - *Taking Sides* by Gary Soto
- *characters* that look, act, speak, and think like children and young adults in contemporary society;
    - *Homecoming* and *Dicey's Song* by Cynthia Voigt
- *themes* that address human needs;
    - *Hope Was There* by Joan Bauer
- *style* that incorporates believable dialogue, accurate and vivid description.
    - *Missing May* by Cynthia Rylant

Contemporary Realistic Fiction: "New Realism" often addresses controversial issues that elicit criticism for its too authentic content. These issues, which Norton calls "New Realism" (370) include sexism, sexuality, violence, profanity, family problems, desertion, divorce, and remarriage, death, growing up, alienation, individuality, racism, peer pressure, physical and emotional survival, and ageism. Norton counsels educators to consider such texts with care. Attention to mores, values, and beliefs of students in the classroom, citizens within the larger community, the social context, culture, ethnicity, and race is essential when evaluating such texts for use in the classroom. Selections of contemporary realistic fiction that contain "New Realism" themes include:

- *sexism*: *Jacob Have I Loved* by Katherine Paterson
  Dicey's Song by Cynthia Voigt
- *sexuality*: *Night Kites* and *"Hello" I Lied* by M. E. Kerr
- *violence*: *Scorpions* and *Shooter* by Walter Dean Myers
- *profanity*: *The Chocolate War* by Robert Cormier
- *desertion*: *Walk Two Moons* by Sharon Creech
- *single-parent*: *Where the Lilies Bloom* by Bill and Vera Cleaver
- *racism*: *The Bluest Eye* and *Beloved* by Toni Morrison

- *war*: *The Things They Carried* by Tim O'Brien
- *prejudice*: *Snow Falling on Cedars* by David Guterson
- *physical survival*: *Into the Wild* by Jon Krakauer
- *emotional survival*: *Caramelo* by Sandra Cisneros

Multicultural Literature is "a body of literature that represents any distinct cultural group through accurate portrayal and rich detail" (Yokota, 1993, p. 157). Multicultural Literature appears throughout all genres and reflects the unique and varied perspectives, cultures, beliefs, traditions, and contributions of each cultural group in an increasingly diverse global society. Examples of multicultural literature appear throughout the various forms explained during previous discussions as well as in Chapter 2: Literature and Language. Additional selections of multicultural realistic fiction include:

- **African American**

  Scorpions, The Mouse Rap, and *Shooter* by Walter Dean Myers

  The House of Dies Drear by Virginia Hamilton

- **Asian American**

  Kira-Kira by Cynthia Kadohata

  Homeless Bird by Gloria Whalen

  Honeysuckle House by Andrea Cheng

- **Native American**

  Walk Two Moons by Sharon Creech

  The Ceremony of Innocence, I Wear the Morning Star, and *Legend Days* by Jamake Highwater

  The Brave by Robert Lipsyte

- **Latino**

  *The House on Mango Stree*t by Sandra Cisneros

  How the Garcia Girls Lost Their Accents and *In the Time of the Butterflies* by Julia Alvarez

  Taking Sides by Gary Soto

  Elya's Home at Last by Susan Middleton

- **New Immigrant**

  Blue Jasmine by Kashmira Sheth

  The Sunita Experiment by Mitali Perkins

  Tangled Threads: A Hmong Girl's Story by Pegi Dietz Shea

Historical Fiction is a body of literature whose characters, setting, conflicts, theme, action, style, and perspectives are consistent with, relevant to, and reflective of the specific historical time period. Authenticity in language, setting, characterization, and theme is essential to effective historical fiction. Selections of historical fiction include:

- *A Gathering of Days: A New England Girl's Journal* by Joan Bios
- *Code Talker* by Joseph Bruchak
- *Dust to Eat: Drought and Depression in the 1930s* by Michael Cooper
- *The Slave Dancer* by Paula Fox
- *Out of the Dust* by Karen Hesse
- *Dragonwings* by Laurence Yep

Nonfiction

Biographies

Historically, biographies for children were texts that educated about politics, religion, and society. Texts tended to depict heroes and "reflected the belief that literature should save children's souls" (Norton 462). Eventually the religious focus was replaced by biographies of heroes that attained the American Dream, heroes in politics, science, music, sports, and other areas. Biographies also documented the struggle of various persons throughout history. Good biographies are engaging, factually accurate, and credible and reliable based on primary sources. Including photographs and illustrations also enhances the appeal of biographies. When read alongside historical fiction, biographies add clarity and authenticity. A selection of biographies includes:

- *Maritcha: A Nineteenth-Century American Girl* by Tonya Bolden
- *Genius: A Photobiography of Albert Einstein* by Marte Ferguson Delano

- *Lincoln: A Photobiography* by Russell Freedman
- *The Voice that Challenged a Nation: Marian Anderson and the Struggle for Equal* by Russell Freedman
- *Rights* by Russell Freedman
- *Walt Whitman: Words for America* by Barbara Kerley
- *Wise Guy: The Life and Philosophy of Socrates* by M. D. Usher
- *Saladin: Noble Prince of Islam* by Diane Stanley
- *Anthony Burns: The Defeat and Triumph of a Fugitive Slave* by Virginia Hamilton

Informational Books are texts that students use as sources for writing reports, enriching understanding in the disciplines or learning about concepts and ideas out of curiosity. Informational books must contain accurate facts, pictures, and illustrations, be free of stereotypes, challenge analytical thinking, organize for understanding, and possess an engaging style (Norton 502). Informational books also present technical vocabulary, which when accompanied by pictures, charts, and illustrations enhance vocabulary understanding for English language learners and native English speakers. Pairing an informational book with fiction text of a specific period also contextualizes the fictive work for readers. A selection of useful informational books includes:

- *The Way Things Work* by David Macaulay
- *Four to the Pole!: The American Women's Expedition to Antarctica* by Nancy Loewen and Ann Bancroft
- *Arrowhawk* by Lola Schaefer
- *Outside and Inside Killer Bees* by Sandra Markle
- *What's the Deal? Jefferson, Napoleon, and the Louisiana Purchase* by Rhoda Blumberg
- *The Golden City: Jerusalem's 3,000 Years* by Neil Waldman
- *Good Women of a Well-Blessed Land: Women's Lives in Colonial America* by Brandon Marie Miller
- *Remember D-Day: The Plan, The Invasion, Survivor Stories* by Ronald J. Drez

- *Scholastic Encyclopedia of the Civil War* by Catherine Clinton
- *Remember: The Journey to School Integration* by Toni Morrison
- *Now Is Your Time! The African American Struggle for Freedom* by Walter Dean Myers

Book Awards

Caldecott Medal: Award given to a children's book for innovative, detailed, vivid, and rich illustrations, drawings, or pictures. The 2009 Caldecott Medal winner was ***The House in the Night***, illustrated by Beth Krommes, written by Susan Marie Swanson. For a list of Caldecott Medal winners since 1938, see <www.ala.org/ala/mgrps/divs/alsc/**awards**grants/bookmedia/>.

Newbery Medal: Award given to a work written in English by an American citizen. Distinguished work is judged by the author's presentation or interpretation of theme with respect to accuracy, organization, clarity, characterization, setting, style, and plot development. The 2009 winner of the Newbery Award is Neil Gaiman's *The Graveyard Book*. For a complete list of Newbery Medal winners since 1922, see <www.ala.org/alsc/**newbery**.cfm>.

The Coretta Scott King Book Award, is presented by the Coretta Scott King Committee of the American Library Association's Ethnic Multicultural Information Exchange Round Table (EMIERT) to an African American author and an African American illustrator for an outstandingly inspirational and educational contribution that is inspirational and promotes understanding and appreciation of the culture of all peoples and their contribution to the realization of the American dream. The 2009 winner is *We Are the Ship: The Story of Negro League Baseball* written and illustrated by Kadir Nelson. For a complete list of award winners, see <http://www.ala.org/ala/mgrps/rts/emiert/>.

Criteria for Evaluating Children's Literature

Donna E. Norton, in *Through the Eyes of a Child: An Introduction into Children's Literature* identifies very specific criteria when evaluating a work of children's literature. She poses a series of questions that address several foci: story, conflict, characterization, setting, theme, style, point of view, and accessibility.

Story: Generally authors develop a story chronologically. Sometimes, however, they use flashbacks or may even follow a storyline that replicates a character's maturation process. Story development also presents **conflicts** that create suspense and demonstrate struggle. Conflicts usually include person-against-person, person-against-society, person-against- nature, person-against-self, and person-against-supernatural.

1. Is the story a good one?
2. Are the story and plot believable; could the story really happen?
3. Is the climax natural?

Characterization: An engaging story has characters that come alive. They are multi-faceted, confront their problems, change and grow as a result, are not all good or all bad. Memorable characters are those who are physically, mentally, emotionally, intellectually, and socially real. We learn about their strengths, weaknesses, points of view, personalities, perspectives, failures, and triumphs.

1. Do the characters seem real?
2. Do the characters change and grow?
3. How easily does the main character solve the problem?
4. When I read the story aloud, do the characters sound like they are actually talking?

Setting: The setting must help the reader see, sense, smell, taste, hear, and touch what the characters see, sense, smell, taste, hear, and touch. Different genres of children's literature require different ways of establishing setting. Setting may be portrayed as mood, via illustrations, pictures, and description that create place and time. Setting may be portrayed as antagonist, especially in texts that pose a person-against-nature, person-against-society or person-against-supernatural. Setting may also be portrayed as historical background, in which accurate description is essential. Setting may also be portrayed as symbolic, such as the magical Hogwarts in the adventures of *Harry Potter* or the garden locked behind the wall in *The Secret Garden*, a symbol of the father's grieving.

1. Is the setting realistic, representing what is truly known about the time and place?
2. Do I feel that I am in the setting's place and time?
3. Do the characters fit into the setting?

Theme: The theme connects setting, conflict, and characters. The author's purpose, message about life, people, and society, must be credible so that children understand the author's purpose and message in the context of their own lives. In younger children's literature theme revolves around emotions and experiences that are relevant to the reader. Changes in the character can also represent theme. Theme can also be revealed through how characters confront and solve conflicts or in how they develop and mature.

1. Is the theme of the story worthwhile?
2. What is the author trying to tell me?

Style: The words, phrases, imagery, and literary devices authors use to develop theme, characters, conflict, and setting are critical in establishing mood, tone, believable characters, and reasonable conflict.

1. Does the language throughout the story sound natural, engaging, inviting?

Point of View: The author, narrator, or speaker tells a story from his/her point of view that reflects specific experiences, values, beliefs, and perspectives. The point of view from which the text is written has significant impact on the reader. An author may choose to use the first person "I" to tell the story, which restricts the author to write about the emotions, experiences, and insights of one character. Or the author may choose to write from an omniscient point of view, which expands the author's ability to write about the experiences, emotions, and insights of all the characters in the text.

1. Do I learn about the different sides of one or all the characters, their personalities, their strengths, and their weaknesses?

Accessibility, Readability, and Interest: Accessibility considers how available texts are to children, in school, at the library, at home. Readability must match the child's reading level or the experience results in frustrations. Interest is critical to engagement and understanding. Children pursue texts that interest them and present experiences that are similar to their own.

Evaluating Multicultural Literature

Norton also identifies particular questions that must be considered when evaluating Multicultural Literature.

Characterization: Are the characters portrayed as individuals rather than a representative of a group? Do the characters transcend stereotypes? Is the culture accurately portrayed and is physical diversity apparent? Do nonwhite characters solve problems without intervention from white characters, portrayed as equals to white characters, and not glamorized? Are females represented fairly and accurately?

Setting: Is the setting authentic, replete with accurate historical and factual details? Are contemporary and historical settings described accurately and do they rectify omissions and distortions?

Theme: Are social issues depicted frankly, honestly, accurately, and complexly? Does the author have a legitimate purpose for writing the text?

Style: Is the dialect accurate and appropriate? Is offensive or degrading vocabulary avoided? Are the illustrations authentic and non-stereotypical?

COMPETENCY 0005

Understand the writing process and formal elements of writing and composition

What Do Good Writers and Speakers Do? What Is Good Writing and Speaking?

Good writers and speakers take risks by posing innovative and original theses, sharing unusual or engaging ideas, or playing with words. Good writers and speakers put themselves on the line, presenting arguments, narrating stories, and describing events that take a stand, demonstrate point of view, and exhibit powerful voice. Good writers and speakers explore questions and probe ideas that engage, interest, and motivate themselves. Good writers and speaker have strong purpose and consider audience carefully. Good writers and speakers play with language, building powerful vocabularies, and manipulate words and language.

Good writing focuses on specificity incorporating details that create pictures or develop the bigger issue. Good writing includes characters that are highly detailed "right down to the color of his socks, her earrings" (Fletcher 58). Good writing demonstrates a distinctive voice and personality, develops argument, mounts suspense, builds conflict, and creates imagery using multiple literary and rhetorical devices and effective diction, and intersects characters, plot, and setting with balance, finesse, and competence. Good writing leaves a lasting impression on the reader/audience accomplishing its established purpose.

The History and Development of Rhetoric

Simply stated, rhetoric is the art of using language or discourse. Discourse is written and spoken language, used to convey meaning. Young, Becker, and Pike suggest that the word rhetoric derives from Greek *eiro*: "I say." The history of rhetoric in Western tradition begins with the ancient, highly inventive societies. Essentially citizens used rhetoric to plead their cases in court. Although the Sophists were the first teachers of rhetoric, Plato, Isocrates, Artistotle, Cicero, Quintillian, and St. Augustine of Hippo are credited for developing modern rhetoric.

Plato (c.428–c.348 BCE)

Plato loathed false rhetoric. The intent of Plato's oratory was to influence humankind's soul, which assumed that he knew the kinds of souls humankind possessed. Given the depths to which humankind's souls have plunged, Plato would indeed have much work to do to influence contemporary souls.

Isocrates (436–338 BCE)

Isocrates founded the first school of rhetoric in Athens. Unlike his contemporary Plato, Isocrates used rhetoric to probe practical problems. He was most interested in the kind of discourse that would defend causes that were good and honorable.

Aristotle (384–322 BCE)

Plato's student Aristotle developed a complete theory of rhetoric called The Rhetoric. Aristotle developed principles of argumentation, which are still used today.

Cicero (106–43 BCE)

Cicero was probably the most influential member of the Roman senate. He used rhetoric to persuade and convince. Cicero believed that a specific style of oratory corresponded to a particular purpose. *Proving* required plain and simple language. *Pleasing* required a language of charm. *Persuading* required vigorous and rigorous language.

Quintilian (c.35–c.100)

Quintilian also a famous Roman rhetorician devoted his life to creating volumes of ancient rhetorical theory. He believed that good orators had to be good men or they would not be able to speak eloquently. Like Plato, he would be disheartened to know that history has seen marvelous orators, whose goodness and character are suspect.

Saint Augustine of Hippo (354–430)

A lawyer and teacher, St. Augustine of Hippo used rhetoric to evangelize. He believed that eloquent rhetoric converted pagans to Christianity rather than simple rhetoric.

Classical Rhetoric

Classical rhetoric is divided into three branches: *deliberative, judicial*, and *epideictic.* The purpose of *deliberative rhetoric* is to convince, persuade, or dissuade as demonstrated in Patrick Henry's *Speech before the Virginia House of Burgesses*. The purpose of *judicial* rhetoric is to accuse, defend, or exonerate. As surmised, this kind of rhetoric is employed in courtrooms. Harper Lee incorporates this type of rhetoric in *To Kill a Mockingbird* when Atticus presents his closing remarks about the innocence of Tom Robinson in the rape of Mayella Ewell. Marc Antony's spoken soliloquy in *Julius Caesar* is an excellent example of *epideictic* rhetoric, whose purpose is to celebrate, commend, or commemorate his slain mentor Julius Caesar.

Cicero defined five overlapping divisions or canons of the rhetorical process.

- *invention:* discovery of valid arguments to support the thesis
- *arrangement:* five parts of the oration which include
    - introduction to position or thesis in which the speaker or writer establishes credibility and the argument's purpose;
    - narrative in which the speaker or writer establishes the sequential account of events;
    - main part in which the speaker or writer presents the arguments in support of the position or thesis;
    - counterargument in which the speaker or writer anticipates possible opposing arguments and presents counter arguments;

  - closing in which the speaker or writer summarizes the arguments and appeals to the audience's pathos.
- *style:* The manner in which a speech or argument is spoken or written. Style includes all figures of speech
- *memory:* "The practice of storing up commonplaces or other material arrived at through the topics of invention for use as called for in a given occasion" (Silva Rhetoricae *http://rhetoric.byu.edu/canons/Memory.htm*).
- *delivery:* The performance or delivery of the speech.

Modern Rhetoric

Although modern rhetoric still employs all the rhetorical devices of classical rhetoric, modern rhetoric has shifted from the speaker to the author and to the audience. Everyday language and communication in its variety of uses comprises rhetoric. In thinking about rhetoric, it is useful to think about the context of rhetoric, or more specifically to assume a rhetorical stance. Context, which includes purpose, audience, subject, and medium, provides the framework for a rhetorical stance.

Audience includes the listener(s) or reader(s). A writer or speaker varies the type of discourse according to the audience. A student explicating a thesis of a literary text to a professor will (hopefully) use academic discourse, that is, rhetoric that follows formal language conventions, employs the appropriate use of literary devices and figurative language, incorporates effective organization, and addresses the principles of unity of thought, coherence, proportion, and emphasis. A student participating in a debate in front of peers may have three audiences: the opposing side, the judge, and the gallery. A skilled debater then must earn points by addressing all three audiences in ways that support a logical, clear, and coherent argument defended in an effective, persuasive, and even expressive manner. A student text messaging a friend will utilize a minimalist form of rhetoric replete with its own codes, abbreviations, and language. In considering an audience, good writer or speaker asks: Who is the reader or listener? What does the reader or listener know about the subject or topic? How receptive is the reader or listener to what I have to say? What is the reader or listener's bias? How can I help my reader or listener understand what I have to say?

Purpose: Kinneavy identifies four purposes of discourse within the realm of communication: expression, persuasion, reference, and literary. These purposes are not mutually exclusive and are often combined in a piece of writing but in a careful and deliberate manner.

Expressive discourse serves the speaker/writer's goal of self-expression. Such discourse in speech includes: conversations, protests, complaints, prayers, etc. Such discourse in writing includes: diaries, myths, journals, creeds, declarations, contracts, and so on.

Persuasive discourse serves the speaker/writer's goal of persuading or convincing the listener(s)/reader(s). Such discourse in speech includes: oratory, debate, political speeches, advertising, homilies, propaganda, marriage proposals, attorney's arguments etc. In writing, persuasive discourse appears in editorials, written appeals, grant writing, etc.

Referential discourse can be exploratory, scientific, or informative. The goal of this type of discourse is to depict the subject matter as clearly, authentically, and realistically as possible.

- *Exploratory discourse* in speech includes interviews, dialogues, seminars, panel discussions, diagnoses, text messages, emails, etc. Written examples would include questionnaires, medical histories, etc.
- *Scientific discourse* in speech or writing would include literary criticism, descriptive analysis, history, taxonomy, etc.
- *Informative discourse* in speech could include news broadcasts, infomercials, weather reports, stock market panels and topic-specific talk shows. Written informative discourse includes summaries, articles, essays, textbooks, websites, etc.

Literary discourse serves the speaker/writer's goal of entertaining or providing pleasure in some way. Such discourse in speech would include comedy routines, television shows, film, plays, poetry reading, songs, jingles, jokes, puns, etc. In writing, examples include the various genres of literature. In considering purpose, a good writer or speaker asks: What is my objective, aim or goal? What is the purpose of my discourse: to explain, persuade, describe, probe, entertain, illustrate, express, discover, learn? How do I want my audience to respond? Do I want them to laugh, take action, agree, disagree, learn?

Subject is the topic or focus of the spoken or written word. The topic also determines or influences the type of discourse. Writing about a controversial subject such as euthanasia requires a different type of rhetoric than writing about a day at the beach. Even within a very specific type of discourse, e.g., persuasive discourse, language conventions will differ according to subject. Proposing a new law and proposing marriage, should require different conventions, vocabulary, grammar, etc., (Although the language in a prenuptial agreement might indeed be similar to that in a piece of legislation.) In considering subject a good writer or speaker asks: What content best serves my purpose? What thesis will I offer? What is my point, message, idea, belief?

Medium is the method or form of delivery, which can range from a campaign speech, academic paper, poem, commercial, letter, to email or website. In today's world, rhetoric is critical to effective communication but is often perceived negatively, as in the term "empty rhetoric," or propaganda. Yet both are forms of rhetoric. By today's standards the medium is the message, which requires writers, readers, speakers, and listeners to attend not only to the text but also to the visuals that accompany the text. The appeal of a webpage, textbook, billboard, commercial, trailer, poster or press conference is as much about visual images as it is about text. Music and special effects may enhance the rhetoric but may also detract from the message. Modern rhetoric, replete with bells and whistles, demands a discerning audience and a skilled rhetor.

Unity, Coherence, and Emphasis

Critical to effective modern rhetoric are three principles also known as the three unities: coherence, and proportion and emphasis. The three "unities" that must be incorporated to render rhetoric effective are: *unity of thought, unity of feeling*, and *unity of purpose*.

- *Unity of thought*: All ideas, arguments, details, and rhetoric must support one main or central idea or thesis in speech and in writing.
- *Unity of feeling*: Manipulating emotions in various ways must work to produce the desired mood or feeling.
- *Unity of purpose*: All spoken or written discourse must enable the purpose, to inform, convince, influence, enlighten, etc.

Of additional importance is the principle of *coherence*. All ideas in speech or composition (writing) must connect and relate logically to each other and to the central idea to create a coherent and consistent whole. Finally, speakers and writers must adhere to the *principles of proportion* and *emphasis*. Speakers and writers must observe the *principle of proportion* to assure that the appropriate amount of text or space is allotted to each part of the whole; an imbalance negatively impacts the symmetry of the work. The principle of *emphasis* asserts that significant and important ideas must appear in prominent positions, at the beginning or at the end, as these are parts of the speech and composition that the listener or reader is likely to remember.

Similarities and Differences between Language Structures in Spoken and Written English

Spoken Language

Spoken language is like thinking aloud. The speaker must make sure that the listener knows *what*, *where*, and *to whom* an utterance refers (deictics). This requires an unambiguous use of pronouns such as *it*, *this*, and *that*. Spoken language can capitalize on affect to enhance appeal to pathos; a speaker can show a specific emotion of excitement through gestures at the same time using words that relate the same emotion. Affect is used to appeal to logos as well; a speaker may show one finger to correspond to text "The first point of my argument is. . . ." Spoken language makes use of pauses, repetitions, and fillers. Spoken language allows the speaker to establish a relationship with the audience, through gestures, facial expressions, and emotion. Irony, ambiguity, statement, implication, emphasis, questioning, imperatives, and exclamation in spoken language are also aided by a speaker's affect. Thus, speaking relies on the immediate and present context, in which talk occurs. Speech in everyday contexts is socially constructed and contributes significantly to enhancing social relationships of all types. Thus, the relationship between speaker and audience is critical. Individual speakers can make different lexical choices in speech depending on the context and purpose of talk. There is an underlying grammar in spoken language but a speaker may make more use of disjointed forms, phrases, fragments, and clauses. Speaking also requires pragmatic competence, being able to differentiate between questions, statements, commands, and statements by using inflection, intonation, pitch, and stress. This competence enables coding, or the speaker's ability to "convey a persona and an attitude towards an audience." (Kantor and Rubin 59). Motivational speakers will employ a different lexicon than a newscaster. *Prosody* (pitch, stress, rhythm, and intonation) is a suprasegmental feature of speech that allows a sound to be extended over several sounds is not easily demonstrated in written language but allows a speaker to switch codes given the context, purpose, and audience.

Written language must also make sure that the reader knows *what*, *where*, and *to whom* language refers (*deictics*). This is accomplished through establishing voice and point of view. Writing also requires an unambiguous use of pronouns such as *it, this,* and *that*. While speakers have the advantage of an immediate context, writers must develop the context, using figurative language, literary devices, and vivid imagery to appeal to pathos. Written language follows a specific organization depending on the purpose, audience, subject, and medium. This organization may involve the use of transitions, topic and clincher sentences, and other language conventions to signal logic and flow. A writer, unable to use gestures and facial expressions, must make use of myriad rhetorical devices to appeal to pathos. Writers must develop irony and ambiguity through use of explicit devices and figurative language. Writers use tools such as punctuation, italics, boldface type, font, and ellipses, to indicate statement, emphasis, questioning, imperative, and exclamation. Like speakers, writers can make different lexical choices in speech depending on the context of the writing. A journalist will employ a different lexicon than a poet. There is a specific grammar in written language, which depends on the type of discourse, subject, purpose, medium, and audience.

The Role of Cultural Factors in Oral and Written Communication

Many theorists have developed hypotheses about second-language acquisition. Krashen (2003) posits two theories about how children develop oral and written communication: learning and acquisition. *Learning language* implies that the writer and speaker are conscious of learning a language, its rules, structures, and conventions. This kind of language development occurs in school. *Acquisition* implies that language learning is subconscious and natural and occurs in and out of school in a variety of contexts.

Subsumed under these views are hypotheses that suggest that there is a natural order to learning language, with certain aspects of language development appearing before others. Second-language development also follows a natural order. For example: second-language learners understand the formation of plural forms designated by "s" before they learn the presence of "s" in the singular verb form in subject-verb agreement. Researchers suggest that the natural order of learning rarely parallels the order in which language is taught.

It is also suggested that speakers and writers use language rules, structures, and conventions to check if what they are saying or writing is correct. Monitoring spoken language is much more difficult than monitoring written language, because spoken language is more spontaneous, and monitoring often impacts fluency of ideas and language flow.

Another hypothesis suggests that there are affective variables that impact language learning. Variables such as an English language learner's accent, nervousness, fear of sounding incomprehensible or making a mistake, and anxiety are just a few of the variables that prevent second language learners from using the language acquisition device (See Chapter 2.).

Other research suggests that language learners not only need to hear and read language in a variety of contexts reflecting a variety of purposes, or more specifically receive language input, but also must speak and write language in a variety of contexts for a variety of purposes, more specifically language output.

Schumann (1978) explored specific cultural factors that may inhibit second language acquisition. He posits that social distance or the capacity for second-language learners to integrate into the dominant culture may impede language learning. For example, if there is a large enough number of immigrants situated in one area, there is more opportunity for that culture to become self-sufficient and closed, requiring less need to integrate into mainstream culture, where opportunities to learn the second-languages are more plentiful. Thus, there is a larger social distance between the second-language learner and the second language. Other factors that impact social distance are culture shock, attitude, and motivation. Research also confirms that we all possess a language ego, as our language is critical to our identity. Learning a new language can be intimidating, impacting our language ego in a negative way, deterring us from learning a new language. Another variable that influences second language learning is fossilization. *Fossilization* is the persistence of particular errors in speech and writing of second-language learners. For example, a native language may not use articles in its written and spoken forms. Although the second-language learner may have developed significant written and spoken output in the second language to communicate intended ideas, the lack of article usage may still remain. In essence, these language errors become fossilized.

The Composing or Writing Process

The National Council of Teachers of English identifies writing as a recursive process, a process that emphasizes prewriting, drafting, revision, peer-editing, self-editing, and publishing.

Prewriting: The composing process actually begins as soon as the writer or speaker assumes a rhetorical stance. This is a critical part of prewriting because the writer has identified the purpose, considered the audience, focused on the subject, and selected the medium. Any activity that the writer does before writing the first draft is *prewriting*. Prewriting includes: thinking, brainstorming, jotting notes, talking with others, interviewing experts, researching in the library or online, gathering and assessing information, listing, mapping, charting, webbing, outlining, and organizing information. Rereading, marking-up, and annotating a text that is the focus of analysis is prewriting. Reading and noting what experts write about a topic is prewriting. Reading poetry before writing poetry is prewriting. Reading memoirs prior to writing a memoir is prewriting.

Fletcher (1999) suggests keeping a writer's notebook to store ideas, notes, phrases, annotations, events, descriptions, quotations, and other fodder for writing. "A writer's notebook gives you a place to live like a writer, not just in school during writing time, but wherever you are, at any time of the day."

Drafting involves committing ideas on paper. This is the point when ideas become phrases, phrases become sentences, sentences become paragraphs, and paragraphs become essays. During the drafting process, writers concentrate on articulating a clear thesis statement and explaining and developing ideas fully, thoughtfully, and thoroughly. During this part of the process the writer seeks unity, coherence, and emphasis. While drafting the writer makes connections within and among the parts of the draft. The writer also attempts to integrate the most appropriate and useful rhetorical devices, incorporating figurative language to create imagery, and using details, facts, illustration, and examples to elaborate major points and elucidate the thesis. It is during this part of the process that the writer writes and reads like a writer. Grammar, punctuation, and spelling are not important during this step in the writing process. It is more important that the writer puts thoughts on paper as oftentimes, the very act of putting words on paper changes original ideas and inspires new ones.

Revision is probably the most difficult step in the composing process. During this part of the process it is critical that the writer read the first draft like a reader. This part of the process must be reader-centered, that is the writer must be cognizant of how the clarity, flow, balance, evidence, organization of the writing impacts the reader. While revising the writer must revisit those questions about purpose, audience, subject, and medium and reread and rewrite to assure that the writing responds to those questions and addresses those tasks in the most effective, explicit, and engaging manner possible. Revision is the most critical step in the writing process.

The follow are questions writers and peer editors should ask of the writing:

1. What is the purpose? What about the purpose is clear, focused and worthy? Is the reader convinced, entertained or informed?
2. Who is the audience? How and why is the writing appropriate to the audience?
3. What is the subject? What new insight, information or interpretation does the writing offer? What has the reader learned that is new

or different? What about the writing is engaging, interesting, or compelling?

4. How does the medium or form of the delivery utilize the most effective rhetorical devices appropriate to that medium? What specific rhetorical and literary devices did the writer incorporate to accomplish purpose, develop subject, and address audience? In what ways does the writing show instead of tell?
5. What is missing? What new ideas, details, examples, illustrations, and evidence could or should be added? What other rhetorical and literary devices would improve the writing?
6. How does the writer command and engage attention throughout the piece?

Honest responses to these questions provide fodder for and guide revision. These questions can be addressed in a variety of ways. One way is through student-teacher conferencing. Conferencing is critical to the revision process. Carl Anderson (2000) suggests that the writer set the agenda for conferencing by "describing her work" and "responding to the teacher's questions" (83) and the follow up by listening carefully to the teacher's responses, asking clarifying questions, and incorporating the teacher's feedback into the next draft.

In working with Somali students, Friedman (2000) used small group work to aid revision, incorporating a peer-editing protocol that involved reading and talking aloud, questioning, and rewriting. In the first step of the process, each student read his/her paper aloud. Peers listened carefully so they might later ask questions to clarify understanding and meaning. Listeners did not have a draft copy because it was just as important for students to improve listening skills. Writers were also instructed to stop and correct any confusing phrases, ideas, and details discovered during their read aloud. This process reinforced self-evaluation and self-correction, and immediate corrections and changes aided in creating a second draft. Before each student read the self-corrected draft, the other students were invited to share at least two positive comments about the writing and to ask at least two questions to help improve writing and help the reader better understand what the writer was thinking and writing. Writers summarized feedback aloud and wrote notes on the second draft. During the next step, writers incorporated and highlighted answers to questions in a new draft, which was later read aloud, as the process was repeated until pieces were proofread and published.

Editing is the next step in the composing process. Editing involves checking or proofreading written work for accurate language conventions of grammar, mechanics, and spelling. Fletcher and Portalupi (2001) suggest several areas that writers should evaluate during the editing process. They include: paragraph indenting, comma usage, use of active voice, precise language and diction, strength of verbs, sentence variety, quotation and dialogue usage, and sentence flow.

Publishing is the final step in the process. During this step writers share and celebrate their work in a public forum.

Criteria of and Strategies for Evaluating the Content and Effectiveness of Written and Spoken Language

The past sections of this chapter have identified and illustrated the more specific components of written and spoken language, the composing process, and rhetorical devices that enhance written and spoken language. The following section addresses traditional paragraph structures and types, essay structures, forms of writing, metrics for evaluating written and spoken language, and the most common language conventions that are essential to effective written and spoken language.

Paragraphs and Essays

The Paragraph

A *paragraph* is a group of sentences assembled together around a main idea or topic. There are several kinds of paragraphs: enumerative, explanatory, "how to," descriptive, comparison, contrast, comparison/contrast, cause and effect, and problem solutions. The "traditional" paragraph contains a *topic sentence, supporting sentences*, and a *concluding sentence*, sometimes called a clincher sentence. The first word in a paragraph is always indented.

The *topic sentence* is the most general sentence that poses the main idea or focus of the paragraph. The topic sentence usually begins the paragraph, but may be found in the middle and sometimes at the end of a paragraph, especially if the paragraph introduces an essay. The *supporting sentences* include reasons, details, examples, evidence, and illustrations that support the main idea or topic sentence of the paragraph. All supporting sentences should relate to the topic sentence. The *concluding sentence* ends the paragraph by reiterating (using different words) or summarizing the main idea of the paragraph. Sentences in a paragraph follow a logical order by including effective transitions.

The Five-Paragraph Essay

The five-paragraph essay is the most traditional form of the written essay. The five-paragraph essay includes an *introductory paragraph*, three supporting or *"body" paragraphs,* and a *concluding paragraph.*

The first paragraph, or *introductory paragraph*, hooks the reader into the essay, provides minimal background information, states the thesis statement, and establishes the framework or blueprint as to how the writer will prove the thesis statement. A *thesis statement* is a statement that takes a stand or position, expresses one main idea, justifies its value, and narrows the topic into a manageable, supportable argument. Generally the thesis statement includes three major points that support the main argument. Each of these points becomes the topic in each of the three body paragraphs.

Each of the *three body paragraphs* has a topic sentence that relates to one of the major points in the thesis statement, supporting sentences that include details, examples, reason, illustrations, and evidence that support the topic sentence and a concluding/transitional sentence that leads the reader into the next body paragraph.

The *concluding paragraph* summarizes the major points of the essay, rewords the thesis statement, and includes a clincher sentence that leaves the reader thinking.

Rubrics: Evaluating Written and Spoken Language

Whether evaluating writing or speaking, evaluative criteria must establish high standards, value originality and diversity, encourage risk-taking, encourage passion and voice, and support revision. There are numerous ways to evaluate writing, but rubrics provide a useful instrument that not only differentiates among quality criteria in writing and speaking but also, and more importantly, offer students clear foci for revision and improvement. Rubrics are usually generic or task-specific. Truly generic rubrics can be used to evaluate any performance. Task-specific rubrics are tailored to the particular performance or purpose.

Holistic rubrics tend to be generic rubrics, which can be used to evaluate many performances. The advantages to such rubrics are that they "emphasize what learners do," are easy to use, save time, and can be applied by trained raters with good coefficients of reliability. (See: *<http://www.carla.umn.edu/assessment/VAC/Evaluation/rubrics/types/holisticRubrics.html>*.). The primary disadvantage is that they provide little useful feedback to students that can improve performance. The Massachusetts Comprehensive Assessment System uses a holistic rubric to evaluate long compositions. See Figures 1 and 2.

Analytic rubrics address the more general categories of generic rubrics but are presented in distinct categories. In such rubrics, a student can receive points for each category, which are totaled at the end to create a final score. The following is a list of performance dimensions commonly found in analytic rubrics:

Speaking & Writing

1. content
2. vocabulary
3. use of grammar, spelling, punctuation
4. originality
5. diction
6. voice
7. organization
8. coherence
9. relationship between form and purpose
10. style
11. fluency
12. intonation
13. pronunciation

References

17 Gough Square. 2007. 2 February 2009. <http://www.17goughsquare.com>.

Adventures in American Literature. New York: Harcourt, Brace & World, 1970.

The American Heritage High School Dictionary, 4th Edition. Boston: Houghton Mifflin. New York, 2008.

Anderson, Carl. *How's it going?: A practical guide to conferencing with student writers.* Portsmouth, NH: Heinemann, 2000.

Appleman, Deborah. Critical Encounters in High School English. New York: Teacher College Press, 2000.

Armstrong, W.P. "Southern California's Vanishing Cypresses." Fremontia 6 (2): 24–29. 1978.

Armstrong, W.P. "The Close-Cone Pines and Cypresses" (Chapter 9, pp. 295–358). In: Terrestrial Vegetation of California, John Wiley & Sons. 1977.

Barilli, Renato. *Rhetoric.* Minneapolis: University of Minnesota Press, 1989.

Bob Craig's Web Home. 2009. 2 April 2009, <http://www.ask.com/bar?q=Rhetorical+Theory&page=1&qsrc=6&ab=1&u=http%3A%2F%2Fwww.colorado.edu%2Fcommunication%2Fmetadiscourses%2FTheory%2Frhetorical_theory.htm>.

Eagleton, Terry. *Literary Theory: An Introduction*, Second Edition. Minneapolis, MN: University of Minnesota Press, 1996.

Ebbers, S. M. *Vocabulary through Morphemes.* Longmont, CO: Sopris West, 2003.

Espenshade, A. Harry. *The Essentials of Composition and Rhetoric*. New York: D.C. Heath & Co., 1904.

Fletcher, Ralph. *What a Writer Needs*. Portsmouth, NH: Heinemann, 1993.

Fletcher Ralph, *A Writer's Notebook: Unlocking the Writer within You*. New York: Avon, 1999.

Fletcher, Ralph. *Live Writing*. New York: Avon, 1999.

Fletcher, Ralph, and Portalupi, JoAnn. *Writing Workshop: The Essential Guide*. Portsmouth, NH: Heinemann, 2001.

Freeman, David, S. and Freeman, Yvonne, S. *Essential Linguistics*. Portsmouth, NH: Heinemann, 2004.

Friedman, A. A. "Agents of Literacy Change: Working with Somali Students in an Urban Middle School." *The Power of Culture: Teaching across Language Difference.* Cambridge, MA: Harvard Educational Publishing Group, 2002, 121–145.

Friedman, A. A. Writing and Evaluating Assessments in the Content Area. *English Journal 90*(1), 2000. 107–116.

Habib, M.A.R. *Modern Literary Criticism and Theory*, A History. Malden: Blackwell Publishing, 2008.

Henning, Martha L. *Friendly Persuasion: Classical Rhetoric--Now! Draft Manuscript.* August, 1998, 25 March 2009, <http://www.millikin.edu/wcenter/workshop7b.html>.

Henry, M. K. *Unlocking Literacy.* Baltimore: Paul H. Brookes Publishing, 2003.

Herrick, James A. *The History and Theory of Rhetoric: An Introduction*. Needham Heights, MA: Allyn and Bacon, 2001.

Honeycutt, Lee. *Aristotle's Rhetoric*. 21 June 2004. 22 March 2009. <honeyl@iowastate.edu>.

Kantor, Kenneth K. and Rubin, Donald L. "Between Speaking and Writing; Processes of Differentiation." *Exploring Speaking-Writing Relationships: Connections and Contrasts*. Urbana, Illinois: NCTE, 1981.

Kennedy, George. *A New History of Classical Rhetoric*, 1994

Kraschen, S. *Explorations in Language Acquisition and Use*. Portsmouth, NH: Heinemann. 2003.

Moore , Andrew. "Structure of Speech." Andrew Moore's Teaching Resource Site. April 7, 2009 <http://www.teachit.co.uk/armoore/lang/speech.htm>.

Nordquist, Richard. *About.com.* "Tool Kit of Rhetorical Analysis," 2009. 16 March 2009. <http://grammar.about.com/od/rhetorictoolkit/Tool_Kit_for_Rhetorical_Analysis.htm>.

Ramage, John D. and John C. Bean. *Writing Arguments. 4th Edition*. Needham Heights, MA: Allyn & Bacon, 1998, 5 April 2009, <http://www.u.arizona.edu/ic/polis/courses021/ENGL_102–78/EthosPathosLogos>.

Rhetoric and Composition: Some Definitions of Rhetoric. 2009, 30 March 2009, <http://www.stanford.edu/dept/english/courses/sites/lunsford/pages/defs.htm>.

Schumann, J. *The Pidginization Process: A Model for Second Language Acqusition.* Rowley, MA: Newbury House. 1978.

Silva Rhetoricae, 2009, 5 April 2009, <http://www.ask.com/bar?q=five+canons+of+rhetoric&page=1&qsrc=0&ab=0&u=http%3A%2F%2Frhetoric.byu.edu%2Fcanons%2FCanons.htm.>

Teaching the Writing Process in High School, National Council of Teachers of English, Urbana, Illinois: NCTE, 1995.

Terban, M. (2002). *Building your vocabulary*. New York: Scholastic Inc., 2002.

Women's Rural Advocacy Program, Battering: The Facts, 2009, 3 March 2009, <http://www.ask.com/bar?q=What+Causes+Men+to+Abuse+Women&page=1&qsrc=6&ab=0&u=http%3A%2F%2Fwww.letswrap.com%2Fdvinfo%2Fwhatis.htm>.

Young, Richard, Becker, Alton, L and Kenneth L. Pike, *Rhetoric: Discovery and Change*, 1970.

YourDictionary.com, 1996–2009 1 April 2009, <http://www.yourdictionary.com/search?ydQ=definition+of+punctuation&area=entries&x=29&y=11

CHAPTER

2 History and Social Science

The MTEL History and Social Science section includes four test objectives. These objectives represent a broad range of integrated social sciences concepts from the content areas of history, geography, political science, and economics. Embedded within each broad objective are a number of essential social science concepts. A thorough understanding of each objective requires deep knowledge of the embedded concepts coupled with the ability to analyze and apply those concepts in a comparative analysis of Massachusetts, U.S., and world contemporary and historic society.

American History

COMPETENCY 0006

Understand major developments in the history of the United States and the Commonwealth of Massachusetts from pre-colonial times to the present.

Indigenous Peoples and European Settlement

European exploration began in earnest after Christopher Columbus landed in the New World in 1492. The Americas may have been "new" to Europeans, but indigenous peoples had been thriving in communities for thousands of years. The Paleo Culture was the earliest known collection of human beings in the New World. Most believe that they had crossed the land bridge from Siberia to Alaska. Much later (800 BCE–600 CE), groups such as the Adena-Hopewell Indians, who are known for creating large burial mounds and using metal tools, traded and moved within a large expanse of North America. The Mesoamerican civilizations (including the Mayans and the Aztecs) occupied Central America and much of Mexico. These peoples developed a strong agricultural system and extensive trade networks, followed a solar calendar, and participated in highly ritualistic religious and political ceremonies. The Aztecs founded present-day Mexico City in 1325. Spanish explorers, such as *Juan Ponce de Leon, Ferdinand Magellan*, and *Vasco Núnez de Balboa* sailed to Central and South America, and parts of North America. By 1519, when the Spanish explorer *Hernan Cortés* arrived in Mexico, the Aztec ruler *Montezuma II* reigned over 5 million people. There were over 30,000 indigenous people living in Massachusetts when Europeans first began exploring the continent. Tribes such as the Wampanoag, Pennacook, and Massachusetts all belonged to the Algonquin language group.

Many European nations began aggressive exploration of the Americas in the late 15th century. The French were interested in establishing lucrative trade routes and formed close allegiances with many indigenous tribes to achieve this goal. The Spanish, interested primarily in precious metals, controlled much of Central and South America. The British worked to control the east coast of North America for permanent territorial expansion.

The Thirteen Colonies

In 1607, the London Group of the Virginia Company established the first English settlement at *Jamestown, Virginia*. Motivated by economic interest, these early settlers spent most of their time prospecting for gold and failed to adequately prepare for the winter months. Consequently, many Jamestown settlers did not survive and the settlement had difficulty thriving in the harsh realities of the New World.

The Pilgrims established a more successful settlement in New England by harnessing the strict work ethic embedded within their stringent religious convictions. The Pilgrims, known in England before their departure as Puritans, were an austere religious group influenced by the teachings of John Calvin. The Puritans fled the religious persecution of King George and landed in Plymouth on December 25, 1619. Before disembarking from the Mayflower, the Pilgrims signed the *Mayflower Compact*, an agreement whereby all signatories would follow the rules established by majority vote; the Compact was both a symbol of the democratic governance to come in America and considered by many to be the first constitution ratified in the colonies.

By 1733 the original 13 colonies had been established. The original 13 colonies in order of establishment include Virginia (1607), Massachusetts (1620), New Hampshire (1623), New Jersey (1623), New York (1624), Maryland (1632), Rhode Island (1636), Connecticut (1636), Delaware (1638), North Carolina (1653), South Carolina (1663), Pennsylvania (1682), and Georgia (1732). Colonies such as Maryland, Rhode Island, and Pennsylvania were known for their religious tolerance, colonies such as the Carolinas and Georgia prospered through the production of rice and tobacco, and many of the northern colonies participated in the manufacturing and trade of textiles.

Even as the colonies grew, the British Government continued to wield great influence over them as it was in Parliament's interest to control and expand British rule in America. Simultaneously, the British had to contend with other European powers interested in continued American conquest. These tensions came to a head during the *French and Indian War* (1754–1763) when the British fought the French and their native allies for control of North America. This protracted war resulted in British supremacy and control of North America.

The American Revolution and the Development of the National Government

After the *Treaty of Paris in 1763* ended the French and Indian War, the British government's purse was heavily drained and the colonists' sense of total dependence on the British Army for protection was lessened. The preceding decade of war gave the colonists their first taste of quasi-independence, thanks to the wartime policy of salutary neglect, whereby the colonies operated and grew relatively unsupervised while the British were busy fighting off French forces. Through this strategic neglect, colonists began to depend and build upon their own resources for self-defense and small-scale self-government. When Parliament sought to defray the debts of war through a system of heavy direct and indirect taxation, the colonists' feelings of resentment for the heavy-handed legislation grew, fostering an urgent desire for independence from Britain.

The *Stamp Act of 1765* imposed a direct tax on documents such as wills, marriage licenses, newspapers, and playing cards. It was enacted to help support the cost of British troops in the colonies. The subsequent Stamp Act Congress of the same year convened to protest this taxation and seek its repeal. The colonists were successful in their efforts and this small victory built self-confidence and an even greater desire for self-rule. In spite of the growing trend towards rebellion in the colonies, the British continued to tax, and colonists continued to dissent, protest, and subvert. The Declaratory Act and the Townshend Act imposed more taxes on the colonists. A group called the Sons of Liberty formed to boycott British goods and organize protests. Samuel Adams was a founder of the Sons of Liberty. In 1770, the *Boston Massacre* occurred. Tensions came to a head when a crowd of colonists in Boston—after harassing guards at the city's Custom's House—were fired upon, making martyrs for the radical cause out of five men (including *Crispus Attucks*, a runaway Mulatto slave and one of the first patriotic heroes of the revolutionary cause) and wounding many others. In 1773, in a symbolic and purposefully incendiary act, colonists threw imported tea overboard into Boston Harbor, refusing to pay even reduced taxes to the British Government. This event is known as the *Boston Tea Party*. Parliament's response was to pass the *Coercive Acts*—known as the Intolerable Acts among *Patriots*—which closed the port city of Boston until the tea had been paid for, increased the power of Massachusetts' royalist officials, and allowed for the quartering of troops anywhere. The Americans in turn called the *First Continental Congress* in 1774, a meeting where the attendants collectively called for a repeal of the Intolerable Acts and the immediate formation and gathering of local militias.

In April of 1775, the very first battle of the Revolution was fought at *Lexington and Concord* in Lexington, Massachusetts. The British had learned that the Patriots had stockpiled weapons in Concord, Mass., and sent approximately 800 troops to seize the munitions. Upon learning of this secret attack, the Patriots sent three men on horseback to sound the warning. They were Paul Revere, William Dawes, and Dr. Samuel Prescott. In June, the *Battle of Bunker Hill* was in actuality fought on Breed's Hill in Boston. The *Second Continental Congress* convened in 1775, and eventually American independence was declared (and officially adopted through the *Declaration of Independence*, largely attributed to the work of Thomas Jefferson) on July 4, 1776.

A number of key developments precipitated the foundation of the National Government. The language in the Declaration of Independence was based on the philosophical argumentation of John Locke, who believed government should inherit powers from the people. Not wanting to recreate the centralized powers of the British government (the very powers the colonists had rebelled against), Americans designed a government that vested significant power in individual citizens.

Before independence had been achieved, important actions that eventually lead to the signing of the *Constitution* had been set in motion. Written in 1777, but not ratified until

1781, the *Articles of Confederation* provided the first constitution for the fledgling nation. However, the Articles allowed each state too much freedom, creating a weak central government. In western Massachusetts, *Shays' Rebellion* (1786), in which poor farmers revolted against existing conditions, helped spur the development of a more unified *Constitution* that would broadened the powers of the national government. Soon after General George Washington and the colonial army defeated the British in 1787, delegates met in Philadelphia for the Constitutional Convention. Delegates worked for two summers drafting our current national Constitution. Once finalized, supporters of the new *Constitution,* such as *Alexander Hamilton* and *James Madison,* circulated the *Federalist Papers* to rally support for the *Constitution* in the colonies. In 1791, the *Bill of Rights*, which enumerated rights of citizens such as freedom of speech and the right to a fair trial, was appended to the *Constitution*. By the end of 1791, all 13 colonies had ratified the new national constitution.

Westward Expansion and Settlement

In 1803, although the United States was still a young and somewhat unformed nation, the purchase of the Louisiana Territory from France (*the Louisiana Purchase*) reflected an ambitious agenda of territorial expansion. Thomas Jefferson's purchase of this land from Napoleon basically guaranteed uninhibited exploration and expansion beyond the Mississippi River. The following year (1804), Lewis and Clark embarked on a highly successful government-funded expedition of the new territory — in the name of scientific and geographic research.

The *War of 1812* was yet another conflict with the British. The American victory helped to create a burgeoning sense of nationalism and also fostered economic independence by eliminating the last commercial ties to and dependency on Great Britain.

In 1823, President James Monroe issued the *Monroe Doctrine*, a declaration that both asserted the new nation's dominance in the Western Hemisphere and instructed European nations to cease their interference on the American continents. Along with a focus on expanding boundaries for the sake of strengthening the economy and the international clout of the nation, *Manifest Destiny*—a sort of divine justification for moving westward into new lands—drove many individuals and their families to seek new lives, land, and opportunities in the unsettled West. While many Americans trail blazed their way into new towns, settlements, and territories, millions of Native Americans were displaced, coerced into signing treaties, and forced to surrender their lands to the American government.

The question of whether to allow slavery in newly settled territories led to the *Missouri Compromise of 1820*. In this series of bills in Congress, Maine was admitted to the Union as a free state and Missouri as a slave state, to preserve the balance of slave and free states, while slavery would be prohibited in any future state created from the Louisiana Purchase, north of the 36° 30′ parallel, Missouri's southern border.

The Origins and Events of the Civil War

In 1849, westward expansion was driven by the search for gold, discovered in California. The gold rush greatly expanded the state's population and led California to apply for admission to the union as a free state. Due to Southern concern for the growing inevitability of Northern—and therefore free-state—control, this application sparked a crisis which led to the *Compromise of 1850*, a law that allowed new territories to decide the matter of slavery for themselves, based on the principle of "popular sovereignty." In further debates over the expansion of slavery into the territories, the Illinois Senator Stephen A. Douglas argued in the *Kansas-Nebraska Act* that any territory desiring to exclude slavery could do so simply by declining to pass laws to protect it. Abraham Lincoln—who became both a Unionist and the President of the United States in 1860—while not advocating the abolition of slavery, argued that the country must restrict slavery's extension into the territories. The controversy was continued in the aforementioned Kansas-Nebraska Act of 1854, which repealed the Missouri Compromise and allowed the people of those territories to decide for or against slavery by popular sovereignty. Fierce fighting later broke out in Kansas as pro- and anti-slavery forces battled for control. The nation's controversy over the issue of slavery was only heightened by the passage of the *Fugitive Slave Act of 1850* and the *Dred Scott Case of 1857*. At the passage of the Fugitive Slave Act, many northerners and abolitionists were outraged, as the law required citizens to capture and return escaped slaves, under penalty of fine and imprisonment, without the option of a jury trial. In the case of the former slave Dred Scott, the Supreme Court ruled that slaves who resided temporarily in free states or territories were still slaves, and that Congress did not have the authority to exclude slavery from a territory. According to the ruling, a person only became a free citizen of the United States through birth or the process of naturalization. Tension continued to brew between the North and South as the balance of power remained precarious and unstable, and in 1861, eleven southern states seceded from the Union with the intention of forming their own nation and government, known as the Confederacy.

On April 12, 1861, confederate troops fired on Union-held Fort Sumter in Charleston, South Carolina, thereby marking the official beginning of the *Civil War*. At its outbreak, both the Union and the Confederacy controlled desirable advantages. The Northern states had a larger population and greater control of factories, industries and railroads. On the other hand, the Southern states were defending territory largely unfamiliar to Union forces.

During the first year of war confederate forces won several battles. However, the *Battle of Gettysburg* in 1863 marked a turning point, as the Confederate Army sustained a crippling loss of manpower in only two days. In that same year, another blow was dealt to the South when President Lincoln issued the *Emancipation Proclamation*, declaring that all slaves residing within the Confederacy would be free. Later, this freedom would be extended to all slaves living within the United States. African American soldiers were allowed to enlist after the Emancipation Proclamation. *The 54th Massachusetts Infantry* was an African American regiment led by *Colonel Robert Gould Shaw*. As the war raged on and hundreds of thousands of men lost their lives, Union troops, under the leadership of *General William Tecumseh Sherman*, blazed a ruthless path of destruction through the states of Georgia and South Carolina, working in tandem with the strategies of Union *Commander Ulysses S. Grant* and draining the resources and supplies of the Confederate Army. As Union soldiers surrounded the South Carolina capital of Richmond, Confederate *General Robert E. Lee* was finally forced to surrender to General Grant at Appomattox Courthouse on April 9, 1865.

Casualties of the Civil War numbered upwards of 600,000, devastated many areas and the economy of the South, and left bitter and lingering resentment. President Abraham Lincoln was assassinated by John Wilkes Booth just three days after the Confederate surrender. Violence against and oppression of former slaves continued, equality was not proffered as promised, and decades of reconstruction for the entire country—on every level—were necessary to repair the rifts and forge both new regional and national identities.

Reconstruction

While the Civil War raged across southern soil, the economy of the South was weakening and eventually collapsed. This physical and geographical, psychological and economic, devastation led to the period known as Reconstruction (1865–77). Before the war officially ended, President Lincoln had announced his plans for Reconstruction. After his assassination, Vice President *Andrew Johnson* carried out Lincoln's plans with minor changes.

Lincoln's government appointed military governors to temporarily oversee the operations of individual rebel states as they were slowly reincorporated into the Union. The Emancipation Proclamation announced the ruin of the southern economy as at its crux laid the practice of slavery. There was no money left over after the war effort and this lack of capital crippled the South's ability to manufacture. Industrialization and the spread of railways—so rampant in northern states—were slow to get going. Many southerners headed west in the search for new life and opportunities.

For the roughly 4 million freed slaves, the reality of a Union victory fell far short of the promises of freedom and equality. In spite of the passage of the Reconstruction Acts, aimed at improving and protecting conditions for former slaves and the Civil Rights Act of 1866, which officially granted blacks citizenship and denied all states the power to restrict or deny them rights, violent oppression and exploitation continued. The 13th, 14th, and 15th Amendments, which abolished slavery, extended citizenship to blacks, and banned race as a voting condition, respectively, produced little real change.

The sharecropping system—essentially still slavery and a system of perpetual debt—established blacks as tenant farmers beholden to white landowners. White opportunists traveling from the North, known as *carpetbaggers*, arrived in the South intent on building successes in the economic and political realms, often times taking advantage of newly freed slaves to reach their goals. *The Ku Klux Klan*, which held its first meeting in 1867, and several other white supremacist groups organized and orchestrated campaigns of terror and intimidation aimed at keeping blacks in a state of inferiority and fear.

In the aftermath of the Civil War, bitterness and resentment were vented as hostility and violence and many blacks lived in fear and lacked almost any improvement in opportunities. It would take years for the impoverished South to rebuild. Meanwhile, the new southern climate, a climate of instability and racial oppression both old and new would continue well into the 20th century.

Industrialism and Beyond

Even while the North and South battled during the Civil War, the seeds of Industrialism were being sown across the country in the form of railroad ties. By 1900, almost 200,000 miles of railroad track crisscrossed the continent, allowing for easy trade and a growing industrialized economy.

Urbanization followed industrialization as people relocated to cities, searching out factory jobs. In Massachusetts factories produced more than one-third of the nation's textiles. Lowell, Lawrence, Fall River, and New Bedford were leaders in the cotton textile industry. The boot and shoe industry and the associated industry of leather tanning also grew. By 1900, the factories of Lynn, Brockton, Haverhill, Marlborough, Worcester, and other Massachusetts cities were making about half the boots and shoes produced in the entire country.

The American economy rapidly grew, but only a small percentage of the population controlled the newly minted wealth. Industrialists such as *John D. Rockefeller* and *Andrew Carnegie* created huge and immensely profitable corporations. However, most laborers endured harsh conditions for which they received little pay. As a result, clashes between unions and management became increasingly common.

Elected President in 1900 as a Progressive candidate, much of Theodore Roosevelt's work aimed at restraining corporate monopolies (or trusts) and promoting economic competition. *The Progressive Era* also attempted a purification of politics, which many believed had become exceedingly corrupt. Journalists, known as *muckrakers,* exposed corruption and greed. Important political reforms, aimed to challenge the decadence of the Industrial or Gilded Age, included the passage of the income tax laws, prohibition, and women's suffrage.

World War I and the Interwar Years

In 1914, when World War I broke out in Europe, many Americans favored neutrality. However, by 1917 Germany had begun brutal attacks on Britain's merchant ships with submarines called U-boats. After one particular submarine attack in which two Americans were killed, *President Woodrow Wilson* began lobbying Congress to declare war. Three million U.S. troops were drafted and quickly deployed to European battlefields. Although the U.S entered the war late, America's presence had a decisive impact on the outcome. After the war's end in 1918, Wilson, an idealist, formulated a peace plan to make the world "safe for democracy." This plan included the formation of the *League of Nations*, an international organization whereby the member nations would unite to ensure peace and security for all. In the end, the United States did not join the League.

The post-World War I period was marked by prosperity. For the first time in U.S. history, suburbs began to grow more rapidly than central cities. New technology, such as streetcars, commuter trains, and automobiles opened the suburbs to working-class families. Large numbers of southern and rural blacks also began migrating to northern cities to find jobs. Unfortunately, the boom years of the twenties ended just as quickly as they had been ushered in. As the decade progressed, a depressed farm economy, the failure of over 5,700 banks nationwide, a decline in new construction, and other factors culminated in the *Great Depression* after the stock market crash of October 29, 1929 (commonly known as Black Tuesday).

By 1932, 24 percent of the American population was unemployed. Elected in the midst of this crisis, *Franklin Roosevelt* enacted huge reforms collectively known as the *New Deal,* including agricultural and business regulation, public works projects, farm relief, and ultimately the establishment of the Social Security system. The New Deal put millions of people back to work and helped turn the struggling economy around; however, many historians credit America's eventual involvement in World War II as the most important aspect of the country's economic turnaround.

World War II and the Cold War Era

World War II was divided into two large campaigns: the European Campaign and the Pacific Campaign. Between 1938 and 1941, America provided aid to the *Allied forces* as they fought against the advancing Fascist armies of the *Axis powers* (Germany, Italy, and Japan). However, since many Americans and politicians supported *isolationism*, the belief that the U.S. should not participate in war outside of the Western Hemisphere, U.S. troops were not involved in either campaign. Not until after the events of Dec. 7, 1941, when Japanese fighter planes attacked Pearl Harbor, did President Roosevelt lead America directly into the war.

The U.S. achieved major victories in the Pacific campaign at the battle of Midway (June 1942), Iowa Jima (1945), and Okinawa (1945). American and British troops began their most successful and aggressive push against the still formidable Germany and the other Axis forces on D-Day—June 6, 1944. By the end of the summer the Axis powers had retreated and surrendered.

Once again, the U.S. focus returned to Japan. Back at home, scientists from the Manhattan Project had developed the first atomic bomb, which was successfully tested in New Mexico on July 16, 1945. In an attempt to hasten a Japanese surrender and to demonstrate American power to the world, President Truman ordered the use of a single atomic bomb to be dropped on Hiroshima on August 6, 1945. When Japan refused to surrender, a second bomb was dropped on Nagasaki three days later. Japan surrendered the very next day. It has been estimated that about 210,000 people died that year from the effects of the bombs.

The term "Super Power" was first used to describe America at the end of World War II. Increased industrial output during the war had stimulated the economy, impressive demonstrations of America's military strength as well as nuclear technology had secured the title of "world's greatest army," and—unlike most of Europe and the East—the war had not ravaged American cities and infrastructure. However, the Soviet Union and its allies quickly emerged as challengers to America's "Super Power" status. By 1948, Poland, Romania, Bulgaria, Hungary, Albania, and Czechoslovakia had all become part of the growing Soviet block. In September 1949, the Soviets detonated their first nuclear bomb. Cold War tensions led to a rise of anti-communist sentiment at home, leading to the imprisonment of leaders of the American Communist party. Senate hearings, led by Senator Joseph McCarthy, sought to root out supposed communists in government. Abroad, the struggle between communism and capitalism led to the Truman Doctrine, which argued that the United States had to support populations who were resisting Communist movements, and to a policy of U.S. opposition to the expansion of communism, (the theory of *containment*).

Similar to containment, the *Domino Theory* posited that if one country in a region fell to communism, surrounding countries would then topple like dominoes. This theory was used as justification for U.S. intervention in much of the world, including the Vietnam War (1964–1975).

Civil Rights and Women's Rights

In the 1950s, the Civil Rights Movement gathered momentum, beginning with the case of *Brown v. Board of Education of Topeka, Kansas*. The *National Association for the Advancement of Colored People (NAACP)* assigned lawyer, *Thurgood Marshall*, to the case. He successfully argued on behalf of Brown and against segregation, winning the Supreme Court ruling in 1954 that "separate but equal" public schools were unconstitutional. This move toward desegregation was resisted in many parts of the South, with federal troops being sent in at times to enforce the Supreme Court's decision. The Civil Rights Movement was emboldened after the ruling and campaigned to end segregation entirely. In 1967, President Johnson appointed Thurgood Marshall as the first African American Supreme Court Justice.

Rigid separation along racial lines, and laws supporting such division, had been in place since after the Civil War. Although outlawed in practice, slavery as a cultural institution was still a way of life in the South and the separation of education (and its inherent inequality) can be dated back to the Jim Crow laws, laws which divided practically every aspect of life into two categories: black and white. Lynching was another brutal way used to maintain the status quo because it kept black people in constant fear. These divisive laws and practices, which dominated for decades, lie at the root of the civil rights movement a century later.

Dr. Martin Luther King, Jr., was a Baptist preacher who preached a philosophy of *nonviolence*. He advocated a peaceful way of protesting against racial injustices by organizing bus boycotts, sit-ins, and freedom rides, which eventually led to the passage of the Civil Rights Act and the Voting Rights Act of 1964 signed by President Lyndon Johnson. The most famous bus boycott was the Montgomery bus boycott of 1955. Rosa Parks, a seamstress and secretary for the NAACP, was arrested for refusing to relinquish her seat in the middle of a bus to a white man. While African Americans were allowed to sit in the middle of the bus, they had to give their seat to a white person if no other seat was available. Arrested at the next stop, she was charged with violating the segregation laws. Civil rights leaders organized the Montgomery bus boycott as a response to her arrest, whereby over the next year, more than 50,000 African Americans in Montgomery avoided the city bus system until the Supreme Court declared that bus segregation was unconstitutional.

The first women's rights meeting was held in Seneca Falls, N.Y., in 1848. *Elizabeth Cady Stanton* was a featured speaker at the *Seneca Falls Convention;* and she proposed resolutions for women's rights in legal and political matters. Among these resolutions was the issue of *suffrage* (the right to vote). The movement had ardent supporters, but there were also many others who felt that women did not require these rights. Therefore, the Civil Rights Act of 1866 and the 13th through 15th Amendments to the Constitution failed to include Native Americans and women. Later, laws were made more comprehensive and extended to protect all people, regardless of race, color, or sex.

Women were granted the right to vote in 1919, at the end of World War I. Women's efforts on the home front during World War II had strengthened the case for gender equality, as women assumed men's roles both at home and at work while soldiers fought abroad. Though the return of these soldiers from World War II and the subsequent decade of the 1950s saw a return to more traditional and binding gender roles, by the 1960s—a decade marked by social upheaval, new demands from historically marginalized groups, and mass protestation of the Vietnam War strongly indicated that radical changes were afoot.

The 1960s saw the true rise of the women's liberation movement. The women's movement gained momentum in 1963 with the publication of Betty Friedan's book *The Feminine Mystique*, which attacked the middle-class "cult of domesticity" and argued that society did not allow women to use their individual talents. The National Organization for Women (NOW), founded in 1966, called for equal employment opportunities and equal pay. It later advocated the Equal Rights Amendment to the Constitution, changes in divorce laws, and the legalization of abortion. The Equal Rights Amendment has not yet passed. It is *not* an amendment to the U.S. Constitution.

Contemporary America

A Cold War mentality and anti-communist fervor continued throughout the 1980s. In 1989, while conservative U.S. President Ronald Reagan was in office, the Soviet Union finally collapsed. The subsequent decade was marked by economic growth, fueled in large part by the emergence of the Internet and the technology boom. *Globalization*—a theory by which the entire planet is deeply connected through the exchange of goods and knowledge—also followed these new technologies.

Bill Clinton, the 43rd president, signed the Family and Medical Leave Act as well as the North American Free Trade Agreement (NAFTA). He signed executive orders that set aside vast expanses of public lands, especially in the West.

The terror bombings of the World Trade Center and Pentagon on September 11, 2001, marked a turning point in American politics and international relations. Much of George W. Bush's presidency between 2000 and 2008 was marked both domestically and internationally by the U.S. War on Terror.

In November 2008, in the 232-year of the United States, a record number of voters elected Barack Obama as the nation's 44th president—and he became the first African American to hold the office. His election coalition included minorities, college-educated whites, and young voters aged 19 to 26. In a *Time* magazine article written just before the election, *Atlantic Monthly* contributing editor Ta-Nehisi Cotes wrote: "Consider this fact: the most famous black man in America isn't dribbling a ball or clutching a microphone. He has no prison record. . . . Words like *hope, change,* and *progress* might seem like naïve campaign sloganeering in a dark age. But think of the way those words ring for a people whose forebears marched into billy clubs and dogs, whose ancestors fled north by starlight, feeling the moss on the back of trees."

COMPETENCY 0007

Understand the founding documents and governmental systems of the United States and the Commonwealth of Massachusetts; the principles, ideals, rights, and responsibilities of U.S. citizenship; and the fundamental principles and concepts of economics.

American Government, Politics, and Economics

America was founded on a strong set of ideals and values. Many of these values are expressed in three essential founding documents: the Declaration of Independence, the U.S. Constitution, and the Bill of Rights.

The purposes and objectives of the U.S. government are written into the Constitution's short preamble: "We the People of the United States, in Order to form a more perfect Union, establish Justice, insure domestic Tranquility, provide for the common defense, promote the general Welfare, and secure the Blessings of Liberty to ourselves and our Posterity, do ordain and establish this *Constitution* for the United States of America." The remaining seven articles of the Constitution delineate how the government shall be organized and function. The U.S. *Constitution* creates a strong central government, but also provides a system of checks and balances among the three branches of government: the legislative, executive, and judicial branches.

The three branches of government work within a system of *checks and balances*. The *legislative branch* makes laws and has the power to declare war. The legislative branch is composed of a Senate and a House of Representatives. At the federal level, there are 100 senators, who serve six-year terms, and 435 state representatives, who serve two-year terms. The *executive branch* enforces laws. At the federal level, the president signs bills into law and serves as the Commander-in-Chief of the Armed Forces. The *judicial branch* interprets the constitutionality of laws. At the federal level, the Supreme Court seats nine members who are appointed for life by the president. Each branch of the government checks the power of the other two branches and all three branches must work together to properly govern and create laws.

Creating Laws

All Americans are governed by the *rule of law*, which means that no individual, organization, of governmental body is above the law. It is the duty of all Americans to understand and follow the law. Because laws are so powerful in America, it is important that they are thoughtfully conceived and written. The process of creating a law involves many steps, primarily involving the Congress. First a representative writes and introduces a bill. Then, the bill goes to one of the 22 House of Representative committees and the bill is discussed, analyzed, and possibly edited. Next, the bill is debated and voted on by the entire House of Representatives before it is debated, edited, and voted on by the Senate. The House version and the Senate version are melded together by a congressional conference committee. Only after both the House and Senate approve the final version does a bill go to the president to be signed into Law. The president has various options when presented with a bill. He can sign the bill, turning it into a law; *veto*, or reject, the bill; or ignore the bill. If the bill is ignored for 10 days and Congress remains in session, then the bill automatically becomes a law. However, if Congress adjourns before 10 days have passed, then the bill is automatically rejected. This is called a *pocket veto*.

The *Constitution* also addresses the role of federal and state governments. Article I, Section VIII of the constitution describes a number of federal powers, including: the power to borrow money from foreign countries, to mint money, maintain a postal service, to raise and support an Army and Navy, and declare war. The first 10 Amendments to the Constitution are called the *Bill of Rights*. These amendments enumerate such indelible rights as freedom of speech, the right to bear arms, and the right to a speedy trial. The amendments were added to prevent the federal government from encroaching on the states' right to self-government. The Tenth Amendment declares that any powers not delegated to the federal government or expressly prohibited by it to the states, are granted to the states. Individual states can decide which powers are held by their respective state and local governments.

The Massachusetts Constitution

Ratified in 1780, the Massachusetts Constitution is the oldest functioning constitution in the world. Similar to the U.S. Constitution, it aims to protect the rights of individual citizens. Article VII of the Massachusetts Constitution reads, "Government is instituted for the common good; for the protection, safety, prosperity, and happiness of the people; and not for the profit, honor, or private interest of any one man, family, or class of men." The Massachusetts Constitution also illustrates a commitment to the principles of federalism and popular sovereignty: "All power residing originally in the people, and being derived from them, the several magistrates and officers of government, vested with authority, whether legislative, executive, or judicial, are their substitutes and agents, and are at all times accountable to them" (Article V or the Massachusetts Constitutions). The 351 cities and towns of Massachusetts are responsible for most of the governmental services that citizens have come to expect. For example, local governments provide fire and police services, maintain school systems, organize waste removal, and allocate building permits. Mayors and City Councils govern the cities of Massachusetts, but towns are usually governed by groups of officials called selectmen. A Board of Selectmen is usually elected for a one-or-two-year term, and town meetings, a tradition from Colonial times, are still held regularly[1]. This system allows citizens direct participation in the democratic process, including ratification of local budgets and the enactment of local ordinances.

America's democratic system of government provides many rights and advantages to its citizens, but it also requires citizen participation. In a true democracy the power of government resides in the populace. In order to enact this power, citizens must participate in the process by voting, paying taxes, serving on juries, participating in local debates, and even running for political office.

Political Parties

America operates within a two party political system. The two dominant parties are the *Democrats*, the oldest and currently the largest party in the U.S., whose platform generally supports a strong central government, government-funded social projects, and a leaning to the leftist politics, and the *Republicans* (also called the GOP or Grand Old Party), the second largest party, whose platform generally supports fiscal and social conservatism and supply side economics. There are three additional parties, however, whose candidates may be listed on voting ballots: the *Constitution Party*, whose platform supports the original intentions of the Founding Fathers; the *Green Party*, whose platform supports environmentalism, non-hierarchical democracy, social justice, and nonviolence; and the *Libertarian Party*, whose platform supports minimal regulation and *laissez-faire*, meaning hands-off, policies and civil liberties.

Economics and Capitalism

Since one of the most important governmental values in America involves restraining individual power, politicians must continually seek reelection. Economics, politics, and government are all enmeshed. The American economy is built upon the theories of

[1] Galvin, William F. "Massachusetts Facts, Citizen Information Services." http://www.sec.state.ma.us/cis/cismaf/mf1b.htm

capitalism. American citizens have the right to own, maintain, and sell private property. The price of this property depends upon the fluctuations of a free market. Although the government does provide some regulations, a market economy is mostly driven through supply and demand—if there is great demand for a commodity and the supply of that commodity is small, then the price will go up. *Scarcity* is a key term in understanding supply and demand economics. Scarcity describes the constant state of affairs in which individual desires may be endless, but resources are always limited. Because of scarcity people must compete over resources, giving each resource a specific value.

Economics could be defined as the study of choices. Because resources and money are both limited, all economic transactions require specific choices. *Opportunity cost* is defined as the value of what was not chosen because every economic choice rejects alternative options. Often when people think of economics they think only in terms of price and profit; however, opportunity cost could also include non-monetary units such as time or energy.

The *capitalist system* encourages innovation, competition, and an entrepreneurial spirit with the aim of increasing productivity and profit. Entrepreneurs start new economic ventures by organizing labor, capital, and resources. Entrepreneurs compete against each other and the best ideas, inventions, and businesses survive and thrive. When entrepreneurs embark on a new project they take on a certain degree of risk because not all projects will be successful.

COMPETENCY 0008

Understand major developments and figures in world history.

Early Human Civilizations

From earliest times, humans lived in hunter-gatherer societies, often nomadic and dependent on local natural resources such as edible plants and game animals. Over time, other forms of social organization developed, such as semi-nomadic livestock herding and subsistence farming, village-based subsistence farming, city-states, kingdoms, and empires. Societies have been classified by their level of technological development based on whether their tools were made of stone, bronze, iron, or more advanced materials. This has led to the designations of Stone Age, Bronze Age, Iron Age, etc. During these periods, civilizations arose in the ancient Middle East to which modern Western civilization can trace its writing system and law codes. These civilizations include Sumeria, Israel, Egypt, Assyria, Babylonia, and Medo-Persia.

Israel

What is known of the origin of Israel is more a compendium of sources than an account based on strictly historical sources, a common issue when evaluating ancient peoples and places. The Israelites' great contribution to religious thought and development was *monotheism*, the belief in one universal God. After a brief respite from Babylonian rule in the 6th century BCE, foreigners dominated the area, that came to be known in the 20th century as the state of Israel, for roughly 2,500 years.

Greece

Of pivotal importance in Western history is the rise of ancient Greek civilization, beginning with the conquest by Alexander the Great in the 4th century BCE of much of the former territory of the previous Middle Eastern empires. This led to the spread of the Greek culture and language. Ancient Greek culture and learning has had an enduring influence on western development in many areas: the sciences, philosophy, scholarship, political thought, and games and sportsmanship, along with lasting literary contributions, notably the epic poems of Homer.

Elements of democracy were developed under the Greeks. The Greek city-state, or *polis*, was an important political feature made up of a city or town and its surrounding countryside. The polis was the center of an individual's social and political life. During the Hellenic Age (612–339 BCE) an aristocrat named *Draco* codified the laws for the Athenian polis and posted them for the public. Though his laws were harsh (the term "draconian" derives from his name due to the strict nature of his rules), his contribution to democracy was the idea that the law belonged to all citizens.

Three of the most important philosophers in terms of the development of western thought lived during the period of Classical Greece. *Socrates* was interested in human behavior and ethics. The "Socratic Method" uses logically constructed questions to challenge ideas. His student, *Plato*, believed in a more personal and transcendental approach to the body, mind, and world affairs. Plato's pupil, *Aristotle*, was a man of logic, reason, and direct observation. The world's first democracy was founded at Athens around 500 BCE.

Rome

The civilization of Rome thrived on preserved and adapted aspects of Greek culture, but over time achieved even greater dominance and influence in the Middle East and the

Mediterranean region. By conquering the Greek dynasty ruling over Egypt in 31 BCE, Rome, under a single government, became the undisputed regional power and, in time, went on to conquer much of the known world. Rome was the first empire to extend the ancient Middle Eastern and Greek cultures northward into Europe.

Julius Caesar, the powerful Roman reform leader (ca. 102–44 BCE), is known for his military conquests and for the institution of a calendar system still in use today (with a few minor changes). The peace of this period led to a flourishing of the visual arts and higher learning, values and concepts at the core of aesthetic and intellectual progress, from the Middle Ages, through the Renaissance, and into our modern world.

The first and second centuries CE (Common Era), was a period known as *Pax Romana* (Latin for "Roman Peace"). Named because it was a time of political peace with no major wars or internal conflicts to threaten the empire, the Pax Romana was a time of much development of new architecture and an extensive system of roads, as well as a postal system, that facilitated transportation and thus favored the expansion of trade. Roman law was based on fairness and constancy, aspects still in demand and debate today.

Sometime during the reign of the Roman Emperor Augustus, Jesus of Nazareth (Jesus Christ) was born. Although crucified around 30 CE, Jesus' followers, (later called Christians), grew in great numbers and the diffusion of this new faith contributed in large part to the eventual fall of Rome. Beginning in the third century, Rome also began a long decline as the succession of emperors grew unstable and the army began to have trouble maintaining control over outlying provinces. In the fifth century, invading Germanic tribes conquered Rome. Remnants of imperial power survived, however, in the Eastern Empire, with its capital in Constantinople (now Istanbul) and in the Roman Catholic Church. The Germanic invaders also preserved and adopted much of what was left of the Roman Empire.

The Middle Ages

Even after Rome's power was broken, its impact was still felt in its former European territories. The Church and the feudal system filled the vacuum of power resulting from Rome's fall. In the *feudal system* of social organization, *nobles* ruled over peasants, called *serfs*, who worked the land. Among the nobles, the less powerful, called *vassals*, swore oaths of loyalty to the more powerful nobles, with the promise of military protection in exchange for their support. The feudal system included group contracts in addition to individual ones. Entire towns of peasants could have contractual agreements with nobles. Charters allowed peasants to govern their own affairs. Tradesmen formed *guilds* to regulate the price, quality, and quantity of goods produced. This system, with many variations, was the dominant economic and social system in Europe throughout the Middle Ages.

The Middle Ages, also known as the Dark Ages, were marked by political instability in the early centuries after Rome's fall. The Emperor *Charlemagne* ruled from 768 to 814, building a huge but also vastly fractured empire (The Holy Roman Empire) stretching across Europe. The *Crusades*, holy wars fought between Christians and Muslims, were fought with both religious and economic motives. After Jerusalem was captured and claimed by European Crusaders at the end of the 11th century, *Saladin*, King of Egypt and Syria, recaptured the Holy Land in 1187 and it remained under Islamist control through the 20th century. The sharp decrease in the spread of knowledge, widespread illiteracy, and disasters such as the population-decimating Black Plague of the 14th century, contributed to the stagnation of the era. Stability was highly valued in the midst of such problems, and medieval worldviews emphasized finding security by accepting one's status on "the great chain of being." In time, however, increasing political stability and the growth of trade and commerce set the stage for the early modern era of western history.

Renaissance and the Reformation

The modern era began around 1450 with the period known as the *Renaissance* (French for "Rebirth"). A cultural movement, the Renaissance began in Florence, Italy, with a renewed interest in, and veneration for, classical Greek and Roman aesthetics. This initial interest led to a flourishing of the arts as well as an interest in the exploration of the human experience. It was a time of creativity and change in Europe. Artists, such as Michelangelo and Leonardo da Vinci, explored the human body to create more realistic paintings. The growth of commerce, banking, and industry favored the spread of knowledge among the rising middle class. The invention of the printing press in Mainz, Germany, by *Johann Gutenberg* in the mid-fifteenth century, revolutionized the way, and to what extent, information was disseminated, helping to raise literacy rates across Europe and beyond. William Shakespeare wrote 37 plays during this time, and Cervantes wrote "Don Quixote."

Closely following the grandeur of the Renaissance, the *Reformation* challenged the dominance and corruption of the Roman Catholic Church and led to the development of

Protestantism, which more closely reflected the values of Northern European cultures and the middle class. A German monk, *Martin Luther*, posted ninety-five arguments against Papal authority and the practices of selling indulgences and salvation. His explanation of *sola fide*—justification by faith alone—led to his excommunication from the Roman Catholic Church. Thus began what became known as the *Protestant Reformation*. In England, *Queen Elizabeth I* (r. 1558-1603) valued political unity and stability over religious unity and harmony and imposed a strictly controlled system upon the Anglican Church. Elizabeth's rule was a success on both the domestic and foreign fronts and she supported exploration abroad. At this time, not only England but also Spain and Portugal began exploring the globe and founding overseas colonies. The interests in discovering new knowledge, and the attitude of challenging traditional views, have continued as western traditions.

The renewed interest in classical learning spurred a great increase of scientific knowledge in the 17th century. *Sir Isaac Newton's* discovery of the laws of gravity and motion, based on previous studies of Galileo's work, established a foundation for the study of physics in place for the next two hundred years. This period was also marked by political change as the feudal system slowly gave way to the development of *monarchies* in Western Europe. In this form of government, power was centralized in the hands of the king (or monarch) rather than divided among the nobles. In France, there was an *absolute monarchy*, where the King ruled by divine right and without any check on his actions other than his own conscience. The other major form of monarchy, *constitutional monarchy*, was in operation in England. In a constitutional monarchy the King, (or Queen), ruled along with the larger body of Parliament. Advances continued in the fields of science, politics, education, and commerce; these advances further removed Europe from its medieval past and favored the growth of the middle class.

The Age of Reason: the Enlightenment

The 18th century saw the development of ideas based on rational thought, reason, logic, and the application of scientific knowledge for the betterment of society. This period, known as the *Enlightenment*, further challenged medieval ideals of stability and order by championing progress and planned change. *John Locke* was an enlightenment thinker who wanted to reform government. He believed that the government should protect the natural rights of the people. *Natural rights* can be defined as those rights belonging to all humans from birth. The growing pressures for progress caused strained relationships between the ruling class and the middle class; such conflict eventually exploded in France, in the French Revolution of 1789. Before the French Revolution, the concept of an individual citizen's rights did not exist. There had merely been certain privileges allowed to, and afforded by, class.

Soon thereafter, the *Industrial Revolution* and *colonialism* began to transform the face of Europe and many other regions of the world. In the 19th century, the unprecedented explosion of industry and technology destroyed the agricultural traditions and society of Europe, led to the process of rapid urbanization, and western civilization expanded its power throughout the rest of the world.

Britain led the Industrial Revolution since it had natural resources and plenty of workers for its new factories and mines. Iron and coal were key components of industrialization. Iron, which could be made faster and stronger by using coal, was used to make machines and steam engines. The textile industry was the first to use machines to make cloth, which had previously been hand-spun in homes. The machines were large and expensive, so spinners and weavers worked in large rooms. These became the first factories. Steam engines provided speedy transportation for people and goods. The engines were used in boats along canals and in steam locomotives, which led to the development of the railroad system.

While Spain and Portugal were losing their colonies in the Americas, many European countries expanded into Africa, Asia, and the Pacific, including areas that had never before been colonized by western nations.

Historic Developments in Recent Times

The competition over resources in overseas colonies was one of the major reasons for World War I, which, in spite of its name, was mainly a European war. Finally sparked by the assassination of the heir to the throne of Austria-Hungary, it soon claimed the lives of millions. In addition, in countries such as Great Britain and Germany, the immense scale of the war meant that for the first time, enlisted men from all walks of life—not only professional soldiers—became casualties of war. In France, about half the men of an entire generation were lost and in one single battle (the Battle of the Somme); the British suffered over 60,000 casualties on the first day alone.

Germany, the major instigator of World War I, fell far short of its attempt to create a global empire. At the end of World War I, German-controlled colonies fell into the hands of Great Britain and France. Germany became economically poor and remained repressed for the next two decades. Bitterness in Germany over the loss of the war, inflation, and the cost of war reparations were factors in the successful cultivation of nationalism and the eventual rise of Adolf Hitler to power. Hitler's Third Reich and Nazi regime eventually killed a staggering 50 million people, including 6 million Jews, and 20 million Soviets. World War II began in 1939 when Hitler invaded Poland. Germany was joined by Japan and Italy to form the Axis powers, which fought against the Allied Forces, mainly Great Britain, the United States, and the Soviet Union. (France, perhaps remembering the dead of World War I, surrendered to Germany early in the war and formed the collaborative Vichy government.) World War II came to an end in 1945 after the Battle of the Bulge, and Russian advancement and subsequent occupation of Berlin.

Almost immediately after World War II, the Cold War, a contentious conflict fought between the superpowers and nuclear threats of the United States and the Soviet Union, began. The process of *decolonization* (the process where formerly European and U.S. colonies rejected foreign rule and protested further interference) also began. Great Britain's most important colony, India, broke away in 1948 under the famously nonviolent leadership of *Mohandas Gandhi*. Britain was also unable to prevent the establishment of the Jewish state of Israel in formerly British Palestine in that same year. Most of Britain's African colonies became independent in the 1950s and 1960s. In the meantime, Europe was divided by a figurative Iron Curtain between capitalist Western Europe and Soviet-controlled Eastern Europe.

China, in which a Communist revolution under Mao Zedong (also known as Mao Tse-tung), succeeded following the great devastation of Japanese occupation during World War II, was solidly in the Soviet camp for many years but remained independent during much of the Cold War. Japan, though not allowed to assemble a military as a condition of its defeat in World War II, became a U.S. ally and a dominant Asian economic power. The U.S. and the Soviet Union waged war through their allies in Korea and Vietnam. The Cold War came to an end through several steps between 1989 and 1991, when the Soviet Union essentially collapsed. The end of the Cold War—which involved conflict on practically every continent—did not, however, bring peace to the world. In the formerly Soviet-controlled state of Yugoslavia, long buried ethnic rivalries led to civil war, genocide, and an eventual split into three separate countries. On the continent of Africa, many formerly French and British colonies began to break apart along tribal lines, often leading to terrible bloodshed, such as Tutsi genocide in Rwanda in 1994. The South African revolution and struggle against the apartheid (Afrikaans for "separateness") regime, led in large part and over decades into the 1990s by *Nelson Mandela*, were relatively peaceful, though the country was rife with inequality, oppression and exploitation — and continues to mend. Most of Africa is still subject to poverty, disease, and war. In the Middle East, ongoing and complicated international conflicts (such as the two Gulf wars), religious fundamentalism, and various political regimes, along with the continually contentious issue of the state of Israel, have led to the spread of radical political Islam. Such extremist groups have wreaked much havoc in the world, notably in the terror attacks on the World Trade Center and Pentagon on September 11, 2001.

Over the past half century, as the many advances in technology have brought people closer together and made people more conscious of the global scale, the process and effects of globalization have become embedded into our everyday lives. Advances in medicine and health care are lengthening life spans the world over and the process of industrialization continues to reach countries of the third world, creating, strengthening, and at times complicating ties to world powers. Such a multi-layered process creates ever more detailed patterns of crisscrossed and vested interests and the modern world still grapples with exploitation, oppression, and equality — issues both moral and economic. The historical tradition of recognizing individuals for their contributions, discoveries, and revolutionizing force continues, only with 21st century advancement, this information is less privileged and more readily available to a connected global audience via the Internet and other improved forms of communication. Global figures perform on a world stage. Improved means of travel, along with changing immigration patterns and policies, designed to meet the realities of our 21st century world, are redefining geographic, ethnic, and cultural boundaries. Nationalism remains an issue of patriotism and identity and it is still a useful political tool, but the rigid lines that have been used for centuries to define people and places seem to be expanding to include amalgams, yet another reflection of our mixed, enmeshed, and entangled global community.

COMPETENCY 0009

Understand basic geographic concepts, phenomena, and processes, and demonstrate knowledge of the major geographic features and regions of the world, the United States, and the Commonwealth of Massachusetts.

Geography

Broadly speaking, geographic concepts can be separated into two categories: physical and social. *Physical geography* includes knowledge of place (capitals and countries), physical features (mountains and rivers), and climate (global warming and rainfall). *Social geography* involves considering how humans interact with their environment; how people have migrated overtime; and how social, political, and religious systems have coalesced into regional divisions.

Mapmakers (cartographers) divide the globe into four hemispheres. The *equator* separates the northern and southern hemispheres. The *Prime Meridian* divides the eastern and western hemisphere. Locations on a globe can be more precisely identified using latitude and longitude. Lines of *latitude* run from east to west (like the rungs of a ladder) and lines of *longitude* run from north to south, meeting at the north and south poles. The landmasses on the globe are divided into seven continents: North America, South America, Africa, Europe, Asia, Australia, and Antarctica. The four oceans, which cover more than two thirds of Earth's surface, are the Pacific Ocean, the Atlantic Ocean, the Arctic Ocean, and the Indian Ocean.

Every continent is home to a number of major physical features. The world's largest and most biodiverse rainforest and longest river are found in the Amazon region of South America. Africa is home to the Sahara desert, the world's largest desert, as well as fertile tropical jungles and grasslands. More than 60 percent of Earth's people live in Asia, the largest continent. Australia, the only continent that is also a country, is home to the Great Barrier Reef—the largest reef in the world. The South Pole rests on Antarctica, which is almost completely covered by ice sheets almost three miles thick.

North America stretches from the frigid arctic of Greenland to the warm tropics of Panama. America's oldest mountain range, the Appalachians, spans much of the east coast, including western Massachusetts. America's longest river, the Mississippi, and the largest lakes, the Great Lakes, are also found in the East. The Plain states of America are flat and fertile, and home to much of the country's farmland. The jagged Rocky Mountains spread across Colorado, Utah, and Wyoming. Carved by the Colorado River, the Grand Canyon of Arizona reaches a depth up to one mile.

Massachusetts extends from the Appalachian Mountains to the Atlantic shores of Cape Cod. The southern islands of Martha's Vineyard and Nantucket are also part of Massachusetts. The coastline is dominated by large bays, hence the nickname "The Bay State." The state capital and most populous area, Boston, is also located on the coast. Areas of central and western Massachusetts, such as the Berkshires and the Connecticut River Valley, are less populated and more heavily forested. Massachusetts has a warm mid-latitude climate, the type of climate in which the majority of humans live today.

Physical geography has always deeply affected human history as well as contemporary actions. Population centers have tended to flourish on the shores of rivers and oceans that aided in trade and provided stable food sources. Huge migrations have resulted from changes in climate and geographic features. The first people to populate America, who crossed the Bering Land Bridge that temporarily connected Siberia and Alaska, are an example of this phenomenon. More than just people migrate; almost everything (plants, animals, ideas) moves into new spaces. This phenomenon is called *diffusion*.

Many current global events arise from the interconnection between people and their environment. For example, water shortages spur conflict in much of the world including the western United States, rising sea levels and eroding coastlines threaten coastal homes, and discoveries of oil fields in remote areas such as Alaska pit environmentalism against resources extraction.

The Five Themes of Geography

There are five themes around which the teaching of Geography in K-12 classrooms is organized. These themes are *location, place, human-environment interaction, movement*, and *region*.

Location: The study of geography generally begins with the study of location of places. *Absolute location* is noted by longitude and latitude, street address, or township, while *relative location* is noted by a place's relationship to other places or its environment.

Place: Place includes the physical and human description of a location. *Physical characteristics* include mountains, rivers, lakes, beaches, flora and fauna. *Human characteristics* include the type of architecture, cultural features, religion, types of work such as agricultural, etc.

Human-environment interaction: Human-environment interaction describes how humans modify and/or adapt to the landscape; these interactions can be positive, such as the establishment of emissions laws, or negative, such as deforestation to construct shopping malls and housing developments.

Movement: Movement addresses movement and migration across the planet.

Regions: Regions divide the world into categories for study. *Formal regions* have official and public boundaries like cities, states, and countries.

Functional regions are defined by purpose and connections. A political district is considered a functional region, as is the circulation area of a local newspaper. A *vernacular region* refers to regions of the country like "the South," "the Midwest" or "the Northeast." A vernacular region conjures up particular perceptions and ideas, but has no official boundary or purpose.

References

Davis, Kenneth. *Don't Know Much About History.* New York: Crown Publishers, 1990.

Jenkins, Philip. *A History of The United States 3rd Ed.* New York: Palgrave Macmillan, 2007.

John, Fahey. *Family Reference Atlas of the World.* New York: Random House, 2009.

Kagan, Donald, Steven Ozment, and Frank Turner. *The Western Heritage Volume 1 10th Ed.* New Jersey: Prentice Hall, 2010.

Kagan, Donald, Steven Ozment, and Frank Turner. *The Western Heritage Volume 2 10th Ed.* New Jersey: Prentice Hall, 2010.

http://www.mass.gov/legis/const.htm

Rosenberg, Matt. The Five Themes of Geography (retrieved 4 January 2010). http//geography.about.com/od/teachgeography/a/5themes.htm

CHAPTER 3

Science and Technology/Engineering

COMPETENCY 0010

Understand and apply basic concepts and principles of life science to interpret and analyze phenomena.

Living Things

All living things are composed of one or more cells. In the mid 1600s, scientist Robert Hooke studied a very thin slice of cork using the newly invented microscope. Because the compartments in the cork reminded him of cells (rooms in a monastery), he named these microscopic, compartments cells. Later that century, Anton van Leeuwenhoek observed that there were different kinds of cells: animal, plant, and microorganisms.

Cell Composition and Cell Structure

A *cell* is the basic structural and functional unit of all living things. Cells have membranes filled with water containing genetic material, proteins, lipids, carbohydrates, salts, and other substances; these chemical building blocks of cells are called organic compounds because they all contain carbon (C). Compounds are composed of molecules, which are the smallest particles of a substance that retain the chemical and physical properties of the substance and is composed of two or more atoms. The molecules that form living organisms are call macromolecules because these compounds often contain hundreds and thousands of elements connected by several types of chemical bonds.

There are four major types of macromolecules in all living things.

1. *Carbohydrates* store and transport energy and provide structural support to the cell. Carbon (C), hydrogen (H), and oxygen (O) are the elements that form carbohydrates. Carbohydrates are categorized according to the number of simple sugars (monosaccharides) they contain. For example, glucose and fructose are monosaccharides, but when they combine they form sucrose, which is a disaccharide. When more than two simple sugars combine, they form polysaccharides. Long chains of polysaccharides form starch, which works more effectively to store energy and support the cell.

2. *Lipids* or fats store energy and are located in the cell membrane. Carbon (C), and hydrogen (H) form lipids. Lipids cannot dissolve in water and include substances such as oils and fat on meat. Saturated fats, usually from animals, solidify at room temperature. If these remain in excess in the body they can raise levels of cholesterol in the body. Unsaturated fats are from plants and fish and remain liquid at room temperature. Unsaturated fats tend to reduce cholesterol levels.

3. *Proteins* are essential components of all living cells and include enzymes, hormones, and antibodies that are necessary for effective functioning of an organism. They are essential in the diet of animals for the growth and repair of tissue and can be obtained from foods such as meat, fish, eggs, milk, and legumes. Carbon (C), hydrogen (H), oxygen (O), nitrogen (N), and almost always sulfur (S) form proteins. The most common and abundant type of protein is collagen, which is present in skin, ligaments, tendons, and bones. Enzymes are specific types of proteins that speed up chemical reactions in organisms, such as breaking down starch into sugar. All proteins contain 20 amino acids, which are considered the building blocks of proteins.

4. *Nucleic Acids* are responsible for storing genetic material that leads to replication of the organism. Nucleic acids store hereditary information. A five-carbon sugar (which is formed of C, H, and O), a phosphate group, which contains phosphorous (P) and oxygen (O), (PO4) and an organic base form nucleic acids. Deoxyribonucleic acid or DNA and ribonucleic acid or RNA are the primary nucleic acids. Both DNA and RNA contain four nitrogen bases. Three of these bases are the same: adenine, cytosine, and guanine. The fourth base differs: DNA has thymine, while RNA contains uracil. DNA carries the genetic code for each organism. RNA has many functions in the cell:

messenger RNA (mRNA) makes a temporary copy of genes that is used as a template for protein synthesis, transfer RNA (tRNA) decodes the genetic code, and ribosomal RNA (rRNA) catalyzes the synthesis of proteins. RNA is the only biological polymer that serves as both a catalyst (like proteins) and as information storage (like DNA). For this reason, it has been suggested that RNA, or an RNA-like molecule, was the basis of life early in evolution.

Cells of most living things use sugar for energy and produce proteins as building blocks and messengers. Cells may exist independently or may form colonies. In more evolved plants and animals, cells may be organized into tissues, which are series of cells that complete a shared function. Tissues can then form organs, which are fully differentiated structural and functional units in an animal that serves a specific function such as the liver, kidney, eye or esophagus. Organs that work together to accomplish a complex series of tasks form an organ system. The circulatory, integumentary, and digestive systems are examples of organ systems. This complex organization of organ systems comprises an organism.

Cell Types and Structure

There are two types of cells: *prokaryotes* and *eukaryote*s. *Prokaryotes* or unicellular organisms are more primitive, consisting of cytoplasm and a plasma membrane (cell membrane) and lacking organelles. Because they have no nucleus, genetic material is dispersed throughout the cytoplasm. Bacteria are the most common type of prokaryote.

Eukaryotes appeared about one billion years ago. They contain cytoplasmic membranous organelles, a nuclear membrane, and chromosomal proteins. Paramecia, skin tissue, and organs are examples of eukaryotes. An *organelle* is a differentiated structure within a cell that performs a specific function. The following chart lists all the organelles and their function.

Organelles and Their Functions

Organelle	Plant	Animal	Function
Nucleus	✔	✔	"brain" of the cell; contains DNA and genetic material; directs protein production; and controls all activities in the cell.
Nucleolus	✔	✔	"sphere" inside nucleus that holds RNA.
Nuclear Membrane	✔	✔	two-layered membrane that surrounds the nucleus; controls traffic in and out of the nucleus.
Chromosomes	✔	✔	"site" of genetic information; contains DNA; specific number of pairs of chromosomes per species; humans have 23 pairs—46 chromosomes
Ribosomes	✔	✔	house the "machinery" for cell function; inside the nucleus; carry out protein synthesis; contains RNA which copies DNA, decodes DNA, and synthesizes DNA.
Endoplasmic Reticulum (ER)	✔	✔	"highway" of networks of membranous cell tissue; Rough ER has ribosomes, the source for proteins; Smooth ER lacks ribosomes and breaks down fats and carries out numerous metabolic processes.
Cell Membrane (aka Plasma Membrane)		✔	"walls" the entire animal cell; regulates entry and exit of substances; maintains internal and external balance; protects inner cell from outside force.
Cell Wall	✔		"walls" the entire plant cell; stronger than cell membrane; regulates entry and exit of substances; maintains internal and external balance; protects inner cell from outside forces; prevents cell from exploding.
Cytoskeleton	✔	✔	"internal framework" of cell; composed of tubules and filaments; organizes all structures in the cell; critical for cell movement and cell division.
Cytoplasm	✔	✔	"gelatin" inside the cell; encases and protects organelles.
Golgi Apparati	✔	✔	"ships" goods from the ER to the rest of the cell.
Chloroplasts	✔		"site of photosynthesis" in plant cells; trap sunlight necessary for photosynthesis.
Mitochondria	✔	✔	"chemical powerhouse" of the cell; site of cellular respiration, which creates energy for the cell.
Lysosomes	✔	✔	"waste disposal" sacs of the cell; break down macromolecules through digestion using water; keeps cell healthy.
Vacuoles		✔	"containers" or holding units in animal cells for water and organic substances.
Central Vacuole	✔		large "holding container" in plant cells for water; helps maintain turgor pressure in plants.
Centriole		✔	Nine triplets of microtubules in animal cells; two centrioles form one centrosome; form spindle fibers to separate chromosomes during cell division.

Plant and animal cells are generally the same except plant cells have *a cell wall* instead of a *cell membrane*, *chloroplasts*, where photosynthesis occurs, and a *central vacuole* instead of several *vacuoles*. An animal cell also has a centriole, which is not present in a plant cell.

Comparison of Animal and Plant Cells

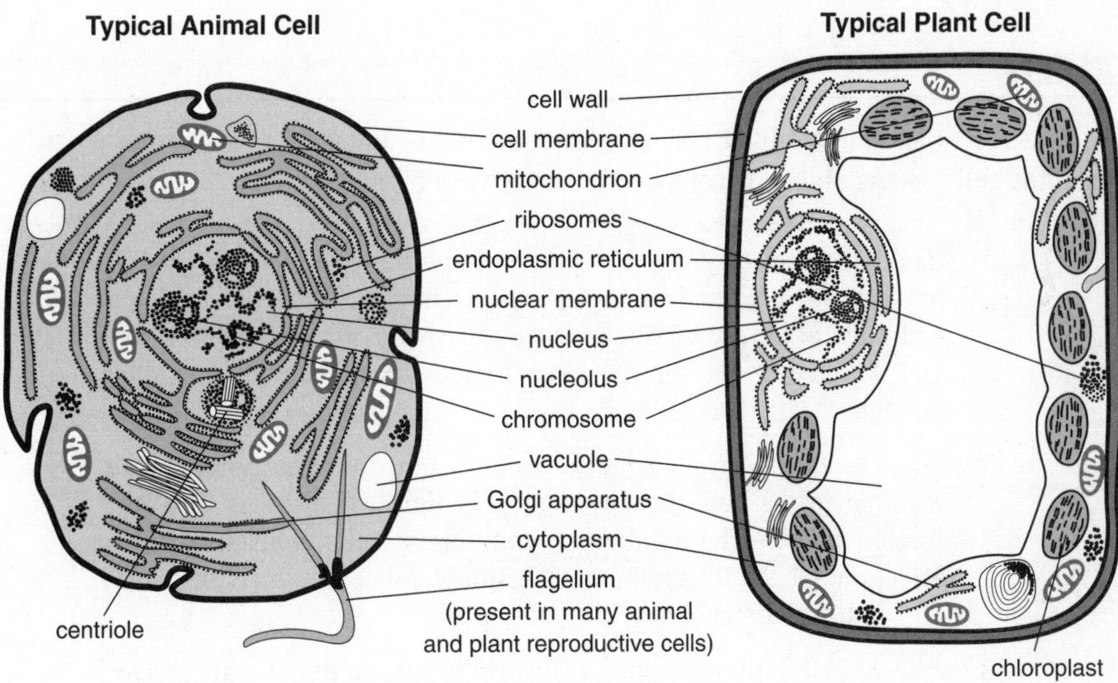

Tissues and Organs

When similar cells group together to perform a specific function, they form tissues. There are four types of tissue in the human body.

1. *Epithelial Tissue*: tightly packed cells from sheets of tissue that line areas of the body and surround the organs keeping them separate from other organs. Examples include the outer layer of skin, the inside of the mouth, and the tissue that surrounds organs.
2. *Connective Tissue:* this type of tissue contains strands of protein and collagen, which add support and structure to the body. Examples include inner layers of skin, ligaments, cartilage, tendons, muscle, bone, fat, and blood.

3. *Muscle Tissue*: specialized, because it can contract, muscle tissue is composed of two proteins, actin and myosin that slide past each other and allow movement. There is muscle tissue throughout the body.
4. *Nerve Tissue*: containing two types of cells, neurons and glial cells, nerve tissue can create and conduct electrical signals, which are managed by the brain and transmitted to the rest of the body via the spinal cord.

Blood

Blood is a specialized fluid that delivers nutrients to the cells and transports wastes from the cells. Human blood is composed of four types of cells:

1. *Red blood cells* (erythrocytes), the most numerous kind of blood cells are manufactured in the bone marrow. In humans, they lack a nucleus and most organelles. They are primarily involved in delivering oxygen, which they get from the lungs to body tissues via the circulatory system.
2. *White blood cells* (leukocytes) are cells of the immune system manufactured in the bone marrow that help fight off diseases and other foreign bodies. The number of white blood cells is an indicator of infection. Generally a number of white blood cells greater than 1.0×10^{10} indicate infection.
3. *Platelets* (thrombocytes) are cells also produced in the bone marrow that release numerous growth factors and aid in clotting.
4. *Plasma* are blood cells that contain salts and various proteins.

All human blood is not the same. Human blood varies according to the combination of antigens and antibodies it contains.

Antigens are substances that the body recognizes as foreign. Antigens are located on the surface of the red blood cells. The degree of foreignness, the size, complexity, dosage, and the person's genetic makeup will determine whether or not the antigen will produce an antibody. There are naturally occurring antigens that are unique to a person's blood.

Antibodies are proteins produced in response to specific antigens. Antibodies are produced by the lymphocytes in the lymphatic organ system and are located in the blood plasma. Antibodies are critical to the immune system. Some antibodies naturally occur in the plasma to help the immune system. Others, called immunogobulins, are antibodies that result from exposure to a specific antigen. Autoantibodies are those that form in response to naturally occurring antigens; these negatively impact the immune system. Individuals have different types and combinations of these molecules.

Blood type or blood group is inherited from parents and is determined by the presence of specific antigens. There are four blood types: A, B, AB, and O.

1. *Blood Type A* carries the A antigen.
2. *Blood Type B* carries the B antigen.
3. *Blood Type AB* carries both A and B antigens. Therefore a person that has AB type blood may receive blood from anyone. Type AB is considered a *Universal Recipient.*
4. *Blood Type O* does not carry any antigens. Therefore a person that has O type blood may donate blood to anyone. Type O is considered a *Universal Donor.*

Blood type is further characterized by the presence or lack of the Rh antigen (called the Rh factor) in the red blood cells. A blood type that contains the Rh antigen is considered positive. Therefore, a person could have A^+, B^+, AB^+, or O^+ blood. About 85% of the population contains the Rh antigen. A blood type that does not contain the Rh antigen is considered negative. Therefore a person should have A^-, B^-, AB^-, or O^- blood. The Rh factor causes a problem in a fetus whose blood is Rh positive and whose mother is Rh negative because the mother's negative blood attacks the positive blood of the fetus. For the same reason, a person with a positive Rh factor cannot be transfused with blood that has a negative Rh factor and vice versa.

The Organ System

Organs contain at least two types of tissue working together to accomplish a specific function. There are numerous organs in the body. The largest organ is the skin. Two or more organs create an *organ system*. The following chart lists each organ system, major organs, and the function of each system.

Organ System, Major Component Organs, and Function

Organ System	Major Component Organs	Function
Skeletal System	Bones, cartilage, tendons, ligaments	Provides support, protects delicate organs, provides sites to which organs attach
Integumentary System	Skin, hair, nails, sweat glands, and sebaceous glands	Provides protection for tissues, cushions tissues, excretes wastes, regulates temperature; largest organ system in the body.
Muscular System	Skeletal and smooth muscles throughout the body	Provides movement, controls movement of matter (food, excrement) through some organs
Circulatory System	Heart, blood vessels, and blood	Transports nutrients, gases, hormones, and waste through the body
Nervous System	Brain, spinal cord, and peripheral nerves	Relay electrical signals through the body, directs behavior and movement, and controls physiological process
Respiratory System	Nose, trachea, and lungs	Provide gas exchange between blood and the environment; oxygen is absorbed and carbon dioxide is expelled
Digestive System	Mouth, esophagus, stomach, small and large intestines	Breaks downs and absorbs nutrients for growth and maintenance
Excretory System	Kidneys, ureters, bladder, and urethra	Filters out waste, toxins, and excess water or nutrients form the circulatory system
Endocrine System	Numerous glands that secrete hormones, among which are the pituitary, thyroid, pancreas, adrenal glands	Relays chemical information along with the nervous system to control physiological processes
Reproductive System		
Male	Testes, seminal vesicles, penis	Manufacture cells that allow reproduction. Male produces sperm; female produces eggs.
Female	Ovaries, oviducts, uterus, vagina, and mammary glands	
Lymphatic/Immune System	Lymph, lymph nodes and vessels, white blood cells, T-cells and B-cells	Destroys microbes and viruses and removes fat and excess fluids from the blood.

What Makes Living Organisms Unique?

Living things have a level of complexity and organization not found in lifeless objects. At its most fundamental level, a living thing is composed of one or more cells and carries out a variety of processes. Metabolism, responsiveness, growth, reproduction, ecology, and evolution are all processes that are unique to all living things.

Metabolism: A living thing can rapidly exchange chemical matter with the external environment and transform organic matter within cells resulting in the release or use of energy.

Responsiveness: A living thing responds to stimuli such as light, heat, sound, chemical and mechanical contact in the external environment, detected by specific receptors such as eyes, ears, and taste buds. Living organisms contain a system of nerves and chemical regulators that control and coordinate effective responses to the environment. Responses generally require energy and occur in patterns that make up the behavior of a living thing.

Growth: A living thing takes in and organizes material from the environment into its own structures. Metabolism allows a living organism to transform material that is unlike itself into materials it can use to build and maintain growth structures.

Reproduction: A living thing can produce a copy of itself via reproduction while the organism is still living. In plants and animals, reproduction is an extension of the growth process. There are two types of reproduction: asexual and sexual. *Asexual* reproduction occurs in organisms like bacteria: one parent bacterium splits into two bacteria. *Sexual* reproduction requires two parents to create offspring. The following are several important terms and processes that relate to reproduction.

Gregor Mendel's work on pea plants provided the basis for understanding heredity. *Heredity* is a set of characteristics an organism receives from its parents. By studying *traits*, a characteristic that distinguishes one individual organism from another, Mendel crossed pea plants that had certain traits with pea plants that had other traits to see what would happen. These crosses are called *hybrids*. Assuming that traits would blend in the new pea plant, he discovered that the traits of only one parent showed in the offspring. This lack of blending suggested to Mendel that there must be some individual unit that determines a specific trait; he called this unit "character"; today these units are called *genes*. Different forms of a gene are called *alleles*. Mendel's work further established the concepts of *dominant* and *recessive*. Through crossing pea plants, Mendel observed that when a tall pea plant was crossed with a short pea plant, the plant was tall, indicating that when an organism has one allele for tallness and one for shortness, the dominant allele (one for tallness) is expressed. The unexpressed allele is called recessive. From this Mendel demonstrated that what a plant looked like or the traits it displayed may not necessarily be what makes up its alleles. The traits that an organism displays is called its *phe-*

notype; the genetic composition of the alleles is the organism's *genotype*. Further research advanced Mendel's work to demonstrate that there can be several combinations of alleles. For example, a tall plant may have a dominant and recessive allele (Tt) (heterozygous, dominant) or two dominant alleles (TT) (homozygous dominant); a short plant will only have two recessive alleles (tt).

Mendel's Principles

- Individual "characters" or genes determine biological characteristics.
- For each gene, an organism receives one allele from one parent and the other allele from the other parent. These alleles separate from each other when reproductive cells are formed; the process is called *segregation*. See discussion of meiosis and mitosis.
- If an organism inherits different alleles for one trait, one allele may be dominant over the other.

Ploidy is the number of complete sets of chromosomes in a cell. Embryonic sex cells or *gametes* such as sperm and egg are *haploid* because each contains one complete set of chromosomes (23). Two gametes (egg and sperm in animals and egg and pollen in plants) combine through fertilization to form a *zygote.* Somatic cells contain two complete sets of chromosomes and therefore are *diploid* (46). *Tetraploidy* (4 sets of chromosomes) is common in plants, amphibians, reptiles, and some insects.

Mitosis and meiosis describe the process by which the body prepares cells to participate in either asexual or sexual reproduction to make an entire organism. *Mitosis* controls the reproduction of skin, heart, stomach, cheek, and hair cells. These are called autosomal or somatic cells. This is also a form of "asexual" reproduction, where one organism or cell reproduces itself such as hydra, bacteria, and single celled organisms. *Meiosis* produces sperm and egg cells (gametes or sex cells). During this process each of these cells divides twice in order to end up with half the number of chromosomes. Each cell passes on genetic information to the offspring through sexual reproduction. Many plants and animals reproduce sexually.

Ecology: A living thing is not only influenced by its surroundings but can also alter its surroundings. Birds migrate to warmer climates when the climate becomes too cold.

Humans alter their environment by emitting excessive hydrocarbons. The relationship between organisms and their environment is *ecology*.

Evolution: A living thing can adapt to changes in the environment through evolution. In most cases, this allows the organism to develop abilities to deal more effectively with the environment. Evolution also creates a greater diversity of organisms than existed previously.

Evolution means a change over a period of time. Based on work by Thomas Malthus, Charles Darwin is credited with conceptualization of the diversity of life, adaptation, natural selection, and survival of the fittest. Based on observations and data gathered on almost a four-year voyage of the *H.M.S. Beagle*, Darwin wrote *The Origin of the Species*. This text not only assembled abundant evidence that supported that life changed and evolved over time, but also a hypothesis about why evolution occurs. He posited that organisms possess particular physical and behavioral traits that enable them to survive; he called these traits *adaptations*. Darwin also used the term *fitness* to describe the ability of an organism to pass on traits to offspring successfully, suggesting that only the fittest organisms survive and continue to exist in nature, a process he called *natural selection*.

Domains and Kingdoms of Living Things

The most current thinking about how the diversity of living things is best represented identifies several categories of organization. Some texts identify five major kingdoms of living things: Monera, Protista, Fungi, Plantae, and Animalia, and these kingdoms fall under three large Domains or Superkingdoms: Bacteria, Archaea, and Eukarya. Other texts identify Archaea as a separate kingdom. Kingdoms are further divided into Phyla when dealing with animals and Divisions when addressing plants. Subsequent categories of organization are Class, Order, Family, Genus, and Species. In the mid 1700s, Carolus Linnaeus developed Taxonomic Classification to organize all living things. Each category of the system includes specific characteristics. Scientists use *binomial nomenclature* (two–name system) to identify an organism by listing the genus and species. In this listing, the genus is always italicized and capitalized, while the species is not capitalized. The following chart outlines the Domains (sometimes called Superkingdoms), kingdoms, common names or categories that refer to phyla and divisions, and general characteristics.

Domains, Kingdoms, Common Name/Category for Phylum or Division, Characteristics, and Member(s)

Domain or Superkingdom	Kingdom	Common Name or Category for Phylum or Division	
Bacteria	Monera		True bacteria Blue-Green algae
Archaebacteria	Crenarchaeota		
Eukarya	Protista		
			Protozoans
			Algae
			Fungal-like protists
	Fungi		Includes yeast, mushrooms, molds, rusts, smuts, and mildew
	Plantae		
		Nonvascular	Mosses and liverworts
		Vascular	Ferns, club mosses, and horsetails
			Gymnosperms, or naked seeds

Characteristics	Member(s)
True bacteria; Most known Prokaryotes; have flagella	Lyme disease; *E. coli*
Prokaryotes of extreme environments	Found in hot springs of Italy
All eukaryotes; either plants or animals, need water-based envt., uni- or multicellular; heterotrophs, and autotrophs, phagocytes	
Phagocytes (ingest prey); use flagella, pseudopods, cilia to move; many are parasitic	Amoebas, paramecia, Plasmodium (causes malaria), Trypanosoma (causes African Sleeping Sickness); diatoms
All have chlorophyll; photosynthetic; some have flagella; can be toxic	Red Tide, Green algae, Euglena, Sirogyra, Volvox, Kelp
Giant, multinucleate mass of cytoplasm; live in decayed wood; move like amoebas; phagocytes	Slime mold
Multicellular; have nuclei; heterotrophs; generally do not move; asexual and sexual; thrive in soil and dead matter; develop from spores; haploid	Lichens, brewers yeast, penicillin, thrush, diaper rash, athlete's foot, bread mold, mushrooms, Downy mildew
Multicellular; haploid and diplod phases; live on land and water; cell walls of cellulose; chloroplasts and other pigments; autotrophs—make food photosynthesis; waxy cuticle; rigid internal support system; spores or seeds; sexual and/or asexual reproduction; vascular or nonvascular; roots, stems, and leaves	
No vascular tissue; sporangium contains spores; stem, leaves, and hairs; seta (foot)	True moss, peat moss, granite moss
Spores no seeds; xylem to transport water sporangia; rhizomes; stems, and leaves	Whisk ferns, horsetails
Cone-bearing; needles; stay green all year; seeds are not enclosed in an ovule but rather a cone; microsporangia and megasporangia; among the oldest plants in the world	Pines, firs, spruces, junipers, cypress, cedar, cycad, ginko, redwoods

Domain or Superkingdom	Kingdom	Common Name or Category for Phylum or Division	
Eukarya *(cont.)*	Vascular *(cont.)*		Angiosperms or flowering plants
	Animalia		
		Invertebrates	Sponges
			Jellyfish, hydras, sea anemones, coral
			Flatworms
			Roundworms
			Annelids or segmented worms
			Mollusks

Characteristics	Member(s)
Flowering; seeds are covered by a fruit; monocots, eudicots or magnoliads; woody or herbaceous; flowers in multiples of 3, 4 or 5; one or two cotyledons; net-veined or parallel-veined; contain stamen (male) and/or pistil (female-includes ovule and ovary), sepal, petal; requires pollination for reproduction	All fruits and vegetables; deciduous trees and shrubs, all flowering plants
cell membrane instead of cell wall; fixed body plan; mobile, heterotrophs [consume other organisms]; multicellular; sexual and asexual reproduction; diploid [two copies of genetic material in the nucleus]	
multicellular; no organs or nervous system; sessile, asexual reproduction; mostly marine; filter feeders; no true body cavity	sponges
Radial symmetry; asexual and sexual reproduction; contain nematocysts (stinging cells); carnivorous or filter feeders; mostly marine; primitive nervous system; no organs; may have skeleton of chitin or calcium carbonate; two life stages: polyp and medusa	Box jellyfish, sea pens; fire coral
Bilateral symmetry; ganglia or "brain"; nervous and excretory system; stomach cavity; some have oral sucker; some are parasitic; hermaphroditic; muscle; suckers	Planaria, tape worms, liver flukes
Largest number of multicellular organisms that live in the soil; structure is a tube within a tube; some are plant, human, insect parasites; others decompose organic matter; others eat bacteria, fungi; nervous and excretory system	Hookworms, ascaris, rat lungworm which can cause meningitis, trichina worms which cause trichinosis
Bilateral; tissues and organs; gut, mouth, and anus; nervous and excretory systems; close circulatory system; live in most environments; segmented	Earthworms, lugworms, ragworms, leeches
Soft bodied animals enclosed by hard shell; bivalves and gastropods; mostly aquatic; nervous, reproductive, excretory, digestive, and primitive respiratory systems; noted for extensive variety and beauty; gills or lungs; sexual reproduction; head-foot structure	Snails, clams, oysters, scallops, sea slugs

→

Domain or Superkingdom	Kingdom	Common Name or Category for Phylum or Division	
Eukarya *(cont.)*	Animalia *(cont.)*	Invertebrates *(cont.)*	Echinoderms
			Arthropods
		Vertebrates	Cartilaginous and Bony Fish
			Amphibian
			Reptiles
			Birds
			Mammals

Characteristics	Member(s)
5-rayed symmetry; gut with anus; variable body shape but no head; no excretory and poorly defined circulatory system; asexual reproduction; marine animals; eats fine particles in water; may have hard exterior	Starfish, sea urchins, sand dollars, sea cucumbers
Segmented body; chitinous exoskeleton; bilateral symmetry; paired segmented appendages; gills, primitive nervous system; sexual reproduction; noted for detailed life cycles; mouth and anus; open circulatory system	Trilobites, crabs, lobsters, insects, spiders, ticks, centipedes
Have backbone and spinal cord; skeleton is either cartilaginous or bony; gills; fresh and marine water; dorsal, lateral, and tail fins; carnivorous; strong jaw and teeth; scales or dermis; cold-blooded; bony fish have scales; sharks have dermal denticles	All sharks, all fish, eels
Cold blooded; smooth skin that must keep moist; 3-chambered hearts; live in both water and land; four limbs; large mouth, small teeth; respiration using lungs and gills; undergo several stages in life cycle and complete metamorphosis; nervous, excretory, digestive, and circulatory system	Frogs, toads, salamanders
Scaly, waterproof skin; molt shells and skins; lungs; 3-chambered heart; generally cold-blooded; closed circulatory system; sexual reproduction; nervous, digestive, excretory; lay eggs; carnivores and herbivores	Turtles, lizards, snakes, crocodiles, alligators, dinosaurs
Warm blooded; skin covered with feathers; hollow bones; 4-chambered heart; forelimbs modified to wings; most can fly; lay eggs; sexual reproduction; bills; webbed feet; toothless; possess wishbone; syrinx (unique voice box); developed respiratory system; acute vision, developed organ systems	Robins, swans, doves, starlings, albatross, ducks, herons, chickens, flamingoes, ostriches
hair, mammary glands, three middle ear bones, diaphragm, 4-chambered heart, large cerebral cortex, single bone for lower jaw, juvenile and adult teeth, warm-blooded; highly developed organ systems	Human, skunk, whale, dolphin, pig, horse, deer, bat, shrew, rabbit, seal, platypus, monkey

Viruses

Viruses do not belong to any kingdom because they are not considered living organisms, as they cannot reproduce without a living host. Once a virus infests its host, it replaces the host cell's original DNA or RNA instructions with its own genetic instructions, which are usually to make as many copies of the virus as possible.

Taxonomic Classification of *Homo sapiens* with Characteristics

Domain	Kingdom	Phylum	Class	Order	Family	Genus	Species
Eukarya: advanced cells that contain organelles							
	Animalia: cell membrane instead of cell wall, fixed body plan, mobile, heterotrophs [consume other organisms], multicellular, sexual reproduction, diploid [two copies of genetic material in the nucleus]						
		Phylum: **Chordata**: notochord—skeletal rod—that provides support, bilateral symmetry, complete digestivdigestive system, segmented body, endoskeleton, closed circulatory system					
			Mammalia: hair, mammary glands, three middle ear bones, diaphragm, 4-chambered heart, large cerebral cortex, single bone for lower jaw, juvenile and adult teeth, warm-blooded				
				Primata: warm-blooded, bear live young, forward and color vision, opposable thumbs and grasping fingers, progressive expansion of cerebral cortex, reduced litter, efficient gestation, facial mobility and voice			
					Hominidae: only includes humans, small front teeth and large molars, bipedal, walks erect, reduced facial musculature, dexterous hands, increased brain		
						Homo: larger, thin, and round cranium, smaller front and back teeth, flatter face, vertical forehead, chin, sunken upper jaw and cheek bones, small brow, delicate postcranial skeleton, smaller chest cavity	
							sapiens: ability to construct and use tools, bipedal, use and understand symbols, large cranial capacity, shorter arms and legs

Livings Organisms and Food Production and Consumption

Living things produce, consume, and acquire food in a number of ways. The following section provides important definitions about energy production and food consumption. Also included are important chemical cycles that describe important processes in photosynthesis and respiration.

Plants, Photosynthesis, and Respiration

Plants are *autotrophs* because they make their own food through a process called *photosynthesis*. All plants need water, nutrients especially nitrogen (N) from the soil, carbon dioxide (CO_2) from the air, and sunlight in order to live. The relationship between plants and animals is a mutually supportive one. Plants manufacture sugar and oxygen through photosynthesis; animals take in oxygen and through respiration give off carbon dioxide which plants use during photosynthesis. Before explaining the processes of photosynthesis and respiration, a general description of plants and their life cycle is helpful.

Angiosperms are divided into two sub-classes. *Monocotyledons,* which include grasses, lilies, irises, orchids, corn, and palms, have flowers that occur in threes, parallel veins in the leaves, little if any woody growth, seeds that have one seed leaf, and flower parts that occur in threes. *Dicotyledons*, which include most of the flowering trees, shrubs, and many non-woody plants have flowers that occur in fours or fives, seeds that have two seed leaves, net-like leaf veins, woody growth, and ring-shaped vascular bundles in their stems.

Just as animals have unique tissues and organs, so do plants. Plant tissues include xylem, phloem, and meristems. *Xylem* conducts water throughout the plant. *Phloem* distributes food throughout the plant. *Meristems* are specialized cells that grow rapidly and undergo continuous cell division. Plants are also unique because each cell contains the necessary DNA for growth, which permits asexual or vegetative reproduction. For example, each cell of a cyclamen has all the genetic information necessary to grow a root system, stem, leaves, and flowers. Because plants are generally sessile (they cannot move around) they rely on other organisms and mediums for pollination and proliferation. *Pollination* is the transfer of pollen (male gamete) from the anther to the stigma. Once in the stigma, the pollen forms a tube, which allows it to transfer the male gamete to the egg for fertilization. Some flowers like salvias and viola can self-pollinate, but most rely on wind, water, insects, birds, bats, and other animals for pollination. These mediums also carry seeds. Seeds contain the sporophyte embryo, food for the embryo, and a protective coat.

Parts of a Plant

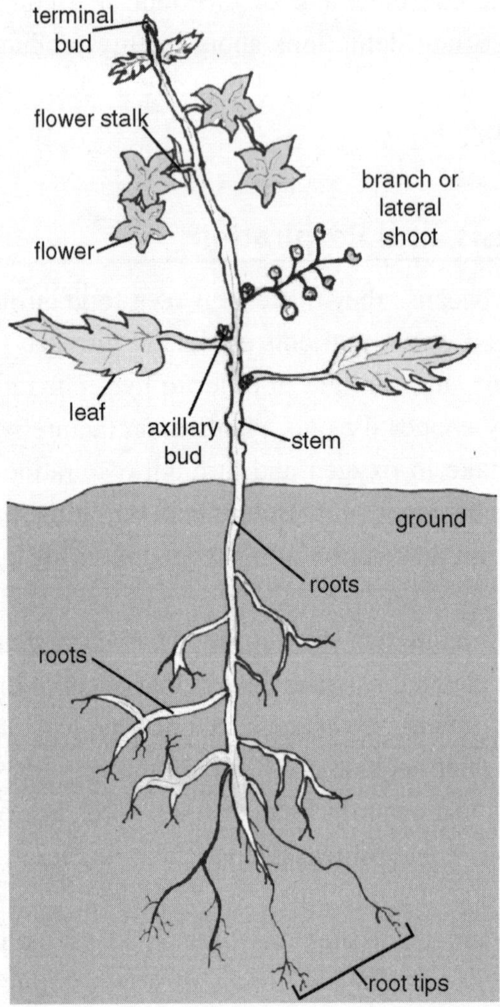

An embryo in a seed is dormant and can survive without additional food or water until conditions are right for growth.

Plants fall into one of three groups according to life cycle. An *annual* is a plant that completes its entire life cycle in one full year. During this time, they grow, bloom, produce seeds, and die. Examples of annuals include marigolds, geraniums, petunias, and zinnias. A *biennial* takes about two full years to complete its life cycle. Examples of biennials include carrots, Sweet William, cabbage, Swiss chard, and celery. A *perennial* lives more than three years. Those that bloom, die and come back the following spring are called herbaceous perennials. Hydrangeas, forsythia, lilacs, and Rose of Sharon are examples. Woody perennials are hardy and can stand cold temperatures. These plants include shrubs, conifers, and fruit trees.

Photosynthesis is the process of converting light energy to chemical energy, which is stored in the chemical bonds of sugar macromolecules. Photosynthesis occurs in plants (Kingdom Plantae), blue-green algae (Kingdom Monera), and other kinds of algae (Kingdom Protista). If you recall the differences between plant and animal cells, you will remember that plant cells contain chloroplasts, organelles that absorb red and blue sunlight in the form of chlorophyll (Chlorophyll looks green because green is the light that is not absorbed and therefore seen by the human eye.). Photosynthesis takes place in plant leaves, which are loaded with chloroplasts. The leaves are effective participants in this process because they contain holes (stomata), which let carbon dioxide, (CO_2) and oxygen (O_2) out.

There are two major reactions that occur during the process of photosynthesis: the *light reaction* and the *dark reaction*.

During the *light reaction*, the light energy is converted to chemical energy in a specific membrane of the chloroplast, where chlorophyll and other pigments are clustered. These pigments absorb light and move its energy to a central chlorophyll molecule in which photosynthesis occurs. Obviously because light energy is essential to this reaction, the reaction occurs in the light.

The *dark reaction* occurs in the stroma within the chloroplast, and converts CO_2 and water absorbed through plant roots into sugar, which is stored as starch. This reaction uses the products of the light reaction ATP (adenosine triphosphate) and NADPH (Nicotinamide adenine dinucleotide phosphate), water (H_2O), and CO_2 during the Calvin cycle to form sugar.

Photosynthesis

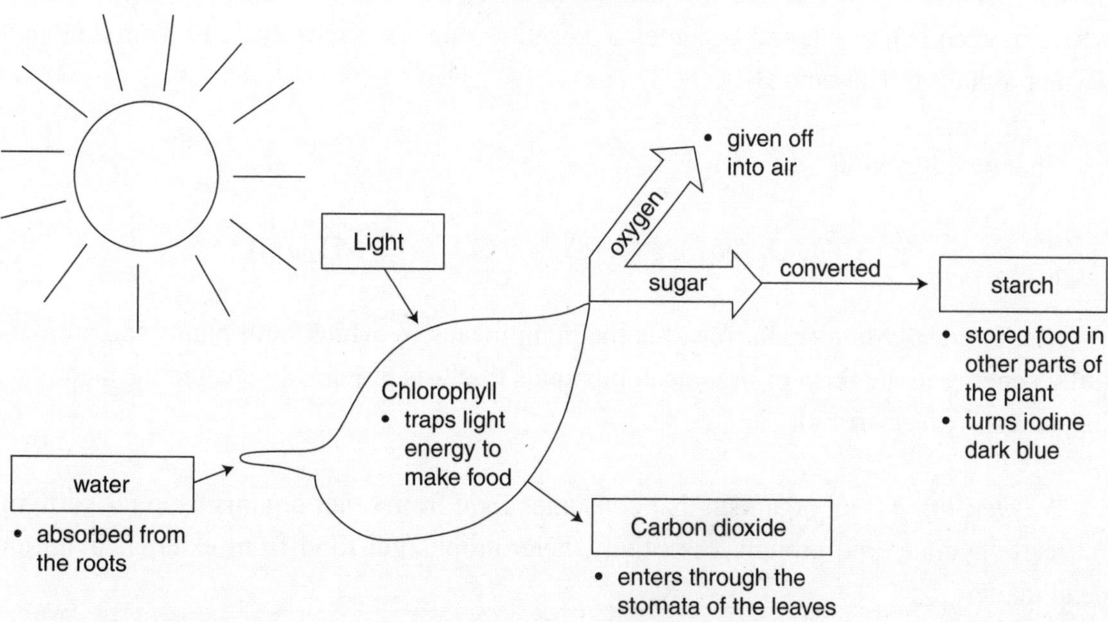

Chemical Reaction of Photosynthesis

$$6CO_2 + 6H_2O \text{ (+ light energy)} \rightarrow C_6H_{12}O_6 + 6O_2$$

Thus plants provide the source of oxygen we breathe, which is an extremely important point to remember as humans and other environmental factors destroy trees and other plants.

Respiration

Respiration is the physiological and chemical process that enables animals to use oxygen to release carbon dioxide into the environment, which is then used by plants during photosynthesis. Respiration is essentially the opposite of photosynthesis. Respiration occurs at several levels. The most significant level occurs at the cell. There are two types of cellular respiration that occur to produce water and carbon dioxide: aerobic (requiring oxygen) and anaerobic (not requiring oxygen).

During respiration, the cell breaks down sugar (glycolysis) in the cytoplasm into a special chemical, pyruvate. Because this process does not require oxygen, it is considered anaerobic respiration. The pyruvate permits the products of this breakdown to enter the mitochondria of the cell. If oxygen is present the pyruvate may become fully oxidized (aerobic respiration). This produces energy in the form of ATP and another important compound acetyl-coA, which leads to the Krebs cycle (Citric acid cycle). If oxygen is not present, pyruvate will ferment to form acetyl-coA, which then enters the mitochondria where oxygen is present, and becomes oxidized during the Krebs cycle to form ATP and waste products of CO_2 and H_2O.

Chemical Reaction

$$C_6H_{12}O_6 \text{ (aq)} + 6\ O_2 \text{ (g)} \rightarrow 6\ CO_2 \text{ (g)} + 6\ H_2O \text{ (l)}$$

Aerobic respiration (red arrows) is the main means by which both plants and animals utilize energy in the form of organic compounds that was previously created through photosynthesis (green arrow).

A *heterotroph* is an organism that consumes food from other organisms in the form of fat, carbohydrate, and protein; essentially, heterotrophs get food from external living or dead matter.

Symbiosis occurs when two or more dissimilar organisms interact. There are four types of symbiosis: mutualism, commensalism, parasitism, and amensalism.

In *mutualism* each organism benefits. As previously mentioned, the relationship between plants and animals is an elaborate example of mutualism. Lichens are another example of mutualism in which a fungus and alga coexist in a mutually beneficial way and is also one of the few examples that involves more than two kingdoms. The major partner in this relationship is a fungus (Kingdom Fungi) and the other partners may be blue-green algae (Kingdom Monera) and other algae (Kingdom Protista). Since the fungus is a heterotroph and cannot make its own food, it benefits by getting sugars from algae created during photosynthesis. The lichen in turn, protects the algae against the weather, providing the algae with a more stable and constant home.

A second type of symbiosis is *commensalism*. In commensalism one living organism benefits, while the other in unharmed. A barnacle, a type of crustacean, adheres itself permanently to the shell of a mollusks, turtle, or even whales. As a result the barnacle has a place to stay, but the host is not harmed in any way. Another example is the relationship between the *remora*, a sucking fish that attaches itself near the mouth of a shark. The remora benefits by eating the shark's food scraps and the shark is unharmed.

Parasitism is another form of symbiosis. In this form of symbiosis, one partner, the parasite, benefits at the expense of the host. The most common examples include tapeworms, flukes, malaria, and fleas. Tapeworms (Kingdom Animalia) affix themselves to the small intestines of humans and other animals and absorb all the nutrients, potentially killing the host. Another parasite, malaria, belongs to Plasmodium (Kingdom Protista). This parasite has two hosts: a mosquito and a vertebrate. When the female mosquito bites a host infected with malaria, the blood contains malarial parasites, which develop in the mosquito's saliva. When the mosquito bites another host, the parasites are then transmitted to another host through saliva, thus infecting another host with malaria. All parasites are eukaryotes except bacteria and viruses.

Amensalism is a type of symbiosis in which one partner is inhibited or destroyed and the other is unaffected. Amensalism does not include the typical intimate relationship of organism-host interaction. *Competition* is one form of amensalism in which a larger or stronger organism excludes a smaller or weaker one from living space or deprives it of food. For example, a taller tree may block out the sunlight, depriving smaller plants of sunlight, which may eventually cause their death. Another example is when animals trample over grass, killing the grass. Another form of amensalism is *antibiosis*, in which one organism is unaffected but the other is damaged or killed by a chemical secretion. An example of this is the bread mold *Penicillium*, which produces penicillin, the antibiotic that kills bacteria.

Biomes, Ecosystems, and Food Webs

A *biome* is a large geographical area that contains distinctive plant and animal groups, which are adapted to that particular environment. Geography and climate determine the type of biome that can exist. Major biomes include deserts, forests, grasslands, tundra, and marine and fresh water environments.

Each biome consists of many ecosystems. An *ecosystem* is a living community that is composed of complex relationships between each member and its surrounding environment. An ecosystem may consist of many *habitats*, which are areas or environments where an organism or ecological community normally lives or occurs. Any change in one part of the environment can have a significant impact on other parts of the environment. Furthermore, a change in one biome can significantly impact another biome.

The living part of an ecosystem is sometimes called a *food web* or *food chain.* Because plants manufacture food they are called *producers* and are at the beginning of the food chain. Next in the chain are *consumers* or organisms that eat plants and other organisms. Consumers are considered predators because they seek out (prey on) other organisms for their food. There are three types of consumers: *carnivores* are living organisms that eat only animals (numerous mammals, sharks); *herbivores* are living organisms that eat plants (rodents, deer, cattle); and *omnivores* are living organisms that eat both plants and animals (humans). The last part of the food chain/web are the *decomposers*, which feed off of dead plants and animals, breaking down this kind of matter into minerals and gases. Decomposers include fungi and bacteria.

Life Cycles

A living thing changes, grows, reproduces, and dies in a cycle. This is called a *life cycle*. Most animals progress through what is called a *simple life cycle* that is comprised of 3 stages: before birth, infancy or young, and adult. In such a cycle the animal is born alive or hatched from an egg, moves through infancy (being simply a smaller versions of a parent) and grows slowly to become an adult.

A Food Web in the Coniferous Forest Biome

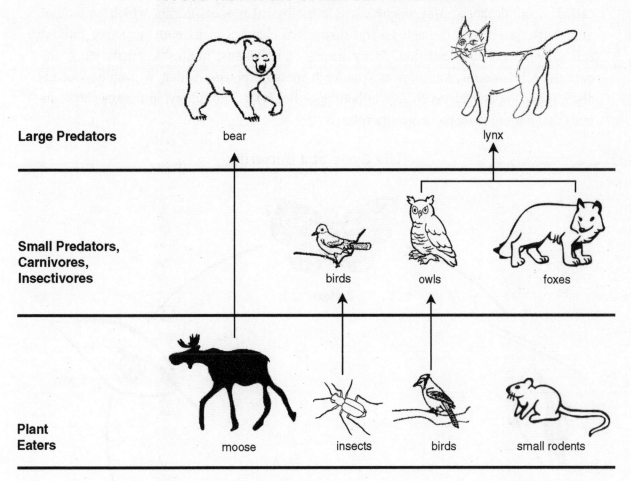

Large Predators

bear

lynx

Small Predators, Carnivores, Insectivores

birds

owls

foxes

Plant Eaters

moose

insects

birds

small rodents

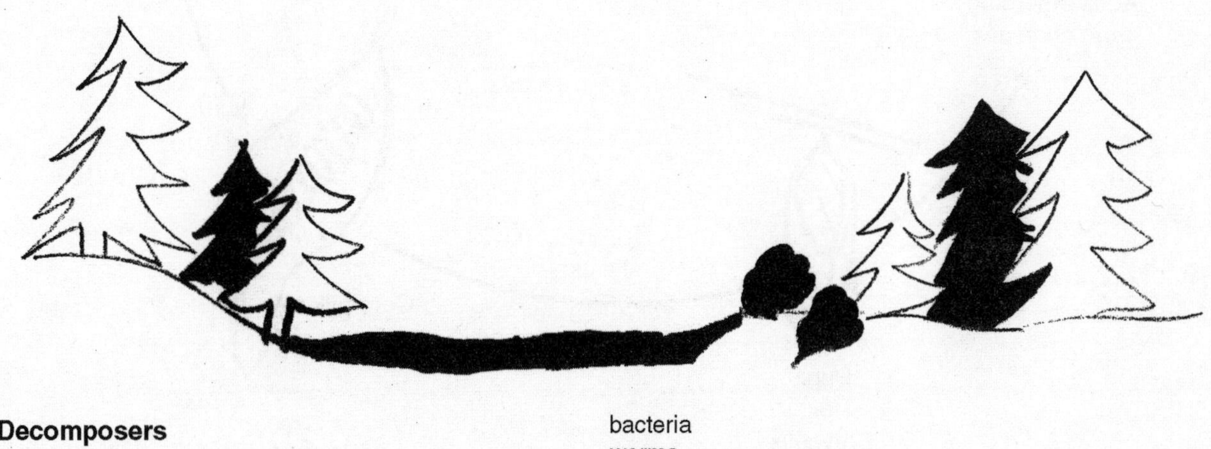

Decomposers

bacteria
worms
fungi

Some animals, however, experience more complex life cycles and undergo a process called metamorphosis. *Metamorphosis* is a biological process during which an animal, after birth, progresses through several distinctive changes in its body structure through cell growth and differentiation. Many insects, amphibians, mollusks, crustaceans, cnidarians, echinoderms, and tunicates undergo metamorphosis, which is usually (but not always) accompanied by a change of habitat or behavior. The following figures show animals that undergo complete metamorphosis.

Life Cycle of a Butterfly

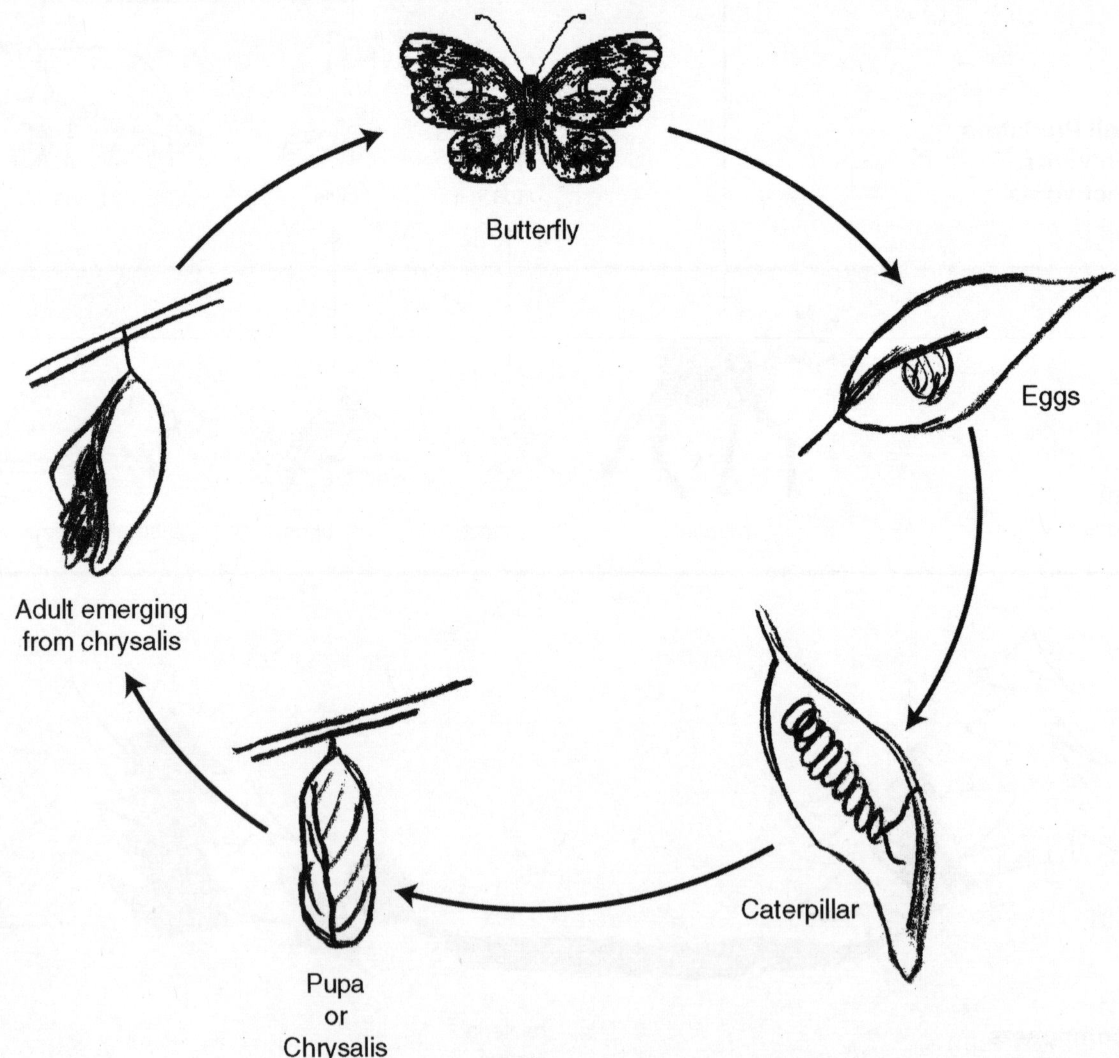

During Stage 1 the butterfly lays eggs. During Stage 2 these eggs hatch into larvae (caterpillars). Larvae are freeform, worm-like moving and eating creatures. Caterpillars are usually brightly colored and spiny. During Stage 3 the caterpillar becomes a chrysalis, which is a hard, protective, cocoon that encases the pupa before it becomes a butterfly. There is no feeding during the pupal stage. During Stage 4 a butterfly emerges from the chrysalis or pupa to go on to lay eggs and continue the cycle.

Life Cycle of an Amphibian

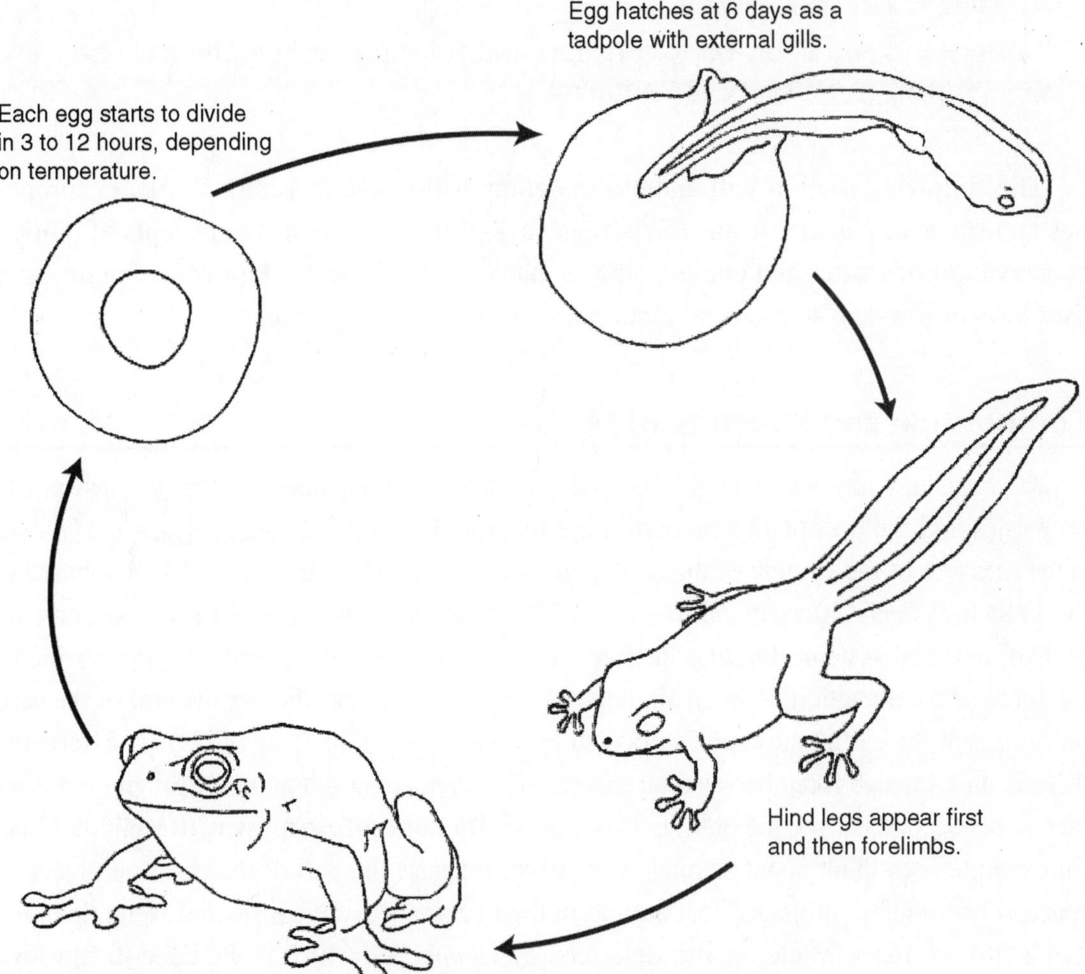
Egg hatches at 6 days as a tadpole with external gills.
Each egg starts to divide in 3 to 12 hours, depending on temperature.
Hind legs appear first and then forelimbs.
Metamorphosis is complete at about 90 days. Frog is a juvenile for one to 2 years. The frog becomes sexually mature at 3 years. Male fertilizes eggs as the female sheds them. A large number of eggs, 500 to 5,000, are fertilized in about 10 minutes.

Some animals undergo incomplete metamorphosis, which includes only three stages: egg, nymph, and adult. These animals include insects like grasshoppers, cockroaches, dragonflies, and termites.

Molting

Many animals *molt* or periodically shed all or part of their outer covering, such a shell, skin, feathers, exoskeleton, and cuticle, which is replaced by new growth. Such animals include insects, crustaceans, amphibians, reptiles, birds, and other mammals.

COMPETENCY 0011

Understand and apply basic concepts and principles of the physical sciences to interpret and analyze phenomena.

The following section will address the composition and structure of matter; properties and states of matters; forms of energy; ways of transferring heat; concepts of motion; conservation of matter and energy; simple machines; and the ways in which engineering uses laws of physical science and matter to solve everyday problems.

Composition and Structure of Matter

Matter is any physical material that occupies space and has mass. All matter has specific properties and the quantitative properties are measured in units of Metric System. *Mass (m)* is the measure of the amount of material in an object. Mass is measured in SI Units (based on the French *Système International d'Unités*). The following tables present selected units and prefixes in the SI system. *Weight* is the force that the mass exerts as a result of gravity, which is the force of the attraction between all masses in the universe, specifically, the pull of the earth on masses at the earth's surface. Discovered by Isaac Newton, his *Law of Gravity* asserts that there is an attractive force between all masses. The standard acceleration of gravity (*g*) is 9.8 meters per second per second or $9.8 m/s^2$ or $32 ft/s^2$. **Do not confuse mass with weight!** A useful example is to think about astronauts in space. Because the pull of the earth on objects in space is negligible, astronauts float around in their cabins and are considered weightless; yet, they still have mass. Matter is also described by *volume* (*v*), which is the three-dimensional space occupied by matter. Because it is three-dimensional, or length x length x length (length x width x height), the basic SI unit is meter cubed (m^3); and *density* (*d*), which is the amount of mass in a unit volume of a substance: density = mass over volume.

Density and weight are also confused. A kilogram of feathers has the same mass as a kilogram of lead, but it takes a greater volume of feathers and only a small volume of lead to form a kilogram because lead has a much higher density than a feather.

Selected SI Units

Physical Quantity	Name of Unit	Abbreviation
Mass	Kilogram	kg
Length	Meter	m
Area	$Meter^2$	m^2
Volume	$Meter^3$	m^3
Time	Second	s^2
Temperature	Kelvin	K*
Amount of substance	Mole	mol
Electric current	Ampere	A

*Three temperature scales are used in daily life and scientific research.
Fahrenheit: (*F*)—ice melts at 32° and boils at 212°
Celsius: (*C*)—referred to as Centigrade—ice freezes at 0° and boils at 100°
Kelvin: (*K*)—ice melts at 273° and boils at 373°

Conversion Formulas:

$$[K] = [°C] + 273.15$$

$$[K] = ([°F] + 459.67) \times 5/9$$

$$[°C] = [K] - 273.15$$

$$[°C] = ([°F] - 32) \times 5/9$$

$$[°F] = [°C] \times 9/5 + 32$$

$$[°F] = [K] \times 9/5 - 459.67$$

Selected Prefixes in the SI System

Prefix	Abbreviation	Numerical Meaning	Example
Mega-	M	10^6 (million)	1 megameter (Mm)=1 x 10^6 m
Kilo-	k	10^3 (thousand)	1 kilometer (km) = 1 x 10^3 m
Deci-	d	10^{-1} (one-tenth)	1 decimeter (dm) = 1 x 10^{-1} m
Centi-	c	10^{-2} (one-hundredth)	1 centimeter (cm) = 1 x 10^{-2} m
Milli-	m	10^{-3} (one-thousandth)	1 millimenter (mm) = 1 x 10^{-3} m
Micro	μ^a	10^{-6} (one-millionth)	1 micrometer (μm) = 1 x 10^{-6} m

Forms and Properties of Matter

Matter exists in 4 forms: solid, liquid, gas (vapor), and plasma. These forms differ in the following ways:

1. *Solids* have a definite volume and a definite shape. Solids cannot be compressed to become smaller. This MTEL prep text is an example of a solid.
2. *Liquids* have a distinct volume and the shape varies according to the container. Liquids cannot be compressed to become smaller. Apple juice is an example of a liquid.
3. *Gases* have no distinct volume or shape; the volume conforms to the shape of the container. Gases can be compressed to occupy a smaller volume or can expand to a larger volume. Carbon dioxide is an example of gas.
4. *Plasma* is like a gas in that its volume and shape conform to the shape of the container, but unlike gas plasma responds to electromagnetic forces because it can conduct electricity. Lightning is an example of plasma.

Most matter with which we come in contact is not in its purest state. Air, seawater, and chemical wastes can usually be broken down to pure substances: substances that have distinct properties and a fixed composition. *Pure substances* cannot be broken down by any chemical or physical means. Of course, any element on the periodic table is a pure substance, but there are other examples of pure substances such as water (H_2O), table salt or sodium chloride ($NaCl$), carbon monoxide (CO), carbon dioxide (CO_2), and methane gas (CH_4).

Every substance has unique physical and chemical properties. *Physical properties* can be measured without changing the substance: taste, odor, density, color, melting and boiling points, and hardness. *Chemical properties* describe how the substance will interact with other substances: flammability, radioactivity, sensitivity to light, oxidation, and toxicity.

Every substance can undergo physical and chemical changes. During a *physical change*, the substance changes its physical appearance but not its identity. When ice melts to form water, and water heats to form vapor, the physical state changes from solid, to liquid, to gas, but the identity (H_2O) does not change. During a *chemical change* (also called a chemical reaction), however, the substance changes to another substance, thus changing its chemical identity. When a substance is burned, like fireworks or logs in the fireplace, or cooked, like an egg, or a car bumper rusts, these are examples of a chemical change. Logs burn and release carbon into the air. Other examples include photosynthesis, respiration, and digestion.

A combination of two or more substances in which each substance retains its own chemical identity is called a *mixture*. Oil and water, sand and water in a cup, and concrete are mixtures. Although concrete hardens, the rocks and gravel in the concrete are still identifiable. Mixtures that are uniform throughout are called *homogeneous* or solutions. Air is a homogeneous mixture of gaseous oxygen (O_2), nitrogen (N), water vapor (H_2O), carbon dioxide (CO_2), and other gases (All substances in the mixture are gases). Other examples of homogeneous mixtures are body lotion, glue, and furniture polish. Mixtures that are not uniform are *heterogeneous* mixtures such as salt and water, cereal and milk, and Oreos.

Pure substances have a constant composition that does not vary. These substances are classified as elements or compounds. *Elements* cannot be decomposed into simpler substances. Scientists have organized all discovered elements in the *Periodic Table of Elements*, first created by Dmitri Mendeleev. Elements on the periodic table are arranged by atomic number (rows) and by similar properties (columns—also known as family or group). *Compounds* are composed of two or more elements that are chemically combined in definite proportions by mass. Water is a compound (H_2O) that regardless of form of matter will always be 11% hydrogen and 89% oxygen. Around 1800, chemist Joseph Proust made this observation, which led to the *Law of Constant Composition* or *Law of Definition Proportions*. Carbon dioxide, carbon monoxide, and sodium chloride are all compounds and regardless of source will always combine in the same proportions by mass.

Atomic Theory

John Dalton, an English teacher, conceived of the Atomic Theory, which provides a conceptual picture of how to visualize an element. His theory incorporates several important principles.

1. Each element is composed of extremely small particles called atoms.
2. All atoms of a specific element are identical.

3. Atoms of different elements have different properties.
4. Atoms are neither created nor destroyed.
5. Atoms of more than one element can combine to form compounds.
6. In any given compound the number and kind of atoms, are constant.

Dalton's theory assumes several important laws:

1. *Law of Conservation of Matter or Mass*: This law asserts that matter cannot be created or destroyed. This mean that the total mass of a substance that is present prior to a chemical reaction will be the same after the chemical reaction. For example, when charcoal burns, its mass and that of the oxygen, which is necessary for combustion, prior to combustion, does not change after these substances are burned.
2. *Law of Constant Composition*: This law asserts that the composition of a substance is always the same, regardless of how the substance was made or where the substance is found. For example, a molecule of pure water will always have 2 atoms of hydrogen and one atom of oxygen (H_2O).
3. *Law of Multiple Proportions*: This law asserts that the masses of one element, which combine with a fixed mass of the second element, are in a ratio of small whole numbers. For example, carbon and oxygen react to form CO or CO_2, but not $CO_{1.3}$.
4. *Law of Conservation of Energy*: This law asserts that energy cannot be created or destroyed. For example, the amount of electrical energy required to light up a bulb is equal to the amount of light and heat energy emitted from the light bulb.

Dalton and colleagues viewed the atom as a tiny indestructible and indivisible object, but by the mid 1800s, new discoveries by Thomson, Millikan, and Rutherford indicated that the atom was composed of even smaller, subatomic particles. Rutherford observed that the atom had a nucleus (much like the nucleus of a cell), which contained the atom's mass, positively charged particles called protons, and particles with no charge called neutrons. The rest of the atom was generally empty with the exception of negatively charged particles called electrons, which were in a constant state of flux/motion orbiting around the nucleus and moving from one ring or shell to another. The following figure shows the basic structure of an atom.

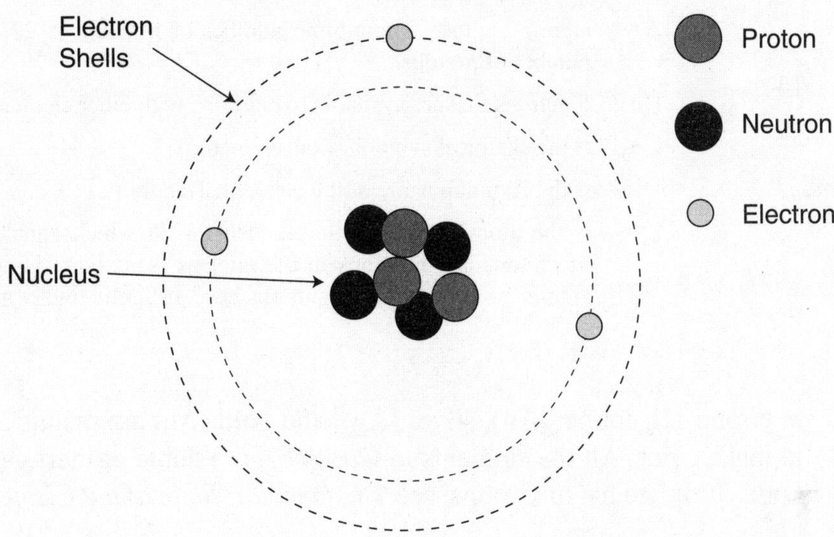

Atoms have several important characteristics.

1. All atoms of an element have the same number of protons in the nucleus. A lithium atom will always have 3 protons in the nucleus. A carbon atom will always have six protons in the nucleus. The number of protons in the nucleus is called the *atomic number*.
2. Because an atom has no electrical charge, this means that the number of electrons (negatively charged particles) orbiting outside the nucleus must cancel out the protons (positively charged particles). Therefore a lithium atom also has 3 electrons, and a carbon atom has 6 electrons.
3. The *mass* of an atom is the total number of protons and neutrons.
4. Mendeleev organized the elements in the *Periodic Table of Elements* according to the atomic number of each element, which moves from left to right. The *Periodic Table* is organized by rows (periods) and columns (family or group). The row indicates that all the atoms of the elements in that row have the same number of electronic shells (orbitals); each element in Row 1 has one shell, each element in Row 2 has two shells, and so on. The column indicates the number of electrons the atom has orbiting in its shell; every element in Group 1A has one electron orbiting in its shell, each element in Group 2A has two electrons orbiting in its shell, and so on. Periods, columns, or families also share certain chemical and physical properties and thus are labeled according to these properties. For example, all the elements

Diagram of Titanium as it appears on the *Periodic Table of Elements*.

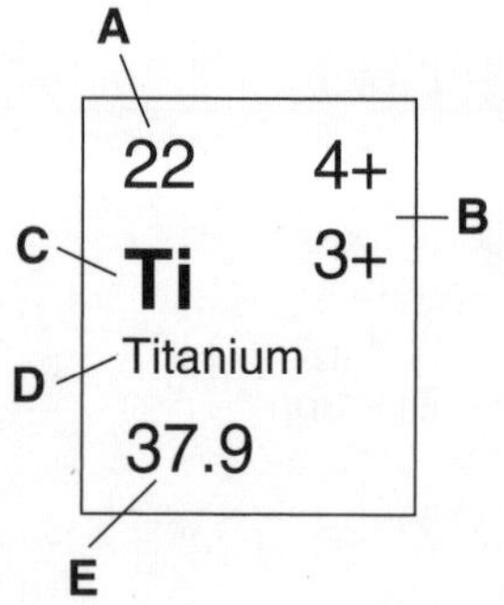

A = atomic number: The atomic number of titanium is 22, which is the number of protons.

B = Electrons that are available to combine with other elements.

C = is the chemical symbol of the element: Ti

D = is the common name of the element: Titanium

E = is the atomic mass of the element: 47.9, which equals the number of protons and neutrons in the nucleus (This mass is not double the atomic number, because neutrons have a slightly higher amu.)

in Group 1B, copper (Cu), silver (Ag), and gold (Au) are metals used to make coins. All the elements in Group 8A are noble or inert gases. For a complete list of Groups, see *The Periodic Table of the Elements*.

5. Protons and neutrons have approximately the same mass, which is incredibly small (1.00073 amu [atomic mass unit] and 1.0087 amu respectively). Electrons are even tinier, 5.486×10^{-4} amu.

A *molecule* is a combination of two or more tightly bound atoms; a molecule acts as a singular object. Many elements in nature are found in their molecular form. For example oxygen in air consists of two atoms of oxygen or one molecule of oxygen. That is why the *chemical formula* of oxygen in air is written O_2. The subscript 2, indicates that there are two atoms of oxygen in each molecule. Because oxygen is made up of two atoms it is called a diatomic molecule. Other examples of diatomic molecules are chlorine (Cl_2), hydrogen (H_2), bromine (Br_2), all of the elements in Group 7A (Halogens).

A *chemical formula* or *molecular formula* is a way of expressing information about the atoms that constitute a particular chemical compound. The chemical formula identifies each element in the compound by its chemical symbol and indicates the number of atoms of each element found in each discrete molecule of that compound. If a molecule contains more than one atom of a particular element, this quantity is indicated using a subscript after the chemical symbol. Developed by Swedish chemist Berzelius chemical formulas are used in chemical equations to describe chemical reactions.

Forms of Energy

Energy is the capacity of a physical system to perform work. Simply when energy is transferred to an object, work is done to that object. Energy can also be transferred in the form of heat. Energy exists in several forms: heat, sound, chemical, nuclear, light, mechanical, electrical, and electromagnetic.

Potential Energy is energy that is "stored" in matter. Although textbooks use the term "stored" many scientists view this term as a misconception because it suggests that the energy is a specific substance present in matter, like red blood cells in blood. There are many forms of potential energy such as gravitational potential energy, elastic potential energy, chemical potential energy, and electrical potential energy. An elastic band is probably the best example of potential energy. For example, a rubber band in a slingshot can be stretched to do work on whatever is being thrown. Until the object is released, the energy is considered potential energy. Once the object leaves the band and flies through the air, the energy becomes kinetic because the energy of the stretched rubber band has been transferred to the object (has done work on the object).

Kinetic energy is the energy contained in a moving mass. Whenever work is being done or heat is being transferred, the energy is considered kinetic. The sling shot object flying through the air is an example of kinetic energy.

According to the *Law of Conservation of Energy*, the total energy of a system remains constant, though energy may transform from one form into another form. Two automobiles meeting in a head-on collision may eventually come to rest, but the mechanical energy that each car brought to the collision results in conserved forms of energy such as sound, heat, or motion. The SI unit of energy is the joule (J) or newton-meter (N * m). The joule is also the SI unit of work.

Transfer of Heat Energy

As previously mentioned, the transfer of heat from one source to another is an example of kinetic energy. There are several ways that heat can be transferred: conduction, convection, and radiation.

- *Conduction*: During conduction atoms and molecules collide to transfer kinetic energy. For example, when hot atoms (atoms moving fast) of one substance collide with cold atoms (atoms moving slowly) of another substance, the fast atoms lose speed and the cold atoms gain speed. The fast atoms transfer kinetic energy to the cold atoms, which is a transfer of heat. This transfer of heat is considered microscopic because the transfer is occurring at the atomic and molecular level.

- *Convection*: During convection heat moves from a hot region to a cold region, but the transfer involves larger amounts of matter, and is therefore considered macroscopic. Heating water is a good example. When water begins to boil, hot bubbles (acting as a region of heat), which are less dense, rise to the top or cooler, less dense region of the water. At the same time, cool, denser water sinks to the bottom where it becomes heated.
- *Radiation*: During radiation, light energy in the form of heat is transferred from the sun to the earth. Light moves in electromagnetic waves, which are oscillating or vibrating electric and magnetic fields. The movement of electromagnetic waves is called radiation. These waves move at a constant speed of 3×10^8 meters/second or more commonly called the speed of light. Waves have specific properties, which are explained in the figure that follows. Each color on the spectrum of light has a specific wavelength and emits a specific amount of energy. Light shining through a prism or a raindrop (rainbow) displays all the colors of light. When electrons move from one orbital to another, they emit light (photons). White light comprises all colors on the spectrum. An object will appear blue because the dye molecules it contains reflects the blue wavelengths in the white light that strikes it. The primary colors are red, blue, and yellow; various combinations of two or all of these colors create all the colors of the spectrum. The light we see is noted as "visible light" on the spectrum.

Description of a Wave

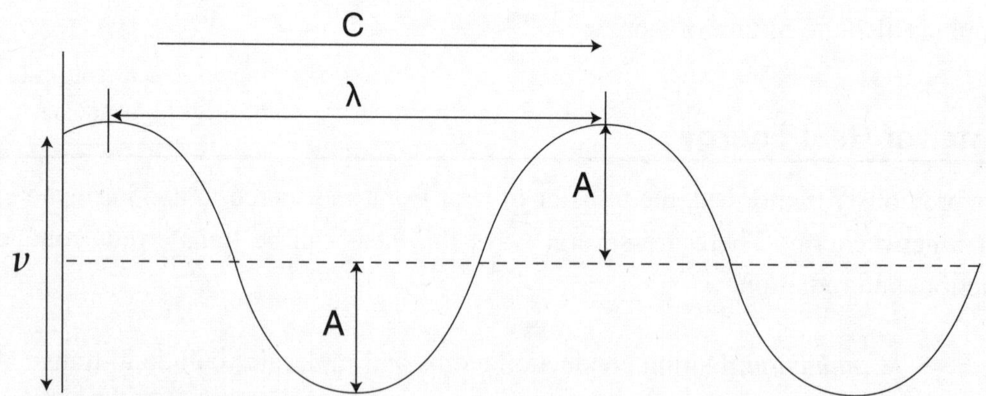

Properties of waves:

λ Wave length—Distance from crest to crest.
C Speed of light, 300,000 km/sec—Rate of motion of crests or troughs.
$\mathcal{T}$ Period—Time between passage of successive crests.
ν Frequency—Number of crest passages per unit time.
A Amplitude—Distance from level of crest to level of trough.

Concepts of Motion

Motion is change in the location or position of a body. Motion is always observed and measured relative to a frame of reference. More generally, the term *motion* signifies any spatial and/or temporal change in a physical system. Change in motion is the result of an applied force. Motion is typically described in terms of velocity, acceleration, displacement, and time. These terms are considered *vectors*: a vector is quantity that has size (magnitude) and direction. An arrow is used to symbolize vector.

1. *Velocity* is the rate of change of an object. A common term for velocity is speed. Velocity is expressed as distance over time: 5 meters/sec.
2. *Acceleration* is the change in velocity over time. Simply, acceleration is the rate at which an object can speed up (accelerate) or slow down (decelerate). The SI unit for acceleration is meters /second^2. Acceleration can also be the rate at which direction changes.
3. *Displacement* is the distance from the point at which the object is at rest to the end point of motion—or the shortest distance between two points. Displacement is measured in meters.
4. *Time* is part of the measuring system used to denote sequence of, duration of, and intervals between events. The SI unit for time is seconds.

Sir Isaac Newton discovered that motion is governed by a set of laws.

1. *The First Law of Motion*: This law, sometimes called the *Law of Inertia*, asserts that object at rest remains stationary and an object in motion moves at the same speed unless it is acted on by an unbalanced force. For example, if you are standing still on the floor, the force of the floor pushes you up and the force of gravity pulls you down. That you are standing still indicates that the forces pushing you up and pulling you down equal out or are *balanced*. Suppose someone running by you accidentally shoves you, exerting a force on you, making the force unbalanced. If the floor is slippery, you may slide and eventually regain your stability. However, if the floor is not slippery, the floor's surface will exert another force, *friction*, which may cause you to fall. Friction is an example of an *unbalanced force*. Put simply, if forces are balanced an object at rest will stay at rest, and an object in motion will stay in motion. The tendency of an object to resist change in motion is called *inertia*.

2. *The Second Law of Motion*: This law states that when a force is placed on an object, it will accelerate in the *direction* of the force, the acceleration will be directly proportional to the force that is applied and inversely proportional to the mass of the object. Simply put, if you push something, it will accelerate and move in the direction you pushed it, and if you push it twice as hard, the acceleration will be two times greater, and if you are pushing two objects, one of which has twice the mass, this object will accelerate at ½ the acceleration of the other. *Momentum*, which is equal to mass x velocity, was originally thought to be only related to Newton's Second Law, but scientists, including Einstein have demonstrated that momentum applies to electrodynamics, quantum mechanics, and relativity.
3. *Third Law of Motion*: This law asserts that every action has an equal and opposite reaction. A simple example of this is the recoil of a gun. The amount of the force that pushes out the bullet is equal to the force of recoil the marksman experiences.

Simple Machines

Simple Machines existed in biblical times; they just weren't called simple machines. Simple machines help us push or pull an object in any direction and more easily, saving us time, energy, and work. There are six simple machines: lever, pulley, wheel and axle, inclined plane, wedge, and screw. A machine has two functions: transmitting relative motion and transmitting force. See the illustrations of the six machines.

1. A *lever* is a rigid bar that rotates around a fixed point called the fulcrum. The bar may be either straight or curved. In use, a lever has both an applied force and a resistance force. There are three classes of levers, which are based on the location of the fulcrum and the input and output forces.
   a. A seesaw, shoehorn, and scissors (double levers) are *first-class levers*: one end of the seesaw is the input, the other end is the output and the fulcrum is somewhere in between the input and the output.
   b. A bottle opener, a nutcracker, and nail clippers are *second-class levers* because the input effort is located at one end of the bar and the fulcrum is located at the other end of the bar.
   c. A baseball bat, broom, stapler, and mousetrap are *third-class levers* because the input effort is higher than the output load, how-

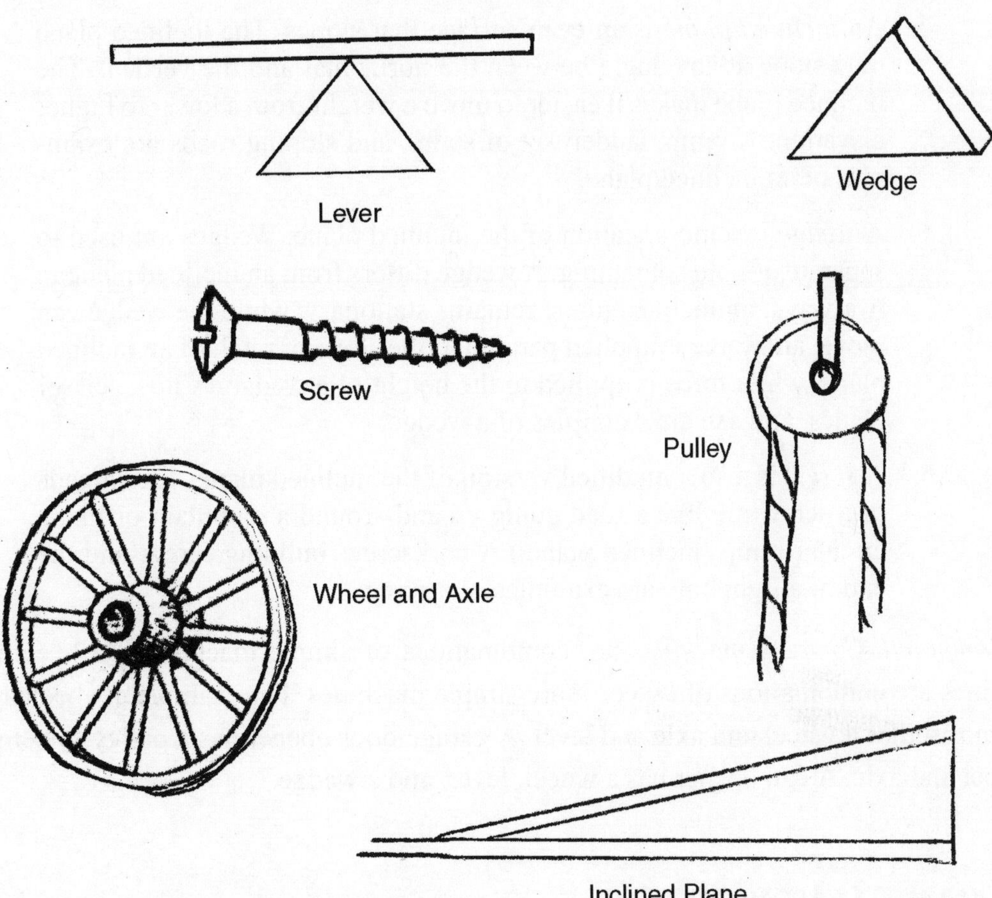

ever, the distance the object moves is greater than the distance of the effort. Think about how a batter swings a baseball bat. The distance the bat moves from the side/back of the batter during the swing is much smaller than the distance the ball moves into the field (provided the batter does not swing and miss).

2. A *wheel and axle* is a simple machine consisting of a large wheel rigidly secured to a smaller wheel or shaft, called an axle. When one part turns, the other part also turns. One full revolution of either part causes one full revolution of the other part. A car, bike, and wagon wheel are examples of a wheel and axle.

3. A *pulley* consists of a grooved wheel that turns freely in a frame called a block. A pulley can be used to change the direction of a force or to gain a mechanical advantage, depending on how the pulley is arranged.

A block and tackle, the system that pulls the flag up the pole, raises the blinds, or hoists the sail on a boat are examples of a pulley.

4. An *inclined plane* is an even surface that slopes. The inclined plane may slope at any angle between the horizontal and the vertical. The inclined plane makes it easier to move a weight from a lower to higher elevation. A ramp, ladder, set of stairs, and sloping roads are examples of an inclined plane.
5. A *wedge* is a modification of the inclined plane. Wedges are used to separate or hold something. A wedge differs from an inclined plane in two ways: an inclined plane remains stationary, while the wedge can move; and force is applied parallel to the slope or pitch of an inclined plane, while force is applied to the height of a wedge. A hoe, scissor blades, and axe are examples of a wedge.
6. A *screw* is also a modified version of the inclined plane. The threads of a screw are like a road going up and around a mountain or like a circular ramp (inclined plane.) A corkscrew, building screw, and the end of a light bulb are examples of a screw.

Compound/Complex machines are combinations of simple machines. ALL complex machines are combinations of two or more simple machines. For example a wheelbarrow is comprised of a wheel and axle and lever. A garage door opener has a pulley system and a wheel and axle. A can opener has a wheel, lever, and a wedge.

COMPETENCY 0012

Understand and apply basic concepts and principles of the earth and space sciences to interpret and analyze phenomena.

The Earth and the Solar System

The Earth is a sphere that looks like it has been flattened (oblate spheroid). The Earth, whose name comes from the Anglo-Saxon word "erdaz," which means ground or soil, is one of 8 planets in the *Solar System* (the Sun, 8 planets and their moons, and inner asteroid belt), which is part of the second largest galaxy in the universe, the Milky Way Galaxy. The Solar System takes about 230 million years to orbit the center of the Milky Way. Earth, (born of stardust almost 4.8 billion years ago) as its name suggests, is an inner terrestrial planet, along with Mercury, Venus, and Mars. The other 4 planets, Jupiter, Saturn, Neptune, and Uranus are giant, gas outer planets; that is why these planets have rings (composed of gas) around them. The Earth is the third planet in distance from the Sun.

Mercury is closest to the Sun and the smallest planet in the Solar System and Neptune is farthest from the Sun, but Jupiter is the largest planet in the Solar System. The following table lists important facts about the Earth, Sun, and Moon.

Important Facts about the Earth, Sun, and Moon

Earth is wider at the equator than from the North to South Pole.	
Equator Circumference	40,076 kilometers (km) (24,902 miles)
Polar Circumferences	40,005 km (24,858 miles)
Diameter at Equator	12,756 km (7,926 miles)
Diameter at Pole	12,714 km (7,900 miles)
Earth is made up of Oxygen, Silicon, Aluminum, Iron, Calcium, Sodium, Potassium, Magnesium, Nickel, and Carbon.	
Land surface area ~29%	148,326, 000 km^2 (57,268,900 square miles)
Water surface area ~71% (97% sea; 3% fresh)	361,740,000 km^2 (139,668,500 square miles)
Mass	5.976 $\times 10^{24}$ kg or ~ 6x10^{21} metric tons
Density ~ densest planet in the Solar System	5.52 g/cm^3 or 5 520 kg/m^3.
The Earth rotates on its axis at a slant as it orbits the Sun (a star), which causes the seasons.*	
Time for Earth to orbit the Sun	~365 days
Time for Earth to rotate on its axis	~24 hours
Distance between Earth and Sun	~150 million km or 93 million miles
Coldest temperature on Earth	362°K, 89.2°C, –128.5° F Vostok, Antarctica, 1983
Hottest temperature on Earth	331°K, 58°C, 136.4°F) Al'Aziziyah, Libya, September 1922
Major components of breathable air	78.084% Nitrogen (N_2), 20.946% Oxygen (O_2)
The Sun, a star, is the largest object in our Solar System, ~99.8% of the total mass of the Solar System, and is composed of 78% Hydrogen, 20% Oxygen, and 2% metals. The 8 planets of the Solar System orbit the Sun.	
Mass	1.989 $\times$ 10 ^{30} kg.
Diameter	1,390,000 km, ~8,637,060 miles
Surface Temperature (where Sunspots are)	5,800°K, 5,526.85°C, 9,980°F
Core Temperature	15,600,000°K, 15,327,000°C, 27,620,000°F
Power, produced by fusion reactions	3.86 $\times$ 10^{33} ergs of energy in the form of gamma rays/second
The Moon (a satellite) orbits the Earth ~28 days, known as months.	
Diameter of the Moon	~3,476 km, ~477,214 miles
Distance between Earth and Moon	384,000 km, ~238 607 miles)

*Because the Earth's spin axis is **NOT** perpendicular (straight from north to south) the Earth's surface changes its position in relationship to the sun and thus the amount of heat delivered to the surface, which causes the seasons. See figure of Earth's Rotation and the Seasons.

Earth's Rotation and the Seasons

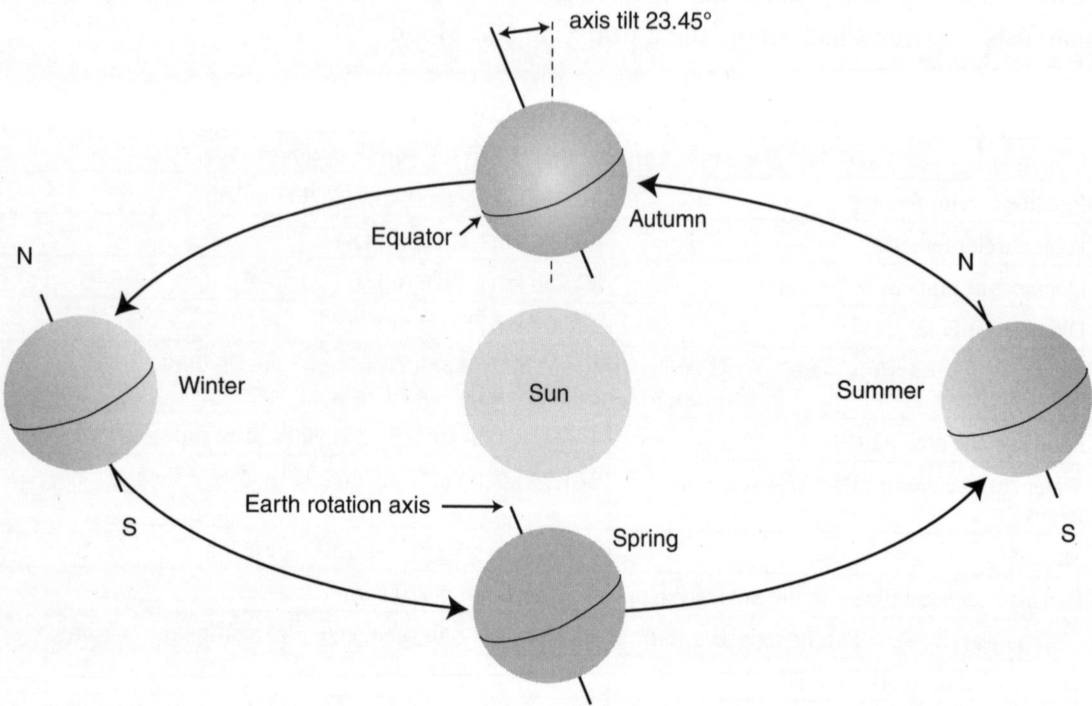

The *Moon* is the most well known natural satellite of the Earth. There are 4 other satellites in addition to the Moon. The Moon has no light, but rather reflects light from the Sun. The position of the Earth in relation to the Sun and Moon causes unusual astronomy events to occur; these events are *eclipses*. An eclipse occurs when one celestial object moves into the shadow of another, partially or fully obscuring it from view. There are two types of eclipses:

A *solar eclipse* occurs when the moon travels between the Sun and the Earth during the middle of the day and blocks the Sun's light from the Earth.

A *lunar eclipse* occurs when the moon moves into the Earth's shadow during the night and blocks the moon from the Earth.

Geosphere: Structure of the Earth

Physical Earth is composed of the inner core, outer core, mantle, upper mantle, and crust.

1. *Core*: The Earth's core has a liquid outer core and a solid inner core. The outer core, 2250 kilometers thick, contains iron, which generates a magnetic field; the inner core, about 1220 kilometers thick, contains nickel.
2. *Mantle*: Right below the crust, this section extends down to the outer core, and is composed of an upper and lower mantle. Luckily the mantle is flexible; otherwise, the Earth would fracture. The upper mantle is about 670 kilometers thick and composed of rock. The lower mantle, ranging in thickness from 670-2900 kilometers, is hot and plastic-like.
3. *Crust*: This is the outermost surface of the Earth. There are 2 types of crust: continental crust, composed of granite, silicon, and aluminum

Physical Structure of the Earth

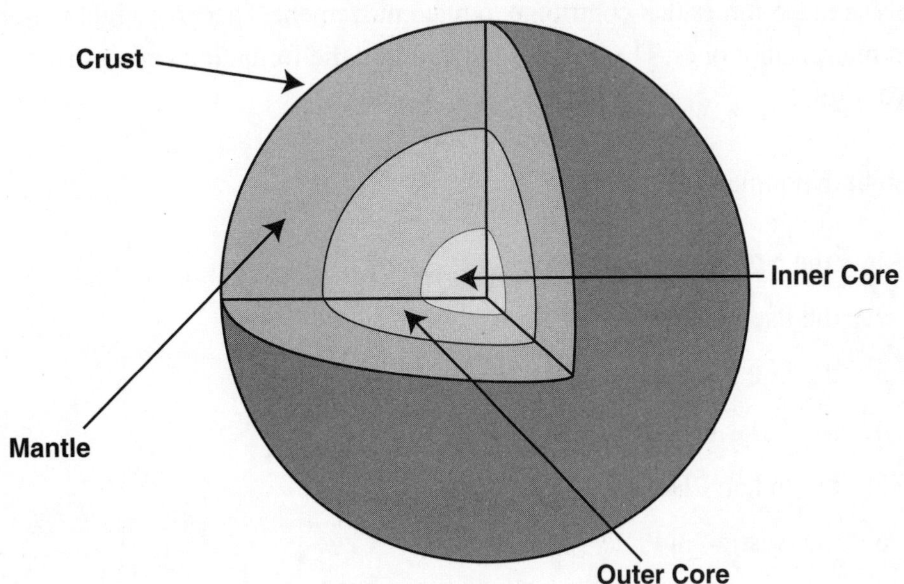

which lies below the continents which is about 20–70 kilometers thick; and the ocean crust, composed of basalt, silicon, and magnesium, which is about 5-10 kilometers thick. The *lithosphere*, which is the layer that includes the crust and part of the upper mantle, is the site of volcanoes, earthquakes, continental drifts, and mountain building.

Forces that Shape the Earth's Surface

The Earth's surface or crust is constantly being shaped and modified by forces that are internal *(endogenous forces)* and external *(exogenous forces)* to the Earth. In order to understand these forces, it is important that you understand important characteristics about the Earth: position within the solar system, general characteristics, and physical structure.

Endogenous Processes: Plate Tectonics

Tectonic Plates: The lithosphere is composed of tectonic plates. Tectonic plates are an example of an *endogenous process*. These plates are 100 kilometers thick and consist of continental and oceanic crust. Convection currents (heat energy from radioactive decay of uranium, potassium, and thorium) cause the plates to move constantly (~2–3 centimeters per year) in different directions, sliding, diverging, passing each other, which results in the modification of the Earth's crust. Such movements are shown in topographic maps. Friction and gravity are also forces that contribute to plate movement. There are eight major tectonic plates and many minor ones. These plates have caused the formation and destruction of continents over time.

The eight major plates are:

1. the North American Plate
2. the Pacific Plate
3. the South American Plate
4. the Eurasian Plate
5. the Indian Plate
6. the Australian Plate
7. the African Plate
8. the Antarctica Plate.

The eight primary plates constitute the bulk of the 7 continents and the Pacific Ocean. Plates meet at what are called *boundaries*, which is where the world's most active volcanoes are located. The *Ring of Fire* contained in the Pacific Plate is the most active and well known of these plate boundaries. The topography of the Earth is a product of endogenous and exogenous processes. *Relief* is simply the difference in elevation between two points. When the surface is relatively flat we say it has low relief. Conversely, mountainous regions have high relief. The relief features of the Earth are divided into three orders based on what created them and their size.

Rocks, Minerals, and Soil

Deep under the Earth's surface, in the magma area, different kinds of rock are produced. A *rock* is an aggregate of one or more minerals. A *mineral* is an inorganic, natural solid found in nature. The natural weathering of rock, wind, rain, wave, and ice erosion produce *soil* and rearrange soil minerals into new types of rock.

There are three types of rocks: igneous, sedimentary, and metamorphic.

- *Igneous rocks*: formed from molten rock deep in the Earth; three types: *intrusive*—large crystals, cooled slowly inside the Earth's crust; includes granite, granodiorite, diorite, gabbro, and peridotite. *Extrusive* rocks—small crystals, cooled rapidly; includes basalt, rhyolite, dacite, and andesite. *Pyroclastic rocks*—volcanic ash and other volcanic debris.
- *Sedimentary rocks*: formed of rocks and minerals resulting from the chemical and physical breakdown of pre-existing rocks; two types: *clastic*—contains rock fragments, feldspar, and quartz; include sandstone, conglomerates, and shale (includes silt and clay); *chemical*—formed from minerals in precipitation; include halite, gypsum, anhydrite, and limestone.
- *Metamorphic rocks*: rocks that have been changed into another kind of rock. These rocks were once igneous or sedimentary that were changed, usually by heat or pressure. They now have new minerals and/or structure. Marble is an example of metamorphic rock.

Properties of Rocks:

1. *Hardness*: ability of one substance to scratch another. Hardest—diamond; softest—Moon rock

2. *Luster*: how light is reflected: glassy, pearly, silky, resinous, waxy, and earthy. The degree of luster: shining, glistening, glimmering, matt, dull.
3. *Density*: mass of substance in a given volume. Densest rocks—gold and platinum; lightest—silicates.
4. *Cleavage*: degree of smooth, shiny surface upon breakage. High cleavage—mica; low cleavage—mud rock.
5. *Fracture*: appearance of mineral when shattered or broken open: smooth, splintered.
6. *Twinning*: appearance of fine, parallel lines.
7. *Transparency*: transparency in visible light: water-clear, transparent, translucent, or opaque.
8. *Color*: variety of color: yellow sulphur, red cinnabar, green malachite, blue azurite.
9. *Special Light Effects*: reflection or diffraction of light by twinning: opalescence (rainbow like opal) and labardorescence (incredible array of blue color).
10. *Streak*: color of colored mineral on white: pyrite

Structure of the Earth's Atmosphere

Layers of the Earth's atmosphere are divided on the basis of temperature. The force of gravity pushes down on the Earth's surface, which creates air pressure. The higher the layer is, the colder its temperature. The layers of the atmosphere include:

- *Troposphere*: 0-12 km thick; contains 75% of the gases in the atmosphere, is where we live and where weather occurs. The layer that separates the troposphere from the stratosphere is called the tropopause, where strong winds blow toward the east and where the jet stream occurs.
- *Stratosphere*: 12-50 km thick; contains the ozone layer, which absorbs the sun's damaging ultraviolet radiation.
- *Mesosphere*: 50-80 km thick; coldest region of the atmosphere; protects Earth from meteoroids, which burn up in this area.
- *Thermosphere*: (heat sphere) 80 km and higher; contains very thin air; ultraviolet radiation turns to heat > 2000 degrees Celsius. The

lower part of this layer is the *ionosphere*, where gas particles absorb ultraviolet and X-ray radiation from the sun and become electrically charged (ions) which bounce off and reflect radio waves, which helps radio communication. The upper part of the thermosphere is the *exosphere,* where satellites orbit the Earth.

- *Magnetosphere*: the area beyond the atmosphere; contains protons and electrons, traps deadly radiation. During a solar flare, which is a rapid, intense, and sudden variation in brightness that releases energy equal to more than one million 100-megaton hydrogen bombs, the subatomic particles collide to create the Aurora Borealis (northern lights)!

The Water Cycle

One of the most critical cycles of living Earth is the Water Cycle (Hydrologic Cycle). See the figure that follows. The cycle describes how water cycles through various states of matter to support life. There are several important processes that occur in the water cycle: accumulation, evaporation, condensation, precipitation, and run-off. Water (liquid H_2O) from surface runoff (rain, snow melt, or other water that flows in surface streams, rivers, or canals) and from subsurface runoff (rain, snow melt, or other water that flows in underground streams, drains, or sewers) *accumulates* and is stored in oceans, lakes, rivers, and glaciers. Due to solar heating and other climate forces, water *evaporates* (forms water vapor) into the atmosphere. Water also evaporates through *transpiration*, a process whereby water is absorbed through the roots of plants, moves to the leaves through phloem, and evaporates into the atmosphere. As the atmosphere cools, water vapor *condenses* to form clouds, which eventually release liquid water in the form of precipitation and falls to earth in rain, snow, hail, and sleet. The cycle continues as water accumulates in oceans, lakes, and so on.

Weather and Climate

Weather is everything that occurs in the troposphere at any given time. Day-to-day weather includes atmospheric temperature, precipitation, humidity, wind, density, and pressure. *Climate* is the average atmospheric conditions over a long period of time or average weather conditions in a specific region. The angle of the sun, which changes according to latitude, causes extreme heat in the tropics and extreme cold in the Polar Regions. These extremes between polar and tropical air cause the jet stream, which are fast moving, narrow air currents. On Earth's surface, temperatures usually range ±40 °C (100 °F to −40 °F) annually. Changes in Earth's orbit affect the amount and distribution

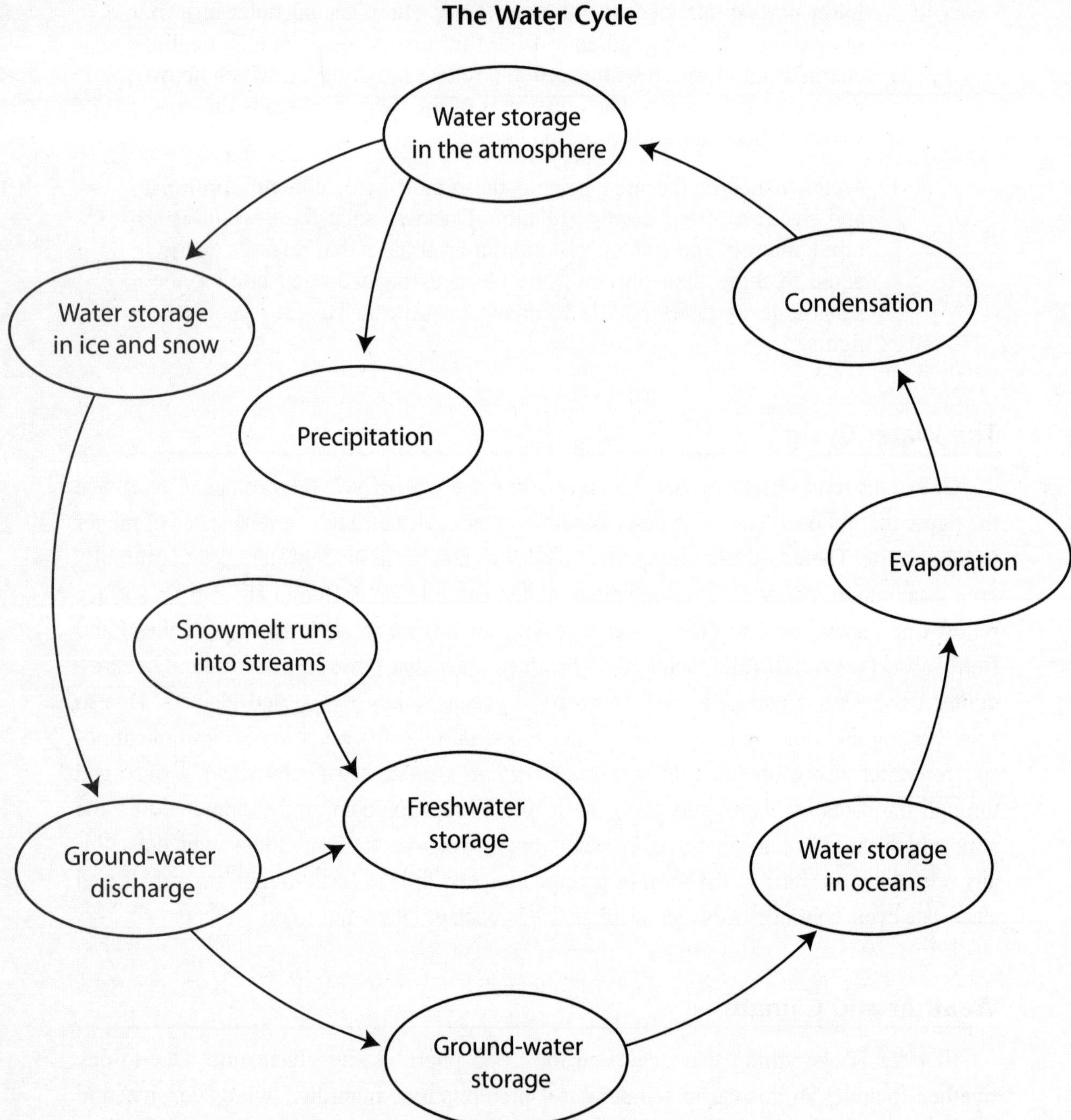

of solar energy received by the Earth and influence long-term climate. The temperature of the Earth's surface causes pressure differences.

Factors that impact weather and climate are latitude, altitude, prevailing winds, distance from the sea, ocean currents, Earth's tilt, mountains, and people. Latitudes that are closer to the Equator have a warmer the climate than those further away. Higher altitudes are cooler; lower altitudes are warmer. Because the Earth tilts on its axis, one hemisphere leans toward the sun during one half of the year and away from the sun the other half of the year. Ocean currents increase or decrease temperatures; the Gulf Stream keeps Europe's west coast ice free in the winter and warmer in the summer than other places of similar latitude. El Niño, a warm current of water in the Pacific Ocean that appears every 3–7 years, forces energy and moisture into the atmosphere, modifying rainfall and wind. Global warming, the average temperature of the Earth's air and oceans, has been increasing over several decades due to deforestation, gas emissions from burning fossil fuels (human causes) and solar radiation and volcanoes (natural causes). Results of global warming are conjectured to cause changes in precipitation, more subtropical deserts, rising sea levels, glacial retreat, extreme weather events, major impact on agriculture and food production, and eventual extinctions of certain species.

Exogenous Processes

External forces that modify and change the Earth's surface are caused by solar energy (energy from the sun). These include wind and rain erosion, ice (glaciers), gravity, waves, and pressure. Those processes acting at the surface of the earth and primarily driven by solar energy are called *exogenous processes*.

Wind on earth, is movement of gases on a very large scale. Wind in outer space is the movement of light energy from the sun through space. Convection currents in the atmosphere, due to changes in density and pressure cause wind. Air always flows from areas of high pressure to areas of low pressure to maintain equilibrium. Winds move in a spiral: inwards and upward in low pressure systems and downward and outwards in high pressure systems. As wind blows, its force separates and transport soil particles, which is *wind erosion*. Wind erosion is therefore an exogenous process. Naturally the speed of wind (velocity) contributes significantly to soil erosion. Obviously high-intensity winds create more soil erosion. Soil erosion disturbs the balance between soil and plant roots, disrupts terrace-cultivation, and impacts agricultural processes. Construction, deforestation, animal grazing, shifting cultivation procedures, and fires also enhance wind erosion. Although the ecosystem allows for some erosion, major soil erosion upsets the balance of nature.

Water erosion has a significant impact on the ecosystem. *Rain*, condensed water vapor (See Water Cycle), causes two kinds of erosion: splash and sheet erosion. *Splash erosion* occurs when rain splashes down and knocks soil particles into the air. Consider all the particles of rich topsoil that become dislodged during one significant rainstorm. In *sheet erosion*, particles unearthed via splashing move downhill to cause sheet-flooding. When combined with rain, the effects are even more devastating, as rain and high winds drive sediment and silt down slopes, into streams, rivulets, and rivers, carrying with it soil nutrients and causing more pores in the Earth's surface. Water velocity is also critical in increasing erosion; the faster water moves, the larger the objects it can move along the way.

Ice, in moving glaciers, is a powerful erosive force. Glacial plucking is a form of erosion whereby water under the glacier freezes and breaks off pieces of rock, which are then carried along by the moving glaciers. Glaciers also abrade: abrasion cuts into rocks under the glacier, which scoops up the rock like bulldozers.

Waves in oceans and large bodies of water can produce more than 2,000 pounds of pressure/square foot, seriously eroding rocks along the coastline. Erosion of sand is an easy task for waves.

Ocean Waves, Tides, and Currents

The properties of waves in other areas of science are the same in ocean waves as shown in the following figure. Like other waves, ocean waves are characterized by wave height, wavelength, period, and speed. Waves carry energy across vast distances. The most common, *wind waves*, occur on the surface of oceans, seas, lakes, rivers, canals, puddles, and ponds. Wind waves range in size from ripples to rogues. The kind of wind waves is determined by wind velocity, fetch (distance over water the wind has blown), width of fetch, time wind blows over area, and depth of water. The greater these variables are, the larger the wave. *Tsunamis* are waves caused by geological occurrences such as volcanoes, earthquakes, landslides, and underwater disturbances. *Tidal waves* are caused by the gravitational pull of the sun and the moon on the Earth. Tidal waves are the largest rogue waves whose height reaches upwards of 100 feet.

Tides, periodic rising and falling of water, are created by the pull of the moon's gravity on the Earth. Ocean levels fluctuate daily as the sun, moon, and Earth interact. Since the Earth is rotating while this is happening, two tides occur each day. Simply put, gravity, inertia, and bulges cause tides. The pull of the Earth's side closest to the moon pulls ocean water and creates a bulge. At the same time inertia tries to keep the water in place, but gravity wins. On the other side of the Earth, gravity is less because the moon is farther away, and inertia wins this battle, pulling the Earth, forming another bulge. These

Diagram of Ocean Wave

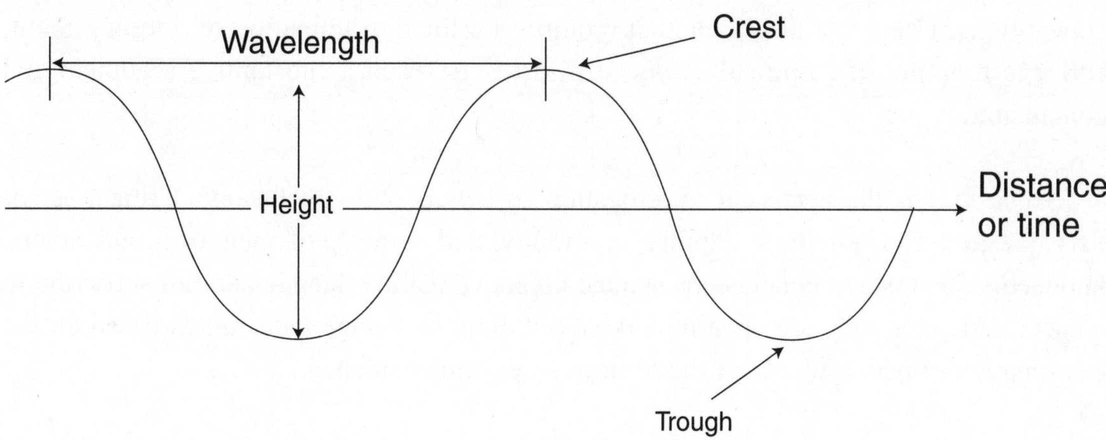

bulges are aligned with the rotation of the Earth. When you are on the coast and the moon is directly overhead and closest to the Earth, you will experience high tide, which occurs about every 12½ hours because the Earth rotates 180 degrees in 12 hours. When the Earth is farthest from the moon, low tide occurs.

COMPETENCY 0013

Understand the foundations of scientific thought; the historical development of major scientific ideas and technological discoveries; and the relationships among scientific discoveries, technological developments, and society.

Foundations of Scientific Thinking: Empiricism, Rationalism, and Skepticism

Science is a way of knowing and learning about our world that is grounded in the work of Aristotle and is based on three critical concepts: empiricism, rationalism, and skepticism.

Simply, *empiricism* is the use of empirical evidence. Empirical evidence is evidence that is based on the senses and is used by scientists because it can be replicated, critiqued, and experienced by other scientists. Evidence is based on laws and principles that have been interrogated, replicated, and experienced by scientists and others throughout time.

Rationalism, or the practice of using logical reasoning, is not instinctive or intuitive. In fact many events that occur in science are counter-intuitive and results in misconceptions. Logic is a discipline that requires a critical examination of, inquiry about, and interrogation of empirical evidence in order to reach a substantive argument and conclusion.

Skepticism is the persistent interrogation of beliefs and conclusions. Critical scientists question and test the reliability, credibility, and veracity of their own and others' knowledge claims and conclusions against objective reality. Skeptics do not subscribe to a specific dogma; they are open-minded and willing to change their minds based on the examination of new evidence or the scrutiny of existing evidence.

Scientific Inquiry

Established by the U.S. Congress by the National Science Foundation Act of 1950, the National Science Foundation is an independent agency of the U.S. government responsible for supporting basic research and education in the sciences, mathematics, and engineering. It grants funding for research and provides support for educational programs in mathematics and sciences. In *Foundations, The Challenge and Promise of K–8 Science Education Reform* (1997), written by the Center for Science Education and Published by the National Science Foundation, inquiry was defined:

The process of "inquiry" is modeled on the scientist's method of discovery. It views science as a constructed set of theories and ideas based on the physical world, rather than as a collection of irrefutable, disconnected facts. It focuses on asking questions, considering alternative explanations, and weighing evidence. It includes high expectations for students to acquire factual knowledge, but it expects more from them than the mere storage and retrieval of information.

Sherry Seethaler identifies several myths of science. K–12 students often come away with these misconceptions about science and scientific inquiry.

1. Science is a step-by-step process in which scientists develop a hypothesis, design an experiment to test it, conduct the experiment, collect data, analyze the data, and accept or refute the hypothesis based on it.
2. Scientific models are visual representations of reality.
3. Science is the progressive accumulation of facts.

4. Disputes among scientists are an indication that there is a problem with the scientific process.
5. The publication of findings is the endpoint of scientific research.
6. Many important ideas have been ignored in the past, so if someone claims to have ideas that are being ignored by the scientific establishment, there is a good chance that their ideas are correct.

Themes in Scientific Discovery

The following chart presents a very brief time-line of scientific discoveries that have occurred since approximately 1000 BCE until the current time. As you study these events please note the following themes:

1. *The relationship and often the tension between science, government, and religion have existed since the beginning of time.* Early in human history, political figures, emperors, and rulers understood, and religious figures such as Jesus, Buddha, Muhammad, and the great prophets, explained all knowledge about how the Earth was formed and how humans evolved through the Holy Scriptures, the Koran, and the Talmud which identified "God" or a supreme being as the creator of the world. Or the cultures created elaborate mythologies that identified many gods as creators of particular aspects and explained the occurrence of unexplainable events in the world. Thus the beliefs of prevailing governments were often inextricably linked to a religious ideology that identified God or gods as the center of all creation and the Earth as the center of the universe, resulting in elaborate control of scientific discovery, deadly inquisitions, support or lack of funding for discovery, and even death. Given such control of knowledge, it is no wonder why Galileo was ordered to cease his support of Copernican astronomy. The Ancient Greeks and Egyptians can be credited with the beginnings of scientific and empirical thinking, using reason and evidence to separate the natural from the supernatural. They developed the foundation for medicine, atomic structure, simple and complex machines, physics, astronomy, and natural history. Persian scientists also saw the logic in scientific explanation of natural events and eventually became discoverers and disseminators of scientific knowledge about the natural world. The Renaissance saw the resurrection of scientific and rational thinking, laying the groundwork for the scientific revolution. Still, however, there was a profound tension between the "Church," prevailing governments, and scientific discovery. Since most European governments reflected the religious beliefs of the period, their support for scientific research

varied from ruler to ruler. One only needs to examine the controversies around stem cell research to note that disagreements still exist among scientific, political, and religious constituencies. You will also see, however, that by the early 1900s governments began to sponsor scientific research to address not only societal needs but also national defense and space exploration.

2. *War and warfare, whose end results are more often than not political, promote advances in technology and engineering.* Although the Chinese invented gunpowder in the late 100s, it was not until the mid 800s that it came into its own when used in battles between dynasties and sects. Catapults—simple levers—jettisoned boulders into enemy walls. Eli Whitney's discovery of assembly line manufacturing of guns enabled the North to overcome the South during the Civil War. During the first and second World Wars, the race to develop chemical agents to destroy conventional forces dominated scientific research for both the allies and axis powers. The Curies' discovery of radium laid the groundwork for subsequent work in nuclear fission and the development of the atomic bomb, which established the U.S. as *the* major political power in the world during WWII. The development of the hydrogen and neutron bombs, nuclear power, reactors, and ballistic missiles serve as constant reminders of the power of science to protect and destroy.

3. *Science, technology, and engineering also demonstrate the power of scientific thinking to enhance communication and further discovery.* Beginning with Marconi's wireless telegraph, to Bell's telephone, to Bush's mechanical and analogue computers, to invention of digital and supercomputers, satellites, to cell phones, wireless Internet, and the World Wide Web, science has not only facilitated the sharing of important knowledge and learning but has also facilitated critical discussion among world leaders, provided up-to-the minute information about weather patterns, natural disasters, and significant life-changing events. Space travel, satellites, and powerful telescopes have opened up the universe for exploration and further discovery. These various forms of communication have made a large world more personal and accessible and provided important intelligence that helps governments protect and defend freedom.

4. *Scientific discovery about nature, evolution, and the human body has led to engineering breakthroughs that pervade all aspects of life and health.* From the primitive lens, to the double helix, to the human genome, to the CAT scan, scientific inquiry has led to improved quality of life. Understanding how the body works from cellular biology to neuroscience, researchers and engineers have worked together to

enhance medical care, create cures for disease, improve agriculture, replace organs, treat psychological illness, find more effective ways to learn, and generally enhancing the quality of life of many of its citizens. An important caveat, however, is that such discovery requires immense funding; and often this funding is informed by specific political and economic agendas.

5. *The most critical theme, however, is the interdisciplinary nature of scientific discovery.* Previous paragraphs have only begun to demonstrate the interconnectedness among science, mathematics, engineering, technology, industry, economics, politics, government, religion, business, medicine, and history. What is even more significant is the interconnection among the various branches and areas of science and mathematics. Just a cursory view of this timeline yields thousands of cause and effect relationships that exist between and among the various discoveries, regardless of field or discipline. One cannot truly understand the form and function of living organisms without understanding the elements, composition of matter, atomic structures, cellular chemistry, relationships between organisms and their environments, astronomy, the relationship of the Earth to the sun and moon, gravity, the physical structure of the Earth and its atmosphere, space, weather, climate, ecology, energy; the list is endless.

A Very Brief Timeline of Major Scientific Discoveries

Date	Event
1000 BCE	The primary source of knowledge about the world lies in the Holy Scriptures.
600 BCE	Thales of Miletos, Greek founder of scientific thinking because he proposes a physical cause for earthquakes: water under the Earth.
570 BCE	Pythagoras theorized the Earth was round; discovered theorem to find angles of right triangles.
500 BCE	Golden Classical Age of Greece and scientific thinking; empirical thinking, however, is tossed out the window; segregation of natural and supernatural beginnings of the world; Age of Access.
460 BCE	Hippocrates is the founder of modern medicine.
400 BCE	Modern scientific thinking; Democritus gives us the word "atom."
350 BCE	Aristotle heralds in golden age of rationality, which means analytical thinking.

Date	Event
205 BCE	Archimedes explains the lever, calculates the area under a parabola, and discovers innovative machines.
200 BCE	Eratosthenes discovers a way to calculate the circumference of the Earth.
77 CE	Pliny writes his 33rd volume of *Natural History.*
140 CE	Ptolemy places the Earth at the center of existence.
150	Galen poses that the brain controls all functions of the body and develops dissection and vivisection techniques.
800	Abu Al-Kindi from Iraq applies scientific inquiry and empiricism to mathematics, pharmacy, physics, and medicine.
850	Although the Chinese invented gunpowder around 180, they used it for war and fireworks displays around the mid 800s.
960	Baghdad becomes the importer of scientific and mathematical thinking.
1200	Jewish philosopher Maimonides proposed philosophic and scientific rationalism.
1350	Italians bring "Black Death" from the Kaffa to Constantinople and to Mediterranean seaports; it eventually reaches London almost 200 years later.
1430	The Renaissance brings the re-emergence of scientific discovery and thinking; Gutenberg invents the printing press.
1450	Leonardo da Vinci is not only a painter and sculptor but also an architect and engineer.
1480	Euclid publishes his work in geometry.
1500	Copernicus disproves the theory of the heavens and establishes that the Earth and other planets revolve around the Sun.
1530	German scientist Zeising writes about the proportionality of human body parts.
1540	Scientific revolution expands through Europe. Vesalius publishes *The Constitution of the Human Body*.
1550	Eustachio publishes tract on sensory organs.
1560	Gesner publishes *History of Animals*, classifying fishes, insects, reptiles, and birds.
1560	Servetus poses that blood moved from heart to lungs and back to the heart.
1600	Francis Bacon establishes the experimental method of scientific inquiry.

Date	Event
1609	Kepler discovers that the orbits of the planets are not circular.
1610	Galileo invents an improved "spyglass" the telescope to discover that moons move around planets in simple orbital paths, which supports the theories of Copernicus. Galileo is considered the father of modern astronomy.
1619	Descartes writes his first treatise on proper scientific and philosophical thinking.
1628	Harvey confirms Vesalius' theory about how blood moves from the heart to other parts of the body.
1633	The Catholic Church orders Galileo to end his support of Copernican astronomy, citing that his research on a sun-centered universe contradicts Holy Scripture (the Inquisition).
1640	Robert Boyle explores "new philosophy" which requires proving and disproving hypotheses, develops gas laws, and advances that matter is composed of particles; also founded the Royal Society.
1651	Hobbes publishes *Leviathan*, supporting reasoning and scientific thinking.
1660	Leibniz invents calculus independent from Newton.
1662	Royal Society of London is established.
1666-1690	Newton describes gravity; laws of conservation of matter and energy; publishes *Principia Mathematica*, changing existing theories of physics and mathematics.
1667	Anton van Leeuwenhoek discovers red blood cells and sperm.
1670	Robert Hooke advances the use of microscope to examine living tissue.
1699	France establishes the Academy of Science, marking support for a new way of thinking about science and nature.
1710	Benjamin Franklin invented the lightning rod, bifocals, Franklin stove, demonstrates that lightning *is* electricity.
1712	Newcomen invents the first most widely used steam engine.
1720	Edward Jenner discovers vaccine for smallpox.
1724	Immanuel Kant attempts to explain scientific knowledge.
1725	Mather's *The Angel* attempts to reconcile scientific discoveries with traditional religious views.

Date	Event
1739	Carol Linnaeus develops binomial nomenclature and works to promote practical applications of scientific discovery.
1740	Pope Benedict XIV decides that scientific discoveries will illuminate rather than diminish God's work.
1743	Antoine Lavoisier discovers oxygen.
1745	Volta discovers the voltaic cell.
1770	Industrial Revolution takes hold in England.
1771	Priestly discovers the influence of plants on the composition of air around them.
1775	George Washington establishes the Army Medical Department.
1780	Cavendish poses revolutionary theories about light and heat.
1790	Lavoisier is guillotined for his scientific discoveries.
1798	Malthus publishes his first essay on population emphasizing that the world will have to regulate its resources to accommodate increasing population growth.
1799	Humboldt and Bonpland establish the study of the geographic distribution of plants.
1800	Thomas Wedgewood creates the first photograph.
1820	Michael Faraday experiments with sound and electromagnetism.
1823	Purkinje discovers the uniqueness of each person's fingerprint.
1842	Clarke uses ether as anesthesia; Wells uses nitrous oxide during a molar extraction.
1851	Crystal Palace in London presents exhibits of scientific discovery.
1855	George Bunsen creates the Bunsen Burner.
1857	Pasteur develops pasteurization.
1859	Charles Darwin publishes the *Origin of the Species*.
1860–1931	Thomas Edison originates the concept of mass production of electric power, invents the telephone, electric light bulb, camera, and is credited with the creation of the first industrial research laboratory. He held almost 1,100 patents.

Date	Event
1866	Gregor Mendel proposes his laws of inheritance.
1866	Alfred Nobel creates dynamite.
1869	Paul Langerhans develops insulin.
1828	George Westinghouse invents air brakes.
1869	Dmitri Mendeleev creates the Periodic Table.
1873	James Maxwell develops the theory of electromagnetism.
1876	Alexander Graham Bell invents telephone.
1878	Albert Michelson calculates the speed of light.
1882	Robert Koch develops the science of bacteriology.
1893	Rudolf Diesel invents the diesel engine.
1893	W. L. Judson invents the zipper.
1895	Conrad Röntgen stumbles on discovering x-rays.
1897	Samuel Langley develops the first experimental airplane.
1897	J. J. Thompson identifies electrons.
1898	Marie and Pierre Curie discover radium.
1900	Max Planck poses the basis of quantum theory
1902	Marconi discovers the wireless telegraph.
1903	Wilbur and Orville Wright fly the first airplane.
1905	Albert Einstein develops work on the Theory of Relativity.
1907	Ernest Rutherford discovers nucleus of the atom.
1908	Henry Ford develops the first moving assembly line to manufacture the Model T Ford.
1913	Niels Bohr proposes a model of the atom.
1916	John Browning invents the automatic rifle.
1920	Einstein develops gravitation theory.

Date	Event
1924	Clarence Birdseye invents the first frozen food.
1924	Raymond Dart uncovers the skull of Australopithecus, the very first human to exist.
1925	Werner Heisenberg discovers the Uncertainly Principle.
1926	Robert Goddard invents the liquid-fuel rocket.
1926	Erwin Schrodinger develops wave theory of matter.
1927	Georges Lemaitre discovers The Big Bang Theory.
1928	Sir Alexander Fleming discovers penicillin.
1928	Vannever Bush invents the first mechanical computer.
1929	Edwin Hubble poses the Law of the Expanding Universe.
1931	Ernest Laurence invents cyclotron.
1932	Vannever Bush invents analog computer.
1932	Robert van de Graff invents van de Graff generator.
1937	Frank Whittle invents jet propulsion.
1939	Igor Sikorsky invents the first helicopter.
1942	Wernher von Braun invents the guided missile.
1942	Enrico Fermi invents the first nuclear reactor.
1943	Oswald Avery proves that DNA is in chromosomes.
1944	Wernher von Braun invents the ballistic missile.
1944	Howard Aiken invents the first digital computer.
1945	J. Robert Oppenheimer et al. creates the first atomic bomb.
1947	Auguste Piccard invents the bathyscaphe.
1951	George Gey propagates the first cancer cell line.
1951	Peter Goldmark develops the first color television.
1951	Atomic Energy Commission creates the first electricity-producing breeder reactor.
1952	Edward Teller and U. S. Govt. develop hydrogen bomb.
1953	Crick and Watson discover the helical structure of DNA.

Date	Event
1954	Jonas Salk develops polio vaccine.
1955	W. F. Libby develops carbon dating.
1956	Ginsberg and Dolby invent videotape.
1957	U.S.S.R. government scientists invent artificial earth satellite: Sputnik 1
1957	Willem Johan Kolff invents the artificial heart.
1957	U.S. government scientists invent sodium-cooled atomic reactor.
1957	Defense Advanced Research Project Agency (DARPA) begins work on inventing the Internet.
1958	U.S. government scientists invent communications satellite.
1958	Samuel Cohen invents neutron bomb.
1959	Jack Kilby and Robert Noyce invent integrated circuit.
1960	Townes, Schowlow, and Gould invent laser.
1961	Russian cosmonaut Uri Gagarin is first man to orbit Earth in space.
1961	Alan Shepard Jr. is first American to orbit Earth a month after Russia's Gagarin.
1964	Cell-Mann and Zweig hypothesize the existence of quarks.
1966	Michael DeBakey invents left ventricle of artificial heart.
1967	Christiaan Barnard completes the first human heart transplant.
1968-75	Har Khorana creates first complete synthesis of a gene.
1969	Neil Armstrong is the first person to walk on the moon.
1970	U.S.S.R. government scientists create the first magneto hydrodynamic power generator.
1971	Ted Hoff invents the first microprocessor.
1971	Berg, Boyer, and Cohen develop recombinant DNA technology.
1973	U.S. government scientists launch Skylab orbiting space station.
1975	Bell Labs develop fiber optics.
1976	Van Tassel and Cray invent supercomputer.
1978	Robert Jarvik creates the Jarvik-7 artificial heart.
1978	Berg, Mulligan, and Howard perform mammal-to-mammal gene transplants.

Date	Event
1979	Sinjou and Doi create the compact disc.
1979	W. F. Anderson and colleagues repair genetic flaw in mouse using recombinant DNA technology.
1980	Alvarez discovers that dinosaurs were killed by an asteroid
1981	National Aeronautics and Space Administration (NASA) develops space shuttle.
1981	HIV Aids is recognized officially.
1982	Robert Jarvik implants first permanent artificial heart.
1984	Bill Gates invents Microsoft Windows.
1992	Internet gives rise to the World Wide Web.
1997	Dolly the sheep is cloned.
2001	First draft of human genome is completed.
2006	Pluto is reclassified as a dwarf planet.

COMPETENCY 0014

Understand the principles and procedures of scientific inquiry and experimentation; the relationships among science, technology, and engineering; and the principles of engineering design.

A Model of Science Inquiry

The following diagram represents the scientific method based on scientists' conceptualization of scientific inquiry.

NSTA Position Statement

The *National Science Education Standards* (*NSES* p. 23) defines scientific inquiry as "the diverse ways in which scientists study the natural world and propose explanations based on the evidence derived from their work," and in essence how scientists come to understand the natural world. As suggested in the diagram, scientific inquiry involves posing questions, gathering evidence/collected data through observations, investigations,

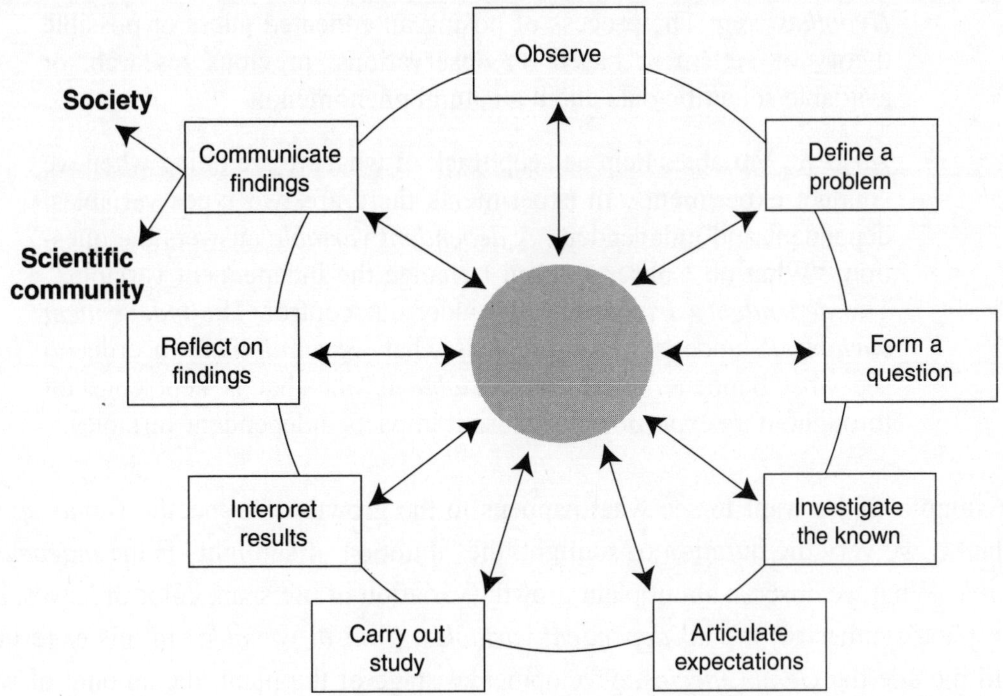

Redrawn from "A Scientific Method Based on Research Scientists' Conceptions of Scientific Inquiry," R. Reiff, W. S. Harwood, T. Phillipson. Proceedings of the 2002 Annual International Conference of the Association for the Education of Teachers in Science.

a variety of sources, explaining and evaluating evidence, drawing and articulating conclusions with other scientists, and policy makers.

The National Science Teachers Association (NSTA) recommends that all K–16 teachers model scientific inquiry and pose it as the mainstay in science classrooms in order to help students generate a deeper understanding of science and scientific inquiry.

Important Definitions Related to Scientific Inquiry

- *Questioning*: The process of posing factual, analytical, and evaluative questions that seek to inquire about events in the natural world.
- *Observation*: The process of using all the senses and technology to gather information about natural phenomena.

- *Hypothesizing*: The process of posing an educated guess or possible theory or statement based on observations, previous research, or available scientific data about a natural phenomenon.

- *Variable*: Variables help us keep track of what we are doing when we conduct experiments. In experiments there are two types variables: dependent and independent. A *dependent variable* answers the question: "What do I observe when I change the independent variable?" The *dependent variable is NOT* under our control. The *independent variable IS* under our control; it is what we *manipulate* in order to see what happens. A *control variable* is one that is kept constant throughout an experiment because it impacts independent variables.

Example: If we want to see what happens to the growth of a specific *Genus species* of plant if we vary the duration of sunlight, the "duration of sunlight" is the *independent variable*. What we observe about plant growth (variation in life span, color of leaves, ability to photosynthesize) are all *dependent variables. Control variables* in this experiment would include the *Genus species*, developmental stage of the plant, the amount of water and nutrients it receives, the way life span is measured, when it is measured, etc.

- *Data:* All the possible results or evidence we collect based on measurement, assessments, replications of trials, observations, and other sources.

- *Replication of Results*: A process, which requires that the experiment be conducted, in the exact same way, numerous times, in order to verify results.

"Understanding Inquiry Science": A synthesis of 20 years of research that assesses the impact—and meaning—of "inquiry science," researchers identify three criteria of rigor to judge the reliability, credibility, and reasoning of scientific inquiry. The three criteria address:

- *Descriptive Clarity*: What is actually known about how this study was conducted?

- *Data Quality*: Are data sources legitimate, credible, and reliable?

- *Analytic Integrity*: Are findings credible, replicable, and trustworthy?

The Principles of Engineering Design

Engineering is the discipline, art, and profession of acquiring and applying technical, scientific, and mathematical knowledge to design and implement materials, structures, machines, devices, systems, and processes that safely realize a desired objective or inventions. *Technology* is the practical application of science to commerce or industry. Historically and currently science, engineering, and technology are inextricably linked. The Accreditation Board for Engineering and Technology (*http://www.abet.org/gov.shtml*) defines engineering as the creative application of scientific principles to design or develop structures, machines, apparatus, or manufacturing processes, or works utilizing them singly or in combination; or to construct or operate the same with full cognizance of their design; or to forecast their behavior under specific operating conditions; all as respects an intended function, economics of operation and safety to life and property.

Engineering began as early as the invention of simple machines, which utilized mathematical principles to develop useful tools. In the 1300s "engineer" meant "one who constructs military engines." A more current definition harkens back to the Latin *ingenium*, which means "innate quality, especially mental acumen, a clever invention." The earliest "civil engineers" who designed structures were the Egyptians who built the pyramids, the Greeks who constructed the Acropolis and the Parthenon, the Romans, who built the Coliseum, Appian Way, and aqueducts, the empires of the Incas, Mayans, and Aztecs, the Chinese Great Wall, and so on. The military engineers of these empires built weapons constructed of simple machines, gears, artillery, gunpowder, and catapults.

It wasn't until the Renaissance that mechanical engineers developed the steam engine, which spurred the Industrial Revolution and eventually the concept of mass production and assembly line technology.

The 1800s saw the *invention* of the electric motor, vacuum tube, and transistors, which gave rise to electronics. This period also saw the development of specialized machinery, tools, and industrial scale production of chemicals, chemical plants, and processes.

By the 1920s, the Wright Brothers' successful flying machine made aeronautical engineering, which was basically empirical, a reality. With the inventions of rockets, rocket fuel, nuclear energy, and computers scientific exploration is limitless.

Engineers apply sciences and mathematics to find solutions to problems or to innovate current technology. Engineers evaluate different design choices and choose solutions that best meet challenges. Engineers must identify, understand, and interpret the constraints on a design in order to produce a successful result given particular resources, real or imagined limitations, cost, safety, versatility, marketability, and maintenance.

Steps in the Design Process:

1. Pre-Production
    a. Statement of design goals
    b. Analysis of current designs
    c. Research similar designs
    d. Specify design solution for a particular purpose
    e. Problem-solve, conceptualize, and collect data
    f. Present design solutions
2. During-Production
    a. Develop and improve design
    b. Test design
3. Post-Production
    a. Implement and introduce design into environment
    b. Summarize and evaluate processes and results
    c. Critique and pose suggestions for improvements
4. *Redesign* by cycling back to *Pre-Production*

References: Life Sciences

http://biology.unm.edu/ccouncil/Biology_124/Summaries/Cell.html

http://library.thinkquest.org/12413/structures.html#chromosomes http://evolution.berkeley.edu/evosite/lines/images/cells.gif

Antigens and Antibodies <http://faculty.matcmadison.edu/mljensen/BloodBank/lectures/blood_bank_antigens_and_antibodi.htm>

The Discovery of Blood Groups.

<http://nobelprize.org/educational_games/medicine/landsteiner/readmore.html>

<http://web.jjay.cuny.edu/~acarpi/NSC/14-anatomy.htm>

<http://www.uq.edu.au/_School_Science_Lessons/9.53.GIF>

<http://www.google.com/imgres?imgurl=http://mac122.icu.ac.jp/gen-ed/higher-plants-etc-gifs/10fl-plant-life-cycle.>

<http://www.google.com/imgres?imgurl=http://mac122.icu.ac.jp/gen-ed/higher-plants-etc-gifs/10fl-plant-life-cycle.

<http://extension.oregonstate.edu/mg/botany/internal.html>

<http://commons.wikimedia.org/wiki/File:Angiosperm_life_cycle_diagram.svg>

Photosynthesis <http://biology.clc.uc.edu/Courses/Bio104/photosyn.htm>

Photosynthesis: <http://ellerbruch.nmu.edu/classes/cs255w03/cs255students/teabbott/p4/pics/photosynthesis.jpg>

Respiration: <http://en.wikipedia.org/wiki/Cellular_respiration>

What Is a Lichen? <http://www.earthlife.net/lichens/lichen.html>

Symbiosis *New World Encyclopedia* <http://www.newworldencyclopedia.org/entry/Amensalism#Type_0.2C-._Amensalism>

<http://www.world-builders.org/lessons/less/biomes/conifers/conifweb.html>

<http://kwiznet.com/images/questions/grade1/science/life_cycle_of_butterfly.gif>

<http://www.scienceclarified.com/images/uesc_01_img0038.jpg>

<http://images.google.com/imgres?imgurl=http://iweb.tntech.edu/mcaprio/life_cycle.jpg&imgrefurl=http://iweb.tntech.edu/mcaprio/grasshopper_photos.ht>

<http://www.animalcorner.co.uk/insects/grasshoppers/grasshopper_lifecycle.html>

<http://waynesword.palomar.edu/trfeb98.htm>

Gordon Ramel <http://www.earthlife.net/inverts/cnidaria.html>

Hickman, J.C. (Editor). The Jepson Manual: Higher Plants of California. University of California Press, Berkeley, 1993.

Holley, D. The Characteristics of Amphibians: Investigating the general characteristics of the class Amphibia. 2008.

<http://reptilesamphibians.suite101.com/article.cfm/the_characteristics_of_amphibians> (retrieved 12 December 2009).

Lecointre, G. and H.L. Guyader. [Illustrated by D. Visset & Translated by K. McCoy.] *The Tree of Life: A Phylogenetic Classification.* Harvard University Press, Cambridge, Massachusetts, 2006.

Margulis, L., K.V. Schwartz, and M. Dolan. *The Illustrated Five Kingdoms: A Guide To The Diversity Of Life On Earth.* HarperCollins College Publishers, New York, 1994.

<http://www.earthlife.net/inverts/echinodermata.html>

Phylum Arthropoda: <http://www.entomology.umn.edu/cues/4015/handouts/Orders.htm>

Mollusca Charateristics, <http://bio.fsu.edu/~bsc2011l/sp_05_doc/Mollusca_2–22–05.pdf>

<http://www.entomology.umn.edu/cues/4015/handouts/Orders.htm>

Mackean, D. J. & Mackean, I. (2004–2010). Characteristics of Fish: An introduction. <http://www.biology-resources.com/fish.html>

The Amazing Diversity Of Living Systems <http://waynesword.palomar.edu/trfeb98.htm

Seed Plants <http://faculty.clintoncc.suny.edu/faculty/Michael.Gregory/files/Bio%20102/Bio%20102%20lectures/Seed%20Plants/seed%20plants.htm>

References: Physical Sciences

<http://www.bcscience.com/bc9/images/0_quiz_element.gif>

<http://www.accessexcellence.org/RC/VL/GG/ecb/ecb_images/03_07_forms_of_energy.jpg>

<http://www.colourtherapyhealing.com/colour/images/electromagnetic-spectrum.jpg>

<https://www.glastonburyus.org/staff/SOCHAF/science/PublishingImages/SimpleMachinesImages.jpg>

<http://www.uark.edu/depts/aeedhp/agscience/simpmach.htm>

The Earth. December 2009. <http://www.google.com/imgres?imgurl=http://www.nationsonline.org/bilder/earth_rotation_axis> (retrieved 8 January 2010).

The Earth's Rotation <http://www.google.com/imgres?imgurl=http://www.nationsonline.org/bilder/earth_rotation_axis>

Plate Tectonics: An Introduction: Continental Drift and the Structure of the Earth (2006) <http://cgz.e2bn.net/e2bn/leas/c99/schools/cgz/accounts/staff/rchambers/> (retrieved 8 January 2010).

The World Atlas.com. Tectonic Plates <http://www.google.com/imgres?imgurl=http://www.worldatlas.com/aatlas/infopage/tectonic>

<http://www.physicalgeography.net/fundamentals/10h.html>

Pidwirny, M. (2006). "Structure of the Earth." *Fundamentals of Physical Geography, 2nd Edition*. <http://www.physicalgeography.net/fundamentals/10h.html> (retrieved 9 January 2010).

Anthoni, J. Floor. (2000). "Classification of Rocks, Soil, and More." <www.seafriends.org.nz/enviro/soil/rocktbl.htm>

"Rock Cycle Diagram" <http://www.okaloosa.k12.fl.us/technology/WOWLessons/WOWResources/RockCycle>

"Atmosphere: The Structure. <http://teachertech.rice.edu/Participants/louviere/struct.htm>

"What is a Solar Flare?" <http://hesperia.gsfc.nasa.gov/sftheory/flare.htm>

Evans, John M. (June 5, 2007)

<http://www.google.com/imgres?imgurl=http://www.windows.ucar.edu/earth/Water/images/water_cycle_usgs_big.jpg&imgrefurl=http://www.windows.ucar.edu/tour/link%3D/earth/Water/water_cycle_climate_change>

Schlanger, Vera. (February 2004). "High Pressure Systems, Low Pressure Systems," <http://www.atmosphere.mpg.de/enid/3sf.html> (retrieved 9 January 2010).

Rosenberg, Matt. "The Agents of Erosion Are Water, Wind, Ice, and Waves" <http://geography.about.com/od/physicalgeography/a/erosion.htm> (retrieved 10 January 2010).

Borade, Gaynor. (March 2009). Facts about Wind Erosion. <http://www.buzzle.com/articles/facts-about-wind-erosion.html>(retrieved 10 January 2010).

Hurley, Brian (November 2002). Where Does the Wind Come From—And How Much Is There? <http://www.claverton-energy.com/where-does-the-wind-come-from-and-how-much-is-there.html> (retrieved 9 January 2010).

<http://www.google.com/imgres?imgurl=http://earthsci.org/processes/weather/waves/Waves_files/Wave_Diagram.jpg&imgrefurl=http://earthsci.org/processes/weather/waves/Waves.>

Ross, D.A. 1995. *Introduction to Oceanography*. New York, NY: HarperCollins. pp. 236–242.

Sumich, J.L. 1996. *An Introduction to the Biology of Marine Life, 6th edition*. Dubuque, IA: Wm. C. Brown. pp. 30–35.

Thurman, H.V. 1994. *Introductory Oceanography, 7th edition*. New York, NY: Macmillan. pp. 252–276.

"Oceans in Motion: Waves and Tides." <http://kingfish.coastal.edu/biology/sgilman/770Oceansinmotion.htm>

"Tides and Water Levels: Gravity, Inertia, and the Two Bulges" <http://oceanservice.noaa.gov/education/kits/tides/tides03_gravity.html>

<http://cires.colorado.edu/education/outreach/rescipe/collection/pdf/inquiryWheel.gif>

Foundations, The Challenge and Promise of K–8 Science Education Reform (1997). Written by EDC's Center for Science Education and Published by the National Science Foundation.

Schafersman, Steven, D. (1994) <http://www.freeinquiry.com/intro-to-sci.html>

Understanding "Inquiry Science"A synthesis of 20 years of research assesses the impact—and meaning—of "inquiry science" (May 31, 2006). <http://www.edc.org/newsroom/articles/understanding_inquiry_science> (retrieved 10 January 2010).

Scientific Timeline: Inventions and Discoveries (May 24, 2008) <http://www.cylive.com/viewContent.do?id=174&savesearch=false&vt=pub&q=1993–2010&x=118&y=90>

<http://www.google.com/search?q=History+of+scientific+thinking&hl=en&client=firefox-a&channel=s&rls=org.mozilla:en-US:official&hs>

<http://www.google.com/search?q=History+of+scientific+thinking&hl=en&client=firefox-a&channel=s&rls=org.mozilla:en-US:official&hs>

<http://en.wikipedia.org/wiki/Timeline_of_the_history_of_scientific_method>

<http://science.howstuffworks.com/scientific-method3.htm>

CHAPTER

Integration of Knowledge and Understanding

4

COMPETENCY 0015

Prepare an organized, developed analysis on a topic related to History and Social Science or to Science and Technology/Engineering.

This section first presents a general approach to writing the essay. Next is a list of possible topics for analysis, presented in thesis statement format for each subject matter area. Then, one topic is selected from each subject matter area, followed by one completed essay.

I. Identify a strong thesis: one that shows an ability to analyze one or more aspects of science, engineering, history, or social sciences; one about which you can provide detailed and/or illustrative examples; and one that shows a strong understanding of the subject matter. It is helpful if your thesis addresses 3 points/reasons that support your argument.

II. Outline the major points of your analysis, including specific examples, details, examples, and events that support each point.

III. Reread the list to assure that you have adequate details and examples to support each major point of your analysis.

IV. Outline the introduction and major body paragraphs (at least one for each major point).

V. Write/Draft your introduction and body paragraphs.

VI. Revise draft for clarity of thesis, support, appropriate use of examples with clarifying explanation, appropriate application of literary lens, consistency of argument, continual reference to thesis, diction, style, and voice.

VII. Edit or Proofread: Review draft for errors in spelling, grammar, and punctuation.

History and Social Science Topics

1. The history of the United States reflects a persistent struggle for independence, achievement, and power.
2. A belief in democracy, a spirit of independence, and consistent innovation has contributed in establishing the United States as a dominant world power.
3. Progress is a double-edged sword; it improves the quality of life for some but diminishes it for others.
4. Throughout the history of the world, civilization has improved and progressed based on selected lessons learned from the past, while simultaneously ignoring other just as significant lessons.
5. Religion has been and continues to be a major influence in World History.

History and Social Science Sample Essay

We have chosen to develop our sample essay on the second choice listed: A belief in democracy, a spirit of independence, and consistent innovation has contributed in establishing the United States as a dominant world power.

Since the first settlement at Jamestown, Virginia (1607), the history of the United States has been marked by democracy, independence, and innovation. Although each has contributed significantly in the advancement and progress the U.S. has enjoyed for the past four centuries, it is the intersection of and interconnection among these beliefs and attributes that have nurtured the development of world-class power.

Along with the Pilgrims came a belief in democracy. Fleeing religious persecution under King George, their voyage on the Mayflower brought them to "Plimoth," but prior to setting sail, they signed the *Mayflower Compact*, an agreement whereby all followed the rules established by majority vote; the *Compact* was a symbol of democratic governance in America and the first constitution ratified in the colonies. This collaboration, augmented by division of labor, where every citizen worked and shared the benefits of work contributed to the long life of this second colony and set an example for the eleven that would follow. By 1733 the original 13 colonies had been established. A belief in the collaborative rule of democracy precipitated the foundation of the National Government. Americans designed a government that vested significant power in individual citizens. Written in 1781 and ratified in 1781 the *Articles of Confederation* provided the first national constitution, but when poor farmers revolted against existing conditions (Shays' Rebellion), a more unified *Constitution* broadening the powers of the national government seemed essential. Soon after colonists defeated the British in 1787, delegates met in Philadelphia for the Constitutional Convention, drafting our current national Constitution. By 1791, the *Bill of Rights*, which enumerated rights of citizens such as freedom of speech and the right to a fair trial, was appended to the *Constitution*. By the end of 1791, all 13 colonies had ratified the new national constitution, establishing a government based on the democratic principles, which established rule of the people, by the people, and for the people. These rights were not guaranteed to all however, especially women and slaves. Although women were granted the right to vote in 1919, it was their work on the homefront during World War II and the activism of Betty Friedan that finally earned women some of the rights their male counterparts had always possessed. Not even the Civil War (1861–1865), Lincoln's signing of the controversial Emancipation Proclamation in 1863, the Civil Rights Act of 1865, and the 13th, 14th and 15th Amendments (1865–1870), which abolished slavery, extended citizenship to blacks, and banned race as a voting condition could achieve minimal rights for African Americans. It was not until the Civil Rights Movement in 1950, resulting in *Brown vs. Board of Education* (1954), which finally rendered "separate but equal" unconstitutional and led to desegregation of schools, that African Americans finally assumed rights that were constitutionally theirs. Finally, the election of the first African American president, Barack Obama, in Nov. 2008, indicated to the U.S. and the world that the U.S. is indeed a country where democracy prevails.

Democracy is inextricably linked to a spirit of independence and freedom. Independence from British rule and religious persecution led the Pilgrims to the New World. An increasing spirit of independence led colonists to build upon their own ingenuity and resources for self-defense and to develop small-scale self-government. The colonists' successful Stamp Act Congress in protest of taxation inspired even more confidence and greater desire for self-rule. Dissent against the British led to the Boston Tea Party and retaliation against the Intolerable Acts resulting in the American Revolution (1775), the formation of the Second Continental Congress, and the subsequent *Declaration of Independence*, on July 4, 1776. U.S. independence and belief in freedom has also motivated our support of others to sustain/acquire freedom and independence. Although participation in World Wars I and II, Korea, Vietnam, Iraq, and Afghanistan are rooted in maintaining the U.S. as a world power, supporting our policy of containment and the Truman Doctrine, and defending national security, it is also rooted in a belief that humankind is entitled to a life without oppression and access to at the very least, a safe environment, education, and basic civil liberties. As of late, "Tea Parties" have occurred all across the U.S., representing people who are opposed to "Government gone Wild!" Although the war in Iraq has gone on too long, March 2010 marked a major turning point in Iraq's history as an emerging democracy and independent nation.

Democracy and independence provide fertile ground for discovery and innovation. Discovery manifested in westward expansion and settlement from the Louisiana Purchase in 1803, to the Monroe Doctrine (1823), the belief in Manifest Destiny, to the California Gold Rush has extended territorial gains, spurring on innovation in transportation from "Iron Horse" railways, to underground subways, to high-speed Acella trains. Industrialization and technology has seen everything from Wilbur and Orville Wright's first flight to space travel, jointly, manned, space stations, satellites that gather critical information about everything from our enemies to the weather, enhancing security and safety. Supercomputers, digital technology, satellites, and sophisticated scientific technology have moved us into the information age at a critical pace, allowing us to see history as it occurs, presenting us with opportunities to aid others and to participate in a global knowledge society. Innovation has brought hybrid crops, genetic engineering, nuclear power, cures for disease, fuel-efficient transportation, cell phones, and technology that permits us to download the entire Library of Congress in one minute. Although technology has established the U.S. as a major world power, it has not been without profound cost. Discovery and innovation usurped lands from the Native Americans, stripping them of dignity and culture. Dropping two atomic bombs ended WWII but at the expense of Japanese civilian women and children who would suffer the consequences for decades and established a nuclear arms race that still looms large as Middle East powers and North Koreans threaten worldwide decimation. Arms sales rank highest among lucrative professions along with Ponzi Schemes. The race to space governed decades of "Cold War." And while affluent neighborhoods and schools forge ahead using the best technologies, urban schools mired in poverty become further marginalized.

The United States has emerged as a superpower due to a genuine belief in democracy, an unmatched spirit of independence, and a commitment to discovery and innovation. The intersection of these factors has and will continue to make the U.S. great and powerful, but with power comes responsibility and events of late fueled by goals of dominance, wealth, and greed, can lead to destruction, if not kept in check. Thus far the U.S. has dominated because it has put freedom, democracy, and people's wills and needs first, and it must continue to serve all its citizens and care for what we have all created or it will fall prey to the errors of historically great empires.

Science and Technology/Engineering Topics

1. There has always been and will always exist a tension between science, government, and religion.
2. War and warfare, whose end results are more often than not political, promote advances in technology and engineering.
3. Science, technology, and engineering demonstrate the power of scientific thinking to enhance communication and further discovery.
4. Scientific discovery about nature, evolution, and the human body has led to engineering breakthroughs that pervade all aspects of life and health.
5. The most critical aspect of the evolution and advancement of science, scientific knowledge, and scientific achievement is the interdisciplinary nature of scientific discovery.

Science and Technology/Engineering Sample Essay

Sample Essay for #5: The most critical aspect of the evolution and advancement of science, scientific knowledge, and scientific achievement is the interdisciplinary nature of scientific discovery.

Humans have always inquired into the nature of the world, life, and themselves. Whether it was to explain their existence, build fire, raise crops, understand how something works, build weapons, explore space or explain human, the Earth's, or the universe's origin, scientific inquiry and science has generally not occurred for the sake of science but rather to answer questions about all aspects of life and humankind. Thus, the evolution and advancement of science, scientific knowledge, and scientific achievement is and continues to be a result of the interdisciplinary nature of scientific discovery.

On a grander scale, scientific discovery has and continues to be connected to religion, politics, history, economics, anthropology, agriculture, and the list goes on. Early in human history, political figures, emperors, and rulers understood, and religious figures such as Jesus, Buddha, Muhammad, and the great prophets, explained, all knowledge about how the Earth was formed and how humans evolved through the Holy Scriptures, the Koran, and the Talmud which identified "God" or a supreme being as the creator of the world. Or, cultures created elaborate mythologies that identified many gods as creators of particular aspects and explained the occurrence of unexplainable events in the world. The beliefs of prevailing governments were often inextricably linked to scientific discovery sometimes to the disadvantage of truth, as in the case of Galileo. The Ancient Greeks and Egyptians can be credited with the beginnings of scientific and empirical thinking, using reason and evidence to separate the natural from the supernatural. They developed the foundation for medicine, atomic structure, simple and complex machines, physics, astronomy, and natural history all seemingly unique but also immensely connected. Persian scientists also saw the logic in scientific explanation of natural events and eventually became discoverers and disseminators of scientific knowledge about the natural world. The Renaissance, a major historical period in Europe, saw the resurrection of scientific and rational thinking, laying the groundwork for the scientific revolution. War, a highly political vehicle for acquiring land and power or defending human rights, has incorporated chemistry, physics, Earth science, and biology to generate some of the most significant discoveries in the world. Invented in the late 100s, Chinese gunpowder came into its own in the 800s, when used in battles between dynasties and sects. Catapults—simple levers—jettisoned boulders into enemy walls. Eli Whitney's discovery of assembly line manufacturing of guns enabled the North to overcome the South during the Civil War. During the first and second World Wars, the race to develop chemical agents to destroy conventional forces dominated scientific research for atlas and axis powers. The Curies' discovery of radium laid the groundwork for subsequent work in nuclear fission and the development of the atomic bomb, which established the U.S. as **the** major political power in the world during World War II. The development of the hydrogen and neutron bombs, nuclear power, reactors, and ballistic missiles serves as a constant reminder of the power of science to protect and destroy.

Beginning with Marconi's wireless radio, to Bell's telephone, to Bush's mechanical and analogue computers, to the invention of digital and supercomputers, satellites, to cell phones, wireless Internet, and the World Wide Web, science not only reflects the intersection of science, math, economics, and political science disciplines in the sharing of important knowledge and learning but also has facilitated critical discussion among experts from all disciplines, provided up-to-the minute information about weather patterns, natural disasters, and significant life-changing events. Space travel, satellites, and powerful telescopes have opened up the universe for exploration and further discovery. These various forms of communication have made a large world more personal and accessible and provided important intelligence that helps governments protect and defend freedom.

From the primitive lens, to the double helix, to the human genome, to the CAT scan, scientific inquiry has led to improved quality of life. Understanding how the body works from cellular biology to neuroscience, researchers and engineers have worked together to enhance medical care, create cures for disease, improve agriculture, replace organs, treat psychological illness, and find more effective ways to learn, generally enhancing the quality of live of many of its citizens. An important caveat, however, is that such discovery requires immense funding; and often this funding is informed by specific political and economic agendas.

Previous paragraphs have only begun to demonstrate the larger interconnectedness among science, mathematics, engineering, technology, industry, economics, politics, government, religion, business, medicine, and history. What is even more significant is the interconnection among the various branches and areas of science and mathematics. Just a cursory view of the timeline of invention and discovery yields thousands of cause and effect relationships that exist between and among the various discoveries, regardless of field or discipline. One cannot truly understand the form and function of living organisms without understanding the elements, composition of matter, atomic structures, cellular chemistry, relationships between organisms and their environments, astronomy, the relationship of the Earth to the Sun and moon, gravity, the physical structure of the Earth and its atmosphere, space, climate, weather, ecology, energy; the list is endless. This same information enables engineers to construct buildings that can potentially withstand an assault like the terror attacks of 9/11, that are energy efficient, and green, helps biomedical engineers create artificial organs, bionic limbs, and disease resistant crops, and develops technology that entertains, informs, gathers intelligence, and keeps humankind linked to each other. Identifying and understanding physics and chemistry of elements enables biologists and biochemists to understand the building blocks of life, cell structures and functions, cell biochemistry, and more recently the human genome. Pharmacists armed with knowledge of chemistry and pharmacology create drugs that cure disease, prolong life, improve stamina, and whiten teeth. Physicians from a variety of specialties within the discipline of medicine use knowledge from nuclear chemistry to cure cancer and control its spread. Laser technology can stop a retina from detaching, eliminate a cataract in seconds, and carve out preparation for a filling in the dental office.

John Donne observed that, "No man is an island." Such is the nature of science and scientific discovery. Just as the first humans recognized the simple connections between fire and cooked food, strength, shape, and properties of rock and the ability of tools made from rocks to plant, draw, communicate, and destroy, and rain, sun, and wind and the growth of crops and migration of animals, subsequent peoples have consistently recognized the intersection of life's major disciplines and the complex interconnection among all scientific and mathematic disciplines. Just as no person is an island, it stands to reason that no single scientific discovery is "an island." In fact, it is the interconnection between and among ideas bred by scientific discovery that continually advances the frontiers of human knowledge.

MTEL General Curriculum:

Review for Mathematics Subtest

CHAPTER

5

Mathematics

COMPETENCY 0016

Understand the number system and the concept of place value.

The History of the Number System

Historians believe that the first number systems originated when people began trading between communities. They most likely used stones, clay tokens, and other physical objects to keep a count of their livestock and agricultural goods. Over time people realized that they could represent these amounts by drawing pictures instead of using tokens. Eventually the pictures were replaced by tally marks; later, symbols were used to represent amounts. These symbols became numbers.

Throughout history, many civilizations—including the Babylonians, Egyptians, Greeks, Romans, Mayans, Arabs, and Chinese—developed different systems for recording numbers. Although Roman numerals became popular during the expansion of the Roman Empire, today we use numbers that evolved from the more advanced system developed by the Arabs, the *Hindu-Arabic number system.*

The Modern Number System

The Hindu-Arabic system is called a *base-10 numeral system*, meaning that each *digit* represents a different value depending on its position within the number. People often confuse numbers and digits. A *digit* is a single numerical symbol; in the Hindu-Arabic system, there are ten digits: 0, 1, 2, 3, 4, 5, 6, 7, 8, and 9. A *number* is a string of one or more digits: 10, 35, 1,209, etc. With these ten digits you can express numbers as high or low as you wish. Using each digit individually, you can count from zero to nine. Any value lower than zero, higher than nine, or in between the individual digits must be expressed in terms of *place value*. Place value assigns each digit a greater or lesser value depending on its position (or place) in the number. Each place within a number is ten times greater than the place to its immediate right. The use of the number ten is based on the fact that people have always used their ten fingers as counting tools.

The place values to the right of a decimal point are ones, tens, hundreds, thousands, ten-thousands, hundred-thousands, millions, ten-millions, hundred millions, etc. For example, the number 45,019 (read forty-five thousand, nineteen) has 4 ten-thousands, 5 thousands, 0 hundreds, 1 ten, and 9 ones. The number can be broken down like this: 45,019 = 40,000 + 5,000 + 0 + 10 + 9. The zero in the hundreds place means that zero hundreds are added to the number. This zero is called a *placeholder*, to keep the other digits in their proper places.

Placeholder Rule: When a 0 appears to the *right* of at least one digit other than 0, it is a *placeholder*. Place-holding zeroes are important, and must be included when writing a number. A zero that appears to the *left* of *every* digit other than zero is called a *leading zero*. Leading zeroes serve no purpose in a number, and should be dropped.

Scientific Notation

Scientific notation is a method used to represent any number by using *exponents* (most useful for very large and very small numbers). An *exponent* is a power or a mathematical notation that indicates how many times a quantity is multiplied by itself. An exponent is symbolized by a superscript. For example, in the expression 10^2, the exponent "2" means that the quantity 10 is multiplied by itself two times: $10 \times 10 = 100$; $10^3 = 10 \times 10 \times 10 = 1{,}000$. Scientific notation permits us to take a large number and represent it using a number between 1 and 10 multiplied by 10 or raised to a power of 10.

Example: 65,000 in scientific notation = 6.5×10^4

To write any number in scientific notation:

1. Write the number as a decimal. For example, to change the number 980,000,000 to scientific notation, first write it as a decimal: 980,000,000.0.

2. Move the decimal point enough places to change the number to a number that is between 1 and 10. To do this, move the decimal to the left until you get a number between 1 and 10, which in this case is 8 places: 9.80000000 (9.8 is between 1 and 10).
3. Multiply the new number by 10 raised to the number of places you moved the decimal point in step 2. Since you moved the decimal 8 places to the left 10 will be raised to a power of 8: 9.8 by 10^8 or 9.8×10^8. If you had moved the decimal to the right, the power would be 10^{-8}.

To write a decimal number in scientific notation, follow the same process.

1. For example, to change 0.00983 into scientific notation, first write the number as a decimal. You will note, however, that 0.00983 is already a decimal so go to the next step.
2. Move the decimal 3 places to the right to get a number between 1 and 10 so that 0.00983 becomes 9.83 dropping the leading zeroes.
3. Because you moved the decimal point 3 places to the right, multiply 9.83 by the 10 raised to the number of places you move the decimal point. 10^3, but because the decimal was moved to the right, the exponent is negative, viz., 9.83×10^{-3}.

Scientific notation saves time writing out extremely large or small numbers. For example, it is easier to state the mass of the Earth in scientific notation, which is 5.976×10^{24} kg rather than writing out a number that has 24 digits after the 5. The chart below gives examples of how scientific notation helps scientists work with large numbers.

Important Facts about the Earth and the Sun

Fact	Numbers written out	Scientific Notation
Land surface area ~29%	148,326, 000 km^2 (57,268,900 sq. mi.)	1.48326×10^8 km^2
Water surface area ~71% (97% sea; 3% fresh)	361,740,000 km^2 (139,668,500 sq. mi.)	3.6174×10^8 km^2
Mass of the Earth	5,976,000,000,000,000,000,000,000 kg	5.976×10^{24} kg

Rounding and Estimating

When working with complicated numbers, it is sometimes easier to simplify by rounding numbers. To *round* a number means to change some of its digits to place-holding zeroes.

Rounding to the nearest ten. To round a two-digit number to the nearest ten, increase or decrease the number to the *nearest* number that ends in zero. Rounding up or down depends on the last digit of the number. If the last number is equal to or greater than 5, round up. For example: 18 becomes 20 because 8 is greater than 5; 61 becomes 60 because 1 is less than 5; 43 becomes 40 because 3 is less than 5. When a number ends in 5, always round up to the next highest number that ends in zero. For example: 15 becomes 20; 45 becomes 50. Two digit numbers in the upper-90s get rounded to 100. For example, 98 becomes 100. To round longer numbers to the nearest ten, focus on the ones and tens digits.

Sometimes, a small change to the ones and tens digits affects all the other digits. For example, 999 becomes 1,000, and 9,995 becomes 10,000.

Rounding numbers to the nearest hundred and beyond. To round numbers to the nearest hundred, or thousand, focus only on 2 digits—the digit in the place you're rounding to and the digit to its immediate right. Change all other digits to the right of these 2 digits to zeroes. To round 642 to the nearest hundred, focus on the hundreds digit (6) and the digit to its immediate right (4). Round these 2 digits as if you were rounding to the nearest 10, and change the digit to the right to a zero: 642 becomes 600.

Estimation means approximating an answer rather than providing an exact answer. Estimation saves time and helps you check you answer. Several strategies for estimating include:

1. *Reasonableness*: Use common sense to determine if a calculation is a reasonable answer to a problem. Use this to double check an attempt to find an exact answer by verifying that an answer could be correct.

   Example: If when multiplying two decimals, 0.1 and 10.4, your answer is 94, revisit your multiplication. It is not reasonable to think that one-tenth (.1) of 10.4 could be 94.

2. *Front-end Strategy*: In this type of estimation, only round and add the leftmost digits (also called the "front-end"). After rounding, all

the digits will be zeroes except the digit in the leftmost place. So, if a number has two digits, you round to the "tens" place before adding the leftmost digits. Note: When you write an approximate answer, use two wavy lines (≈), which means "approximately equal to."

Example: $78 + 33 \approx 80 + 30 \approx 110$

If a number has three digits, round to the nearest "hundreds" place before adding the leftmost digits.

Example: $868 - 153 \approx 900 - 200 \approx 700$

http://www.basic-mathematics.com/front-end-estimation.html

3. *Clustering Strategy*: To find the sum of multiple numbers that are all close to (or "cluster" around) a common value, cluster the number.

   Example: to add 19.25 + 20.3 + 18.7 + 20.8. Since all of the numbers are close to 20, the sum is about 4×20 or 80.

4. *Compatible Numbers Strategy*: Change the numbers to make them easier to use.

   Example: To add 848 + 367, you could just take 2 away from the 367, leaving 365, and add it to the 848 to get 850. Now you add 850 + 265, which is easier to calculate.

Estimating is useful but can also lead to results that are not very close to the right answer. Your estimates are likely to be "off" if you round numbers that are too near the middle of the range, multiply or divide rounded numbers, or round too many numbers in the same direction.

Integers

Integers include all whole numbers, negative whole numbers, and zero. For example, 43,434,235, 28, 2, 0, –28, and –3030 are integers, but numbers like $\frac{1}{2}$, 4.00032, 2.5, pi, and -9.90, are *not* integers. We can say that an integer is in the set: {. . . -3, –2, –1, 0, 1, 2, 3 . . .}

Integers are points along a number line:

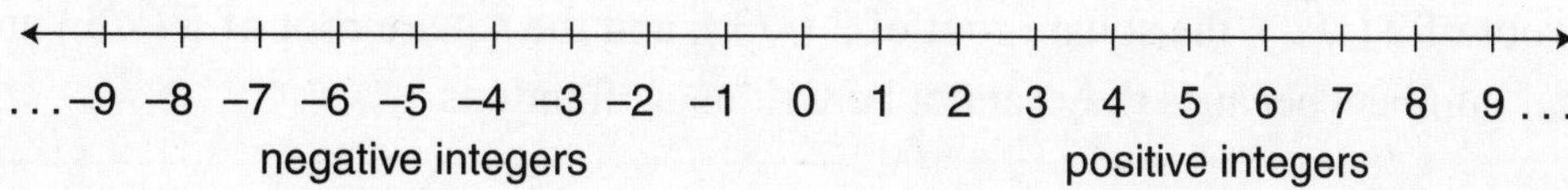

Note: Zero is neither *positive* nor *negative*.

The terms *even* and *odd* only apply to integers. For example, 6.5 is neither even nor odd. Zero is even. To check whether a number is odd, see whether it is one more than an even number. For example, 3 is odd because it is 1 more than 2, which is an even number.

Another way to say this is that zero is even since it can be written in the form $2 \times n$, where n is an integer. Odd numbers can be written in the form $2 \times n + 1$.

Rational Numbers

A *rational number* is any number that can be written as a ratio of two integers. A rational number can be written as a fraction where the numerator (top number) and denominator (bottom number) are both integers. The name "rational" comes from the word "ratio," because the rational numbers can be written in the ratio form $\frac{p}{q}$ where p and q are integers. Logically, *irrational* just means all the numbers that are not rational.

All integers are rational numbers, because each integer n can be written in the form $\frac{n}{1}$ or a ratio. For example $5 = \frac{5}{1}$ and 5 is a rational number. Numbers like $\frac{1}{6}$, $\frac{636}{4{,}627}$, and $\frac{5}{9}$ are also rational numbers, because their numerators and denominators are integers. All *repeating decimals*, all *integers*, and all *finite decimals* are rational numbers.

Irrational Numbers

Irrational numbers are numbers that can be written as decimals but not as fractions. An irrational number is any real number that is not rational. A *real number* is a number that is somewhere on the number line; any number on a number line that is not a rational number is irrational. An irrational number is a *non-repeating decimal.* No matter how many decimal places you write down, you can always write down more; the digits in this decimal do not repeat or fall into any pattern.

For example, pi (π) is an irrational number because it cannot be expressed as a fraction, and has no *exact* decimal equivalent, although 3.14 is used in most applications. The square root of 2 ($\sqrt{2}$), the square root of 3 ($\sqrt{3}$), and the square root of 5 ($\sqrt{5}$) are other irrational numbers because they cannot be written as fractions.

COMPETENCY 0017

Understand integers, fractions, decimals, percents, and mixed numbers.

Integers: Please see previous section for an explanation of integers.

Fractions

Every *fraction* is made up of two numbers separated by a line, or fraction bar. The number above the line is called the *numerator*. The number below the line is called the *denominator*. In the fraction $\frac{3}{4}$, 3 is the numerator, and 4 is the denominator.

Fraction terms and rules:

1. *Reciprocals* are fractions flipped over. For example, $\frac{2}{7}$ and $\frac{7}{2}$ are reciprocals; $\frac{4}{4}$ is its own reciprocal.
2. *Proper and improper fractions*: When the numerator is less than the denominator, the value of the fraction is less than one. Such fractions are called *proper fractions*. However, when the numerator is greater than or equal to the denominator, the fraction is greater than or equal to 1, and therefore, is an *improper fraction*. For example, $\frac{5}{6}$ and $\frac{3}{8}$ are proper fractions. $\frac{7}{6}$ and $\frac{11}{11}$ are improper fractions.
3. *Ones and Zeroes*:
   - When the denominator of a fraction is 1, the fraction is equal to the numerator by itself. Any whole number can become a fraction by adding a fraction bar and placing a 1 under it. For example, $\frac{8}{1} = 8$, and $9 = \frac{9}{1}$.
   - When the numerator and denominator are the same, the fraction equals 1. Think of slicing a pizza into 8 slices, and then keeping all eight slices. You have eight eighths, or $\frac{8}{8}$ of the pizza, which is the whole (1) pizza.

- When the numerator of a fraction is zero, the fraction equals zero.

Note: the denominator of a fraction can **never** be zero. Fractions with zero in the denominator are *undefined* and have no mathematical meaning.

4. *Equivalent Fractions*: Equivalent fractions are fractions that are the same quantity but are expressed in different forms. For example, look at the fraction bars below:

Bar 1 is divided into 6 sections; each section is $\frac{1}{6}$ of the entire bar. Let's shade in $\frac{3}{6}$ of the Bar.

Bar 1.

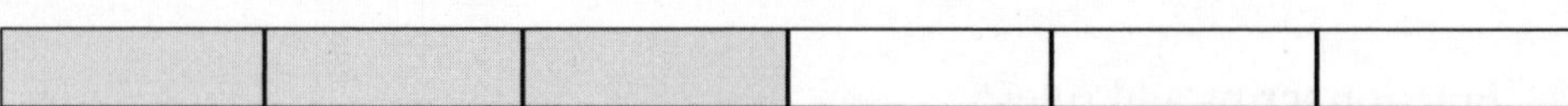

Bar 2 is divided into 2 sections; each section is $\frac{1}{2}$ of the entire bar. What happens if we shade in $\frac{1}{2}$ of the Bar 2? The shaded part is exactly the same. Therefore $\frac{3}{6}$ and $\frac{1}{2}$ are equivalent fractions.

Bar 2.

5. *Reduced Fractions*: A reduced fraction is an equivalent fraction in which the numerator and the denominator are as small as possible. In the example above, we noticed that $\frac{3}{6}$ and $\frac{1}{2}$ are equivalent fractions. Of the two fractions, however, $\frac{1}{2}$ is the fraction in its *reduced* form because the numerator "1" and denominator "2" are smaller than the corresponding numerator "3" and denominator "6."

Fraction word problem

Example: Sharing a pizza pie.

You often have to add or subtract fractions in problems that involve splitting up parts of a whole. For example, consider this problem:

Sam ate $\frac{1}{6}$ of a pizza, Joey ate $\frac{1}{4}$, and Ben ate $\frac{1}{3}$. What fraction of the pizza was left when they were finished eating their portions?

First: jot down the information that is given:

Sam = $\frac{1}{6}$, Joey = $\frac{1}{4}$, and Ben = $\frac{1}{3}$

These fractions are part of one total pie. To solve the problem, you need to figure out how much all three of them ate:

All 3 = $\frac{1}{6} + \frac{1}{4} + \frac{1}{3}$

You will notice that each of these fractions has a different denomination. In order to add these fractions, you must make the denominator the same by finding the *lowest common denominator (LCD)* for each fraction. The lowest common denominator of two or more **non-zero** denominators is actually the *smallest whole number* that is *divisible by each* of the denominators. There are two widely used methods for finding the LCD.

1. One way is to simply list the multiples of each denominator (multiply by 2, 3, 4, etc.) then look for the lowest number that appears in each list.

   We want to add $\frac{1}{6} + \frac{1}{4} + \frac{1}{3}$, so *first* we list the multiples of each denominator.

   Multiples of **6** are 12, 18, 24, 30, 36, 42, 48...

   Multiples of **4** are 8, 12, 16, 20, 24,...

   Multiples of **3** are 6, 9, 12, 15, 18, 21,...

   The lowest denominator that appears in all three sets of multiples is **12**, so **12** is the least common denominator.

Now that we know the LCD, we can change each fraction so it has the same denominator. We can do this by dividing the denominator of each fraction into the LCD to find out what the numerator of the fraction will be.

For the fraction $\frac{1}{6}$, we divide 12 by 6, which equals 2; 2 then becomes the numerator giving us the fraction $\frac{2}{12}$. In other words, $\frac{1}{6}$ and $\frac{2}{12}$ are the same quantity.

Repeating the process for $\frac{1}{4}$ and $\frac{1}{3}$, we get:

$\frac{1}{4} = \frac{3}{12}$ and $\frac{1}{3} = \frac{4}{12}$

Adding $\frac{2}{12}+\frac{3}{12}+\frac{4}{12}=\frac{9}{12}$. Because the goal of the problem is to find out how much pizza is left, we must subtract $\frac{9}{12}$ from $\frac{12}{12}$ (1 whole pie). $\frac{12}{12}-\frac{9}{12}=\frac{3}{12}$. *Remember*: reduce all fractions. Using shaded fraction bars to illustrate, we see that $\frac{3}{12}$ and $\frac{1}{4}$ are equivalent fractions and that $\frac{1}{4}$ is the fraction with the smallest numerator and denominator. So our final answer is $\frac{1}{4}$ pizza is left after Sam, Joey, and Ben devour the rest.

$\frac{3}{12}$

$\frac{1}{4}$

$\frac{3}{12} = \frac{1}{4}$

Decimals

Decimals allow people to work with numbers smaller than one: tenths, hundredths, thousandths, etc. A simple way to think about decimals is to think in terms of money. A $1.00 is one dollar or 100 cents, that $.25 is a quarter of a dollar or 25 cents, $.50 is 50 cents or half a dollar, and $.75 is three quarters or three fourths of a dollar or 75 cents; .25, .50, and .75 are decimals because they represent a portion of a 100.

Decimal word problem

Example: Buying by the pound

Albert bought 4.53 pounds of pistachios and 3.1 pounds of peanuts. Lou bought 5.24 pounds of pecans and 0.7 pounds of walnuts. Which of them bought the most nuts, and how many more pounds of nuts did that person buy?

To solve the problem, first figure out how much each person bought:

Albert = 4.53 + 3.1 = 7.63 pounds of nuts

Lou = 5.24 + 0.7 = 5.94 pounds of nuts

To find out how much more meat Albert bought than Lou, find the difference (subtract).

7.63 lbs – 5.94 lbs = 1.69 lbs

Answer: Albert bought 1.69 more pounds of nuts than Lou.

Percents

Percents offer another way of talking about parts of a whole. Percent means out of 100. If you have 50 percent (or 50%) of $\times$ (a variable) then you have 50 out of 100, or half of it. A percent smaller than 100 means less than a whole; a percent greater than 100 means more than a whole.

Percent word problem

Example: Splitting the vote

In a recent mayoral election, 5 candidates were on the ballot. Fred Johnson won 30% of the vote, Greg White won 22%, Isaac Miller won 18%, Don Wright won 12%, Oscar Lehane won 9%, and the remaining votes went to write-in candidates. What percentage of voters wrote in their selection?

The candidates were in a single election, so all the votes must add up to 100% total. The first step is to add up the 5 percentages we are given and then subtract that value from 100%.

$30\% + 22\% + 18\% + 12\% + 9\% = 91\%$

$100\% - 91\% = 9\%$

Answer: 9% of the voters wrote in their choices for mayor.

Mixed Numbers

Mixed Numbers are combinations of whole numbers and fractions. For example, the mixed number $3\frac{2}{3} = 3 + \frac{2}{3}$. To do *word problems* with mixed numbers, convert the mixed number into an improper fraction and then continue to solve the problem.

Conversions

Converting decimals into fractions: 0.6734

1. Put a fraction bar under the decimal, and put a 1 under it: $\frac{0.6734}{1}$
2. Move the decimal point as many places to the right as necessary to make the numerator a whole number, which in this case is 4 places.
3. Count how many places to the right you had to move the decimal point and write the same number of zeroes to the right of the 1 in the denominator.

   $\frac{6{,}734}{10{,}000} = \frac{3{,}367}{5{,}000}$

Converting fractions into decimals:

Write the fraction as a decimal division, dividing the numerator (top number) by the denominator (bottom number).

a. Example: write $\frac{2}{4}$ as $2 \div 4$ and divide = .5

Converting percents into decimals:

Eliminate the percent sign, and move the decimal point two places to the left.

Examples: 6.7% = 0.067

.125% = .00125

Converting decimals into percents:

Move the decimal point two places to the right, and add a percent sign.

Example: .06 = 6% because $.06 = \frac{6}{100} = 6\%$

.00125 = .125% because $.00125 = \frac{125}{100{,}000} = \frac{.125}{100} = .125\%$

Converting percents into fractions:

Use the number in the percent as the numerator and the number 100 as the denominator. Reduce the fraction or change an improper fraction into a mixed number. If the original percent involves a decimal (example: .125%), follow the same procedure, but move the decimal point in the numerator as many places to the right as necessary to make the numerator a whole number. Then move the decimal in the denominator that same number of places to the right by adding the same number of zeroes.

Example: $34.43\% = \frac{34.43}{100} = \frac{3{,}443}{10{,}000}$

Converting fractions into percents (2 steps):

1. Convert the fraction to a decimal (as shown above).
2. Convert the decimal into a percent (as shown above).

Example $\frac{4}{5} = 0.8 = 80\%$

COMPETENCY 0018

Understand and apply principles of number theory.

Prime Numbers

A *prime number* is a number divisible only by 1 and itself. For example, the number 13 is only divisible by 1 and 13. The first twenty-six prime numbers are:

2, 3, 5, 7, 11, 13, 17, 19, 23, 29, 31, 37, 41, 43, 47, 53, 59, 61, 67, 71, 73, 79, 83, 89, 97, and 101.

Characteristics of prime numbers

- The number 1 is not considered a prime number because it only has one divisor, 1.
- The only even prime number is 2, because any larger even number is divisible by 2. Odd prime refers to any prime number greater than 2.
- There is an infinite number of prime numbers.

Prime numbers are mainly used in information technology.

Composite Numbers

A *composite number* is divisible by at least three numbers (including 1 and the number itself). For example, 6 is a composite number because it is divisible by 1, 2, 3, and 6.

Every composite number less than 100 is divisible by at least one of the following numbers: 2, 3, 5, and 7.

A number's *prime factors* are the set of prime numbers (including repeats) that equal that number when multiplied together.

For example, here are the prime factors of the numbers 64 and 48:

$64 = 2 \times 2 \times 2 \times 2 \times 2 \times 2$ (or 2^6)

$48 = 2 \times 2 \times 2 \times 2 \times 3$ (or $2^4 \times 3$)

The easiest way to break a composite number down into its prime factors is by creating a *factorization tree.*

1. Split the number into any two factors and put a check mark next to the original number.
2. If either of these factors is prime, circle it.
3. Repeat steps 1 and 2 for each number that is neither circled nor checked off.
4. When every number in the tree is either checked or circled, then the tree is finished and the circled numbers are the prime factors of the original number.

The factor tree for 72 is as follows:

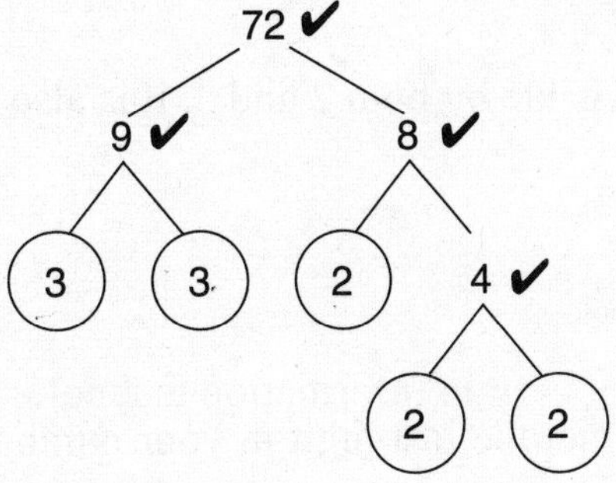

http://www.schoolworkout.co.uk/ks3work/Factors.htm

There are several "tricks" that can help you figure out if a number is divisible by a certain factor.

Divisible by 2:

All even numbers are divisible by 2. (All numbers that end with 0, 2, 4, 6, or 8.)

Divisible by 3:

1. Add up all the digits in the number.
2. If the sum of all the digits is divisible by 3, so is the number.

3. For example: 12,123 (1+2+1+2+3=9). 9 is divisible by 3, therefore so is 12,123.

Divisible by 4:

1. If the last two digits in the number are divisible by 4, the number is also.
2. For example: 827,612 ends in 12, which is divisible by 4, thus so is 823,612.

Divisible by 5:

A number is divisible by 5 if and only if it ends in 0 or 5.

Divisible by 6:

If the number is divisible by both 2 and 3, it is also divisible by 6.

Divisible by 7: (2 Tests)

First test:

1. Double and subtract the last digit in your number from the rest of the digits.
2. Repeat the process for larger numbers.

Example: 357 (Double the 7 to get 14. Subtract 14 from 35 to get 21 which is divisible by 7 and we can now say that 357 is divisible by 7.

Second test:

1. Multiply each digit beginning on the right side (ones place) by 1, 3, 2, 6, 4, 5.
2. Add the products.
3. If the sum is divisible by 7, so is your number.

Example: Is 2,016 divisible by 7?

6(1) + 1(3) + 0(2) + 2(6) = 21

6 + 3 + 0 + 12 = 21, which is divisible by 7 so 2,016 is also divisible by 7.

Divisible by 8:

If the last 3 digits in a number are divisible by 8, so is the number.

Example: 6,224: 224 is divisible by 8, therefore, so is 6,224.

Divisible by 9:

1. Add up all the digits in the number.
2. If the sum is divisible by 9, so is the number.

   Example: 43,785 (4+3+7+8+5=27) 27 is divisible by 9, therefore so is 43,785.

Divisible by 10:

A number is divisible by 10 if and only if it ends in a zero.

Divisible by 11:

1. Add up the alternate digits of a number, and then add up the other set of alternate digits.
2. If the sums equal each other then the whole number is divisible by 11.
3. Also, if the difference between the two sums is a multiple of 11, then the whole number is divisible by 11.
   a. Example: Look at 123,456,322.
   b. 1 + 3 + 5 + 3 + 2 = 14, and 2 + 4 + 6 + 2 = 14.
   c. Therefore, the whole number is divisible by 11.

Divisible by 16:

If the last four digits in a number are divisible by 16, so is the whole number.

Why do they work?

The primary reason that divisibility rules work is because our number system uses a base of 10. Therefore, the digits that make up a number (a string of digits) are actually the coefficients of a polynomial where 10 substitutes for the variable in the polynomial.

For example:

$1233 = 1 \times 10^3 + 2 \times 10^2 + 3 \times 10^1 + 3 \times 10^0$ which comes from the polynomial

$(1)(x^3) + (2)(x^2) + (3)(x^1) + (3)(x^0)$ which $= x^3 + 2x^2 + 3x + 3$. You see that in the first expression $x = 10$.

Divisibility can often be broken up into two or more simpler problems.

For a comprehensive explanation of why the tests and tricks work, see:

http://nsdl.org/resource/2200/20061219123513312T

Least Common Multiple (LCM)

The *least common multiple* (LCM) of a set of numbers is the lowest positive number that is a multiple of every number in the set.

1. To find the LCM in a set of numbers jot down a list of its first multiples in order.
    a. List the first multiples in order; the LCM is the first number on each list that is the same.

Example: if you want to find the LCM of 18 and 24, list the multiples of each number

18 = 36, 54, 72, 90 . . .

24 = 48, 72, 96 . . .

The LCM of 18 and 24 is 72.

2. A second way to find the LCM of a set is to use the prime factorizations of each number:

   a. List the prime factors of each number.

   Example: if you want to find the LCM of 18 and 24, start by listing the prime factors of each number

   $18 = 2 \times 3 \times 3$

   $24 = 2 \times 2 \times 2 \times 3$

   b. For each prime number listed, underline the number that is repeated most in each of the prime factorizations. The number 2 appears once in the factorization of 18, but three times in the factorization of 24, so underline the three 2's. Similarly, the number 3 appears twice in the prime factorization of 18, but only once in the factorization of 24, so underline the two 3's.

   $18 = 2 \times \underline{3} \times \underline{3}$

   $24 = \underline{2} \times \underline{2} \times \underline{2} \times 3$

   c. Multiply all the underlined numbers.

   Example: Here is the product: $2 \times 2 \times 2 \times 3 \times 3 = 72$.

   So, the LCM of 18 and 24 is 72.

Greatest Common Factor (GCF)

The *greatest common factor* (GCF) is the largest number that is a factor of all the numbers in the set. There are two ways to find the GCF. One way is to list all of the factors of each number, and then simply find the largest number that appears in each list.

To generate all of a number's factors:

1. Begin with 1 and end the list with the number itself.

2. Test whether the number 2 is a factor (whether or not it is an even number). If so, add 2 to the list, along with the original number divided by 2 as the second-to-last number on the list.
3. Test whether the number 3 is a factor the same as you did with 2 in the last step.
4. Continue testing numbers until the beginning of the list meets the end of the list.
   a. Example: Generating the factors of the number 24
      i. 1……….24
      ii. Test if 2 is a factor: $24 \div 2 = 12$, so:

          1, 2, ……12, 24
      iii. $24 \div 3 = 8$, so:

          1, 2, 3, ….. 8, 12, 24
      iv. $24 \div 4 = 6$, so

          1, 2, 3, 4, ...6, 8, 12, 24
      v. 24 is not divisible by 5, and we already have 6 as a factor, so we have our completed list. The factors of 24 are:

          1, 2, 3, 4, 6, 8, 12, and 24

Another way to find the GCF is by using *prime factorization.* List the prime factors of each number (as discussed above).

1. Circle every common prime factor, every prime factor that is a factor of every number in the set.
2. Multiply all the circled numbers—the result is the GCF.
   a. Example: To find the GCF of 24, 32, and 40.
      i. First list the prime factorization of each number, and circle the factors the appear in each number:

$$24 = \textcircled{2} \times \textcircled{2} \times \textcircled{2} \times 3$$

$$32 = \textcircled{2} \times \textcircled{2} \times \textcircled{2} \times 2 \times 2$$

$$40 = \textcircled{2} \times \textcircled{2} \times \textcircled{2} \times 5$$

ii. Multiply the circled numbers—in this case, three 2s are circled in each line, so we multiply $2 \times 2 \times 2$ and we find our greatest common factor which is 8.

Knowing how to calculate LCM and GCF in real-world situations is a useful skill. Here are some examples:

Example: You are buying hot dogs for a cookout. Hot dogs are sold in packs of 10. Hot dog buns are sold in packs of 8. Assuming that none of your guests is on a low-carb diet, and everyone needs a bun for each hot dog, what is the smallest number of hot dogs and buns you can buy to have an equal number of each?

To solve this problem, you need to find the least common multiple of 8 and 10.

8 = 8, 16, 24, 32, 40,...

10 = 10, 20, 30, 40,...

40 is the LCM.

$$\frac{40\ \cancel{\text{hotdogs}}}{10\ \cancel{\text{hotdogs}}/\text{pack}} = 4\ \text{packs}$$ *You will need 4 packs of hotdogs.*

$$\frac{40\ \cancel{\text{hotdog buns}}}{8\ \cancel{\text{hotdog buns}}/\text{pack}} = 5\ \text{packs}$$ *You will need 5 packs of hotdog buns.*

So you would need to buy 4 packs of hot dogs, and 5 packs of buns.

Example: You are baking sweet potato pies for the bake sale. Piecrusts are sold in packs of 3. Pie filling is sold in 4-can packages. What is the least number of piecrusts and filling that you can buy to have the same number of each? How many packages of each should you buy?

Again you need to find the LCM of 3 and 4.

$3 = \underline{3}$

$4 = \underline{2}, \underline{2}$

$2 \times 2 \times 3 = 12$

To make 12 pies you need 12 piecrusts and enough filling for 12 pies.

$\dfrac{12\ \text{\sout{piecrusts}}}{3\ \text{\sout{piecrusts}}/\text{package}} = 4$ *packages* *You need to buy 4 packages of piecrusts.*

$\dfrac{12\ \text{\sout{cans of filling}}}{\text{\sout{4 cans of filling}}/\text{pack}} = 3$ *packs* *You need to buy 3 packs of pie filling.*

You will need to buy 4 packages of piecrusts and 3 packs of pie filling.

Example: Jeffrey is packaging up presents to give to his friends. He has 45 pencils and 36 stickers. All of the packages need to contain the same amounts of stickers and the same amount of pencils. What is the greatest number of packages that he can make? How many of each item is in each bag?

For this problem, you need to find the GCF of 45 and 36.

45 = (3), (3), 5

36 = 2, 2, (3), (3)

The GCF is 9 so Jeffrey can make 9 bags.

$\frac{45 \text{ pencils}}{9 \text{ bags}}$ = *5 pencils/bag*   *Jeffrey can put 5 pencils in each bag.*

$\frac{36 \text{ stickers}}{9 \text{ bags}}$ = *4 stickers/bag*   *Jeffrey can put 4 stickers in each bag.*

So, Jeffrey can make 9 bags. Each will contain 5 pencils and 4 stickers (36 ÷ 9 = 4).

COMPETENCY 0019

Understand operations on numbers.

Operations

Operations tell us what to do with the numbers. The four main operations are addition, subtraction, multiplication, and division.

Addition

Addition is the process of combining or "adding" two or more numbers together to form one sum. Addition is indicated by a plus sign (+). The form in which we write and solve an addition example includes *addends* and a *sum*:

2 (addend) + 3(addend) = 5(sum)

Subtraction

Subtraction is the inverse of addition. Subtraction is denoted by a minus sign (–). Subtraction can be shown on a number line by moving backwards or from right to left.

The form for a subtraction example includes a *minuend*, a *subtrahend*, and a *difference*. (The terms "minuend" and "subtrahend" are not used very often, but "difference" is a common term.)

5(minuend) – 2(subtrahend) = 3(difference)

Multiplication

Multiplication is essentially the same as repeated addition. For example, 3 multiplied by 4 (verbally said as "3 times 4") can be shown by adding 4 copies of 3 together:

$$3 \times 4 = 3 + 3 + 3 + 3 = 12$$

The same mathematical sentence can also be demonstrated as 3 copies of 4:

$$3 \times 4 = 4 + 4 + 4 = 12$$

In the above example 3 and 4 are called *factors*, and the result of the operation (12) is called the *product*. Multiplication is denoted by a multiplication sign, which can take two forms: "x" or "•"Another helpful way to understand multiplication is to think of the multiplication symbol as the word "of." This is helpful when multiplying fractions and decimals. For example, if you are multiplying $\frac{1}{2} \times 16$, it may be helpful to read this to yourself as "$\frac{1}{2}$ of 16" instead of "$\frac{1}{2}$ times 16." The product, $\frac{1}{2}$ of 16, is 8.

Division

Division is the inverse of multiplication. This means that if $c \times b = a$, then $a \div b = c$. The form of a division example includes a *dividend*, *divisor*, and the resulting number, which is called a *quotient*:

$$8(\text{dividend}) \div 2(\text{divisor}) = 4(\text{quotient})$$

Division is also expressed in the form of a fraction. For example $7 \div 15$ could also be written as $\frac{7}{15}$.

Properties

Properties of the number system and operations:

Multiplicative identity property of 1: Any number multiplied by 1 remains the same.

Example: $1 \times 2 = 2$

Property of reciprocals: Any number (except zero) multiplied by its reciprocal is 1. The *reciprocal* of a number is 1 divided by that number.

Example: $\frac{7}{2} \times \frac{2}{7} = 1$

The additive identity property of zero: Adding zero to a number does not change the number.

Example: $1 + 0 = 1$

Commutative property for addition and multiplication: The order in which addends are added or factors are multiplied does not determine the sum or product. Division and subtraction are not commutative.

Example: $6 + 2 + 5$ gives the same sum as $5 + 2 + 6$

$3 \times 7 \times 6$ gives the same product as $6 \times 3 \times 7$

Associative property for addition and multiplication: Associating, or grouping, 3 or more addends or factors in a different way, does not change the sum or product. Division and subtraction are not associative.

Example: $(3 + 6 + 2) + 10 = 21$ is the same sum as $3 + (6 + 2 + 10) = 21$

Example: $(2 \times 4 \times 9) \times 3 = 216$ is the same product as $2 \times (4 \times 9 \times 3) = 216$

Distributive property of multiplication over addition: A number multiplied by the sum of 2 other numbers can be distributed to both numbers, multiplied by each of them separately, and the products added together. The simple notation form of the distributive property is: $a(b + c) = (a \times b) + (a \times c)$

Example: $7(3 + 4) = (7 \times 3) + (7 \times 4)$

If you find procedures, which you can apply easily and accurately and learn how to apply them to a variety of problems, you will have the tools to solve almost any math problem. If you commonly lose track of procedures, it is helpful to approach difficult problems by *deconstructing* or *breaking down* the problem into simpler parts that you can manage more easily. You will develop strategies that work for you, but here are a few examples of alternative ways to solve problems by breaking them down into smaller more manageable parts. When you get stuck trying to solve a problem, think of any relevant *number relationships that you already know* or can easily calculate "in your head" that might help. It is often helpful to use a diagram to think about the method you use to break up a problem. Other learners like to use stories, pictures, and arrays to visualize the parts of the problem.

For example, to solve 64×27, you might think of the following situation:

> I work at a grocery store, and I need to fill 64 bags with 27 lemons in each bag. It might be helpful to break down the numbers in the problem into the following parts:
>
> $60 \times 20 = 1{,}200$
>
> $60 \times 7 = 420$
>
> $4 \times 20 = 80$
>
> $\underline{4 \times 7 = 28}$
>
> 1,728 lemons will fill 64 bags with 27 lemons in each.

Use the properties outlined above as tools to break a complex problem into several smaller problems to make it easier to understand. Think of number problems as practical real-life situations and use stories or pictures to understand the operations that you are actually performing on the numbers.

Number operations can be represented in graphs, pictures, and verbally.

Here's an example of a graphic representation of mathematical values:

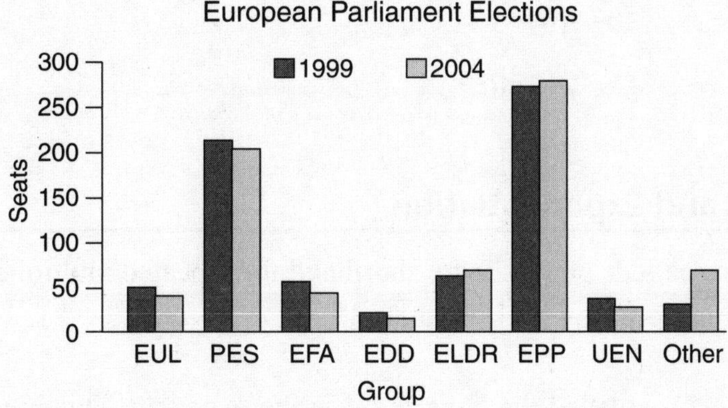

http://en.wikipedia.org/wiki/Bar_chart.

Relationships Among Operations

Inverse Operations

Addition and subtraction are *inverse* operations. For example, here are two inverse equations:

a) $1 + 7 = 8$

b) $8 - 7 = 1$

In (a) add 1 to 7, which = 8. In (b) subtract 7 from 8, which brings us back to 1.

Another example: a) $15 - 10 = 5$

b) $5 + 10 = 15$

Multiplication and Division are also *inverse* operations. If multiply 4 by 3 and then divide by 3, you get back to 4.

$4 \times 3 = 12$

$12 \div 3 = 4$

Similarly, if you divide 30 by 10, and then multiply by 3, you get back to 30.

$$30 \div 10 = 3$$

$$3 \times 10 = 30$$

Multiplication and Exponentiation

Exponents (also called "powers") are shorthand for repeated multiplication. For example, 3^4 means, to multiply 3 by itself 4 times: $3^4 = 3 \times 3 \times 3 \times 3 = 81$.

In this example, 3 is called the *base* and 4 is the *exponent*. This is read "three to the fourth power," or "three to the power of four." When the base is the number 10, finding out the exponent by writing the number 1, and the same number of zeroes as the exponent after it. Learning this will help you use scientific notation.

For example:

$$10^0 = 1$$

$$10^1 = 10$$

$$10^2 = 100$$

$$10^3 = 1{,}000$$

$$10^4 = 10{,}000$$

Any non-zero number raised to the power of zero equals one.

Postulates of Equality

1. Reflexive Property of Equality: $a = a$
2. Symmetric Property of Equality: if $a = b$, then $b = a$
3. Transitive Property of Equality: if $a = b$ and $b = c$, then $a = c$

Postulates of Equality and Operations

1. Addition Property of Equality: if $a = b$, then $a + c = b + c$
2. Multiplication Property of Equality: if $a = b$, then $a \times c = b \times c$
3. Substitution Property of Equality: if $a = b$, then a can be substituted for b in any equation or inequality
4. Subtraction Property of Equality: if $a = b$, then $a - c = b - c$

Postulates of Inequality and Operations

1. Addition Property of Inequality: if $a < b$, then $a + c < b + c$; if $a > b$, then $a + c > b + c$
2. Multiplication Property of Inequality:

   if $a < b$ and $c > 0$, then $a \times c < b \times c$

   if $a < b$ and $c < 0$, then $a \times c > b \times c$
3. Equation to Inequality Property:

   if a and b are positive, and $a + b = c$, then $c > a$ and $c > b$

   if a and b are negative, and $a + b = c$, then $c < a$ and $c < b$
4. Subtraction Property of Inequality:

   if $a < b$, then $a - c < b - c$

   if $a > b$, then $a - c > b - c$
5. Transitive Property of Inequality:

   If $a < b$ and $b < c$, then $a < c$

   If $a \le b$ and $b \le c$, then $a \le c$

   If $a > b$ and $b > c$, then $a > c$

   If $a \ge b$ and $b \ge c$, then $a \ge c$
6. Transitive Property of Equality

   If $a = b$ and $b = c$, then $a = c$

The Order of Operations

When a mathematical expression involves more than one operation, there are certain rules we need to follow regarding which to do first. These rules are called the *Order of Operations:*

1. First, complete all the operations that are in **P**arentheses.
2. Next, do any **E**xponents or **R**adicals.
3. Next, working from left to right, do all **M**ultiplication and **D**ivision.
4. Last, working from left to right, do all **A**ddition and **S**ubtraction.

   In steps 3 and 4, multiplication does not take precedence over division, and addition does not take precedence over subtraction; the order for the operations listed in each step just goes from left to right.

To help them remember the order of operations, people often use the acronym PEMDAS, which stands for the mnemonic, *"Please Excuse My Dear Aunt Sally."*

Applying the Order of Operations:

Example:

$4 \times 3^2 + 14 \div (5 + 2)$

1. First, complete the operation in *parentheses*: $5 + 2 = 7$:

   $4 \times 3^2 + 14 \div 7$

2. Next, complete the operation with the *exponent*: $3^2 = 9$

   $4 \times 9 + 14 \div 7$

3. Next, going from left to right, complete all multiplication and division: $4 \times 9 = 36$, and $14 \div 7 = 2$

   $36 + 2 = 38$

The Laws of Exponents

The following laws of exponents are important to learn and understand:

1. *Multiplying Exponents with the Same Base*

   $a^m \times a^n = a^{(m+n)}$

To multiply two exponents with the same base, add the powers. In other words, if you wanted to multiply 3^4 by 3^6, you would get 3^{10}.

$3^4 = 3 \times 3 \times 3 \times 3$

$3^6 = 3 \times 3 \times 3 \times 3 \times 3 \times 3$

If you multiply them together, you get $(3 \times 3 \times 3 \times 3)(3 \times 3 \times 3 \times 3 \times 3 \times 3)$, which means there are ten 3's multiplied together, or 3^{10}.

2. *Dividing Exponents with the Same Base*

$$\frac{(a^m)}{(a^n)} = a^{(m-n)}$$

To divide two exponents that have the same base, subtract the power in the denominator from the power in the numerator. To divide B^4 by B^2, subtract exponents $B^{(4-2)}$ or B^2.

It proves the same way as the first rule. If there are four B's in the numerator ($B \times B \times B \times B$) and two in the denominator ($B \times B$), two Bs will cancel each other out, leaving two B's in the numerator.

3. *Raising a Product to a Power*

$(a \times b)^n = a^n \times b^n$

To raise a product of several numbers to a power, raise each number to the power. To raise 2B to the third power, you would have to raise the 2 and the B to the third power, so your answer would be $8B^3$. To prove it, write out $(2 \times B) \times (2 \times B) \times (2 \times B)$. Remove the parentheses and combine the 2's and the B's: $2 \times 2 \times 2 \times B \times B \times B$, which is $2^3 \times B^3$ or $8B^3$.

4. *Raising a Quotient to a Power*

$$\left(\frac{a}{b}\right)^n = \left(\frac{a^n}{b^n}\right)$$

To raise a quotient of two numbers to a power, raise each number to the power. To raise $\frac{3}{5}$ to the third power, you would have to raise the 3 and the 5 to the third power, so your answer would be $\frac{(3)^3}{(5)^3}$ or $\frac{27}{125}$.

5. *Raising an Exponent to an Additional Power*

$$(a^m)^n = a^{(m \times n)}$$

To raise an exponent to an additional power, multiply the two powers. To raise x^2 to the third power, multiply the two powers, 2 and 3. This would leave you with the answer x^6.

Operations on Fractions

To *add and subtract fractions*, first find a common denominator, which is the same in both fractions, by finding the lowest common multiple (LCM) of the denominators. Once you find a common denominator, multiply the numerator by the same number you had to multiply the denominator by to reach the common denominator. Once both fractions have the same denominator, simply add or subtract the numbers in the numerators, and keep the denominator the same.

Add $\frac{2}{3}$ and $\frac{7}{8}$:

- Find the lowest common multiple of 3 and 8. (See the earlier section on generating lowest common multiples.)
- The LCM is 24, so we need to change each fraction so that the denominators are both 24.
- To change $\frac{2}{3}$ to a fraction with 24 in the denominator, we need to multiply both the numerator and the denominator by the same number.
- Multiply the denominator, 3 by 8 to get 24; then multiply the numerator by 8 as well. $\frac{2}{3} \times \frac{8}{8} = \frac{16}{24}$. We just converted the fraction $\frac{2}{3}$ to $\frac{16}{24}$.
- To convert $\frac{7}{8}$ we multiply the fraction by $\frac{3}{3}$ (one) to give it a denominator of 24. $\frac{7}{8} \times \frac{3}{3} = \frac{21}{24}$.
- Finally, add $\frac{16}{24} + \frac{21}{24}$ (our two converted fractions): $\frac{16}{24} + \frac{21}{24} = \frac{37}{24}$.

  We have an improper fraction here, so our next step is to make it a proper fraction. If you think of $\frac{24}{24}$ as 1, then you take $\frac{24}{24}$ out of $\frac{37}{24}$ (subtract $\frac{24}{24}$ from $\frac{37}{24}$, you are left with $\frac{13}{24}$). The complete number $\frac{37}{24}$ as a mixed number is 1 and $\frac{13}{24}$ or $1\frac{13}{24}$.

When *multiplying or dividing fractions,* first convert the fractions, if they are mixed numbers, into improper fractions. To convert a mixed number into an improper fraction, first look at the denominator of the fraction. Multiply the whole number by the denominator; then add the resulting number to the numerator.

For example, to convert $5\frac{1}{2}$ to an improper fraction, first multiply 5×2 (to get 10), then add that to 1. So the resulting improper fraction is $\frac{11}{2}$.

Once you have fractions instead of mixed numbers, to *multiply the fractions*, you just multiply the numerators and multiply the denominators.

For example: $\frac{3}{5} \times \frac{4}{3} = \frac{12}{15}$.

$$\frac{3}{5} \times \frac{4}{3} = \frac{12}{15} = \frac{4}{5}$$

(This fraction has been reduced to $\frac{4}{5}$ by dividing the numerator and denominator by 3.)

To divide fractions first convert both numbers into fractions if they are mixed numbers. Next, switch the numerator and the denominator of the second fraction, to get its *reciprocal.* Then multiply the first fraction by the reciprocal of the second fraction.

For example: $\frac{3}{5} \div \frac{4}{3} = \frac{9}{20}$

$$\frac{3}{5} \times \frac{3}{4} \left(\frac{3}{4} \text{ is the reciprocal of } \frac{4}{3}\right) = \frac{9}{20}$$

The last step in performing any operation with fractions is always to simplify or reduce the fraction at the end of the problem, and convert any improper fractions back into mixed numbers.

Absolute Value

The mathematical definition of absolute value is:

$|x| = x$, if $x \geq 0$

Or

$|x| = -x$ if $x < 0$

The absolute value of a number is the positive value of that number. The symbol for absolute value is a set of vertical bars | |.

The absolute value of a positive number does not change the number's value.

For example, |3| (read "the absolute value of 3") = 3

$|12| = 12$

$|45| = 45$

Because an absolute value is never negative, taking the absolute value of a negative number changes it to a positive number. For example:

$|-3| = 3$

$|-12| = 12$

$|-45| = 45$

Using Proportions in Real Life

Imagine you are watching the food network and your favorite chef is cooking an awesome meal for 4 people. If you wanted to cook the same meal, but for only 2 people, you could cut all the ingredients in half. Imagine you wanted to make the chef's recipe, for 10 people. You would need to figure out how many times 4 is contained in 10 (and you would come up with 2.5), and then multiply all the ingredients in the recipe by 2.5 to make the meal suitable for 10 people. Scaling a recipe up or down depending on the number of people you plan to feed is a very common scenario when you would use proportional thinking in real life.

Another example of when ratios are used in real life is in medicine. Ratios are used to determine the proper doses of medicine for a patient depending on the patient's age, weight, or other factors.

COMPETENCY 0020

Understand algebra as generalized arithmetic.

Variables

Any letter that is used to stand for a number is called a *variable,* which means its value can vary, hence the word variable. Although any letter can be used to designate a variable, the most commonly used letter is x. Numbers are called *constants*, because their value is fixed.

Functions

A function is a "mathematical machine" that takes in one number and gives back exactly one other number. For example, imagine a function called "trippler" that multiplies any number you put into it by three. When you input the number 5, machine or function outputs the number 15.

Trippler (5) = 15

Trippler (.25) = .75

Trippler (47) = 141

Equality

An important concept in mathematics and science is the concept of equality. *Equality* means that two values are mathematically the same. For example, in the following relationship the value on each side of the relationship is equal.

300 blue M&Ms = 2(150) blue M&Ms

Equations

An *equation* is simply a sentence in mathematics; instead of using words to make the sentence, we use numbers and letters (variables). The sentence is an equation when the equal sign (=) is included in the sentence. The equal sign links two mathematical expressions that have the same value.

For example, $6x + 3 = 45 - x$ is an equation. Any number that satisfies the equation, in other words, makes the equation *true*, is called a *solution*. For example, 6 would make the equation $6x + 3 = 45 - x$ true, because if you substitute 6 for x, you get $36 + 3 = 45 - 6$. This is true because $6(6) + 3 = 45 - 6$, or $39 = 39$.

Solving Equations

Solving the equation means finding the solution that makes the equation true. An equation can have only one or several solutions. If an equation has more than one solution, then the set of all solutions to an equation is called the *solution set*, which is indicated by a pair of braces, {}. So, in the above example {6} is the *solution set* because 6 makes the equation true.

A *linear equation* is a mathematical equation that, when graphed, creates a line. A linear equation, one variable takes the form: $ax + b = 0$, where a and b are real numbers, and a does not equal 0. For example, in the equation $x + 9 = 0$, the variable is x, $a = 1$ (because there is no other constant before x), and $b = 9$. Notice that as long as a is not = 0, this is a linear equation. We will come back to solving this equation later.

To solve a linear equation, we use the properties learned in the "Numbers and Operations" section. The steps for solving a linear equation are:

1. Use the distributive property to remove any parentheses.
2. If different fractions are present, use the multiplication property of equality and multiply each term by the Least Common Denominator (LCD). This will eliminate the denominators from the equation.
3. Combine all like terms.
4. Use the addition (or subtraction) property of equality to move all constants to one side of the equation and all terms with variables to the other side of the equation. This is called balancing the equation.

5. Use the multiplication or division property of equality to isolate the variable to create the solution.
6. Check your solution by replacing the variable in the original equation to see if your solution makes the equation true.

Examples:

1. Solve $x + 9 = -8$ for x:

$x + 9 = -8$	
$-9 = -8 + (-9)$	Use the subtraction property of equality to move the 9 to the right side.
$x + 9 - 9 = -8 - 9$	Simplify to $x + 0 = -17$; then to $x = -17$.
$x = -17$	Check the solution: $-17+ 9 = -8$. This is true, so the solution set is $\{-17\}$.

2. Solve $3 = g - 3$ for g:

$3 = g - 3$	
$+3 + 3$	Use the addition property of equality to move the -3 to the left side.
$3 + 3 = g - 3 + 3$	Simplify to $6 = g + 0$; then to $6 = g$.
$6 = g$ *or* $g =6$	Check the solution. $3 = 6 - 3$; $3 = 3$ is *true*. The solution set is $\{6\}$.

3. *Solve* $2x + 8 = 2 + x + 5$ for x:

$2x + 8 = 2 + x + 5$	
$2x + 8 = x + 7$	Combine like terms on the right.
$-x - 8 -x - 8$	Use the subtraction property of equality to move the variable to the left side, and the 8 to the right. $2x - x + 8 - 8 = x - x + 7 - 8$
$x = -1$	
$-2 + 8 = 7 - 1$	
$6 = 6$	Check the solutionl $-2 + 8 = 7 - 1$; $6 = 6$ is true. The solution set is $\{-1\}$.

4. Solve $x + 3 = x - 4$ for x:

$x + 3 - 3 = x - 4 - 3$	Subtract 3 from each side.
$x + 0 = x - 7$	Simplify
$0 = -7$	Subtract x from each side. This statement is false. Therefore, there is no solution. The result is the null set, written as $\varnothing$.

Using algebra to solve word problems

Algebra can be used to solve many types of problems, including those involving fractions, ratios, proportions and percents.

Example 1

A Grade 4 class has 28 students. Exactly $\frac{1}{4}$ of the students passed their last math test. How many students passed the last math test?

1. Make sure you understand the question; read it carefully several times.

   We are looking to find out how many students passed the math test.

   We will let x = *number of students.*

2. Devise a plan; translate the problem:

   We need to find a number (x) that is $\frac{1}{4}$ of 28:

   $x = \frac{1}{4}$ of 28

   We can re-write the fraction as a decimal:

   $x = .25 \times 28$

3. Solve the problem:

   $x = 7$

4. Check your answer:

   7 is $\frac{1}{4}$ of 28

Answer: 7 students passed the test. Based on this information, the teacher needs to re-teach the math lesson in a different way.

Example 2

The total number of students in Grades 1–5 in Summit Elementary School is 725.

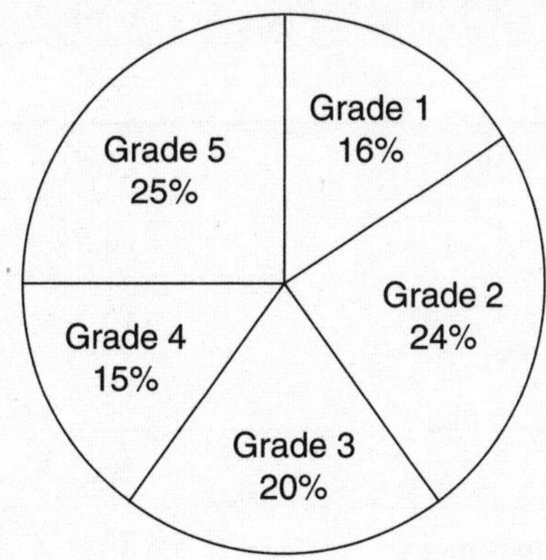

Using the pie chart above, calculate the number students in each grade at Summit Elementary School for 2010.

Let x = the number of students in 1st grade (this is what we want to know). We know the percentage of students in the 1st grade is 16% (a) and we know that the total number of students in the school is 725 (b). Therefore: $x = ab$, where $a = 16\%$ and $b = 725$.

$x = 16\% \ (725)$

$x = .16(725)$ Remember that 16% is the same as .16

$x = 116$ students

	Equation	Number of students in each grade
1st	$x = .16(725)$	116
2nd	$x = .24(725)$	174
3rd	$x = .20(725)$	145
4th	$x = .15(725)$	109
5th	$x = .25(725)$	181
	Total	725 students

Example 3

The table below shows the results of a survey taken about hot beverages at Joe's Coffee Shop in 2009 and 2010. Each customer voted for only one beverage.

Hot Beverages	2009 (%)	2010 (%)
"Regular Joe"	33	30
"Decaf Joe"	21.5	26
Chai	16.5	17.5
Cocoa	16	15.5
Tea	13	11
	100%	100%
Total number of customers:	8932	9332

Approximately how many customers preferred chai in 2009?

The table indicates that 16.5% of the customers (8,932) preferred chai.

To answer the question, we need to figure out, what is 16.5% of 8,932?

$x = 16.5\% \times 8{,}932$ Convert 16.5% into a decimal: .165

$x = .165 \times 8{,}932 = 1{,}473.78$

$x = 1{,}473.78$ (Since we are talking about people, round this number to the nearest whole number, which is 1,474.)

Answer: 1,474 people preferred chai in 2009.

COMPETENCY 0021

Understand the concept of function.

As previously defined, a function takes in one number and gives back exactly one other number. The number that the machine takes in is called the *input*, and the number it gives back is called the *output*. Functions can be represented as a formula, graph, or table of values.

Representations and Methods

A function represents a relationship between members of a set of elements (domain) and another set of elements (co-domain). The first element in the domain corresponds to the first element in the co-domain. For example, given the domain $\{x, y, z\}$ and the co-domain $\{6, 7, 8\}$, x is associated with 6, y with 7, and z, 8. A common example of a function is $f(x) = 2x$. This means that any real number in the domain is associated with a real number that is twice as large as that number in the co-domain; therefore, $f(5) = 10$.

The graph of a linear function, $4x - 3y = 12$ is

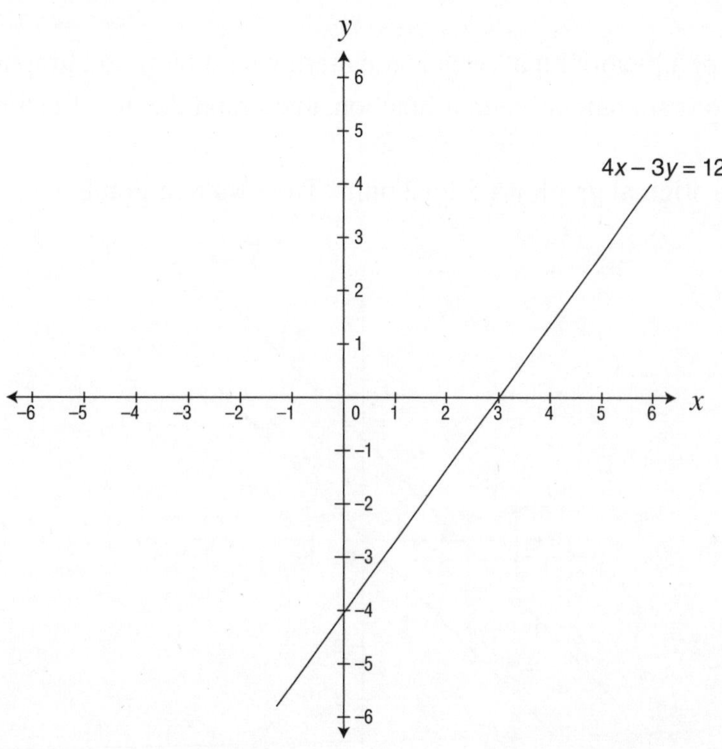

Input and Output Tables

The following table represents the input and output chart for the equation $f(x) = 2x$.

Input	Output
1	2
2	4
3	6
4	8
5	10

Recognizing verbal, numeric, pictorial, and algebraic patterns

Patterns can be found in many places in math. Any multiple of 10 ends in 0: 10, 20, 30, 40, 50, 60. . . . . Identifying patterns helps to complete a sequence of numbers. Using the same example, counting by tens: ten, twenty, thirty, forty, fifty, sixty. . . , we see the ending "ty" and hear the ending "tee." For example, looking at the sequence 3 5, 7, 9, 11, we see that each subsequent number is 2 larger than the previous number. Using this pattern, we can add to the sequence 3, 5, 7, 9, 11, 13, 15, 17. . . .

An example of a pictorial mathematical pattern would be if you graph a function, and then you add a constant number to that function, and graph the new function. Example:

Move the original graph $y = x$ up 2 units. The resultant graph is $y = x + 2$.

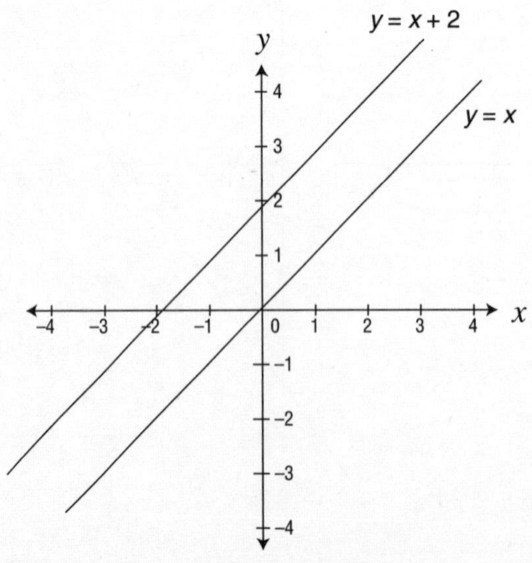

Direct and Inverse Relationships

Direct variation describes a simple relationship between two variables. This means that if x increases y increases, and if x decreases y decreases. Below is a graph of a direct variation.

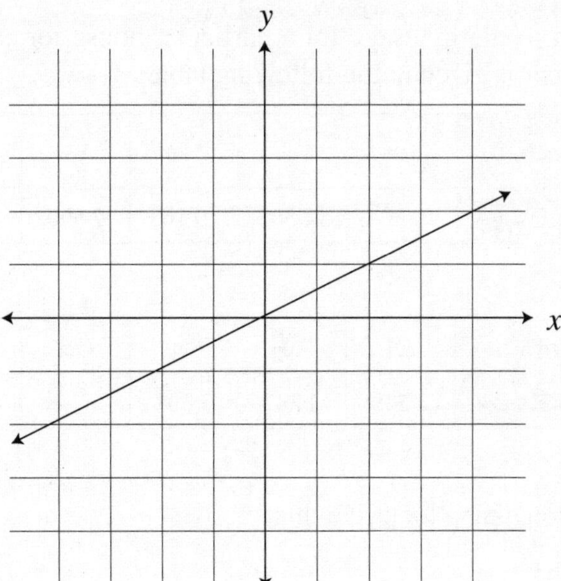

An inverse variation is a relationship where as x increases y decreases or as x decreases y increases.

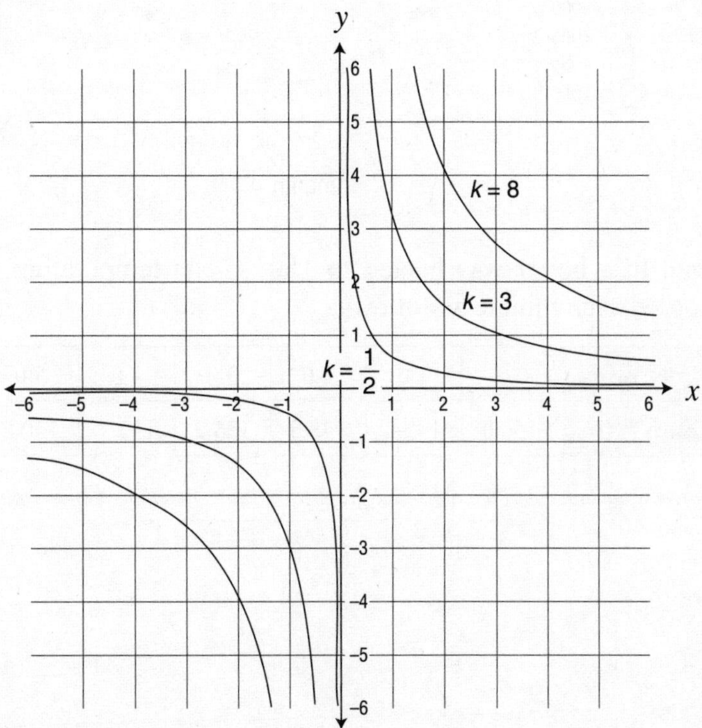

Using qualitative graphs to represent functional relationships in the real world

Here are some examples of when function graphs might be used in the real world:

1. The electric energy usage for a particular house for each month of a certain year is given in the following table:

Month	Jan	Feb	Mar	Apr	May	Jun
Energy Usage	10 504	12 363	10 168	7 500	4 825	3 568

Month	Jul	Aug	Sep	Oct	Nov	Dec
Energy Usage	2 548	2 887	3 301	5 748	7 302	9 706

These data plotted on a map look like this:

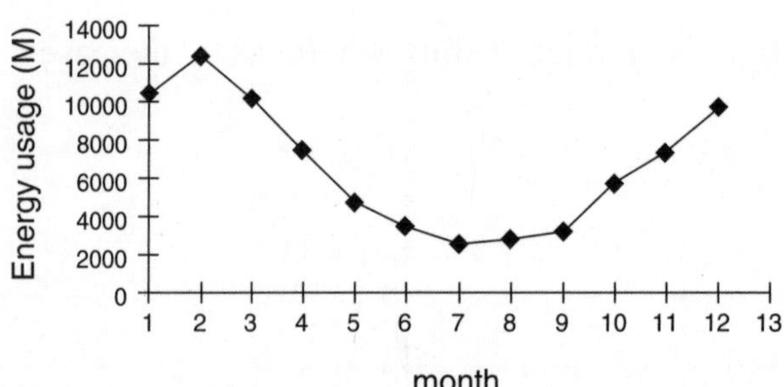

2. Steam in a boiler was heated to 150° C. Its temperature was then recorded each minute as follows:

Time (min)	0.0	1.0	2.0	3.0	4.0	5.0
Temp (°C)	150.0	142.8	138.5	135.2	132.7	130.8

http://www.intmath.com/Functions-and-graphs/6_Graphs-functions-tables-data.php

This data plotted on a graph look like this:

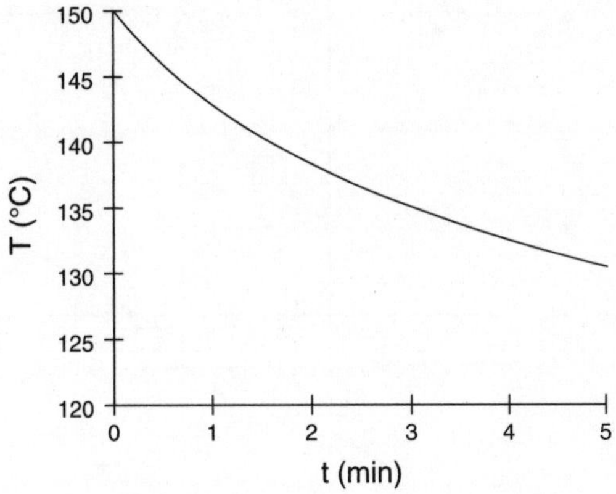

Since the temperature changes in a continuous way, the values in the intervals between the points designate a temperature, and the points are connected by a curve.

COMPETENCY 0022

Understand linear functions and linear equations.

Linear functions are most commonly found in "slope-intercept form." The formula for this function is $y = mx + b$. In this equation, m is the slope of the line, and b is where the line crosses the y-axis (the vertical axis) in a coordinate graph. The *slope* is the ratio of change in the y coordinates of a line, to the x coordinates, sometimes called the rise/run or $\Delta y/\Delta x$, where Δ (delta) or the change in y is over the change in x.

Slopes can be positive or negative.

- A positive slope means that the line moves up to the right and down to the left.

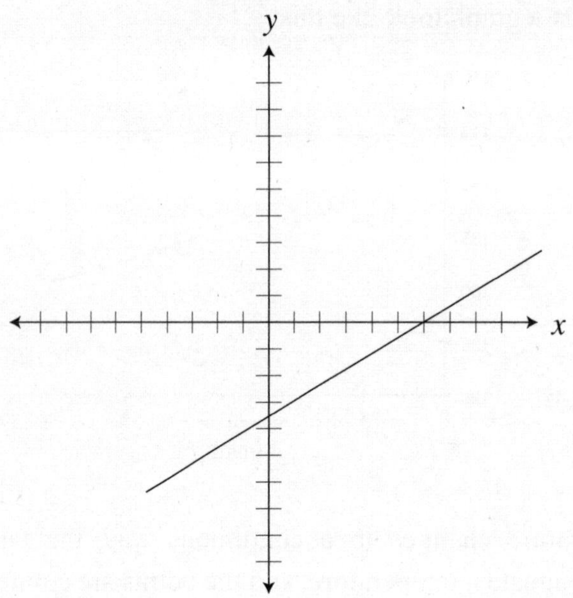

- A negative slope means that the line moves up to the left and down to the right.

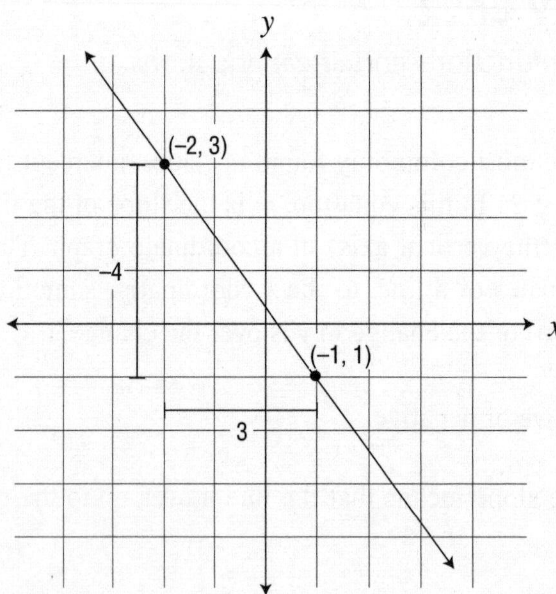

Linear and Nonlinear Functions

A linear function must either be in the form $y = mx + b$, or able to be converted into this form. All other functions are non-linear. To find the linear equation that represents a graph, you must simply find the slope, and the y intercept. Once you have the slope and y-intercept of a line, you can write the equation as in the form $y = mx + b$, using the slope as m and the y-intercept as b.

Analyzing the relationships among proportions, constant rates, and linear functions

Scientists use equations and functions to describe real-world situations in areas such as biology, economics, and physics. One example is the *rate of change,* which shows the proportion of the change of one variable to another.

A *rate* is a ratio that compares two measurement values that have different units. The graph of a linear function shows a *constant* rate of change. In a linear function, the slope reflects the constant rate of change for each interval on the graph.

Here's a graph of a linear function showing constant rate of change:

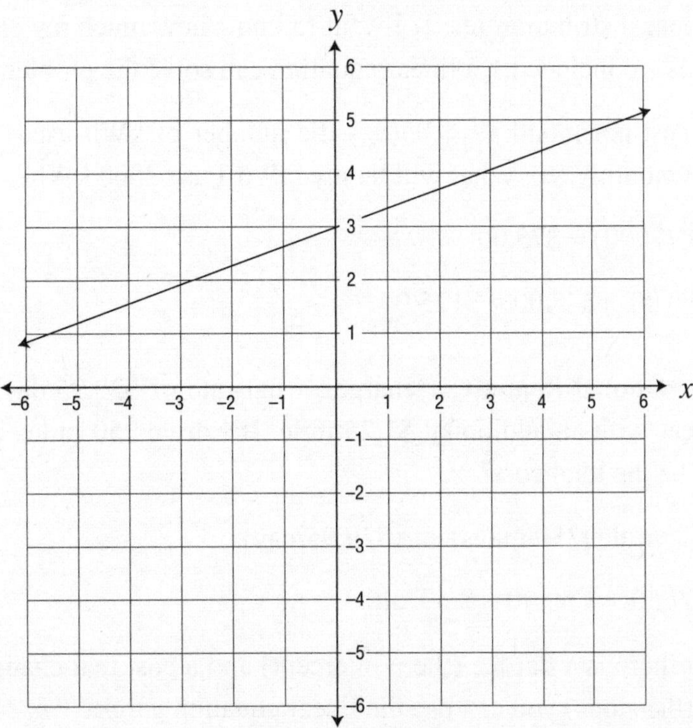

The graph of a non-linear function shows a *variable* rate of change. This means the rate of change varies for each interval of the graph.

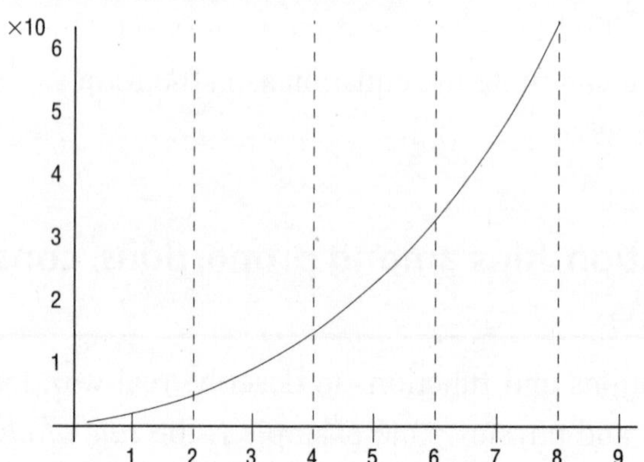

http://www.understandingcalculus.com/chapters/04/4-3.php

Interpreting the meaning of the slope and the intercepts of a linear equation in a real-world situation

Example: National Electric charges a set fee of \$75.00/month and \$.05/kilowatt hour distribution fee. If I want to know how much my electric bill is (no taxes are included.), a linear equation can solve the problem.

y (the cost per month) = \$.05(x = the number of kWh used) + \$75.00 (the set monthly fee. What will be my bill if I use 2000 kWh?

y = \$.05(2000) + \$75.00

y = \$100.00 + \$75.00 = \$175.00

Example: National Rent-a-Car charges a flat rate of \$29.95/day to rent a compact car with an additional \$1.25/mile. If I drive 350 miles in 2 days, what will be the total cost?

y = \$1.25/mile (350 miles) + 2(\$29.95/day)

y = \$437.50 + \$ 59.90 = \$ 497.40

Whenever there is a flat fee (the y-intercept) and a cost that changes based on usage (the slope) you can use the linear equation $y = mx + b$.

COMPETENCY 0023

Understand and apply concepts of measurement.

In the United States, the units of measurement for distance are inches, feet, yards, and miles. The units of measure for volume are teaspoons, tablespoons, fluid ounces, cups, pints, quarts, and gallons. The units of measure for mass are ounces, pounds, and tons.

There is no logic to the U.S. system of measurement; therefore, you will need to memorize the conversions. See Chart 1. The metric system, which is used throughout the rest of the world, is derived from a Base 10 system. The standard metric unit of distance is meter; the standard metric unit for volume is liter; and the standard metric unit for mass is gram. Increase or decrease in these units is determined by powers of 10. Chart 2 lists common prefixes that denote power of 10.

Chart 1

Variable	U.S. Conversion and Abbreviations	Metric System Conversion and Abbreviations
Distance		
	1 foot (ft.) = 12 inches (in.)	1 in. = 2.54 centimeters (cm.)
	1 yard (yd.) = 3 ft. = 36 in.	1 yd. = .914 meters (m.) = 91.4 cm.
	1 mile (mi.) = 5,280 ft.	1 mi. = 1.6 kilometers (km.) = 1600 m. = 160,000 cm.
Volume		
	1 tablespoon (tbsp.) = 3 teaspoons (tsp.)	1 tbsp. = 15 cubic cm. (cc) = 15 milliliters (mL)
	2 tbsp = 1 fluid ounce (oz.)	1 oz. = 29.5 cc. = 29.5 mL.
	1 cup (c.) = 8 oz.	1 c. = 236 cc. = 236 mL.
	1 pint (pt.) = 2 c. = 16 oz.	1 pt. = 473 cc. = 473 mL.
	1 quart (qt.) = 4 c. = 32 oz.	1 qt. = 946 cc.= 946 mL. = .95 liters (l.)
	1 gallon (gal.) = 4 qt. = 128 oz.	1 gal. = 3,785 cc. = 3,785 mL. = 3.785 l.
Weight		
		1 oz. = 28.3 grams (g.)
	1 pound (lb.) = 16 oz.	1 lb. = 453.5 g. = .453 kilograms (kg.)
	1 ton (T.) = 2,000 lb. =32,000 oz.	1 T. = 907.1 kg.

Chart 2

Prefix	Symbol	Factor Number	Factor Word
Kilo	K	1,000	Thousand
Hecto	H	100	Hundred
Deca	da	10	Ten
Deci	D	0.1	Tenth
Centi	C	0.01	Hundredth
Milli	M	0.001	Thousandth

For example, in the metric system:

A *meter* is the basic unit of length.

A *kilometer* is 1000 meters.

A *hectometer* is 100 meters.

A *decameter* is 10 meters.

A *decimeter* is 1/10 meter.

A *centimeter* is 1/100 meter.

A *millimeter* is 1/1000 meter.

These prefixes are applied the same way to liters and grams.

For more information on this topic to to: *http://www.aaamath.com/mea.html.*

Nonstandard units of measurement

We can estimate measurements by making comparisons that are familiar. For example, if you know that a football field is 100 yards long, and your friend's house is 1,200 feet away, you could say, "My friend's house is 4 football fields away from my house." If you are trying to measure the length of your bureau and do not have a ruler, but know that each floor tile is 1 foot long, you could say, "My bureau is 5 floor-tiles long."

Using unit conversions and dimensional analysis to solve measurement problems

Here are two sample word problems that require simple conversions:

1. Grandma sometimes feeds the hummingbirds during the summer. Usually, she fills the feeder with 2 cups of liquid each day. If she feeds the birds for 30 days, how many fluid ounces of food will she need?

   We know (from above) that there are 8 fluid ounces in 1 cup. If Grandma fills the feeder with 2 cups for 30 days, then she will use up 480 fluid ounces.

   $2 \ \cancel{\text{cups}} \times 8 \text{ fl. oz.} = 16 \text{ fl. oz.} \times 30 \text{ days} = 480 \text{ oz.}$

2. Jasmine's new puppy weighs 5 lbs. 4 oz. The veterinarian said that the puppy should gain 4 ounces per week. At that rate, how many pounds should the puppy weigh in 2 months (8 weeks)?

   We know (from above) that there are 16 ounces in a pound. If the puppy gains 4 ounces per week for 8 weeks, it will gain a total of 32 ounces. To figure out how many pounds it will gain, we divide 32 by 16, which equals 2, so the puppy will gain 2 pounds in 8 weeks. If we add 2 pounds to the puppy's original weight of 5 lbs. 4 oz, the puppy will weigh 7 lbs. 4 oz.

   $8 \ \cancel{\text{weeks}} \times \frac{4 \text{ oz.}}{\cancel{\text{week}}} = 32 \text{ oz.}$

   $32 \text{ oz.} \div \frac{16 \text{ oz}}{\text{lb}} = 32 \ \cancel{\text{oz.}} = 2 \text{ lbs.}$

   Initial weight 5 lbs. and 4 oz. + 2 lbs. = 7 lbs. and 4 oz.

Formulas for calculating the length, perimeter, area, volume, and surface area

Formulas commonly used in geometry:

Area formulas:

Note: *ab* means *a* multiplied by *b* or $a \times b$ or $a \bullet b$; a^2 means *a* squared or $a \times a$ or $a \cdot a$.

square = a^2	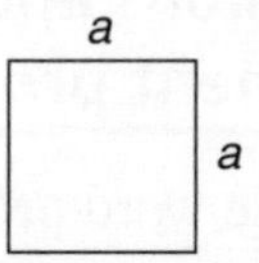 a, a
rectangle = ab	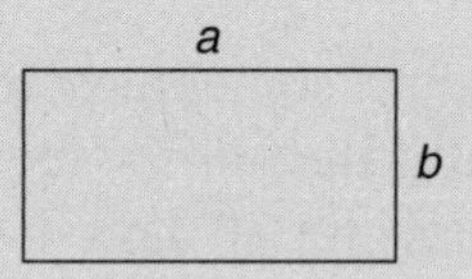 a, b
parallelogram = bh	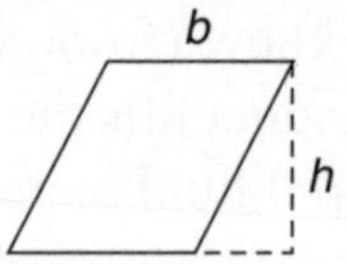 b, h
trapezoid = $\frac{h}{2}(b_1 + b_2)$	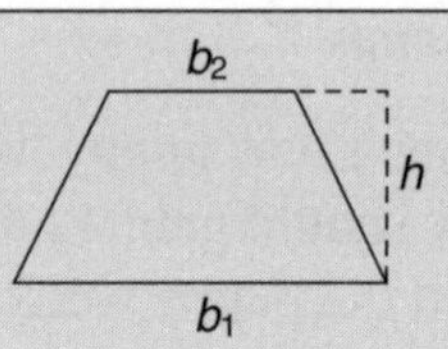 b_2, h, b_1
circle = πr^2 ($pi \approx 3.14 = \pi$)	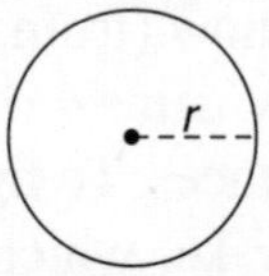 r
ellipse = $\pi r_1 r_2$	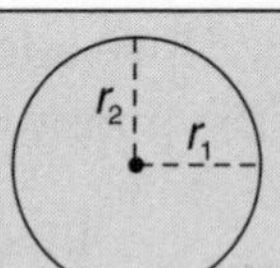 r_2, r_1
triangle = $\frac{1}{2}(bh)$ one-half times the length of the base times the triangle's height	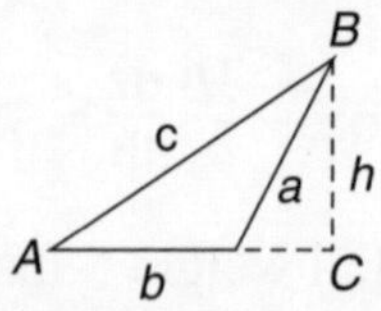 B, c, a, h, A, b, C
equilateral triangle = $\frac{\sqrt{3}}{4}(a^2)$ Each side has the same measurement.	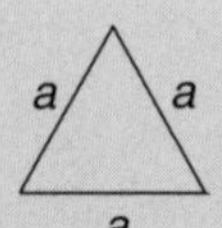 a, a, a

Area is measured in "square" units.

Area of a square = side × side. Since each side of a square is the same measurement, the area is the measurement of one side squared.

If one side of a square measures 6 inches, the area of the square is 6 inches × 6 inches, or 36 square inches. (Square inches can also be written in^2.)

Use the same units for all measurements. If one side measures 4 feet, and another measures 36 inches, you must either convert feet to inches or inches to feet before finding the area.

Perimeter formulas:

The perimeter is the distance around an object or the sum of the sides.

square = $4a$ $a + a + a + a$	a a
rectangle = $2a + 2b$ $a + a + b + b$ OR $a + b + a + b$	a b
triangle = $a + b + c$	B c a h A b C
circle = $2\pi r$ (r = radius) circle = πd (d = diameter, which is twice the radius)	r

The perimeter of a circle is also called the "circumference" or the distance around the circle.

Volume formulas:

cube = a^3 $a \times a \times a$	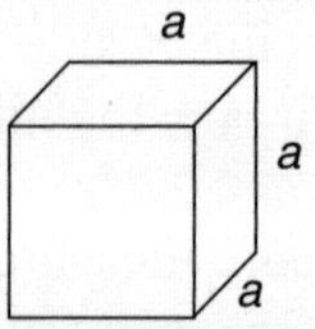
rectangular box = abc $a \times b \times c$	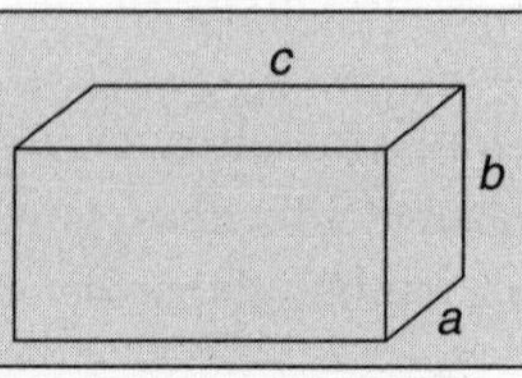
irregular prism = bh	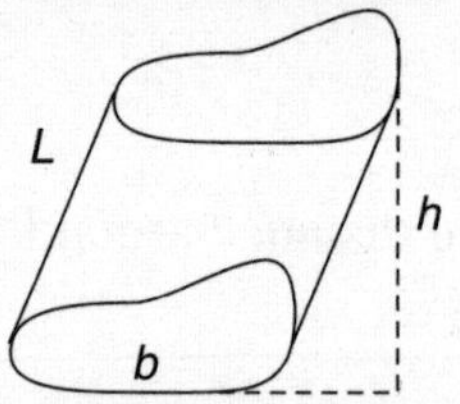
cylinder = $bh = \pi r^2 h$	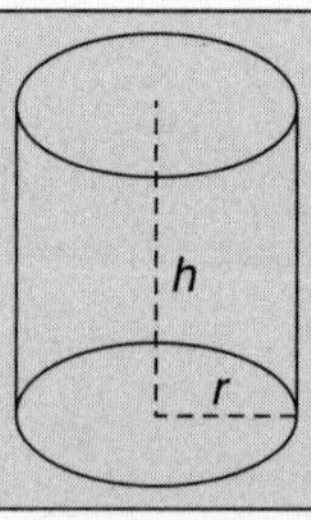
pyramid = $(\frac{1}{3})bh$	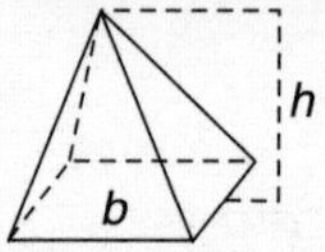
cone = $(\frac{1}{3})bh = \frac{1}{3}\pi r^2 h$	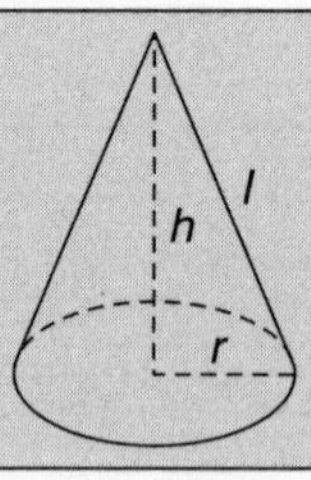
sphere = $(\frac{4}{3})\pi r^3$	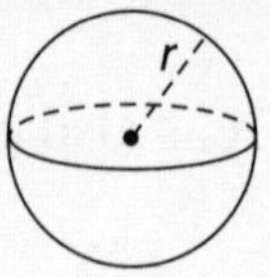

Volume is measured in "cubic" units.

Changing a figure's dimensions changes the figure's area and volume. If the dimensions increase, so will the area and volume; if the dimensions decrease so will the volume and area.

Examples of measurement problems in real-world situations:

1. For her birthday Sonja received a crystal vase. In order to fill the vase, she must pour 16 oz. into the vase 4 times. How many quarts of water does it take to fill the vase? Answer: 2 quarts

   Explanation: The vase holds 4 times 16 ounces of water: 4 × 16 oz. = 64 oz. We know that one quart = 32 oz. (1 cup = 8 oz; 1 pint = 2 cups = 16 oz.; 1 qt. = 2 pints = 4 cups = 32 oz.). To determine the number of quarts, divide the total or 64 oz. in the vase by 32 oz. 64 oz. divided by 32 oz./qt = 2 quarts

   $$4 \times 16 \text{ oz.} = 64 \text{ oz.}$$

   $$64 \text{ oz.} \div 32 \text{ oz./qt.} = \frac{64 \cancel{\text{oz.}}}{32 \cancel{\text{oz.}}/\text{qt.}} = 2 \text{ qts.}$$

2. Mr. Macomber has decided to plant a vegetable garden on a plot of land in his back yard. He wants to plant marigolds around the perimeter to keep the rodents away. The plot is 24 long and 14 feet wide. What is the perimeter of his garden? Answer: 76 feet

   Explanation: Mr. Macomber's garden is a rectangle because the length of each of two sides is 24 ft. and the length of each of the other two sides is 14 feet. To find the perimeter, we simply add the lengths of all the sides: 24 ft. + 24 ft. + 14 ft. + 14 ft. = 76 feet OR we can use the formula 2a + 2b, where a = 24 ft. and b = 14 ft.: (2 × 24 ft.) + (2 × 14 ft.) = 48 ft. + 28 ft. = 76 ft.

3. To qualify for the regional track meet, Kaitlyn must run at least 6.0 feet/second. At this rate, how long will it take her to run 200 yards? Answer: 100 seconds

   Explanation: Because all units of measurement must be the same, first we must convert yards to feet. We know that 1 yd. = 3 ft., so 200 yds. = 600 ft. or 3 × 200. To figure out how long it will take Kaitlyn to run 600 ft. we must divide 600 ft by 6.0 feet/second, because Kaitlyn runs 6 ft in a second. 600 ft. divided by 6 ft/sec = 100 seconds.

4. Danica Patrick is an accomplished racecar driver. If she races her car at a speed of 162 miles/hr., what distance will she travel in 24 minutes? Answer: 64.8 miles

   Explanation: We must first convert minutes to hours. If there are 60 minutes in an hour, then 24 minutes = 24 divided by 60 = .4 hr. ($\frac{4}{10}$ hr.) To find out how far Danica can travel in .4 hr. we need to calculate $\frac{4}{10}$ (.4) of 162 miles, which equals 64.8 miles.

5. Fresh Water Springs totals water sales during the summer months. In the first week of July, Fresh Water Springs sold 850 quarts of water. In the second week it sold 1,264 quarts, 1,536 quarts in the third, and 1,346 quarts in the fourth week. What was the average weekly amount in gallons of water sold during the month of July? Answer: 312.25 gallons

   Explanation: Units are important in this problem, especially since the answer requires average gallons per week. The first step is to find the sum of quarts of water sold in July: 850 qt . + 1,264 qt . + 1,536 qt . + 1,346 qt . = 4,996 qt . The next step is to find the average number of quarts per week. The average = sum divided by the number of entries (in this case, the number of weeks). 4,996 qt. divided by 4 = 1,249 qts/week. Fresh Water Springs sold an average of 1,249 quarts/week. To determine the average number of gallons per week, convert quarts to gallons. There are 4 quarts in a gallon; therefore, we must divide 1,249 qts/4 qt./gal. = 312.25 gallons per week.

COMPETENCY 0024

Understand and apply concepts of geometry.

Polygons

A *polygon* is a many-sided figure that has at least three sides. Each side is considered a segment of the polygon. The number of sides and angles determines how a polygon is named. Examples of polygons include: triangle, square, rectangle, rhombus, trapezoid, diamond, and octagon. Another characteristic of polygons is that they contain diagonals. Segments or sides of a polygon connect at a vertex. A diagonal is a line that is drawn from one vertex to a nonadjacent vertex. One diagonal of a square separates the square into two triangles. A polygon can be regular or irregular. A regular polygon has equal angles and sides such as a square and equilateral triangle. An irregular polygon has sides that are not equal. The following chart lists polygons that have 3 to 10 sides.

1. Triangle

   3 sides, 3 angles, 3 vertices, 0 diagonals

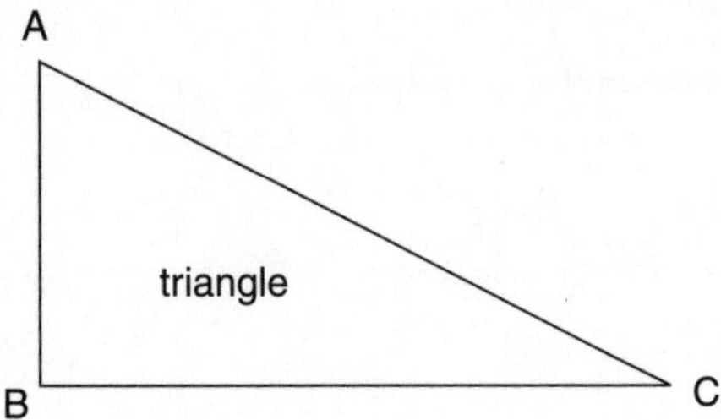

2. Quadrilateral

   4 sides, 4 angles, 4 vertices, and 2 diagonals

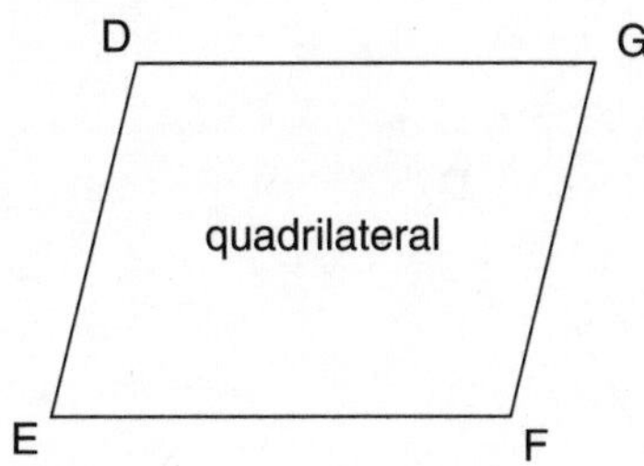

quadrilateral with two diagonals

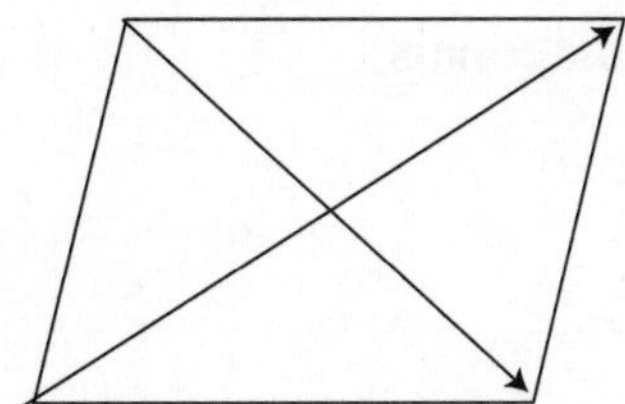

3. Pentagon

   5 sides, 5 angles, 5 vertices, 5 diagonals

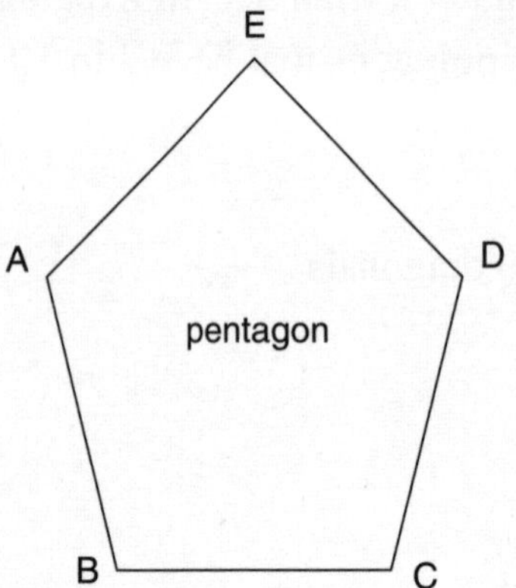

4. Hexagon

   6 sides, 6 angles, 6 vertices, 9 diagonals

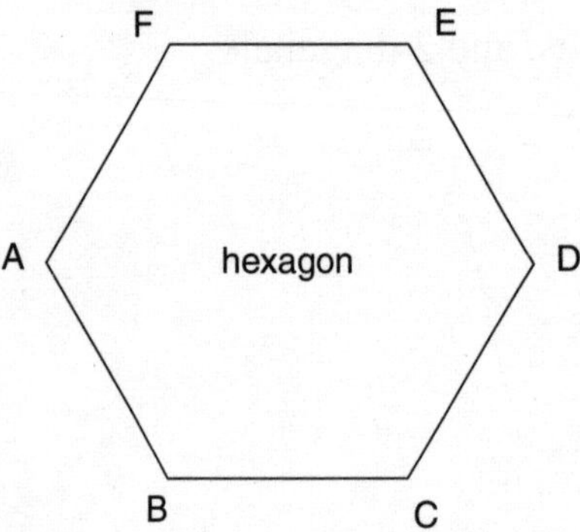

5. Heptagon

   7 sides, 7 angles, 7 vertices, 14 diagonals

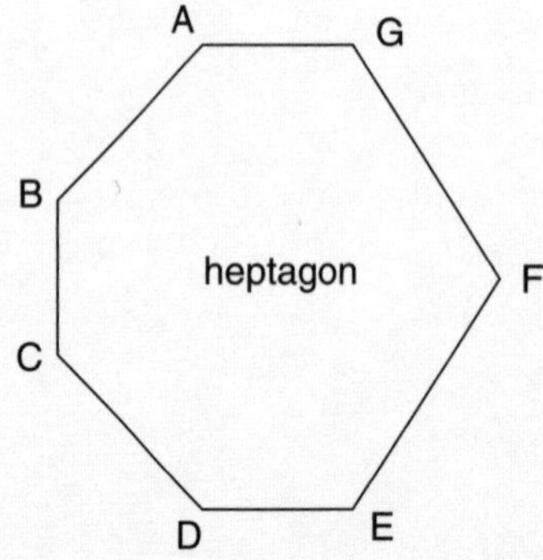

6. Octagon

   8 sides, 8 angles, 8 vertices, 20 diagonals

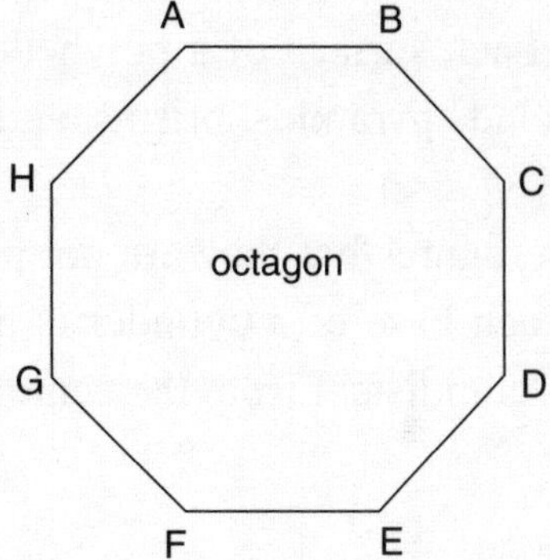

7. Nonagon

   9 sides, 9 angles, 9 vertices, 27 diagonals

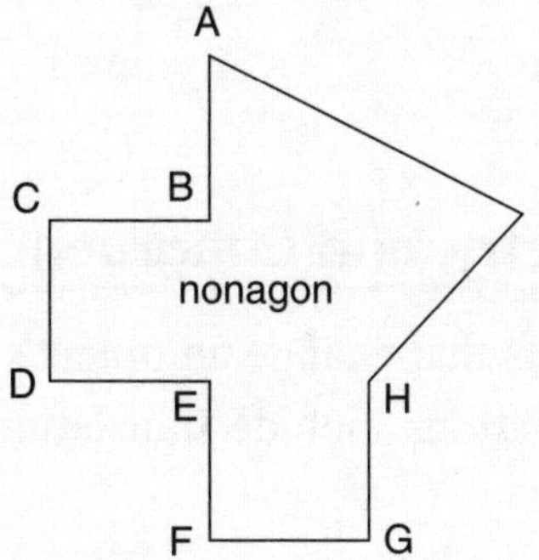

8. Decagon

   10 sides, 10 angles, 10 vertices, 35 diagonals

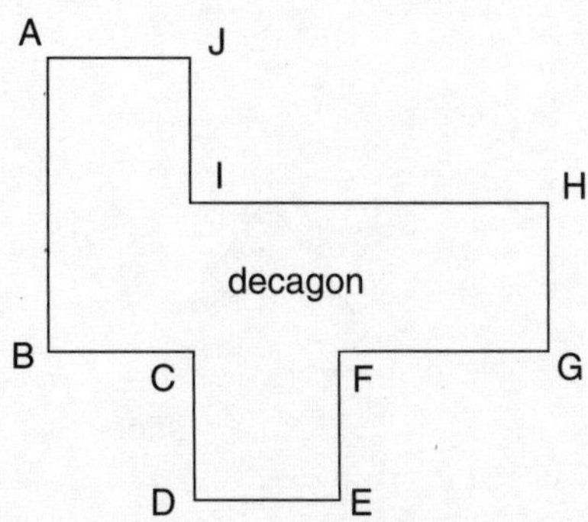

Three-dimensional figures

Three-dimensional figures or "space figures" are figures whose points do not all lie in the same plane. Therefore, space figures are 3-dimensional and have volume (l × w × h). One type of space figure is a *polyhedron.* Each surface of a polyhedron is called a face, and each face is a polygon. Polyhedrons include pyramids, prisms, and cubes.

Cylinders, cones, and spheres are space figures but they are not polyhedrons because they have curved surfaces. For example, each base of a cylinder is a circle. A cone has one circular base. Each point on a sphere is equidistant from the center of the sphere.

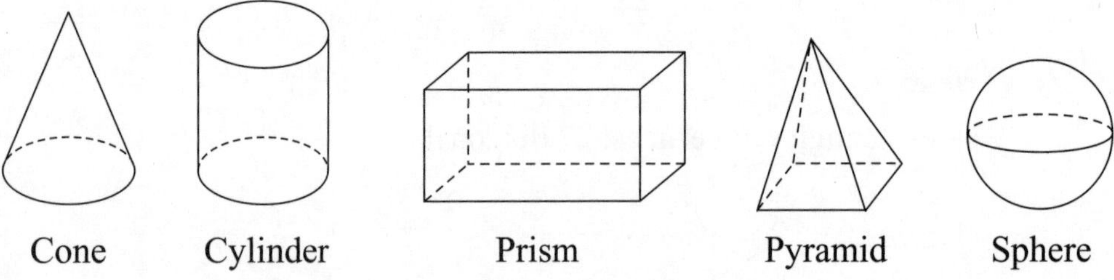

Geometric Transformations, Symmetry, and Congruence

Geometric *transformations* are movements that change an object's position or orientation or its size, but not its shape. Transformations include translations, rotations, reflections, and dilations.

A *translation* moves the object a fixed distance in the same direction.

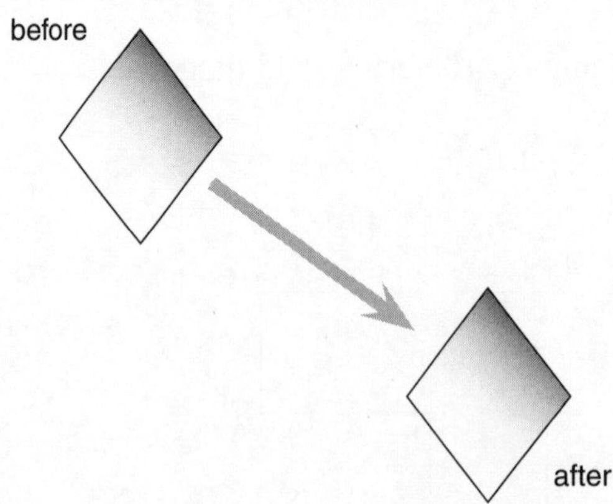

A *rotation* turns the object around on a fixed point called the center of rotation; all rotations move in a counterclockwise or clockwise direction. Ninety and 180 degrees are the most common rotations.

A *reflection* is the mirror image of an object. A reflection of *d* is *b*. For two-dimensional figures, the "mirror" is a line, which is also called the "axis of reflection."

Dilation (sometimes called *dilatation*) enlarges or expands the figure.

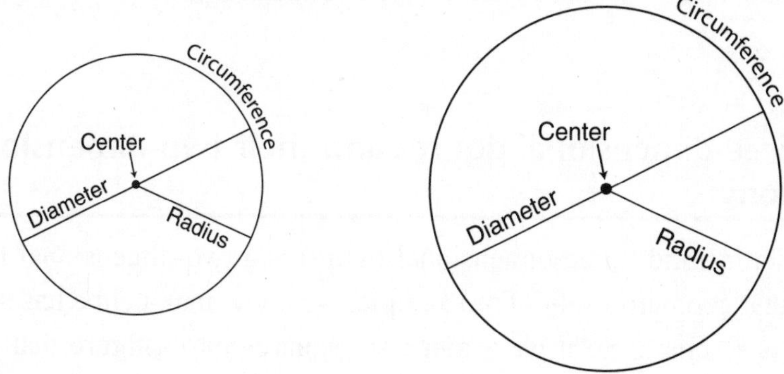

Symmetry is when a figure has two sides that are mirror images of each other. For example, if you draw a perpendicular line from the vertex of an equilateral triangle to center of the base, one side of the triangle is symmetric to the other side of the triangle because it is a mirror image of the other. The perpendicular line is called the line of symmetry. There are two kinds of symmetry: *bilateral* and *radial.* The previous triangle example is an example of bilateral symmetry. A good example of radial symmetry is a circle; any line drawn through the center of the circle will divide the circle into mirror images.

Similarity: Two geometrical objects are similar if they both have the same shape, which means corresponding sides of similar polygons are in proportion, and corresponding angles have the same measure. The two equilateral triangles below are similar because they have the same shape, their sides are proportional, and their corresponding angles are 60°.

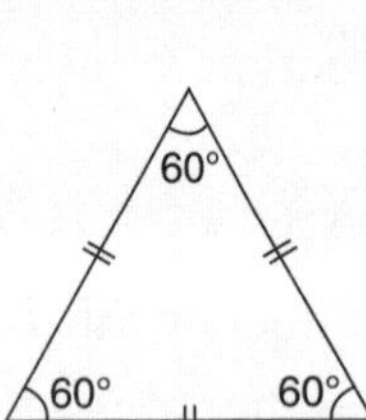

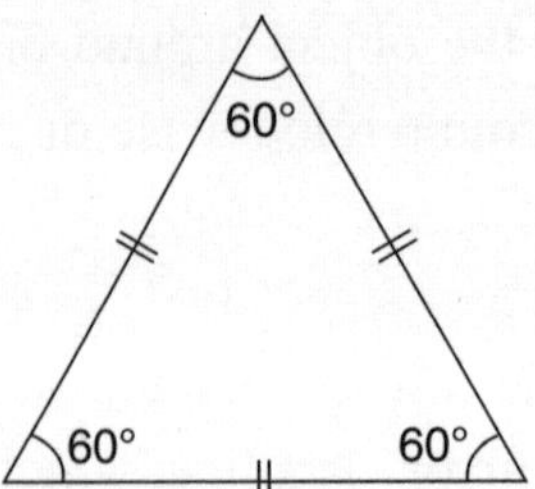

Congruence: Two figures are congruent if they have the same shape and size, but are in different positions (for instance, one may be rotated, flipped, or simply placed somewhere else).

Matching three-dimensional figures and their two-dimensional representations

A net geometric solid (three-dimensional figure) is a two-dimensional figure that can be folded into that geometric solid. For example, we know that a cube has six sides. Each side of a cube is a square. So if we arrange six squares into a figure that can be folded into a cube, we have a *net* for a cube.

Here are two examples of nets of cubes:

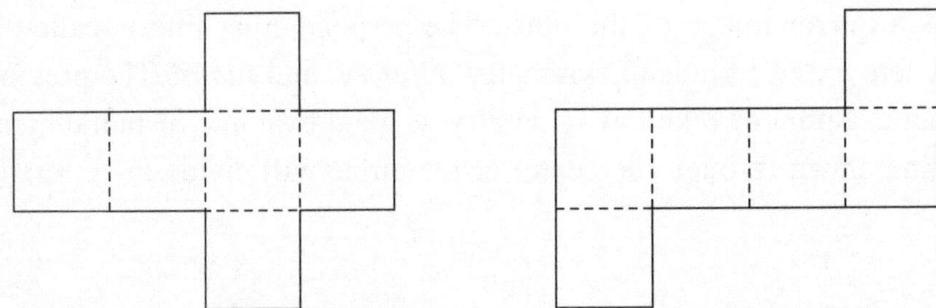

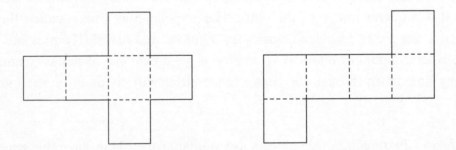

Examples of nets and the solid figures they can be folded to form:

A rectangular prism or cuboid is formed by folding a net as shown.

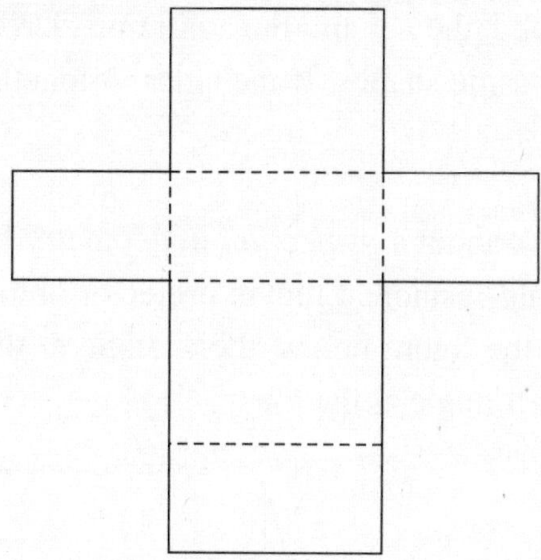

Here are some examples of nets and their corresponding solids:

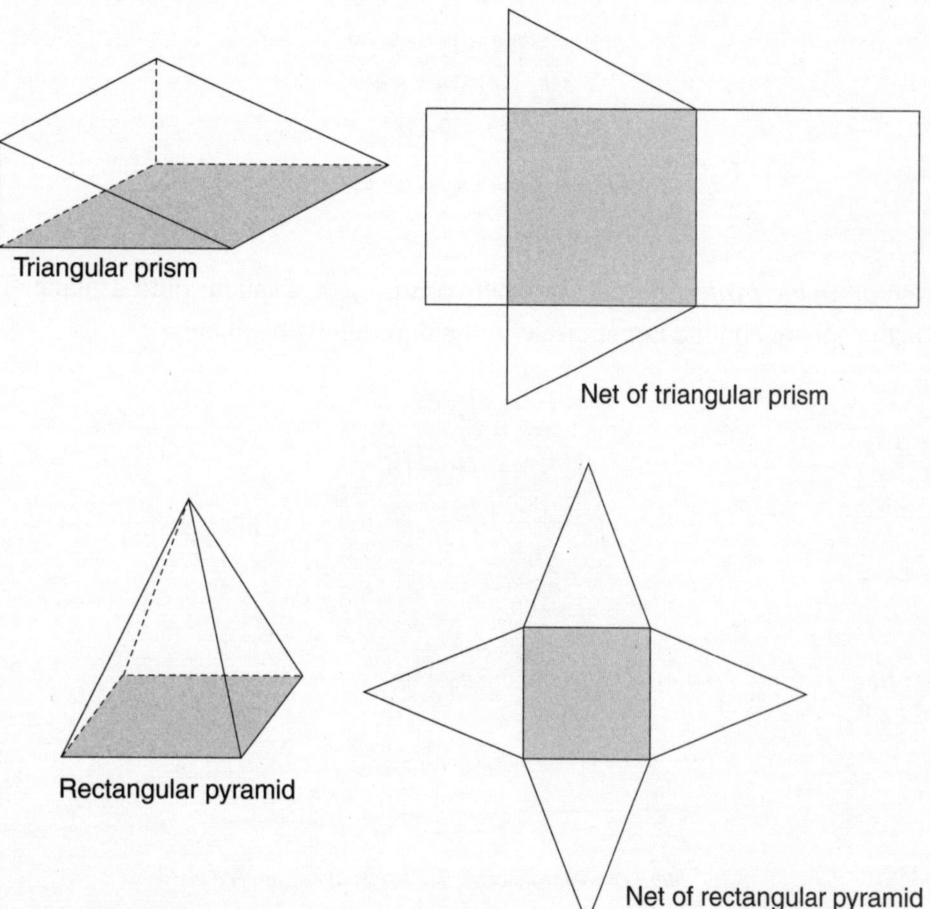

http://www.onlinemathlearning.com/geometry-nets.html

In order to form a net solid, the net and the solid must have the same number of faces and the faces must have the same shapes. If the sides fit together correctly, then you have a net solid.

The simplest way to think about a *projection* in geometry is to visualize an image that is being projected from an old-fashioned movie projector onto a movie screen or to think about perspective in art. In the figure below, the triangle at the bottom of the figure is a larger version of the smaller triangle at the top.

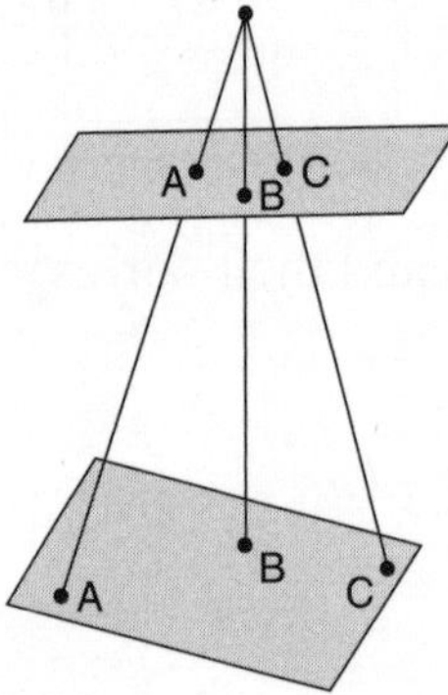

http://www.britannica.com/EBchecked/topic/478464/projection2

A *stereographic projection* occurs when you project a sphere onto a plane. The basketball is the sphere and the larger circle in the diagram is the plane.

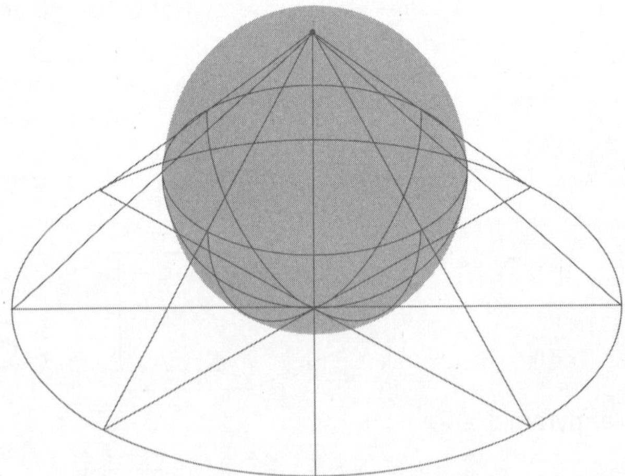

http://en.wikipedia.org/wiki/Stereographic_projection

Connections between algebra and geometry

These are general categories on connections between algebra and geometry:

Geometric formulas: Area, perimeter, etc. are expressed in algebraic form. The Pythagorean Theorem falls into this category. The Pythagorean Theorem: $a^2 + b^2 = c^2$

Another example is the slope intercept equation of a line: $y = mx + b$

Algebraic proofs of geometric theorems: Many proofs use algebraic manipulation. An example of this is the Side Angle Side (SAS) Postulate in geometry. To prove that a given set of triangles is congruent, we compare the relationship between two sides and the included angle of one triangle to two sides and the included angle of another triangle. This relationship is expressed algebraically. If the Side-Angle-Side of one triangle is congruent with the Side-Angle-Side of the other, then the two triangles are congruent.

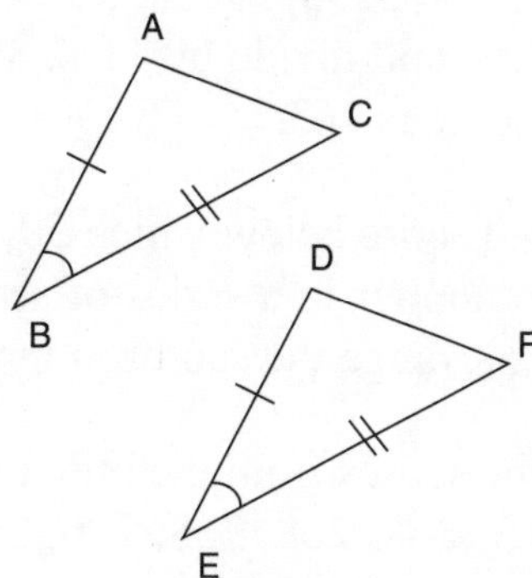

http://hotmath.com/hotmath_help/topics/SAS-postulate.html

IF: $\overline{AB} \cong \overline{DE}$, $\overline{BC} \cong \overline{EF}$ and $\angle B \cong \angle E$, THEN by the SAS Postulate $\Delta ABC \cong \Delta DEF$

Analytic geometry: Geometric figures can be described in terms of coordinates.

Graphing: We can represent an algebraic problem graphically, solving an equation by first finding a geometric intersection.

Geometric representation of an expression: The ancient Greeks used geometry to do "algebra." For example, a quadratic equation is really a question about squares and rectangles. Historically the line between geometry and algebra is often very thin.

COMPETENCY 0025

Understand descriptive statistics.

Mean, Median, and Mode: Measures of Central Tendency

Mean, median, and mode are descriptive statistics. Also called measures of "central tendency" because these measures are closest to the average score, these statistics describe particular trends and patterns in a set of data. It is likely that these statistics terms will be used to describe the data set of test results for the MTEL.

Mean: What is the average test score based on the scores of everyone that took the test? To find the *mean* you simply compute the average of all the scores.

> Example: N or the number of people who took the MTEL is 11. Their scaled scores (from a range of 100–300) were: 171, 250, 250, 263, 268, 268, 268, 280, 290, 290, and 295. To find the mean score, add up all the scores and divide by 11. 2,893 divided by 11 = 263. The *mean* scaled score is 263.

Median: What is the scaled score below which 50% of the scores fall? The *median* is the middle number in a series of scored sorted by value. To determine the median, arrange the scores in increasing order.

> Example: Using the scores from the previous example, the order is: 171, 250, 250, 263, 268, 268, 268, 280, 290, 290, and 295. Since there are eleven scores, the median score is the middle number in the set or the 6th number, which is 268. Finding the median score in a series of ten scores is different. Using first ten numbers in the previous example, find the middle pair of numbers, add them together, and divide by 2. This will yield the median.

> Example: 171, 250, 250, 263, 268, 268, 268, 280, 290, 290. The middle pair are the 5th and 6th numbers: 268 and 268. Adding these two numbers together and dividing by 2 = 268, which is the *median*.

Mode: Which score did most students get on this test? The *mode* is the score that appears the greatest number of times in the set of scores. The number 268 appears the most times in the series; therefore the mode is 268.

In a bell curve, which is a perfect distribution of scores, the mean, median, and mode are the same.

Range, Variance, and Standard Deviation: Measures of Dispersion

Measures of "dispersion" are statistics used to describe the spread away from the average score.

Range: What is the range in this set of scores? The *range* or spread is found by subtracting the lowest score from the highest scores. In the set of scores: 171, 250, 250, 263, 268, 268, 268, 280, 290, 290, and 295, 295 is the highest score and 171 is the lowest score. Subtracting 171 (the lowest score) from the 295 (the highest score) is 124, which is the range.

Variance: What is the difference between each score and the average score? Are there scores that vary a great deal or do they vary in a way that is expected? *Variance* is the measure of difference between each score in the set of scores and the mean of the scores or the sum of squared deviations of the mean score.

Standard Deviation: What is the average variance among the set of scores? A low standard deviation indicates that the scores are close to the mean. A high standard deviation indicates that the scores are far away from the mean. The *standard deviation* is the square root of the variance.

Reliability, another important term in testing, is the degree to which a measurement or set of measurements is consistent or repeatable. *Reliability* answers the question: Will we get the same result using a specific measure time and time again? A physician relies on the sphygmomanometer (blood pressure cuff) to measure a patient's blood pressure accurately, time and time again.

Validity answers the question: Is the measure we are using a good measure for what we are measuring? A sphygmomanometer is a good instrument for measuring blood pressure; therefore it is a valid instrument. On the other hand, a weight scale is not a valid instrument for measuring blood pressure.

Correlation is the relationship between two variables. For example, a teacher may introduce a new reading strategy in one of her classrooms that focuses on drawing inferences. After several weeks, she finds that her students have become better at drawing inferences. A good question to ask: Is there a relationship between using this strategy and students' performance in drawing inferences? If so, what is it? Is there a causal relationship? Is the relationship parallel, positive, or negative? Finding the correlation between two variables helps us answer this question.

As a teacher, you will need to be able to identify and interpret these statistics in order to get an overall picture of student performance, especially when interpreting standardized test scores. Important statistical information includes: N, mean, mode, median, range, and standard deviation.

Using tables, graphs, line plots, and Venn diagrams to present data

There are several ways to present statistical data visually.

Table: Creating a table is often the simplest way to represent statistical data. The following table represents data from the MTEL example. Generally, the variable such as the year, gender, subtest appears on the first column and the statistics to be included in the table run across the rows.

Descriptive Statistics for MTEL Scaled Scores

	N	Mean	SD	Range	Mode	Median
2008 Scores	11	263	34.4	124	268	268

http://support.sas.com/documentation/cdl/en/grnvwug/61307/HTML/default/p1onmh62dcccaqn1a4tf0n7bpwqs.htm

Graphs: Graphs are useful visuals for representing data.

- Bar charts/graphs or histograms incorporate grid, horizontal, and/or vertical columns, to represent quantitative data.

Example of Bar Chart/Graph

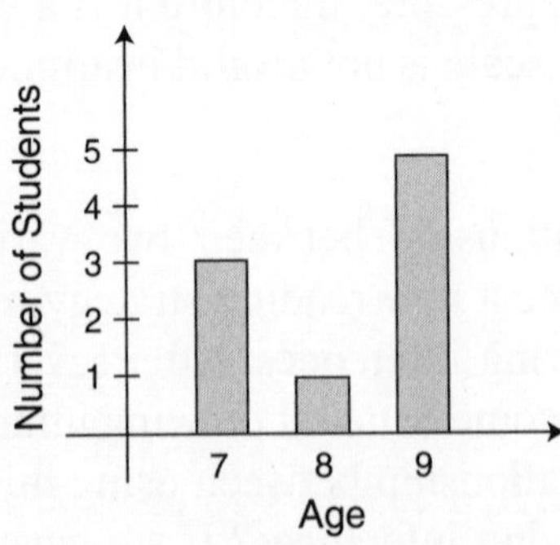

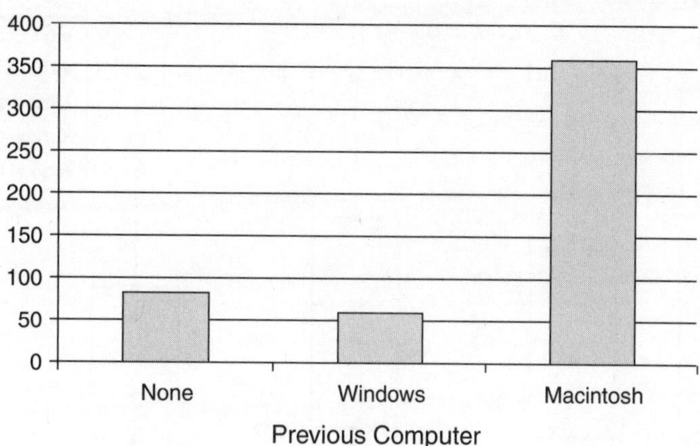

http://cnx.org/content/m10217/latest/

- A histogram is a special kind of bar chart/graph that shows the frequency of an event.

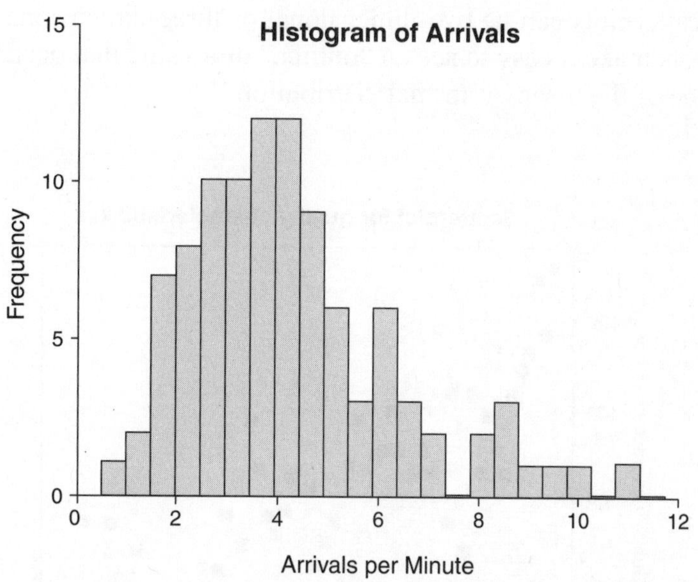

http://en.wikipedia.org/wiki/File:Histogram_of_arrivals_per_minute.svg

- Box plots or box-and-whiskers plots summarize statistics for the distribution of a variable or set of variables. Several pieces of data are usually needed to create this graph: minimum and maximum N, the lower quartile or lowest percentile, the median, and the upper quartile or highest percentile.

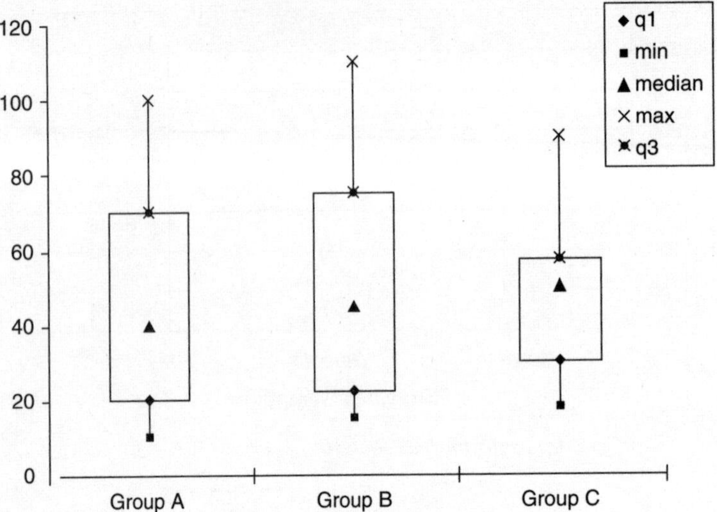

http://www.coventry.ac.uk/ec//~nhunt/boxplot.htm

- Scatterplots use dots to present each observation in a set of data. Scatterplots can be two-dimensional or three-dimensional. Scatterplots make it easy to see an "outlier," or a value that occurs far outside of the mean or normal distribution.

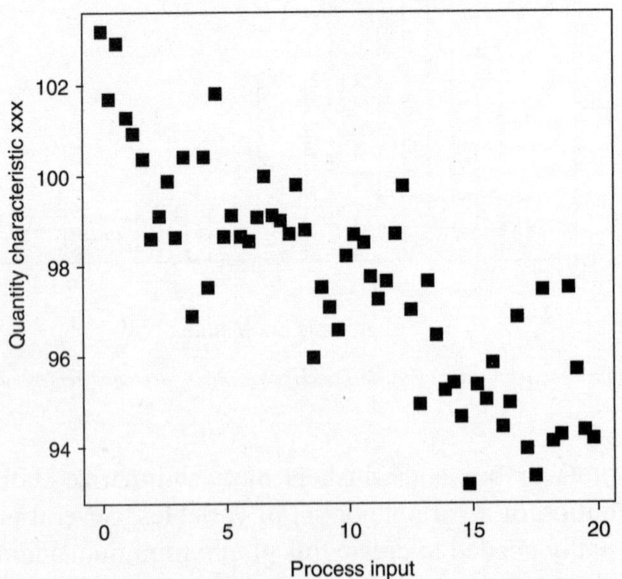

http://en.wikipedia.org/wiki/Scatter_plot

Venn Diagrams, also called set diagrams, are useful visual tools that present the commonalities between 2 or more sets of data. In the example below, the part where set A, set B, and set C, intersect demonstrates values or characteristics that are common to all three sets of data.

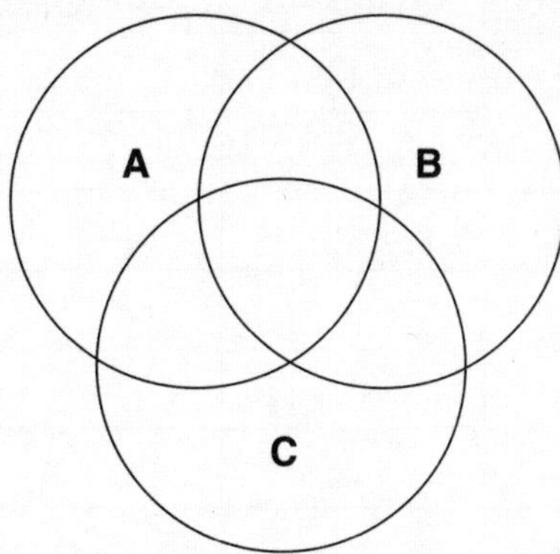

http://en.wikipedia.org/wiki/File:Venn_diagram_cmyk.svg

Frequency Distributions and Percentiles

Frequency distributions show the number of data points or values that fall into several ranges of values. Using the previous MTEL data, we can create a simple frequency distribution chart. The 1st column lists scores highest first, lowest last, the 2nd column tallies (using tally marks) the number of each score, and the 3rd column provides the numerical total of each score. The N is written on the bottom row.

Data Set: 171, 250, 250, 263, 268, 268, 268, 280, 290, 290, 295.

Score	Tally	Frequency
295	*l*	1
290	*ll*	2
280	*l*	1
268	*lll*	3
263	*l*	1
250	*ll*	2
171	*l*	1
	N =	11

Cumulative Frequency Distribution: the 4th column indicates the total number of scores up to and including a particular score. The number 11 indicates that there is 1 score at 295 and 10 below 295.

Score	Tally	Frequency	Cumulative Frequency
295	*l*	1	11
290	*ll*	2	10
280	*l*	1	8
268	*lll*	3	7
263	*l*	1	4
250	*ll*	2	3
171	*l*	1	1
	N =	11	

Grouped Frequency Distributions allow data to be grouped according to specific ranges. This distribution is useful when reporting large frequencies of data. Each interval must be mutually exclusive (a value can fit in only one interval); there should be 7–20 intervals, and the range for each interval should be an odd number.

	Score Interval	Tally	Interval Midpoint	Frequency
1	275–300	llll	288	4
2	249–274	llll	262	4
3	225–250	ll	238	2
4	199–224		212	
5	173–198		186	
6	147–172	1	160	1
			N=	11

Percentages offer another way to report and compare data. For example, of the total sample of 11 students that took the MTEL, we can calculate the percentage of students that scored at each interval. Remember that percentages are based on 100%, so 4/11 or .3636 (rounding to the nearest hundredth) .36 × 100% = 36% of the students scored between 275 and 300. The same percentage scored between 249 and 274. 2/11 or .1818 (rounding to the nearest hundredth) .18 × 100% = 18% scored between 225 and 250, and 1/11 or ~10% scored between 147 and 172. If the passing score on the MTEL is 240, then using Frequency Distribution data, we see that 10/11 or ~90% of students passed the MTEL.

Percentiles also present another way to report and compare data. Standardized tests like the SAT and GRE report numerical scaled scores and percentiles. There is no standard definition of a percentile, except that it is a number from 1st to 99th that shows the percentage of students that scored higher or lower than a specific rank. If you scored at the 95th percentile on your GREs, it means that 95% of students that took the test scored lower than you and 5% scored higher. Sometimes scores are reported in quartiles: the 1st quartile—25%; the 2nd quartile –50%, and so on. Sometimes scores are reported using "stanines" or "standard nines" which means that the distribution of scores is divided into nine sections or parts.

Distribution Curves: Bell Curve or Gaussian Curve

Discovered by Carl Friedrich Gauss, the Bell, or Gaussian Curve represents the normal distribution of data of any variable that tends to cluster around the mean such as height, blood pressure, or test scores. The area under the curve = 1; therefore, each interval on the × (horizontal) axis represents 10% of the scores. The graph shows that most of the scores will cluster around the mean and as the scores move away from the mean, the percentage of those scores diminishes.

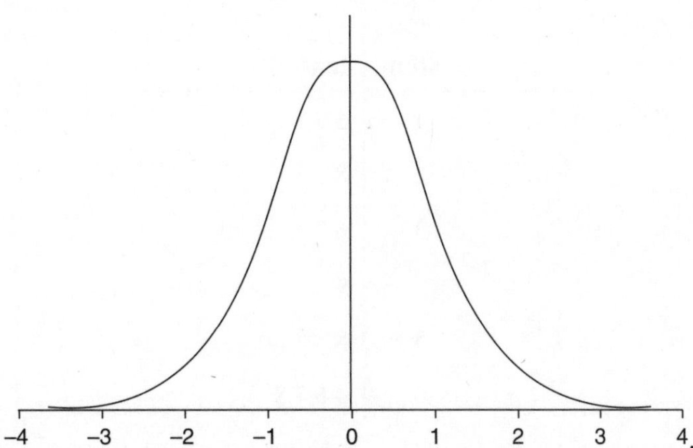

Important terms to remember about distributions include

- center: the point where 50% of the values are on either side.
- spread: how the range of values vary. If the values cover a wide range, the spread is large; if they cluster near one value, the spread is small.
- shape: the symmetry, skewness (left tail is longer (negatively skewed) or right tail is longer (positively skewed), the number of peaks or humps.

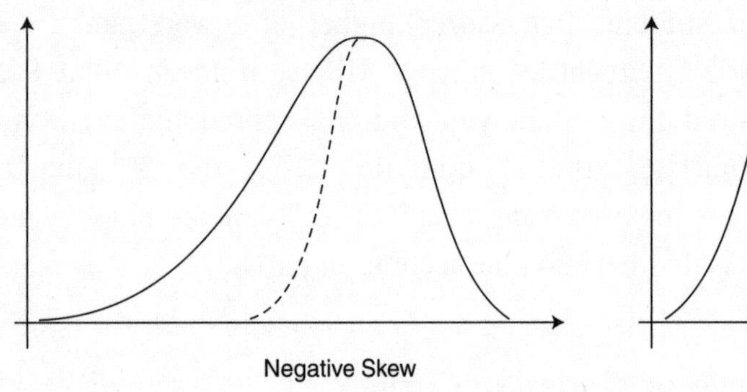
Negative Skew

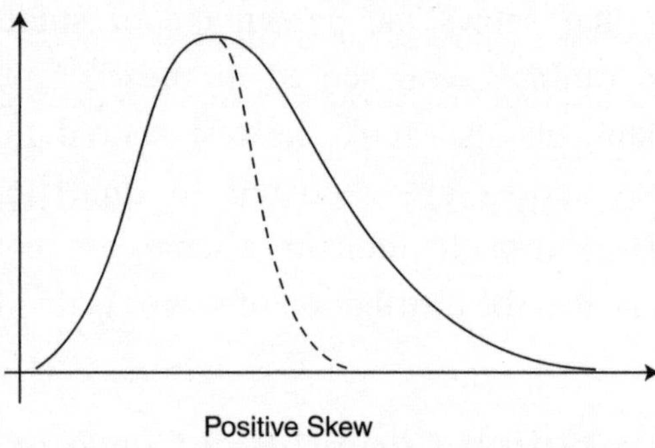
Positive Skew

http://en.wikipedia.org/wiki/Skewness

Stem-and-leaf plots offer still another way to view and compare data. The stem (Column 1) contains the tens digit and the leaf (Column 2) contains the units digit. Below is a stem-and-leaf plot of the following set of scores: 15, 28, 36, 37, 38, 49, 58, 64, 66, 67, and 68. 15 is represented by "1" in the tens column and "5" in the units column.

Test Grades

stem	leaf
1	5
2	8
3	6 7 8
4	9
5	8
6	4 6 7 8

COMPETENCY 0026

Understand and apply basic concepts of probability.

Probability of a Simple Event

Probability is the likelihood or chance that an event will occur. If you listen to the evening weather report, you might hear the meteorologist say that the probability or chance of precipitation occurring is 60%. National, regional, and local weather bureaus suggest that there are 60/100 chances that it will rain. Of course the weatherman will either be right or wrong, which means he has a 50% chance of being right or wrong. The same applies to a true-false test. You can guess either "true" or "false" and therefore have a 50% chance (1 out of 2) that you will guess correctly. Another example where probability applies is rolling a die. A die is a cube with six sides, or faces. On each face is a different number of dots, ranging from 1 to 6. Thus when you roll a die, there are six possible outcomes (1, 2, 3, 4, 5, or 6), and it is likely that any one of these numbers will come up when you roll the die. Suppose you are playing a board game and you need to roll 4 to move your piece to a safety zone. What is the probability that you will roll 4? Because there are 6 possible outcomes, you have a 1 out of 6 or .166 or 16.6% probability that you will roll a 4. Suppose you need to roll a 3 or a 4? Since each has a $\frac{1}{6}$ chance of being rolled, the probability that either a 3 or 4 will be rolled is 2 out of 6 or $\frac{1}{3}$ or .33 or 33%. Although the probability of rolling a 3 or 4 is higher than rolling a 1, you still may not roll either. It is just more likely or probable that you will, but there are no guarantees.

The probability formula is $p = \frac{n}{N}$ where N is the total set of values/members, and n is a subset of the total elements. For example, in a jar that contains 100 orange, 60 red, 40 blue, 30 green, and 10 brown M&Ms, what is the probability that you will pull out a blue one? The total number of M&Ms in the jar (N) is 100 + 60 + 40 + 30 + 10 = 240. The subset n (the number of blue ones) is 40. Therefore, $p = \frac{40}{240} = \frac{1}{6} \approx .16$ or 16% probability that you will pull out a blue M&M.

In Monopoly throwing doubles (two dice, each with the same number of dots) gives a player another chance to roll the dice. What is the probability that you will throw a set of doubles? All 36 possible outcomes are listed in the table below. There are 6 pairs of doubles. Therefore, if N=36 (total possible throws) and n=6 (subset of possible doubles), the probability (p) of throwing doubles is $\frac{6}{36}$ or $\frac{1}{6}$ or about .16 or 16%.

Die 1	Die 2	Die 1	Die 2	Die 1	Die 2
1	1	3	1	5	1
1	2	3	2	5	2
1	3	3	3	5	3
1	4	3	4	5	4
1	5	3	5	5	5
1	6	3	6	5	6
2	1	4	1	6	1
2	2	4	2	6	2
2	3	4	3	6	3
2	4	4	4	6	4
2	5	4	5	6	5
2	6	4	6	6	6

Probability of Two (or more) Independent Events

Two events are considered *independent events* if the probability of one event occurring has no impact on the probability of the other occurring. For example the probability of throwing doubles the first time you throw the dice (first event) is .16. The probability of throwing doubles on the second throw (second event) is still .16. When two events are *independent*, the probability of *both* occurring is the product of the probabilities of the individual events or $\frac{1}{6} \times \frac{1}{6} = \frac{1}{36}$.

To figure out the probability of an event NOT occurring, simply subtract the probability of the event occurring from 1.0, the highest probability. Therefore, the probability of *not* throwing doubles is $1 - \frac{1}{6} = \frac{5}{6}$.

Conditional Probabilities

When two events are dependent on each other this is called *conditional probability*. This means that the probability of the first event impacts the probability of the second event occurring. For example, what is the chance that the two cards you draw randomly from a deck will be two Jokers? Because there are 2 Jokers in a deck of cards, if the first card drawn in a Joker, the probability of drawing a Joker as the second card is lowered because now there is only 1 Joker left in the deck. The probability of drawing a Joker for the second card depends on the *condition* that the first card being drawn is a Joker.

Permutations and Combinations

A permutation is a particular order of a set of elements. The number of *permutations* of a set is the number of different ways in which the elements of the set can be arranged. For example, the set of three elements/numbers {4, 5, 6} can be ordered {4, 5, 6}, {4, 6, 5}, {5, 4, 6}, {5, 6, 4}, {6, 4, 5}, and {6, 5, 4}; therefore, this set has 6 permutations or 6 ways it can be ordered. The notation for permutation of n elements is $n!$, where n = the number of elements in the set and ! is the factorial function, which means to multiply a series of descending natural numbers. In this case n = 3! or $3 \times 2 \times 1 = 6$. For example, 6 pictures on a shelf can be arranged in 720 ways: $6 \times 5 \times 4 \times 3 \times 2 \times 1 = 720$.

On the other hand, *combination* is the number that can be selected from a given set of elements, or numbers, without regard to order. The number of combinations of {4, 5, 6} is 1. Because order is **NOT** important, there is only 1 combination. The lottery is a good example for computing combinations. Suppose there are 40 possible numbers, but you to choose only 5. How many combinations of 5 numbers are possible?

The answer is $\dfrac{40!}{(35!)(5!)} = 658{,}008$.

No wonder it is so difficult to win the lottery!

Source for Algebra

Barker, Vernon; Aufmann, Richard N, and Joanne Lockwood. *Essential Mathematics with Applications: Student Support Edition*. Florence, KY: Brooks/Cole, Cengage Learning, 2005.

Claudia, Allen. *Thinking Quantitatively: The Number Line and Measurement*. Dubuque, IA: Kendall Hunt Publishing, 2008.

Geometry: Concepts and Skills. New York: Houghton Mifflin. 2008.

Selby, Peter H. and Steve Slavin. *Practical Algebra: A Self-Teaching Guide, 2nd Edition*. New Jersey: John Wiley & Sons. 1991.

Mathematics References

(MFD p. 32), and http://www.britannica.com/EBchecked/topic/155116/decimal-number-system

(MFD p. 12)

Practice Test 1

MTEL General Curriculum

ANSWER SHEET FOR PRACTICE TEST 1
MULTI-SUBJECT SUBTEST

1	______	12	______	23	______	34	______	45	______
2	______	13	______	24	______	35	______	46	______
3	______	14	______	25	______	36	______	47	______
4	______	15	______	26	______	37	______	48	______
5	______	16	______	27	______	38	______	49	______
6	______	17	______	28	______	39	______	50	______
7	______	18	______	29	______	40	______	51	______
8	______	19	______	30	______	41	______	52	______
9	______	20	______	31	______	42	______	53	______
10	______	21	______	32	______	43	______	54	______
11	______	22	______	33	______	44	______	55	______

ANSWER SHEET FOR OPEN-RESPONSE QUESTION PRACTICE TEST 1 MULTI-SUBJECT SUBTEST

ANSWER SHEET FOR OPEN-RESPONSE QUESTION PRACTICE TEST 1 MULTI-SUBJECT SUBTEST

ANSWER SHEET FOR OPEN-RESPONSE QUESTION PRACTICE TEST 1 MULTI-SUBJECT SUBTEST

PRACTICE TEST 1
MULTI-SUBJECT SUBTEST

The practice test is separated into two subtests according to the latest version of the MTEL General Curriculum Test: multi-subject (part 1) and mathematics (part 2). Use the answer sheet to record your answers.

You are free to work on the multiple-choice questions and open-response item assignment in any order that you choose. Be sure to watch your time as you work. When you take the actual MTEL General Curriculum (03) test, you will have one four-hour session in which to complete the test.

1. In the lines from his poem "Stopping by Woods on a Snowy Evening," Robert Frost uses what literary device in the lines: "My little horse must think it queer/to stop without a farmhouse near"?

   A. Personification

   B. Metaphor

   C. Simile

   D. Alliteration

Read the sentence below; then answer the question that follows.

The artist's growing fascination with African sculpture, and his interest in mysterious and enigmatic themes, were evident not only in the bold contours of his later paintings but also in the juxtaposition of unexpected elements.

2. The above sentence is an example of formal diction rather than colloquial diction because

   A. its structure is governed by rigorous rules

   B. it contains a "not…but also" construction

   C. it uses words such as "unexpected" and "mysterious"

   D. it talks about an academic subject such as the fine arts

3. The poetic genres of epic poetry, elegies, and ballads can be distinguished in that

   A. elegies and epic poems celebrate heroic deeds or philosophical ideas; ballads have a songlike structure

   B. ballads commemorate the life of someone who has died; elegies and epic poems have a narrative structure

   C. epic poems may consider philosophical ideas; elegies and ballads usually consider lively or comical subjects

   D. elegies commemorate the life of someone who has died; ballads and many epic poems have a narrative structure

4. A teacher presents the following sentences to her class. Which one is correct?

   A. I do not like hiking as much as I like cross-country skiing.

   B. I do not like to hike as much as I like cross country skiing.

   C. I do not like hiking as much as I like to ski cross-country.

   D. I do not like to hike as much as I like going cross-country skiing.

5. In the word *prediction*, "dict" means

   A. find

   B. begin

   C. test

   D. say

6. Which of the following statements about the writing process is NOT true?

   A. Prewriting can lay the groundwork for the structure of a paper by organizing ideas and data.

   B. Research and the formulation of the thesis should always be finished when drafting begins.

   C. Multiple revisions allow for refining the paper's coherence and unity.

   D. Final edition should focus on how clearly the paper's wording or style conveys its thesis.

Read the poem below; then answer the two questions that follow.

"Richard Cory" by Edwin Arlington Robinson

Whenever Richard Cory went down town,
We people on the pavement looked at him;
He was a gentleman from sole to crown,
Clean favored, and imperially slim.

And he was always quietly arrayed,
And he was always human when he talked;
But still he fluttered pulses when he said,
"Good-morning," and he glittered when he walked.

And he was rich—yes, richer than a king—
And admirably schooled in every grace;
In fine we thought that he was everything
To make us wish that we were in his place.

So on we worked, and waited for the light,
And went without the meat, and cursed the bread;
And Richard Cory, one calm summer night,
Went home and put a bullet through his head.

7. Richard Cory represents the

   A. wisdom of age

   B. happiness of love

   C. deception of appearance

   D. contentment of youth

8. Which type of irony best describes a major event in the poem?

   A. Dramatic irony

   B. Situational irony

   C. Verbal irony

   D. Simple irony

9. Which of the following demonstrates an incorrect method of combining two simple sentences?

   A. Jason's breath was horrible, so he bought some gum.

   B. Jason's breath was horrible, he bought some gum.

   C. Jason's breath was horrible; he bought some gum.

   D. Since his breath was horrible, Jason bought some gum.

10. Which sentence uses faulty subject-verb agreement?

    A. Neither the team nor the coach was happy with the game's outcome.

    B. Nobody at the game expects the away team to win.

    C. Jill, along with all of her teammates, sit on the bench.

    D. The time is running out.

11. Which of the following is a form of discourse?

    I. A cable news television show

    II. A political speech

    III. An autobiography

    IV. A blockbuster movie

    A. II and III only

    B. II only

    C. I, II, III, and IV

    D. I, II, and III only

Read the following paragraph and answer the next two questions that follow.

[1] One potential hideaway that until now has been completely ignored is De Witt Isle, off the coast of Australia. [2] Its assets are 4,000 acres of jagged rocks, tangled undergrowth, and trees twisted and bent by battering winds. [3] Settlers will have avoided it like the plague, but bandicoots (rat-like marsupials native to Australia). Wallabies, eagles, and penguins think De Witt is just fine. [4] Why De Witt? [5] So does Jane Cooper, 18, a pert Melbourne high school graduate,

who emigrated there with three goats, several chickens, and a number of cats brought along to stand guard against the bandicoots. [6] "I was frightened at the way life is lived today in our cities," says Jane. [7] "I wanted to be alone, to have some time to think and find out about myself."

12. Which of these changes is grammatically correct?

    A. Sentence 1—Change "has been" to "have been."

    B. Sentence 7—Delete "to have."

    C. Sentence 3—Change "will have" to "have."

    D. Sentence 4—Change "emigrated" to "immigrated."

13. Which of these changes would make the passage flow more logically?

    A. Put Sentence 5 before Sentence 4.

    B. Begin the passage with Sentence 4.

    C. In Sentence 1, delete "off the coast of Australia."

    D. Begin a passage with Sentence 2

14. Which of the following properly pairs an author with his characteristic writing technique or thematic interest.

    I. Jack London—Man's struggle against nature

    II. Ralph Waldo Emerson—Transcendentalism

    III. Herman Melville—Whaling and Romanticism

    IV. Mark Twain—Satire and humor

    A. I and II only

    B. I, II, and III only

    C. I, III, and IV only

    D. I, II, III, and IV

15. Which of the following properly pairs an important literary era with its characteristic theme or representative authors?

    I. The Realist Period—Realistic depictions of nature settings

    II. The Colonial Period—William Bradford, Anne Bradstreet, and Jonathan Edwards

    III. The Revolutionary Period—Political pamphlets, themes of independence and reason

    IV. The Romantic Period—Scientific themes derived from the Enlightenment

    A. II and III only

    B. I, III, and IV only

    C. I, and II only

    D. I, II, III, and IV

Read the poem below; then answer the following two questions that follow.

"Because I could not Stop for Death" ("the Chariot") by Emily Dickinson

Because I could not stop for Death
He kindly stopped for me
The Carriage held but just Ourselves
And Immortality.

We slowly drove, he knew no haste
And I had put away
My labor and my leisure too,
For his civility.

We passed the School, where Children strove
At recess in the ring
We passed the fields of gazing grain
We passed the setting sun.

Or rather, he passed us
The dews drew quivering and chill
For only Gossamer, my gown
My tippet only tulle.

We paused before a house that seemed
A swelling of the GROUND
The roof was scarcely visible
The cornice in the ground.

Since then 'tis centuries and yet
Feels shorter than the DAY
I first surmised the horses' heads
Were toward eternity.

16. In the final stanza, how is it that the narrator believes centuries have passed, yet the passage of time "feels shorter than the DAY"?

    A. Because a long journey makes time feel as if it has slowed down

    B. Because a century is a very short amount of time when compared to eternity

    C. Because cold from the "dew" and "chill" make the carriage ride seem excruciatingly long, even though the narrator knows only a few hours have passed

    D. Because the narrator has lost her sense of time.

17. The imagery in stanza four primarily serves what purpose?

    A. It further personifies Death and Immortality.

    B. It foreshadows the narrator's upcoming death.

    C. It creates a contrast between the narrator's situation and her environment

    D. It shows how much the narrator wishes she were still alive.

Read the poem below; then answer the following three questions that follow.

"We Real Cool" by Gwendolyn Brooks

We real cool. We
Left School. We

Lurk late. We
Strike straight. We

Sing sin. We
Thin gin. We

Jazz June. We
Die soon.

18. Which of the following rhymes is not used in "We Real Cool"?

    A. Slant rhyme

    B. End rhyme

    C. Internal rhyme

    D. Masculine rhyme

19. Which of the following pairs of words from "We Real Cool" is an example of alliteration?

    A. Jazz and June

    B. Thin and Gin

    C. Die and Soon

    D. Real and Cool

20. The development of an expansive trade network, creation of large burial mounds, and use of metal tools, best describe the culture of

    A. the Adena-Hopewell

    B. the Sioux

    C. the Aztecs

    D. the Wampanoag

21. Prior to its official establishment as a state in 1948, which country controlled Israel's territory?

    A. Germany

    B. The United States

    C. France

    D. Great Britain

22. Which of the following best describes how the Gold Rush became an important origin of the civil war?

    A. Whether to admit California to the Union as a free or slave state created division and tension in the country.

    B. Suffering abuse at the hands of Southerners, many runaway slaves fled west in the search of gold.

    C. For the first time in U.S. history, slave ships began landing on the California coast.

    D. All of the above.

23. Following the Civil War in which of the following ways did life change for many freed slaves?

    A. Freed slaves were granted the right to vote.

    B. Freed slaves labored within a sharecropping system.

    C. Freed slaves faced intimidation from white supremacist groups such as the Ku Klux Klan.

    D. All of the above.

24. When making investments, entrepreneurs must measure possible profits against

    A. economic laws

    B. international competition

    C. possible risks

    D. demand for goods

25. A key function of the Prime Meridian is to

    A. divide the western and eastern hemispheres
    B. divide tropic and temperate climate zones
    C. divide the northern and southern hemispheres
    D. divide the Atlantic and Pacific Oceans

26. The legacy of Jim Crow laws divided the country in terms of

    A. males and females
    B. upper and lower classes
    C. black and white
    D. Republicans and Democrats

27. The theory by which the entire planet is deeply connected through the exchange of goods and knowledge is best described by the term

    A. internationalism
    B. connectivity
    C. modernism
    D. globalization

28. Read the excerpt below from the Massachusetts Constitution; then answer the question that follows.

    Article VII. Government is instituted for the common good; for the protection, safety, prosperity and happiness of the people; and not for the profit, honor, or private interest of any one man, family, or class of men.

    To which two principles of government does the excerpt above best illustrates the state's commitment?

    A. The rule of law and individual rights
    B. Federalism and popular sovereignty
    C. Individual rights and separation of powers
    D. Separation of church and state and popular sovereignty

29. Which of the following documents guarantees that all American citizens have the privilege of a speedy trial and free speech?

    A. The Constitution
    B. The Declaration of Independence
    C. The Emancipation Proclamation
    D. The Bill of Rights

Read the scenario below; then answer the following two questions that follow.

The development of a thriving new strain of wheat, combined with good growing conditions, leads to an abundance of grain on the U.S. market.

30. According to the theory of supply and demand, the price of wheat should

    A. remain constant
    B. decrease temporarily
    C. increase sharply
    D. increase temporarily

31. If traveling from a longitude of 0 degrees to a longitude of 50 degrees, one would expect the average temperature to

    A. remain constant
    B. increase
    C. decrease
    D. none of the above

32. What is the oldest mountain range in the United States?

    A. The Appalacians
    B. The Andes
    C. The Grand Tetons
    D. The Rockies

33. The Coercive Acts were known among patriots as

   A. the Insolent Acts
   B. the Stamp Act
   C. the Intolerable Acts
   D. the Incendiary Acts

34. The Colorado River has formed which of the following geographic features?

   A. The Rocky Mountains
   B. The Colorado Delta
   C. The Grand Canyon
   D. Colorado Arches

35. Which of the following were two factors that led to the election of Hitler in Germany?

   A. Inflation and the high cost of war reparations
   B. A flush economy and a national sense of stability
   C. The cultivation of nationalism and an economic boom
   D. Hitler's love of France and his platform of tolerance

36. Which of the following best describes the primary purposes of the U.S. government as outlined in the Constitution?

   A. To create and enforce local laws and regulations
   B. To establish a parliamentary system of rule
   C. To promote the general welfare, security, and liberty of all citizens
   D. To provide a centralized, authoritarian government

37. The development of new architecture, creation of extensive roadways and postal system, and absence of internal conflict best describes the societal conditions during which of the following periods of the Roman Empire?

   A. Roman Expansion
   B. The Golden Age of Rome
   C. Pax Romana
   D. Hellenistic Rome

38. Which of Earth's following attributes accounts for the changing seasons?

    A. Changing weather patterns
    B. Earth's tilted axis of rotation
    C. Shifting of tectonic plates
    D. Distance from the Moon

39. Which of the following natural processes can lead to erosion?

    A. Wind
    B. Rain
    C. Glacial movements
    D. All of the above

40. What naturally occurring process is slowed by beach grass?

    A. Sedimentation
    B. Erosion
    C. Deforestation
    D. Rip tides

41. Which of the following is described in terms of height, period, and frequency?

    A. Mountains
    B. Earthquakes
    C. Winds
    D. Waves

42. Organic compounds such as proteins, lipids, carbohydrates, and salts are found in what structural unit?

    A. Atoms
    B. Electrons
    C. Cells
    D. Molecules

43. What is the primary purpose of human blood?

    A. Fight infection and improve the immune system
    B. Deliver nutrients to cells and transport waste from cells
    C. Prevent clotting and aid in plasma function
    D. Deliver oxygen to the lungs

44. Mammals, reptiles, and amphibians are best described by which classification

    A. Kingdom: Animal; Phylum: Invertebrate
    B. Superkingdom: Animal; Phylum, vertebrate
    C. Kingdom: Animal; Phylum: vertebrate
    D. Superkingdom: Animal; Phylum, invertebrate

45. What distinguishes viruses from all other living organisms?

    A. They cannot reproduce without a living host.
    B. They are parasitic and destructive.
    C. They have the highest metabolic rate of all living organisms.
    D. They are the most common organisms.

46. Which property of matter explains why astronauts are able to float in space?

    A. Mass
    B. Density
    C. Weight
    D. Volume

Directions: Use the information below to answer the three questions that follow.

An experiment is planned to test the effect of microwave radiation on the success of seed germination. One hundred corn seeds will be divided into four sets of twenty-five each. Seeds in Group 1 will be microwaved for one minute, seeds in Group 2 for two minutes, and seeds in Group 3 for ten minutes. Seeds in Group 4 will not be placed in the microwave. Each group of seeds will be soaked overnight and placed between the folds of water-saturated newspaper.

47. When purchasing the seeds at the store, no single package contained enough seeds for the entire project; most contain about thirty seeds per package. Which of the following is an acceptable approach for testing the hypothesis?

I. Purchase one packet from each of four different brands of seed, one packet for each test group.

II. Purchase one packet from each of four different brands of seed and divide the seeds from each packet equally among the four test groups.

III. Purchase four packets of the same brand, one packet for each test group.

IV. Purchase four packets of the same brand, and divide the seeds from each packet equally among the four test groups.

A. I and II only

B. II and IV only

C. III and IV only

D. IV only

48. During the measurement of seed and root length, it is noted that many of the roots are not growing straight. Efforts to manually straighten the roots for measurement are only minimally successful, as the roots are fragile and susceptible to breakage. Which of the following approaches is consistent with the stated hypothesis?

A. At the end of the experiment, straighten the roots and measure them.

B. Use a string as a flexible measuring instrument for curved roots.

C. Record the mass instead of length as an indicator of growth.

D. Record only the number of seeds that have sprouted, regardless of length.

49. In presenting the results of this experiment, which of the following could be used to present the data to confirm or refute the hypothesis?

    I. A single bar graph with one bar for each test group indicating the number of days until the first seed sprouts.

    II. A pie chart for each test group showing the percent of seeds in that group that sprouted.

    III. A line graph plotting the total number of sprouted seeds from all the test groups vs. time (experiment day).

    IV. A line graph for each test group plotting the number of germinated seeds vs. the minutes of time exposed to the microwave.

    A. I only
    B. II only
    C. II and IV only
    D. III and IV only

50. The greatest source of moisture entering the atmosphere is evaporation from the surface of

    A. the land
    B. the oceans
    C. lakes and streams
    D. ice sheets and glaciers

51. Which of the following describes amensalism?

    A. A larger or stronger animal outcompetes a weaker animal, depriving it of food, living space, and possibly leading to its death.

    B. A tapeworm adheres to the intestine of an animal, depriving the host animal of nutrients.

    C. A fungus and a lichen coexist; fungus provides a food resource for the lichen and the lichen protects the fungus from the elements.

    D. A barnacle adheres to the shell of a turtle, but the turtle does not even notice its presence.

52. What role do fungi and bacteria play in the food chain?

A. They produce or manufacture food for carnivores to eat.
B. They break down dead matter into minerals and gasses.
C. They transform plant molecules so herbivores can more easily digest them.
D. They act as parasites, slowing down the production of more food.

53. Atoms are differentiated due to their number of

A. protons
B. bonds
C. properties
D. electrons

54. A cue ball is shot across a pool table. It collides with a stationary ball that takes off in the same direction as the cue ball while the cue ball slows down and quickly comes to a halt. What laws of motion have been demonstrated in this example?

I. The Law of Inertia
II. The Law of Direction
III. The Law of Equal and Opposite Reaction

A. II only
B. II and III only
C. III only
D. I, II, and III

55. When a meteor is flying through the atmosphere, what type of energy is being displayed?

A. Potential energy
B. Kinetic energy
C. Celestial energy
D. Atomic energy

Directions for the Open-Response Item Assignment

This section of the test consists of one open-response item assignment that appear on the following page. You will be asked to prepare a written response of approximately 150 to 300 words (1 to 2 pages) for this assignment.

For each assignment, read the topic and directions carefully before you begin to work. Think about how you will organize your response.

As a whole, your response to the assignment must demonstrate an understanding of the knowledge of the field. In your response to each assignment, you are expected to demonstrate the depth of your understanding of the subject area by applying your knowledge rather than by merely reciting factual information.

Your response to the assignment will be evaluated based on the following criteria:

- **PURPOSE:** the extent to which the response achieves the purpose of the assignment
- **SUBJECT KNOWLEDGE:** appropriateness and accuracy in the application of subject knowledge
- **SUPPORT:** quality and relevance of supporting evidence
- **RATIONALE:** soundness of argument and degree of understanding of the subject area

The open-response item assignment is intended to assess subject knowledge. Your response must be communicated clearly enough to permit valid judgment of the evaluation criteria by scorers. Your response should be written for an audience of educators in this field. The final version of your response should conform to the conventions of edited American English. Your responses should be your original work, written in your own words, and not copied or paraphrased from some other work.

Be sure to write about the assigned topics. Please write legibly. You may not use any reference materials during the test. Remember to review your work and make any changes you think will improve your response.

Open-Response Assignment

Use the information below to complete the exercise that follows.

Mrs. Whalen, a fifth-grade teacher, is assessing Demetrius, a new student to the school, for reading fluency and comprehension. She has him read the following passage aloud.

> My name is Jake. That's my first name, obviously. I can't tell you my last name. It would be too dangerous. The controllers are everywhere. Everywhere. And if they knew my full name, they could find me and my friends, and then . . . well, let's just say I don't want them to find me. What they do to people who resist them is too horrible to think about.
>
> I won't even tell you where I live. You'll just have to trust me that it is a real place, a real town. It may even be *your* town.
>
> I'm writing this all down so that more people will learn the truth. Maybe then, somehow, the human race can survive until the Algonites return and rescue us, as they promised they would.
>
> Maybe.
>
> My life used to be normal. Normal, that is, until one Friday night at the mall. I was there with Marco, my best friend. We were playing video games and hanging out at this cool store that sells comic books and stuff. The usual.

Demetrius has trouble pronouncing nearly every word longer than two syllables: "obviously," "controllers," and "Algonites," for example. He also needs help in pronouncing the word "resist." He reads with some expression and fairly quickly, except for the words he stumbles over. When questioned about the content of the passage, he answers as follows:

Mrs. Whalen:	Can you tell me something about what you were just reading?
Demetrius:	There's a guy who likes video games. I think his name is Jake.
Mrs. Whalen:	What can you tell me about Jake?
Demetrius:	Well, he's scared. He's in trouble.
Mrs. Whalen:	How do you know he's in trouble?
Demetrius:	He can't give out his last name.
Mrs. Whalen:	Do you have any idea what he's afraid of?
Demetrius:	Not really—they're An-guh- . . .
Mrs. Whalen:	The Algonites?
Demetrius:	Yeah, them. I guess they're after the whole world.

Based on your knowledge of reading comprehension, write a response that:

- identifies two comprehension needs demonstrated by this student;
- provides evidence for the needs you identify;
- suggests two different instructional strategies to address the needs you identify; and
- explains why these strategies might be effective.

ANSWER SHEET FOR PRACTICE TEST 1 MATHEMATICS SUBTEST

1	______	10	______	19	______	28	______	37	______
2	______	11	______	20	______	29	______	38	______
3	______	12	______	21	______	30	______	39	______
4	______	13	______	22	______	31	______	40	______
5	______	14	______	23	______	32	______	41	______
6	______	15	______	24	______	33	______	42	______
7	______	16	______	25	______	34	______	43	______
8	______	17	______	26	______	35	______	44	______
9	______	18	______	27	______	36	______	45	______

ANSWER SHEET FOR OPEN-RESPONSE QUESTION PRACTICE TEST 1 MATHEMATICS SUBTEST

ANSWER SHEET FOR OPEN-RESPONSE QUESTION PRACTICE TEST 1 MATHEMATICS SUBTEST

PRACTICE TEST 1
MATHEMATICS SUBTEST

1. How would you express the number 435.62 in scientific notation?

   A. 43562×10^{-2}

   B. 4.3562×10^{2}

   C. 435.6

   D. 4.3562×10^{-2}

2. Round 143,675 to the nearest hundred.

   A. 143,700

   B. 144,000

   C. 143,000

   D. 143,680

3. Bill is sharing a cake with Aaron and Christopher. If Aaron eats half of the cake, and Christopher eats one third, what fraction of the cake will Bill get?

   A. $\frac{1}{3}$

   B. $\frac{1}{6}$

   C. $\frac{1}{4}$

   D. $\frac{1}{5}$

4. If Tony buys 1.5 pounds of American cheese, 0.75 pounds of Swiss cheese, and 1 pound of mozzarella cheese, how many pounds of cheese does he have?

   A. 3.75 pounds

   B. 2.75 pounds

   C. 3 pounds

   D. 3.25 pounds

5. If 450 students vote for student council, and 63 of them vote for Jim, what percent of the vote does Jim get?

A. 7%

B. 6.9%

C. 14%

D. 28%

6. How would you express $\frac{4}{5}$ as a decimal?

A. 0.8

B. 0.2

C. 80%

D. 0.4

7. How would you express $\frac{11}{20}$ as a percent?

A. 18%

B. 1.8%

C. 55%

D. 50%

8. Which of the following numbers is prime?

A. 27

B. 4

C. 33

D. 17

9. What is the prime factorization of the number 42?

A. $2 \times 3 \times 7$

B. $3^2 \times 7$

C. $2^2 \times 21$

D. 6×7

10. Which of the following numbers is *not* divisible by 6?

 A. 11,412

 B. 45,321

 C. 906

 D. 15,630

11. What is the least common multiple of 12, 6, and 8?

 A. 26

 B. 48

 C. 2

 D. 24

12. What is the greatest common factor of 15, 39, and 27?

 A. 9

 B. 3

 C. 5

 D. 15

13. $4^2 \times 4^3 =$

 A. 96

 B. 4

 C. 1,024

 D. 256

14. $|-36| + 27 =$

 A. 63

 B. –9

 C. 9

 D. 18

15. Solve the equation for x. $3x + 5 = 5x - 15$

A. $x = 5$

B. $x = 10$

C. $x = -5$

D. $x = 15$

16. Fill in the missing numbers in the sequence: 80, 40, 20, __, __, 2.5, 1.25

A. 0, 0.5

B. 15, 10

C. 10, 7.5

D. 10, 5

17. What is the slope of this line: $y = 12x + 36$

A. 36

B. 3

C. 12

D. 9

18. Jim and three college friends are evenly dividing the cost of a four-bedroom apartment. The cost of rent is n dollars. What expression can you write to represent Jim's share?

A. $\frac{n}{3}$

B. $4n$

C. $3n - 1$

D. $\frac{n}{4}$

19. Which of the following is a point on the line $2y = 5x + 6$?

A. (4, 13)

B. (2, 5)

C. (2, 6)

D. (4, 26)

20. If x varies **inversely** with y, then as x goes up, y will

    A. go up

    B. go down

    C. stay the same

    D. we don't have enough information to answer the question

21. At the local toy store, there are 12 green bikes, 15 pink bikes, 10 blue bikes, and 10 black bikes. What is the ratio of pink bikes to blue bikes?

    A. 3:2

    B. 2:3

    C. 1:3

    D. 5:4

22. A football field is 100 yards long. How many inches long is a football field?

    A. 1,200 inches

    B. 300 inches

    C. 3,600 inches

    D. 36,000 inches

23. If side a of a rectangle is 12 inches, and side b is 4 inches, what is the area of the rectangle?

    A. 48 square inches

    B. 32 square inches

    C. 144 square inches

    D. 16 square inches

24. If a cube has a side of 1 foot, what is the volume of the cube?

    A. 1 square foot

    B. 3 cubic feet

    C. 12 cubic inches

    D. 1 cubic foot

25. If a movie is 120 minutes long, how many seconds long is the movie?

A. 200 seconds

B. 3,600 seconds

C. 7,200 seconds

D. 432,000 seconds

26. Which of the following objects could not be symmetrical?

A. The letter "M"

B. A human hand

C. A can

D. A nose

27. If a triangle has two angles that are 60 degrees each, how many degrees is the third angle?

A. 90 degrees

B. 30 degrees

C. 60 degrees

D. 120 degrees

28. For the past 5 days, Melissa has been counting the number of calories she eats each day. The numbers have been 1200, 800, 1000, 1500, and 1300. What is the average amount of calories Melissa has been consuming each day?

A. 1,160

B. 1,200

C. 1,000

D. 1,250

29. If you have flipped a coin 3 times, and it landed heads-up all three times, what is the probability that it will land heads-up on the fourth time?

A. 1 out of 6

B. 1 out of 8

C. 1 out of 16

D. 1 out of 2

30. You have 10 socks in a drawer. Five are black and 5 are blue. You reach in and pull out one black sock and put it on. What are the chances that the next sock you pull out will also be a black sock?

    A. 1 out of 2

    B. 4 out of 9

    C. 2 out of 5

    D. 1 out of 5

31. In the given figure, assume that *AD* is a line. What is the measure of angle *AXB*?

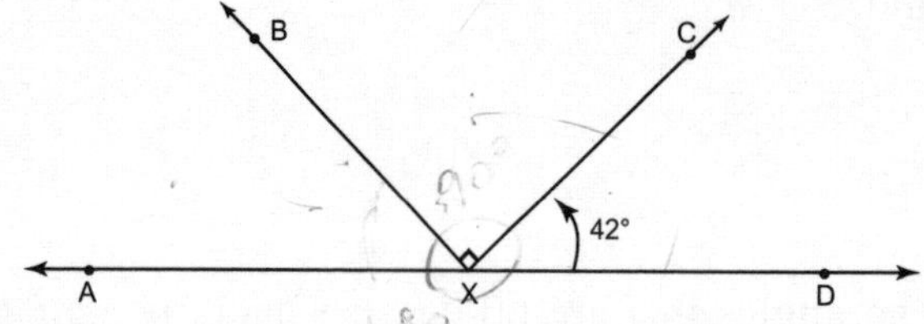

    A. 48°

    B. 90°

    C. 42°

    D. There is not enough information given to answer the question.

32. What is the greatest common divisor of 120 and 252?

    A. 2

    B. 3

    C. 6

    D. 12

33. Round the following number to the nearest hundredths place: 287.416.

    A. 300

    B. 290

    C. 287.42

    D. 287.4139

34. If the two triangles, *ABC* and *DEF*, shown below, are similar, what is the length of side *DF*?

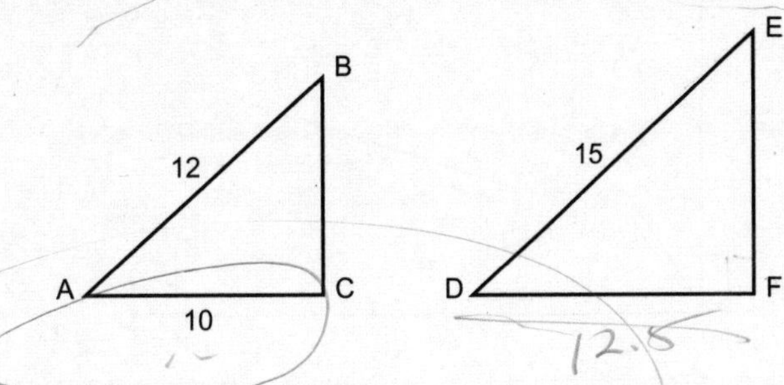

A. 12.5 units

B. 13 units

C. 12 units

D. 13.5 units

35. What is the solution to the equation $\frac{x}{3} - 9 = 15$?

A. 18

B. 8

C. 36

D. 72

36. Which equation could be used to solve the following problem?

Three consecutive odd numbers add up to 117. What are they?

A. $x + (x + 2) + (x + 4) = 117$

B. $1x + 3x + 5x = 117$

C. $x + x + x = 117$

D. $x + (x + 1) + (x + 3) = 117$

37. Which of the following scenarios could be represented by the graph shown below?

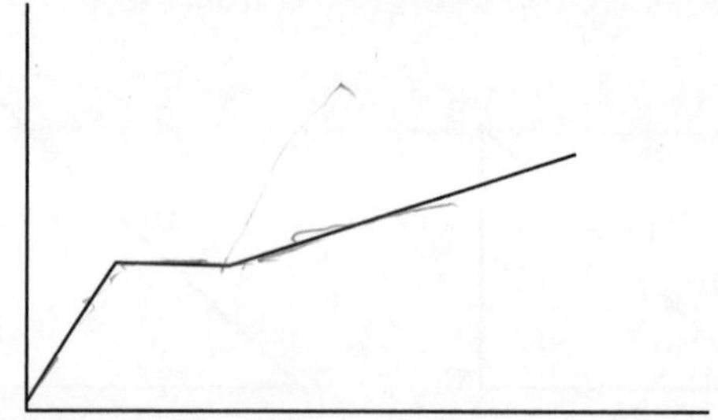

A. Mr. Cain mowed grass at a steady rate for a while, took a short break, and then finished the job at a steady but slower rate.

B. Mr. Cain mowed grass at a steady rate for a while, mowed at a steady but slower rate, and then took a break.

C. Mr. Cain mowed grass at a variable rate for a while, took a short break, and then finished the job at a variable rate.

D. Mr. Cain mowed grass at a steady rate for a while, took a short break, and then finished the job at a steady but faster pace.

38. Which equation could be used to solve the following problem?

Acme Taxicab Company computes fares for riders by the following formula: A passenger is charged three dollars for getting into the cab, then is charged two dollars more for every mile or fraction of a mile of the ride. What would be the fare for a ride of 10.2 miles?

A. $3 \times (2 \times 10.2) = y$

B. $3 + (2 + 11) = y$

C. $3 \times (2 + 10.2) = y$

D. $3 + (2 \times 11) = y$

39. What does it mean that multiplication and division are *inverse operations*?

A. Multiplication is commutative, whereas division is not. For example: 4×2 gives the same product as 2×4, but $4 \div 2$ is not the same as $2 \div 4$.

B. Whether multiplying or dividing a value by 1, the value remains the same. For example, 9×1 equals 9; $9 \div 1$ also equals 9.

C. When performing complex calculations involving several operations, all multiplication must be completed before completing any division, such as in $8 \div 2 \times 4 + 7 - 1$.

D. The operations "undo" each other. For example, multiplying 11 by 3 gives 33. Dividing 33 by 3 then takes you back to 11.

40. The daily high temperatures in Frostbite, Minnesota, for one week in January were as follows:

Sunday:	−2°F
Monday:	3°F
Tuesday:	0°F
Wednesday:	−4°F
Thursday:	−5°F
Friday:	−1°F
Saturday:	2°F

What was the mean daily high temperature for that week?

A. 7

B. −7

C. −1

D. 1

41. How many lines of symmetry do all nonsquare rectangles have?

A. 0

B. 2

C. 4

D. 8

42. Bemus School is conducting a lottery to raise funds for new band uniforms. Exactly 1,000 tickets will be printed and sold. Only one ticket stub will be drawn from a drum to determine the single winner of a big-screen television. All tickets have equal chances of winning. The first 700 tickets are sold to 700 different individuals. The remaining 300 tickets are sold to Mr. Greenfield. Given this information, which of the following statements are true?

I. It is impossible to tell in advance who will win.

II. Mr. Greenfield will probably win.

III. Someone other than Mr. Greenfield will probably win.

IV. The likelihood that Mr. Greenfield will win is the same as the likelihood that someone else will win.

A. I and II only

B. I and III only

C. II and IV only

D. III and IV only

43. How many ten thousands are there in 1 million?

A. 100

B. 10

C. 1,000

D. 10,000

44. The following graph shows the distribution of test scores in Ms. Alvarez's class.

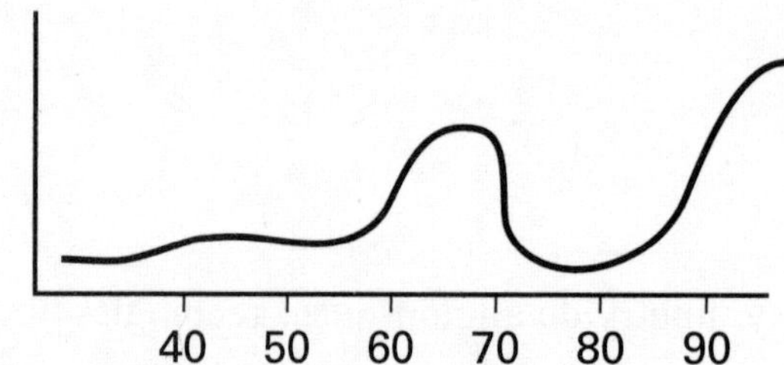

Which of the following statements do you know to be true?

I. The majority of students scored higher than 60.

II. The test was a fair measure of ability.

III. The mean score is probably higher than the median.

IV. The test divided the class into distinct groups.

A. I and II only

B. I and IV only

C. I, III, and IV only

D. IV only

45. Given the numbers –2, –1, –½, 0, 1, 3, which Venn diagram expresses the characteristics of the numbers correctly by type?

A.

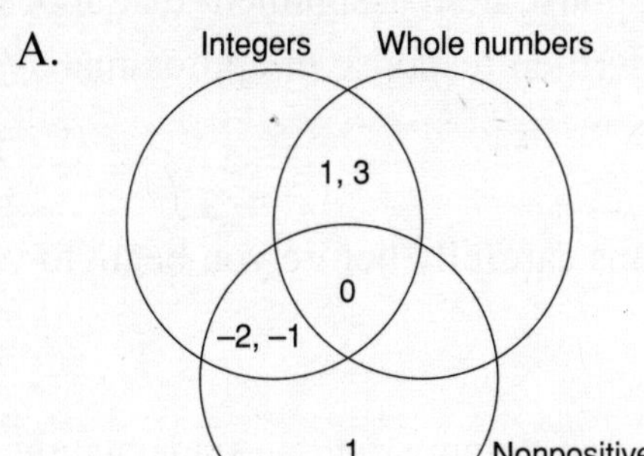

B.

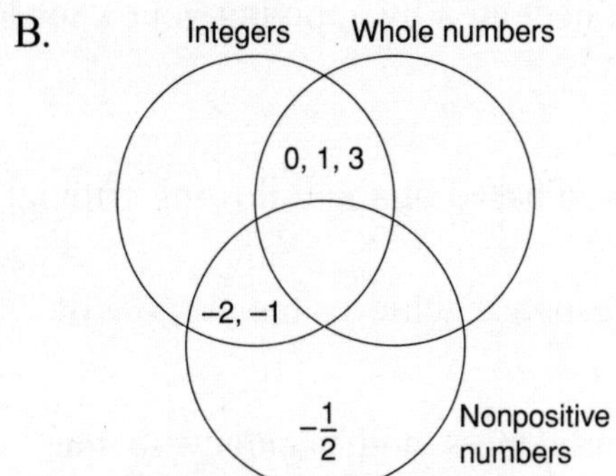

C.

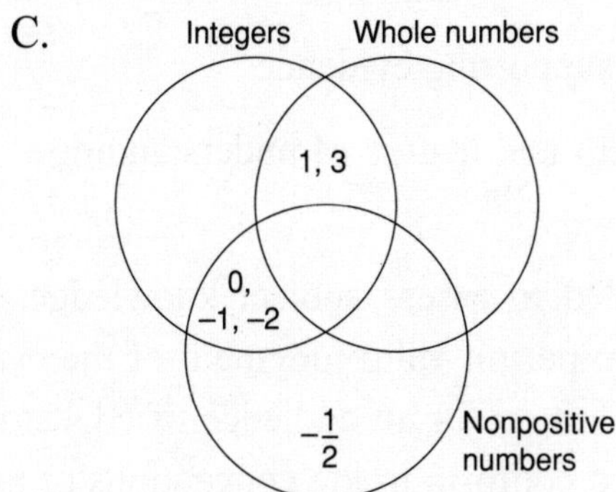

D.

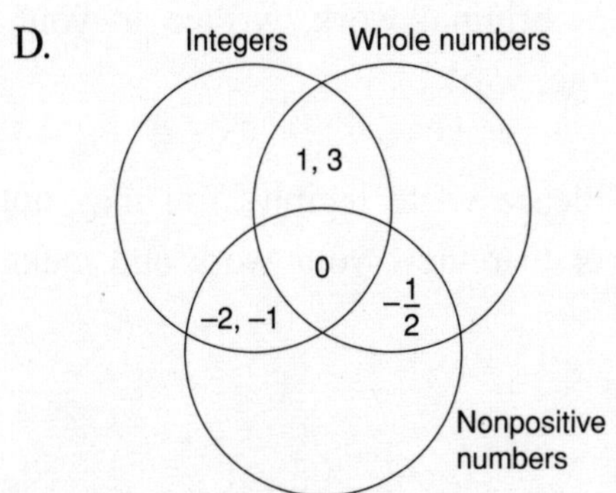

Directions for the Open-Response Item Assignment

This section of the test consists of one open-response item assignment that appear on the following page. You will be asked to prepare a written response of approximately 150 to 300 words (1 to 2 pages) for this assignment.

For each assignment, read the topic and directions carefully before you begin to work. Think about how you will organize your response.

As a whole, your response to the assignment must demonstrate an understanding of the knowledge of the field. In your response to each assignment, you are expected to demonstrate the depth of your understanding of the subject area by applying your knowledge rather than by merely reciting factual information.

Your response to the assignment will be evaluated based on the following criteria:

- **PURPOSE:** the extent to which the response achieves the purpose of the assignment
- **SUBJECT KNOWLEDGE:** appropriateness and accuracy in the application of subject knowledge
- **SUPPORT:** quality and relevance of supporting evidence
- **RATIONALE:** soundness of argument and degree of understanding of the subject area

The open-response item assignment is intended to assess subject knowledge. Your response must be communicated clearly enough to permit valid judgment of the evaluation criteria by scorers. Your response should be written for an audience of educators in this field. The final version of your response should conform to the conventions of edited American English. Your responses should be your original work, written in your own words, and not copied or paraphrased from some other work.

Be sure to write about the assigned topics. Please write legibly. You may not use any reference materials during the test. Remember to review your work and make any changes you think will improve your response.

Open-Response Assignment

Read the problem below, then complete the exercise that follows.

Mr. Del Guercio's class of 22 students had a mean score of 81.8 on the second-quarter district math assessment. Mrs. Prudhomme's class has 23 students, but 4 were absent on the day of the test (all of Mr. Del Guercio's students were present). Mrs. Prudhomme's students who were present earned a mean score of 78.7 on the test. The maximum score on the test is 100. The 4 students who were absent will be making up the test today. Can Mrs. Prudhomme's class overtake Mr. Del Guercio's, and if so, what is the lowest mean score these 4 can attain if Mrs. Prudhomme's class is to have a higher mean than Mr. Del Guercio's?

Use your knowledge of mathematics to create a response in which you analyze and solve this problem. In your response you should:

- describe two prerequisite mathematical skills necessary for solving this problem;
- identify two mathematical concepts involved in solving this problem; and
- solve the given problem, showing your work and justifying the steps you used in arriving at your solution.

ANSWER KEY—PRACTICE TEST 1
MULTI-SUBJECT SUBTEST

Question	Answer	Objectives
1	A	01–05
2	A	01–05
3	D	01–05
4	A	01–05
5	D	01–05
6	B	01–05
7	C	01–05
8	B	01–05
9	B	01–05
10	C	01–05
11	C	01–05
12	C	01–05
13	A	01–05
14	D	01–05
15	A	01–05
16	B	01–05
17	C	01–05
18	A	01–05
19	A	01–05
20	A	06–09
21	D	06–09
22	A	06–09
23	D	06–09
24	C	06–09

Question	Answer	Objectives
25	A	06–09
26	C	06–09
27	D	06–09
28	C	06–09
29	D	06–09
30	B	06–09
31	C	06–09
32	A	06–09
33	C	06–09
34	C	06–09
35	A	06–09
36	C	06–09
37	C	06–09
38	B	10–14
39	D	10–14
40	B	10–14
41	D	10–14
42	C	10–14
43	B	10–14
44	C	10–14
45	A	10–14
46	C	10–14
47	B	10–14
48	D	10–14
49	C	10–14
50	B	10–14

Question	Answer	Objectives
51	A	10–14
52	B	10–14
53	A	10–14
54	D	10–14
55	B	10–14

PROGRESS CHART— PRACTICE TEST 1 MULTI-SUBJECT SUBTEST

Objectives 01–05: Language Arts —/19

1	2	3	4	5	6	7	8	9	10	11	12

13	14	15	16	17	18	19

Objectives 06–09: History and Social Science —/18

20	21	22	23	24	25	26	27	28	29	30	31

32	33	34	35	36	37

Objectives 10–14: Science and Technology/Engineering —/18

38	39	40	41	42	43	44	45	46	47	48	49

50	51	52	53	54	55

OPEN–RESPONSE QUESTION
Objective 015: Integration of Knowledge and Understanding

DETAILED EXPLANATIONS FOR PRACTICE TEST 1 MULTI-SUBJECT SUBTEST

1. **A.**

Frost supposes his horse to have human opinions—to think that something is "queer" or unusual —when it is really just the poem's narrator who knows that the situation is unusual. There is no comparison, either stated or unstated, which would be necessary for simile or metaphor, nor is there any alliteration.

2. **A.**

Formal diction is characterized by more rigorous rules of grammar. "Not only… but also" constructions, and words such as "unexpected" and "mysterious," are often used in colloquial (informal) speech. Also, painting and other fine arts can be discussed using colloquial diction.

3. **D.**

Elegies do not necessarily celebrate heroic deeds or philosophical ideas. Ballads do not necessarily commemorate the life of one who has died, and elegies are not characterized by a narrative structure, nor do they consider comical subjects. Ballads do have a narrative structure, though, as do epic poems that consider heroic deeds and historical events.

4. **A.**

These sentences illustrate the grammatical rule of parallelism. When making a comparison or writing a list each part of the comparison must use the same grammatical form, i.e., nouns are paired with nouns and prepositional phrases are paired with prepositional phrases. Sentence A correctly pairs the gerund "hiking" with the gerund "skiing."

5. **D.**

The Latin root "dict" means "to say" as in the words *dictate* and *dictator*, who is a person with the power to "say" or "proclaim" what is right and wrong.

6. **B.**

Choice B is not true because additional facts can be gathered and the thesis can be further refined after drafting has begun.

7. **C.**

Robinson shows the reader that although Richard Cory seemed to have everything—riches, grace, and respect—he was very unhappy and eventually committed suicide.

8. **B.**

Because there is a discrepancy between the expected result and actual result, this is a case of situational irony.

9. **B.**

This is an example of a comma splice. If you use a comma to combine two independent clauses, you must include a coordinating conjunction (for, and, but, nor, or, yet, so) after the comma in order to indicate the logical relationship between the two ideas.

10. **C.**

The subject of this sentence is "Jill," not "teammates." Jill is singular so the verb should be in its singular form: sits. The subject of the sentence should not be confused with other nouns located in phrases or clauses.

11. **C.**

Any medium used to disseminate ideas, language, and thoughts is considered discourse. Even a piece of visual art that employs no words is a form of discourse, because it speaks through non-verbal signs. Furthermore, discourse does not have to be academic or the product of high culture. All of the four examples are forms of discourse.

12. **C.**

The verb phrase "will have avoided" implies that an action will occur in the future. However, it is clear that the author is describing what has already happened; therefore, "have avoided" is the correct verb usage.

13. **A.**

Paragraph 1 ends by describing all of the animals who have made De Witt Island their home. The best transition to Paragraph 2 introduces Jane Cooper and then explains why she chose this particular place.

14. **D.**

All four of these pairs are correct.

15. **A.**

Item I is incorrect because the realist authors avoided the false beauty of former writing, going to extremes to point out the cruel and ugly side of real life. Item IV is incorrect because the romantic authors replaced scientific reason with emotion.

16. **B.**

Presumably, the narrator has died and is traveling on an eternal journey with Death as her guide. The "horses heads/were toward eternity" meaning the journey will never end. In this scenario, even a century would feel like a relatively short period of time.

17. **C.**

The images of children playing, a fertile field, and the sun are all very life-like. These images contrast the image of death driving the narrator towards eternity. Answer D is incorrect because the narrator does not demonstrate any longing to return to this vibrant scene.

18. **A.**

Slant rhymes are slightly imperfect rhymes and are not used in "We Real Cool."

19. **A.**

Alliteration is the repetition of a consonant sound at the beginning of words.

20. **A.**

Native groups such as the Adena-Hopewell Indians, who are known for creating large burial mounds and using metal tools, traded and moved within a large expanse of North America.

21. **D.**

Following World War II, the United Nations granted Great Britain the control of the Palestine territories, including what would become the state of Israel.

22. **A.**

In 1849, westward expansion was driven by the search for gold, discovered in California. The gold rush greatly expanded the state's population and led California to apply for admission to the union as a free state. Due to Southern concern for the growing inevitability of Northern—and therefore free-state—control, this application sparked a crisis which led to the Compromise of 1850, a law that allowed new territories to decide the matter of slavery for themselves, based on the principle of "popular sovereignty."

23. **D.**

Although the abolition of slavery was, in principle, a major improvement for the plight of southern blacks, many freed slaves did not see a vast improvement in their lives. Groups like the Ku Klux Klan continued to intimidate and even murder. Many Southern blacks and many freed blacks continued to labor under the control of white landowners through the system of sharecropping. Freed slaves were given the right to vote, but many faced intimidation and bureaucracy hurdles that made it difficult to exercise this new privilege.

24. **C.**

All investments carry a certain amount of risk.

25. **A.**

The prime meridian is a distinction used by cartographers to divide the eastern and western hemisphere.

26. **C.**

Rigid separation along racial lines and laws supporting such division had been in place since the end of the Civil War. Although outlawed in practice, slavery as a cultural institution was still a way of life in the South and the separation of education (and its inherent inequality) can be traced back to the Jim Crow laws, laws which divided practically every aspect of life into two categories: black and white.

27. **D.**

Globalization—a theory by which the entire planet is deeply connected through the exchange of goods and knowledge—has been greatly accelerated through the development of new technologies.

28. **C.**

The separation of powers helps prevent any single person or group of people from wielding too much power in the government. This, in turn, helps protect individual rights.

29. **D.**

The first ten amendments to the Constitution, known as the Bill of Rights, enumerate such indelible rights as freedom of speech, the right to bear arms, and the right to a speedy trial.

30. **B.**

The theory of supply and demand states that price is a function of supply and demand. If supply exceeds demand, then prices fall because the market provides more choices for consumers.

31. **C.**

The equator is the line of latitude given a value of zero degrees. If you move either north or south away from the equator, the average yearly temperature will decrease.

32. **A.**

The Appalachian Mountains located on the East Coast of the United States are far older than the Rocky Mountains of the West. The Appalachians are not nearly as high as the Rockies because they have been slowly eroding for many thousands of years.

33. **C.**

Following the Boston Tea Party, Parliament's response was to pass the Coercive Acts—known as the Intolerable Acts among Patriots—which closed the port city of Boston until the tea had been paid for, increased the power of Massachusetts' royalist officials, and allowed for the quartering of troops anywhere.

34. **C.**

Carved by the Colorado River, the Grand Canyon of Arizona reaches a depth up to one mile.

35. **A.**

Bitterness over the loss of the war, inflation, and the cost of war reparations were factors in the successful cultivation of nationalism and the eventual rise of Adolf Hitler to power.

36. **C.**

The Constitution provides a broad outline of how the government is to divide power and work for the well being of all citizens.

37. **C.**

In the first and second centuries C.E. (Common Era), the period known as Pax Romana (Latin for "Roman Peace") saw the development of new architecture and an extensive system of roads, as well as a postal system, that facilitated transportation and thus favored the expansion of trade. This was also favored by a relative absence of internal conflicts, enforced by Roman troops.

38. **B.**

Earth rotates on an axis that is tilted at approximately 23.5 degrees. As the Earth moves around the sun (one rotation per year), certain parts of Earth's surface are closer to the sun than other parts of the Earth. For example, when the Northern Hemisphere is tilted towards the sun, we experience summer.

39. **D.**

Wind, rain, and glaciers all contribute to the movement of soil particles (more formally known as erosion).

40. **B.**

Sandy areas such as beaches are extremely vulnerable to erosion. Erosion is a natural process, but human development along coastal areas has sped up the process. Planting beach grasses is one way to help stem erosion.

41. **D.**

Waves, such as sound waves or ocean waves, are measured by their height, period, and frequency.

42. **C.**

Any molecule that contains a single carbon atom is considered an organic molecule; however, it takes many molecules to form a compound. Cells are large enough structures to contain fats, proteins, salts, and other organic compounds.

43. **B.**

The primary function of blood is to deliver oxygen to cells and to carry away carbon dioxide and other waste products.

44. **C.**

Mammals, reptiles, and amphibians belong to the Kingdom Animalia and since they all have bones, the phylum is Vertebrata.

45. **A.**

Viruses are the only living organism that requires a host to reproduce. All other organisms produce either sexually or asexually. Although viruses are often considered parasitic, many other living organisms are also parasites (a tick or a flea).

46. **C.**

Weight is a force exerted by the pull of gravity. Because there is very little gravitational pull in space, astronauts become "weightless." However, mass, volume, and density are constants and do not change.

47. **B.**

The experiment requires a control of all variables other than the one identified in the hypothesis—exposure to microwave radiation. Seeds from different suppliers may be different; for example, one brand may be treated with a fungicide. While it is likely that item II might be acceptable, without confirming that all packages are from the same year and production run, the four packages may be significantly different from each other. The best solution is to randomly divide the available seeds equally between the four test groups.

48. **D.**

The hypothesis is to evaluate seed germination as a function of microwave irradiation. Recording the overall growth or length of the seed root, while interesting, is not related to the stated hypothesis.

49. **C.**

The presentation of data must address the stated hypothesis. Items I and III correlate germination with time (in days), rather than with amount of exposure to radiation. Items II and IV both maintain a distinction among test groups instead of aggregating all of the data.

50. **B.**

Approximately 80% of Earth's evaporation occurs from the oceans, which cover over 70% of Earth's surface. The rate of oceanic evaporation is highest in tropical climates because of elevated temperatures.

51. **A.**

Amensalism is a form of symbiosis in which one species out competes another species; however, the two species do not have to directly interact with each other as in a parasitic relationship.

52. **B.**

Fungi and bacteria are like the recyclers of a food web. They decompose dead matter into simple compounds and gasses, which are then reincorporated back into the food web through plant growth.

53. **A.**

The atomic number is based on the number of protons in an atom. However, when an atom is in a neutral state, the positive charge of the proton is balanced by an equal number of electrons, electrons can jump from one atom to another. If an atom loses an electron it becomes positively charged (it now has more protons than electrons). If an atom gains an electron it becomes negatively charged (it now has fewer protons than electrons). A charged atom is called an ion.

54. **D.**

All three of Newton's laws of motion have been demonstrated in the pool table example. Both balls were inert before a force was placed upon them. The second ball accelerates in the same direction as the cue ball and it does so with a force equal to the force lost by the cue ball upon contact.

55. **B.**

Kinetic energy is the energy displayed in a moving mass.

A Strong Sample Response to the Open-Response Assignment

For Demetrius to read this text at an independent level, he needs better word identification skills and better acquaintance with the passage's genre.

If he does not know the meaning of the word "obviously," he not only misses a clue about Jake's personality, but he also goes into decoding mode, which prevents him from enjoying the text and from making connections between the text and other experiences.

Although Demetrius has two major word identification problems—decoding words phonologically and simply not having a sufficient vocabulary to read this passage—the inability I will concentrate on here is the insufficient vocabulary. Two of the words Demetrius had trouble with—"obviously" and "resist"—should be in a fifth grader's vocabulary, and they both follow somewhat unusual phonological models.

Even with better skills in this area, however, Demetrius will still have trouble with comprehension. This passage appears to be from a science fiction book, and he definitely seems unfamiliar with the genre. Thus, his first response to Mrs. Whalen's question concerning what the passage is about is Jake's affinity for video games, which may be the only thing Demetrius grasps well about the passage. When asked what else he knows about Jake, he concentrates on Jake's trouble rather than the trouble for the human race, probably because Demetrius is more accustomed to reading books in which individuals are in trouble of their own (or maybe he's just used to being "in trouble" himself).

Both strategies that Mrs. Whalen should try could be done on either an individual basis just with Demetrius or on a class-wide (or small-group) basis, depending on how many other readers in the class are at Demetrius's level. The first strategy, to increase his vocabulary, is to work with the student(s) to analyze new and unfamiliar words in all their reading. Assuming Demetrius will be worked with on an individual basis, he should read a book that is at his current instructional level (that is, one that he can read independently). He should make word lists of the words that he is unfamiliar with. He should define them and try to think of (or find) other words that have similar phonemes. For instance, his words and their phonemic analogies in this passage might be "obviously ↔ previously" and "resist ↔ insist." He may need help finding meanings or analogies, so Mrs. Whalen should have occasional short conferences with him to assess whether the word lists and their analogies are useful or even possible. This strategy will theoretically increase the number of words he knows and his ability to decipher unfamiliar words as well.

A second strategy is one that Mrs. Whalen would probably want to do with the whole class, and that would be to introduce the science fiction genre. Surely many students in the class will be acquainted with science fiction at least through movies and television shows, and they will be able to list a number of standard science fiction plots. Mrs. Whalen should diagram some of these plots on a board or overhead so that students will know what to expect as they read science fiction—for example, that big matters such as human survival are often at stake.

Demetrius already shows that he can make connections between what he reads and his own life, but his connections are flawed because he relies too much on his own life and too little on the text. By learning better word-recognition strategies and by recognizing conventions of the genre he is reading, he can raise his comprehension to a higher level.

A Strong Sample Response to the Open-Response Assignment

Purpose. The purpose of the assignment has been achieved. All four bullet points listed in the assignment have been addressed in an orderly way. The essay begins by stating the two comprehension needs, then gives evidence for these needs. It goes on to discuss two strategies, with reasons that the writer expects each to have a chance for success.

Subject Matter Knowledge. By indicating specific methods for implementing both strategies, this essay shows that the writer has an idea of how to improve reading, and how to assess whether the proposed methods are successful.

Support. Specific examples from the reading assessment are cited in describing the needs, and specific examples are given for the supposed strategies.

Rationale. In a sense, the "rationale" part of the scoring is covered by the other three areas: it would be hard to give a convincing argument without answering the question, demonstrating knowledge, or supporting your points. However, this area also includes the organization of the argument, and this essay methodically elucidates its points in a manner that helps the reader keep track of the overall argument.

ANSWER KEY—PRACTICE TEST 1 MATHEMATICS SUBTEST

Question	Answer	Objectives
1	B	16–19
2	A	16–19
3	B	16–19
4	D	16–19
5	C	16–19
6	A	16–19
7	C	16–19
8	D	16–19
9	A	16–19
10	B	16–19
11	D	16–19
12	B	16–19
13	C	16–19
14	A	16–19
15	B	20–22
16	D	20–22
17	C	20–22
18	D	20–22
19	A	20–22
20	B	20–22
21	A	20–22
22	C	20–22
23	A	20–22
24	D	20–22

Question	Answer	Objectives
25	C	20–22
26	B	23–24
27	C	23–24
28	A	23–24
29	D	25–26
30	B	25–26
31	A	23–24
32	D	16–19
33	C	16–19
34	A	23–24
35	D	20–22
36	A	20–22
37	A	20–22
38	D	20–22
39	D	16–19
40	C	16–19
41	B	23–24
42	B	20–22
43	A	16–19
44	B	25–26
45	A	25–26

PROGRESS CHART— PRACTICE TEST 1 MATHEMATICS SUBTEST

Objectives 16–19: Numbers and Operations —/19

1	2	3	4	5	6	7	8	9	10	11	12

13	14	32	33	39	40	43

Objectives 20–22: Functions and Algebra —/16

15	16	17	18	19	20	21	22	23	24	25	35	36

37	38	42

Objectives 23–24: Geometry and Measurement —/5

26	27	28	34	41

Objectives 25–26: Statistics and Probability —/5

29	30	31	44	45

DETAILED EXPLANATIONS FOR PRACTICE TEST 1 MATHEMATICS SUBTEST

1. **B.**

4.3562×10^2. To express a number in scientific notation, move the decimal point to the place where there is one and only one digit to the left of the decimal point. In this case, that place is between the 4 and the 3. Then multiply the number by 10 raised to the power that is the same as the number of places you moved the decimal point. Remember, if you moved the decimal to the left, the power to which you raise the 10 will be positive, but if you moved it to the right, the power will be negative. In this case, we moved the decimal 2 places to the left, so the 10 is raised to the power of 2 (or 10^2).

2. **A.**

143,700. When we round numbers to a certain place (in this case, the nearest hundred) we round the digit in that place, and change all the digits to the right of that place to zero. To round to the nearest hundred, we need to look at the digit to the right of the hundreds place, which is the tens place. In this case, it is a 7. Because 7 is closer to ten than to zero, we round the 6 in the hundreds place up to 7, and we change all the digits to the right to zero.

3. **B.**

$\frac{1}{6}$. Here we know that Aaron eats $\frac{1}{2}$ of the cake, and Christopher eats $\frac{1}{3}$ of the cake. To find out how much of the cake is left, we need to convert the fractions so that they both have the same denominator. To do this we have to find the lowest common denominator (LCD). In this case, the LCD of 2 and 3 is 6. We can see that 2 and 3 can both go into 6 evenly. So, we convert the fraction of the cake that Aaron ate by multiplying it by $\frac{3}{3}$ (which is equal to one). $\frac{1}{2}\times\frac{3}{3}=\frac{3}{6}$. Then we convert the fraction of the cake that Christopher ate by multiplying it by $\frac{2}{2}$. $\frac{1}{3}\times\frac{2}{2}=\frac{2}{6}$. We also need to change the fraction, which represents the original whole cake into sixths. The whole cake is represented as $\frac{6}{6}$. The amount eaten by Aaron and Christopher is $\frac{3}{6}+\frac{2}{6}=\frac{5}{6}$. We subtract $\frac{5}{6}$ from the whole cake to see how much is left for Bill. $\frac{6}{6}-\frac{5}{6}=\frac{1}{6}$. $\frac{1}{6}$ of the cake is left for Bill.

4. **D.**

3.25 pounds. This is a simple example of adding decimals together. If you don't have a calculator, the easiest way to do this is to write the numbers on top of each other, and the *key* is to make sure that the decimal points are all aligned in the amounts added and also in the answer. It is also helpful to write out all the amounts to the same number of decimal points.

$$\begin{array}{r} 1.50 \\ 0.75 \\ +\,1.00 \\ \hline 3.25 \end{array}$$

5. **C.**

14%. In this problem we need to find out, what percentage 63 is out of 450. We divide 63 by 450 to get 0.14. Then we convert it into a percent by multiplying it by 100, to get 14%.

6. **A.**

0.8. To express $\frac{4}{5}$ as a decimal, simply divide 4 by 5. The answer is 0.8.

7. **C.**

55%. To express the fraction $\frac{11}{20}$ as a percent, it's easiest to first convert the fraction into a decimal, and then from a decimal into a percent. To convert $\frac{11}{20}$ into a decimal, simply divide 11 by 20 = 0.55. To convert 0.55 to a percent, we multiply by 100, and get 55%.

8. **D.**

17. Seventeen is a prime number because is has no factors other than 1 and itself.

9. **A.**

$2 \times 3 \times 7$. To find the prime factorization of a number, we first split the number into any two factors that we know of. We know $6 \times 7 = 42$, so our first step is to break 42 into 6×7. Next we break down 6 and 7. 7 is a prime number so it cannot be broken down any further. We know that $2 \times 3 = 6$. We have now broken down 42 into all prime numbers, and we have $2 \times 3 \times 7$.

10. **B.**

45,321. You can find this answer without using your calculator by using the math divisibility tricks. The divisibility rules tell you that a number is divisible by 6, if it is divisible by both 2 and 3. It is easy to see if a number is divisible by 2, based on whether the last digit is even or odd. To see if a number is divisible by 3, add up all the digits in that number, and if the resulting number is more than one digit, add those digits together. Keep doing this until you have one single digit number. If that number is 3, 6, or 9, then the original number is divisible by 3. In this case, it is easy to see that option B is not divisible by *both* 2 and 3 because even though the digits add up to 15, showing that it is divisible by 3, the original number is odd, so we know it is not divisible by 2.

11. **D.**

24. To find the least common multiple (LCM) of a set of numbers,
first figure out the prime factorization of each number.
$12 = 3 \times 2 \times 2$
$6 = 3 \times 2$
$8 = 2 \times 2 \times 2$

Second, for each prime number listed, underline the most repeated occurrence of this number in any of the prime factorizations. Here, the number 2 appears once in the factorization of 6, and twice in the factorization of 12, but three times in the factorization of 8, so underline the three 2's. The number 3 appears only one time each in the factorizations of 12 and 6, so underline one of the 3's. That leaves us with 2, 2, 2, and 3 underlined.

Third, multiply all the underlined numbers. $2 \times 2 \times 2 \times 3 = 24$. So the LCM of 12, 6, and 8 is 24.

12. **B.**

3. To find the greatest common factor (GCF) of a set of relatively low numbers like we have here, the easiest way is to write out all the factors for each number in the set. The factors of 15 are 1, 3, 5, and 15. The factors of 39 are 1, 3, 13, and 39. The factors of 27 are 1, 3, 9, and 27. The GCF is the highest factor that all 3 numbers have in common. In this case, the GCF is 3.

13. **C.**

1,024. To solve this problem, we need to remember that according to the rules of exponents, when a number raised to an exponent (1) is multiplied by itself raised to an exponent (2), it is the same as raising the number to the power of exponent (1) plus exponent (2). The rule in mathematical form is $(a^m) \times (a^n) = a^{(m+n)}$. Applying the rule to solve this problem, we need to solve $4^{(2+3)} = 4^5 = 1{,}024$.

14. **A.**

63. To solve this problem we simply need to remember that absolute value means the distance from zero. So, the absolute value of –36 is 36. We then substitute 36 for $|-36|$ and the problem becomes 36 + 27 = 63.

15. **B.**

$x = 10$. To solve this equation first we want to put like terms one the same sides of the equals sign. If we subtract 3x from both sides, we get $5 = 5x - 15 - 3x$. If we then add 15 to both sides, we get $5 + 15 = 5x - 3x$. We can simplify this by writing it as $20 = 2x$. Then, we divide both sides of the equation by 2, and the result is $x = 10$.

16. **D.**

10, 5. The pattern in the sequence is to divide each number by 2. 20 ÷ 2 gives us 10. 10 ÷ 2 gives us 5.

17. **C.**

12. To figure out the slope of the line, the equation must be in slope-intercept form $y = mx + b$. When the equation is in slope-intercept form, the slope is represented by m. The equation we are given in the problem is already in slope-intercept form, so the m, or slope, is 12.

18. **D.**

$\frac{n}{4}$. To solve this problem, we need to write an expression that means one fourth of n. We can express this as $n \div 4$, or $\frac{n}{4}$.

19. **A.**

(4, 13) The easiest way to answer this question is by using trial and error. Try substituting the x coordinate and the y coordinate for x and y in the equation, and if the equation is true, then it is a point on the line. In this case, substitute 4 for x and 13 for y to get $2(13) = 5(4) + 6$, or $26 = 26$. Because this is true, we know that (4, 13) is a point on the line.

20. **B.**

Go down. This is simply a question of vocabulary. If two variables vary **inversely**, as one goes up, the other will go down.

21. **A.**

3:2. First with this problem, we need to determine which information is relevant. To find the ratio of pink bikes to blue bikes, we only need to know the number of pink bikes and the number of blue bikes, and the rest of the information can be ignored. There are 15 pink bikes and 10 blue bikes, so the ratio of pink bikes to blue bikes is 15.10. However, we have to reduce the ratio, the same as we would a fraction, so we divide both numbers by 5 to get a ratio of 3.2.

22. **C.**

3,600 inches. To convert 100 yards to inches, first we need to convert to feet. Because each yard = 3 feet, then 100 yards = 300 feet. We know that there are 12 inches in a foot, and we need to know how many inches there are in 300 feet. 300 × 12 = 3,600 inches.

23. **A.**

48 square inches. We know that a rectangle is a 4-sided figure, with two sets of equal sides. To find the area of a rectangle, we multiply one side (the base) by another side (the height). Here, we multiply 12 × 4 = 48 square inches.

24. **D.**

1 cubic foot. To find the volume of a cube we multiply the height × width × depth, and because it's a 3-deminsional figure our answer will be in cubic units. Because all sides of a cube are the same length, we know that the height and width and depth are each 1 foot. 1 × 1 × 1 = 1 cubic foot.

25. **C.**

7,200 seconds. To figure out how many seconds are in 120 minutes, we need to multiply 120 by 60, because we know there are 60 seconds on one minute. 120 × 60 = 7,200 seconds.

26. **B.**

A human hand. This is a question of vocabulary. *Symmetry* is when a figure has two sides that are mirror images of each other. It would then be possible to draw a line through the object and along either side of the line the image would look exactly the same. It would not be possible to draw such a line anywhere on a human hand.

27. **C.**

60 degrees. The 3 angles of a triangle always add up to 180 degrees. The two angles we are given, 60 degrees and 60 degrees, add up to 120 degrees. 180 – 120 = 60 degrees.

28. **A.**

1,160. To find the average amount of calories, we add up all the calories and divide by the number of days in which Melissa has been counting calories. The sum of all the calories is 5,800. 5,800 divided by 5 (the number of days she has been counting calories) gives us 1,160.

29. **D.**

1 out of 2. The probability of the coin landing heads-up is that same every single time you flip the coin. Each coin flip is independent so the previous results have no effect on the current flip.

30. **B.**

4 out of 9. The answer to this problem is the number of possible favorable outcomes out of the total possible outcomes. After removing a black sock from the drawer, there remain 4 black socks out of a total of 9 socks in the drawer; therefore the probability of picking a black sock is 4 out of 9.

31. **A.**

You must know two things to answer the question. One is the meaning of the small square at the vertex of angle *BXC*. That symbol means that angle *BXC* is a *right angle* (one with 90°). The second is that a straight line, such as *AXD*, can be thought of as a *straight angle*, which measures 180°. Therefore, because the sum of the angles *DXC* (42°) and *BXC* (90°) is 132°, the remaining angle on the line must measure 48° (180° – 132°).

32. **D.**

To find the greatest common divisor (GCD), factor both numbers and look for common factors. The product of these common factors is the GCD. The GCD here is the greatest integer that divides both 120 and 252.

$$120 = 2^3 \times 3 \times 5 \text{ and}$$
$$252 = 2^2 \times 3^2 \times 7,$$

so the GCD $= 2^2 \times 3 = 12$.

33. **C.**

Place values are as follows: 1,000's, 100's, 10's, 1's, decimal point, 10ths, 100ths, 1,000ths. The 1 is in the hundredths place. If the number to the immediate right of the 1 (i.e., the number in the thousandths place) is greater than or equal to 5, we increase 1 to 2; otherwise, we do not change the 1. Then we leave off all the numbers to the right of the 1. In our problem, a 6 is in the thousandths place, so we change the 1 to a 2 to get 287.42 as our answer.

34. **A.**

If two triangles are similar, they have the exact same shape (although not necessarily the same size). This means that the corresponding angles of the two triangles have the same measure and the corresponding sides are proportional. To find the missing side (side *DF*), set up the proportion:

$$\frac{AB}{AC} = \frac{DE}{DF}$$

or, by substituting the given values,

$$\frac{12}{10} = \frac{15}{x}$$

where x is the length of side *DF*. This can be read as "12 is to 10 as 15 is to x." The problem can be solved by using cross multiplication. Thus, $12x = 150$, or $x = 12.5$.

35. **D.**

Using the rules for solving one-variable equations, the original equation is transformed as follows:

$$\frac{x}{3} - 9 = 15$$

Adding 9 to each side of the equation gives

$$\frac{x}{3} = 24$$

Multiplying both sides by 3 gives

$$x = 72$$

36. **A.**

The correct equation must show three consecutive odd numbers being added to give 117. Odd numbers (just like even numbers) are each two units apart. Only the three values (x, $x + 2$, $x + 4$) given in choice (A) are each two units apart. Because the numbers being sought are odd, one might be tempted to choose (D). However, the second value in choice (D), ($x + 1$), is not two units apart from the first value (x); it is different by only one.

37 **A.**

The somewhat steep straight line to the left tells you that Mr. Cain worked at a steady rate for a while. The completely flat line in the middle tells you he stopped for a while—the line does not go up because Mr. Cain did not cut grass then. Finally, the line continues upward (after his break) less steeply (therefore more flatly), indicating that he was working at a slower rate.

38. **D.**

All riders must pay at least $3, so 3 will be added to something else in the correct equation. Only choices (B) and (D) meet that requirement. The additional fare of $2 "for every mile or fraction of a mile" tells you that you will need to multiply the number of miles driven (use 11 because of the extra fraction of a mile) by 2, leading to the correct answer of (D).

39. **D.**

It is true that multiplication is commutative and division is not (A), but that is not relevant to their being inverse operations. Choice (B) also contains a true statement, but again the statement is not about inverse operations. Choice (C) gives a false statement; in the example shown, the order of operations tells you to compute $8 \div 2$ before any multiplication. As noted in choice (D), two operations being inverse indeed depends on their ability to undo each other.

40. **C.**

To find the average (mean) of a set of values, first add them together. In this case, the negative and the positive integers should be added together separately. Those two sums are –12 and 5. (The zero can be ignored; it does not affect either sum.) Then –12 and 5 should be added together for a sum of –7. To complete the work, the sum of –7 must be divided by the number of values (7), giving –1.

41. **B.**

If you can fold a two-dimensional figure so that one side exactly matches or folds onto the other side, the fold line is a line of symmetry. The figure below is a nonsquare rectangle with its two lines of symmetry shown.

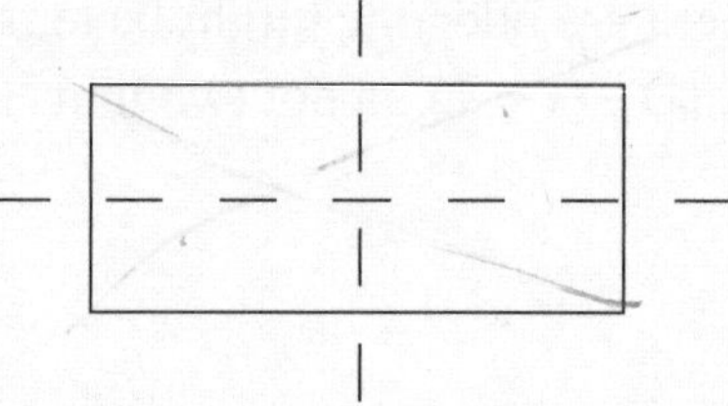

One might think that lines drawn from opposite corners are lines of symmetry, but they're not. The two halves would be the same size and shape, but wouldn't fold onto each other. Note that the question asked about nonsquare rectangles. Squares (which are rectangles) have four lines of symmetry.

42. **B.**

Statement I is true because the winner could be Mr. Greenfield and it could be someone else. Statement II is not true, even though Mr. Greenfield bought many more tickets than any other individual. He still has a block of only 300; 700 ticket stubs in the drum aren't his. This tells us that statement III is true. Finally, statement IV is false. Don't confuse the true statement "all tickets have an equal chance of winning" with the false statement that "all persons have an equal chance of winning."

43. **A.**

You know that 10,000 contains 4 zeros, or 10^4 in place value. The number 1,000,000 contains 10^6, or 6 zeros. Thus, 10^6 divided by 10^4 is 10^2, or 100. You may divide 10,000 into 1,000,000, but that is the laborious way to solve this. Choice (A) is correct.

44. **B.**

Just from looking at the graph, it's clear that most of the space under the curve is past the 60 mark on the *x*-axis, so answer (D) is eliminated because it doesn't include statement I. Statement II can't be answered by what the graph shows. It appears possible that certain questions were too hard for many in the class and that there weren't enough questions to differentiate B students from C students, but perhaps the class performed exactly as it should have, given the students' ability and Ms. Alvarez's teaching. The distribution can give a teacher many clues about the test and the students, and even herself, but by itself, it tells us nothing about the fairness of the test. Thus, answer (A) can be eliminated. Statement III is also false; in left-skewed distributions such as this one, the median is higher than the mean. This is true because the mean is lowered by the lowest scores, while the median is relatively unaffected by them. Statement IV is true: one fairly large group has scored in the high 80s and 90s and another discernible group in the low to mid-60s, whereas few students fall outside these two groups. Thus, the answer has to be (B).

45. **A.**

Venn diagrams are overlapping circles that display elements of different sets. They show elements common to more than one set as well as elements unique to only one set.

–2, –1, 0, 1, 3 are integers

–2, –1, –½, 0 are nonpositive numbers (Note: Zero is neither positive nor negative.)

0, 1, 3 are whole numbers

A Strong Sample Response to the Open-Response Assignment

The first step to solving this problem is to figure out how many total points each class has attained on this test. Because the mean score is calculated by adding all scores together and then dividing by the number of students, we can reverse the process to find the total points for Mr. Del Guercio's class. That is, mean = total score/(number of students), so total score = mean × (number of students).

Mr. Del Guercio has 22 students, so multiplying 22 by 81.8 gives his class's total: 1800 points. Mrs. Prudhomme's class so far has 19 students with an average of 78.7, for a total of 1496 points (rounding up to the nearest point).

To attain a mean of 81.8, Mrs. Prudhomme's class of 23 will have to get a total of 23 × 81.8 = 1881 points, so her class will need 1882 total points to surpass the other class. Since the class total now stands at 1496 points, the 4 students taking the make-up test will need to score a total of 386 points (an average of 96.5) to put Mrs. Prudhomme's class ahead of Mr. Del Guercio's. Thus, her class can still overtake his, but only if the 4 students average over 96.5 on the test. (Needless to say, competitions of this sort have very little to do with effective teaching, but they are sometimes fun.)

Two mathematical skills necessary to solve this problem are (1) how to calculate a mean (addition and division) and (2) how to find an unknown quantity in an equation (by reversing the order of operations).

Two mathematical concepts involved in solving this problem are (1) understanding that knowing the total scores is necessary to compare the classes and (2) understanding the relationship between the mean score and the total number of points.

Features of the Strong Sample to Open-Response Assignment

Purpose. The purpose of the assignment has been achieved. All three bullet points listed in the assignment have been addressed, and most important, the problem has been solved correctly. The essay begins by stating how to solve the problem, and it goes through the problem clearly, without omitting any steps. The required mathematical skills and concepts are listed clearly at the end of the essay.

Subject Matter Knowledge. By indicating the specific method for implementing the solution, this essay shows that the writer has a clear idea of how to solve this and similar problems, and is likely capable of teaching the concepts involved.

Support. Specific calculations involved in solving the problem are detailed, and the reasons for doing those calculations are clearly explained.

Rationale. In a sense, the "rationale" part of the scoring is covered by the other three areas: it would be hard to give a convincing argument without answering the questions, providing a solution, or supporting your points. However, this area also includes the organization of the argument, and this essay presents its points in a manner that helps the reader keep track of the overall argument.

Practice Test 2

MTEL General Curriculum

ANSWER SHEET FOR PRACTICE TEST 2 MULTI-SUBJECT SUBTEST

1	______	12	______	23	______	34	______	45	______
2	______	13	______	24	______	35	______	46	______
3	______	14	______	25	______	36	______	47	______
4	______	15	______	26	______	37	______	48	______
5	______	16	______	27	______	38	______	49	______
6	______	17	______	28	______	39	______	50	______
7	______	18	______	29	______	40	______	51	______
8	______	19	______	30	______	41	______	52	______
9	______	20	______	31	______	42	______	53	______
10	______	21	______	32	______	43	______	54	______
11	______	22	______	33	______	44	______	55	______

ANSWER SHEET FOR OPEN-RESPONSE QUESTION PRACTICE TEST 2 MULTI-SUBJECT SUBTEST

ANSWER SHEET FOR OPEN-RESPONSE QUESTION PRACTICE TEST 2 MULTI-SUBJECT SUBTEST

ANSWER SHEET FOR OPEN-RESPONSE QUESTION PRACTICE TEST 2 MULTI-SUBJECT SUBTEST

PRACTICE TEST 2
MULTI-SUBJECT SUBTEST

The practice test is separated into two subtests according to the latest version of the MTEL General Curriculum Test: multi-subject (part 1) and mathematics (part 2). Use the answer sheet to record your answers.

You are free to work on the multiple-choice questions and open-response item assignment in any order that you choose. Be sure to watch your time as you work. When you take the actual MTEL General Curriculum (03) test, you will have one four-hour session in which to complete the test.

1. The novel *The Adventures of Huckleberry Finn*, by Mark Twain, has been a subject of controversy because:

   A. it contains graphic descriptions of violence considered unsuitable for young readers.

   B. it challenged attitudes toward race in America, and used graphic racial slurs.

   C. it portrays a hostile relationship between a young boy and an escaping slave.

   D. it was thought to have influenced the outcome of the Civil War.

2. The Japanese form of poetry called haiku is known for its

   A. brevity and concision

   B. elaborate and flowery description

   C. logic and directness of statement

   D. humor and lifelike detail

3. Contemporary writers of world literature, such as Chinua Achebe, have emphasized which of the following themes?

   A. Imperialism and the impact of Western culture on traditional societies
   B. Conflicts between traditional and modern ways of life
   C. The living conditions and problems of everyday life in developing nations
   D. All of the above

4. Which pair of prefixes has the same meaning?

   A. Sub and ultra
   B. Ante and pre
   C. Intra and circum
   D. Hyper and tele

5. The proverb "Death is a black camel, which kneels at the gates of all" is an example of

   A. alliteration
   B. simile
   C. metaphor
   D. hyperbole

6. What is the difference between a phrase and a clause?

   A. A phrase is shorter than a clause.
   B. A clause is more complex than a phrase.
   C. A clause contains a subject and a verb, but a phrase contains only one or the other.
   D. A clause can always stand alone as its own sentence, but a phrase cannot.

7. The unrhymed, iambic lines in the following example are an example of what?

Nine times the space that measure day and night
To mortal men he, with his horrid crew,
Lay vanquished, rolling in their fiery gulf,
Confounded though immortal. But his doom
Reserved him to more wrath; for now the thought
Both of lost happiness and lasting pain
Torments him: round he throws his baleful eyes,
That witnessed huge affliction and dismay,
Mixed with obdurate pride and steadfast hate.

A. Heroic Verse
B. Shakespearean Verse
C. Free Verse
D. Blank Verse

8. Which of the following incorrectly pairs a literary device with an example?

A. Euphemism: My grandfather has recently passed on.
B. Malapropism: That is inappropriate to say at the dinner table!
C. Hyperbole: It is so cold out my feet have turned to ice.
D. Assonance: The cheap creep leaps to his feat.

9. Fantasy is considered an important genre of children's literature because it

A. exposes the mind to new possibilities
B. encourages imaginative thinking
C. often presents rich descriptions and vivid imagery
D. All of the above

10. Which of the following best illustrates editorializing?

    A. An extremely likable man, Robert McGee was given a well-deserved round of applause after his speech.

    B. Also discussed at the board meeting was the condition of the South Street School.

    C. The company received its charter in 1912.

    D. Just before he sat down, Mr. McPherson asked in a loud voice, "Has the homework been completed?"

11. Which of the following statements most accurately describes the history of the English language?

    A. The publication of the first dictionaries in the 15th century accelerated the standardization of the English language and created a precedent to which modern language must adhere.

    B. Since the beginning of time language has constantly been in a state of flux.

    C. The English language uses formal diction today because throughout history the most accessible printed book has been the Bible.

    D. The integration of foreign words into the English language is a modern phenomenon.

12. In formal writing, which of the following punctuation marks can be used to end a sentence?

    I. A period (.)

    II. An exclamation point (!)

    III. A question mark (?)

    IV. An ellipsis (…)

    A. I and III only

    B. I, II, and IV only

    C. I, II, III, and IV

    D. I, II, and III only

13. Which of the following properly matches an author with their characteristic writing technique or thematic interest?

    I. Jonathan Edwards—Subdued rhetoric and religious themes

    II. Walt Whitman—Conventional poetic techniques and grandiose themes

    III. William Faulkner—Terse, concise prose

    IV. Robert Frost—Themes concerning the class of nature and industrialization

    A. I, II, III, and IV

    B. I, II, and IV only

    C. IV only

    D. II and III only

14. Which of the following properly matches an important literary era with its characteristic theme or representative authors?

    I. Modernism—F. Scott Fitzgerald and T.S. Eliot

    II. Harlem Renaissance—Zora Neale Hurston and Langston Hughes

    III. 20th Century American Literature—Ray Bradbury, James Baldwin, Gwendolyn Brooks

    IV. Latin American Literature—Polyglossic (or multi-voiced) literary techniques

    A. I, II, III, and IV

    B. II and IV only

    C. II, III, and IV only

    D. IV only

Read the passage below from *The Scarlet Letter* by Nathaniel Hawthorne; then answer the question that follows.

> Before this ugly edifice, and between it and the wheal-track of the street, was a grass-plot, much overgrown with burdock, pig-weed, apple-pern, and such unsightly vegetation, which evidently found something congenial in the soil that had so early borne the black flower of civilized society, a prison. But on one side of the portal, and rooted almost at the threshold, was a wild rose-bush, covered, in this month of June, with its delicate gems, which might be imagined to offer their fragrance and fragile beauty to the prisoner as he went in, and to the condemned criminal as he came forth to his doom, in token that the deep heart of Nature could pity and be kind to him.

15. Which of the following statements is most accurately supported by a formalist (or textual) analysis of this passage?

    A. Nathaniel Hawthorne believed prisons were an evil creation of society.

    B. The passage uses natural imagery to highlight society's hypocrisy and heartlessness.

    C. Nathaniel Hawthorne enjoyed describing nature.

    D. Nature is used allegorically in *The Scarlet Letter* to represent political and religious struggles in the mid 1800s.

Read the following excerpt; then answer the question that follows.

> HOG Butcher for the World,
> Tool Maker, Stacker of Wheat,
> Player with Railroads and the Nation's Freight Handler;
> Stormy, husky, brawling,
> City of the Big Shoulders:

16. This excerpt from Carl Sandburg's poem "Chicago" uses direct and simple language to depict the city in what way?

    A. As a dirty and nasty place

    B. As a powerful and proud place

    C. As a complicated and cultured place

    D. As a tired and weak place

17. When composing a speech, an author should take which of the following into consideration?

    I. Audience
    II. Purpose
    III. Subject
    IV. Duration or Time

A. I, II, and III only
B. I, II, III, and IV
C. I and III only
D. I, III, and IV only

18. Which of the following is a prewriting activity?

    I. Interviewing
    II. Thinking
    III. Outlining
    IV. Annotating

A. III only
B. II and III only
C. I, II, III, only
D. I, II, III, and IV

19. A thesis statement should do which of the following?

    I. Take a stand on an issue.
    II. Narrow the topic to an appropriate size
    III. Justify its value
    IV. Be supportable by evidence

A. I only
B. I and III only
C. I, III, and IV only
D. I, II, III, and IV

20. The U.S. Constitution breaks the government into three branches in order to

 A. prevent the consolidation of power
 B. create a system of checks and balances
 C. help insure that laws are not enacted impetuously
 D. All of the above

Read the passage below; then answer the question that follows.

The Emancipation Proclamation announced the ruin of the southern economy —as at its crux lay the practice of slavery. With little money left over after the Civil War, the southern economy was crippled. Many southerners headed west in the search of new jobs.

21. Information presented in the passage above can best be used to illustrate which of the following periods in American history?

 A. The Progressive Era
 B. The Reconstruction
 C. The Gilded Age
 D. The New Deal

22. The highest levels of biodiversity in the world are found in

 A. wetlands
 B. the Nile River Valley
 C. temperate zones
 D. the Amazon River Valley

23. Which of the following best describes the "domino theory"?

 A. The support of anticommunist governments through weapons and covert military operations
 B. Direct military intervention to prevent the spread of communism in a region
 C. The rooting out of communists in American government
 D. Use of sanctions and propaganda to suppress communist sympathizing

24. During her reign, what did Queen Elizabeth I of England value above all else?

   A. Political unity over religious unity
   B. Catholicism and the Church
   C. Religious unity over political unity
   D. Alliance with the Holy Roman Empire

25. Which of the following most accurately describes an important geographic feature of a major region of Massachusetts?

   A. The state's highest point is found in central Massachusetts.
   B. The coastal region is marked by a number of large bays.
   C. The Connecticut River valley is arid and unfertile.
   D. Cape Cod and Martha's Vineyard are peninsulas.

26. Which of the following best outlines the chronological progression of a House bill into law?

   A. The bill moves from a House subcommittee, to a Senate floor debate, to the White House, to a congressional conference committee.
   B. The bill moves from a House floor debate, to a House subcommittee, to the White House.
   C. The bill moves from a House subcommittee, to a Senate floor debate, to a congressional conference committee, to the White House.
   D. The bill moves from a House subcommittee, to a House floor debate, to the White House, to a congressional conference committee.

27. What percentage of the Earth's surface is covered by the four major oceans?

   A. 25%
   B. 50%
   C. 60%
   D. 71%

28. Which of the following are examples of physical geographic concepts?

 A. Place and climate
 B. Migration and sea level
 C. Diffusion and migration
 D. All of the above

29. Which of the following resulted from an American belief in Manifest Destiny?

 A. The revolutionary war
 B. Coerced treaties with native groups
 C. Isolationism
 D. Settlement of territories west of the Mississippi River

30. How is the President most directly involved in the making of a law?

 A. The President introduces ideas that he desires to become law.
 B. The President campaigns to win popular support of new laws.
 C. The President participates in congressional debate.
 D. The President signs a bill into law or vetoes a bill.

31. Epic poetry, emphasis on games, sportsmanship and physical prowess, and the world's first democracy best describes the contributions made by

 A. Sumeria
 B. Assyria
 C. Greece
 D. Rome

32. Which of the following best describes an important relationship between physical geography and patterns of human history?

 A. Migrating peoples have tended to settle on the banks of rivers and oceans.
 B. Oceans have prevented the spread of biodiversity among continents.
 C. Disease is restricted by geographic region.
 D. The majority of the world's population has lived in tropical climates.

42. Intending to test a hypothesis about plant growth, students design an experiment, collect data, chart this data, and keep notes of their methods so the process can be replicated. This is an example of what type of study?

    A. Theoretical
    B. Philosophical
    C. Logical
    D. Empirical

43. Nucleic acids (DNA and RNA) are primarily responsible for?

    A. Storing, copying, and decoding hereditary information
    B. Storing and decoding hereditary information
    C. Copying hereditary information only
    D. Storing hereditary information only

44. Which of the following is the best description of an organelle?

    A. A small organ
    B. A single-celled organism
    C. A structure within a cell
    D. A structure composed of many cells

45. Which of the major organ systems transports nutrients, gases, hormones, and waste through the body?

    A. The respiratory system
    B. The circulatory system
    C. The transportation system
    D. The digestive system

46. When a bee collects nectar from one flower and then moves to another flower to collect more nectar, the bee is inadvertently helping the flowers by participating in what process?

    A. Seed distribution
    B. Mitosis
    C. Pollination
    D. Meiosis

47. Jellyfish, flatworms, and sponges are best described by which classification?

    A. Kingdom: Animal, Phylum: invertebrate

    B. Superkingdom: Animal, Phylum: vertebrate

    C. Kingdom: Animal, Phylum: vertebrate

    D. Superkingdom: Animal, Phylum: invertebrate

48. Around the time of World War II, the chemical industry developed several new classes of insecticide that were instrumental in protecting our soldiers from pest-borne diseases common to the tropic regions in which they were fighting. These same insecticides found widespread use at home to increase production of many agricultural crops by reducing the damage from insects like cotton weevils and grasshoppers. While farmers continued to use the same levels of insecticide, over time it was found that the insect population was increasing. Identify the best explanation for this observation.

    A. Insecticides, like most chemicals, lose their potency when stored.

    B. The insect population was increasing to reach the carrying capacity of an ecosystem.

    C. The initial doses of pesticide were too low to effectively kill the insects.

    D. Insects with a tolerance to insecticide survived the initial doses and lived to produce insecticide-resistant offspring.

49. Which of the following statements is NOT true?

    A. Heredity is the study of how traits are passed from parent to offspring.

    B. The chemical molecule that carries an organism's genetic makeup is called DNA.

    C. Sections of DNA that determine specific traits are called chromosomes.

    D. The genetic makeup of an organism is altered through bioengineering.

50. Which of the following sources of energy is nonrenewable?

    A. Hydrogen-cell
    B. Nuclear
    C. Geothermal
    D. Hydroelectric

51. To move a heavy book across a tabletop at a constant speed, a person must continually exert a force on the book. This force is primarily used to overcome which of the following forces?

    A. The force of gravity
    B. The force of air resistance
    C. The force of friction
    D. The weight of the book

52. The Earth's moon is

    A. generally closer to the Sun than it is to the Earth
    B. generally closer to the Earth than to the Sun
    C. generally equidistant between the Earth and Sun
    D. closer to the Earth during part of the year, and closer to the Sun for the rest of the year

53. Which of the following statements is NOT true?

    A. Cancers and hereditary diseases can be infectious.
    B. Infectious diseases are caused by viruses, bacteria, or protists.
    C. Environmental hazards can cause disease.
    D. The immune system protects the body from disease.

54. Which of the following types of pollution or atmospheric phenomena are correctly matched with their underlying causes?

    I. Global warming-carbon dioxide and methane

    II. Acid rain-sulfur dioxide and nitrogen dioxide

    III. Ozone depletion-chlorofluorocarbons and sunlight

    IV. Aurora borealis-solar flares and magnetism

    A. I and II only

    B. II and III only

    C. I and IV only

    D. I, II, III, and IV

55. Which of the following statements best describes the process of metamorphosis?

    A. A mammalian fetus grows in its mother's womb.

    B. A human progresses through puberty.

    C. A caterpillar grows into a chrysalis.

    D. A snake molts, or sheds its skin, when growing.

Directions for the Open-Response Item Assignment

This section of the test consists of one open-response item assignment that appears on the following page. You will be asked to prepare a written response of approximately 150 to 300 words (1 to 2 pages) for this assignment.

For each assignment, read the topic and directions carefully before you begin to work. Think about how you will organize your response.

As a whole, your response to the assignment must demonstrate an understanding of the knowledge of the field. In your response to each assignment, you are expected to demonstrate the depth of your understanding of the subject area by applying your knowledge rather than by merely reciting factual information.

Your response to the assignment will be evaluated based on the following criteria:

- **PURPOSE:** the extent to which the response achieves the purpose of the assignment
- **SUBJECT KNOWLEDGE:** appropriateness and accuracy in the application of subject knowledge
- **SUPPORT:** quality and relevance of supporting evidence
- **RATIONALE:** soundness of argument and degree of understanding of the subject area

The open-response item assignment is intended to assess subject knowledge. Your response must be communicated clearly enough to permit valid judgment of the evaluation criteria by scorers. Your response should be written for an audience of educators in this field. The final version of your response should conform to the conventions of edited American English. Your responses should be your original work, written in your own words, and not copied or paraphrased from some other work.

Be sure to write about the assigned topics. Please write legibly. You may not use any reference materials during the test. Remember to review your work and make any changes you think will improve your response.

Open-Response Assignment

Read the information below; then complete the exercise that follows.

The study of different genres enables students to compare and contrast different types of literature. Although the myths within different cultures appear unique on the surface, most have common elements and themes.

- Choose one type of myth from a variety of cultures and describe its common elements and themes.
- Use this information to write a simple one page myth of the type you choose.
- Describe the prerequisite skills necessary to fulfill the tasks above.

ANSWER SHEET FOR PRACTICE TEST 2 MATHEMATICS SUBTEST

1	______	10	______	19	______	28	______	37	______
2	______	11	______	20	______	29	______	38	______
3	______	12	______	21	______	30	______	39	______
4	______	13	______	22	______	31	______	40	______
5	______	14	______	23	______	32	______	41	______
6	______	15	______	24	______	33	______	42	______
7	______	16	______	25	______	34	______	43	______
8	______	17	______	26	______	35	______	44	______
9	______	18	______	27	______	36	______	45	______

ANSWER SHEET FOR OPEN-RESPONSE QUESTION PRACTICE TEST 2 MATHEMATICS SUBTEST

ANSWER SHEET FOR OPEN-RESPONSE QUESTION PRACTICE TEST 2 MATHEMATICS SUBTEST

PRACTICE TEST 2
MATHEMATICS SUBTEST

1. How would you express the number 127.3 in scientific notation?

   A. 1.273

   B. 1.273×10^{-2}

   C. 1.273×10^{2}

   D. 12.7

2. Round 4,358,765 to the nearest thousand.

   A. 4,358,800

   B. 4,330,000

   C. 4,358,700

   D. 4,359,000

3. Emily is sharing a pie with her mom and dad. If her mom eats a quarter of the pie, and Emily eats an eighth of the pie, how much pie is left for Emily's dad?

   A. $\frac{3}{8}$

   B. $\frac{1}{4}$

   C. $\frac{5}{8}$

   D. $\frac{1}{2}$

4. If Mary buys 3.5 pounds of ham, 2.25 pounds of turkey, and 2.5 pounds of roast beef, how much meat does Mary have?

   A. 8.25 pounds

   B. 7.25 pounds

   C. 7.5 pounds

   D. 8 pounds

5. 520 people at the mall voted on their favorite flavor of ice cream. If chocolate got 60% of the vote, how many people voted for chocolate?

   A. 86

   B. 300

   C. 208

   D. 312

6. How would you express 72% as a fraction?

   A. $\frac{3}{4}$

   B. $\frac{18}{25}$

   C. $\frac{100}{72}$

   D. $\frac{36}{72}$

7. How would you express $\frac{45}{95}$ as a percent (nearest integer)?

   A. 2.11%

   B. 21%

   C. 47%

   D. 45%

8. Which of the following numbers is *not* prime?

   A. 15

   B. 17

   C. 29

   D. 2

9. What is the prime factorization of the number 36?

A. $3^2 \times 4$

B. $2^3 \times 3$

C. 3^3

D. $3^2 \times 2^2$

10. Which of the following numbers is *not* divisible by 9?

A. 273

B. 5,463

C. 6,021

D. 72,045

11. What is the least common multiple of 2, 7, and 12?

A. 168

B. 84

C. 42

D. 21

12. What is the greatest common factor of 8, 36, and 48?

A. 4

B. 8

C. 9

D. 92

13. $3^7 \div 3^5 =$

A. 531,441

B. 6

C. 9

D. –9

14. $56 - |-8| =$

A. 48

B. 64

C. –48

D. 7

15. Solve the equation for x. $5x - 12 = 3x - 4$

A. $x = 3$

B. $x = -4$

C. $x = 8$

D. $x = 4$

16. Fill in the missing numbers in the sequence: –12, –6, __, __, 12, 18

A. –3, 3

B. 0, 6

C. 0, 3

D. 3, 6

17. What is the slope of the line $4y = 16x + 8$?

A. 12

B. 8

C. 16

D. 4

18. The regular price of a new jacket is p dollars. The jacket is on sale for 30% off. What expression would you write to indicate the sale price of the jacket?

A. $p - 0.3$

B. $1.3p$

C. $0.7p$

D. $0.3p$

19. Which of the following is a point on the line $3y = 2x - 12$?

A. (3, 12)
B. (0, –4)
C. (3, 2)
D. (–12, 2)

20. If x varies **directly** with y, then as x goes up, y will

A. go up
B. go down
C. stay the same
D. Insufficient information to answer the question.

21. Ted is sitting on his front steps, watching cars drive by on his street. He counts 24 black cars, 6 silver cars, 10 blue cars, and 15 cars of other colors. Of the cars Ted counted, what is the ratio of black cars to silver cars?

A. 24: 31
B. 4:1
C. 24:55
D. 1:4

22. A mile is 5,280 feet. How many yards are in a mile?

A. 63,360 yards
B. 440 yards
C. 15,840 yards
D. 1,760 yards

23. If side a of a parallelogram is 10 inches, and side b is 6 inches, what is the perimeter of the parallelogram?

A. 60 square inches
B. 32 inches
C. 16 inches
D. 60 inches

24. If a rectangular prism is 6 inches wide, 4 inches tall, and 3 inches deep, what is the volume of the prism?

A. 24 square inches

B. 26 cubic inches

C. 72 cubic inches

D. 13 square inches

25. How many minutes are in one week?

A. 604,800 minutes

B. 2,880 minutes

C. 1,440 minutes

D. 10,080 minutes

26. If you take a small sponge and drop it into some water, and it grows into a larger sponge of the same shape and proportions, this illustrates the concept of

A. dilation

B. symmetry

C. translation

D. reflection

27. If a triangle has an angle of 90 degrees and an angle of 45 degrees, how many degrees is the third angle?

A. 90 degrees

B. 45 degrees

C. 60 degrees

D. Insufficient information to answer the question.

28. Five students took a math test. Their scores were 98, 89, 75, 82, and 92. What was the average (mean) score?

A. 89

B. 90

C. 86.5

D. 87.2

29. If you roll two 6-sided dice, what is the probability that you will roll a combination that adds up to exactly 5?

    A. 1 out of 12
    B. 1 out of 6
    C. 1 out of 9
    D. 1 out of 18

30. Again, you roll two 6-sided dice. What is the probability that you throw snake-eyes (1 and 1)?

    A. 1 out of 36
    B. 2 out of 36
    C. 1 out of 6
    D. 1 out of 9

31 Divide 8.2 by 0.05.

    A. 1.64
    B. 164
    C. 16.4
    D. .164

32. The number 14 is approximately 22% of which of the following numbers?

    A. 56
    B. 60
    C. 308
    D. 64

33. Simplify to a single term in scientific notation.

$$(2 \times 10^3) \times (6 \times 10^4)$$

    A. 12×10^7
    B. 12×10^{12}
    C. 1.2×10^8
    D. 1.2×10^{12}

34. A red rose bush is 39 inches tall and a yellow rose bush is $36\frac{3}{4}$ inches tall. The red rose bush is growing at a rate of $\frac{1}{2}$ of an inch per week, and the yellow rose bush is growing at a rate of $\frac{3}{4}$ of an inch per week. How long will it be before they are the same height?

A. 6 weeks

B. 8 weeks

C. 9 weeks

D. 12 weeks

35. You have a square piece of paper that has a perimeter of 20 cm. What is the area of the paper?

A. 400 square cm

B. 25 square cm

C. 16 square cm

D. 24 square cm

36. What is the approximate volume of the following cylinder? Use 3.14 as an approximation for pi.

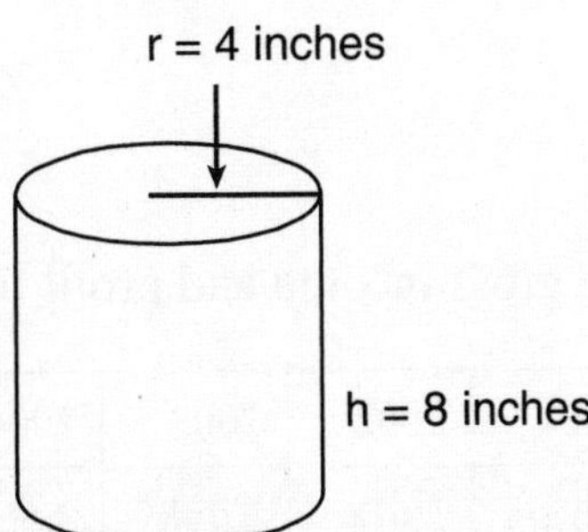

A. 401.92 cubic inches

B. 3215.36 cubic inches

C. 37.68 cubic inches

D. 100.48 cubic inches

37. Use the figure given to answer the question that follows. Assume that AD is a line.

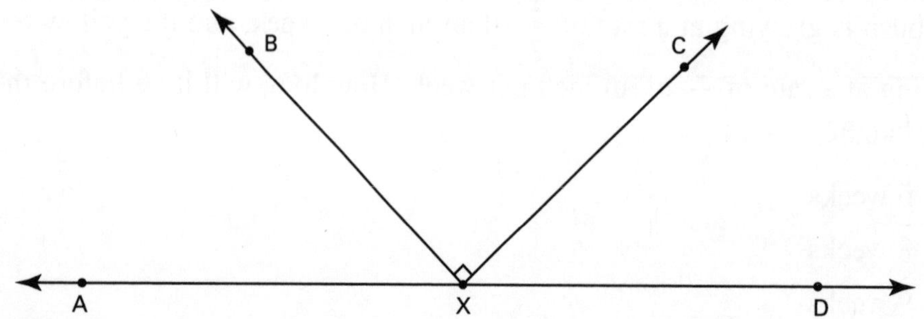

What is the sum of angle AXB and angle CXD?

A. 45°

B. 90°

C. 180°

D. There is not enough information to answer the question.

38. A bag contains 9 red marbles, 7 blue marbles, and 8 white marbles. Without looking at the color, you choose one marble from the bag. What is the approximate likelihood that the marble is white?

A. 50%

B. 38%

C. 33%

D. 29%

39. The following table lists the gross income and profit for the Bailey Company.

Year	2000	2001	2002	2003	2004	2005	2006
Gross Income	1,315	1,625	2,018	2,758	3,566	4,459	5,034
Profit	143	172	222	1,327	1,464	1,562	2,709

In which year was the difference between gross income and profit the greatest?

A. 2001

B. 2003

C. 2005

D. 2006

40. Camille bought a bracelet from her favorite store. The price of the bracelet was \$31.99, and sales tax was 6.5%. She gave the cashier \$35.00. How much change did Camille receive?

A. \$0.93

B. \$0.78

C. \$1.12

D. \$1.03

41. A survey was taken to determine the amount of time children spent watching TV each day. The results were: 1 hour or less (18.4%), between 1 and 5 hours (68.8%), 5 or more hours (12.8%). If you considered 415 children, about how many would you expect to watch television for 1 hour or less each day?

A. 72

B. 76

C. 80

D. 84

42. Solve for q:

$$\frac{1}{4}q - 9 = 3$$

A. $q = 12$

B. $q = 27$

C. $q = 48$

D. $q = 108$

43. What are the solutions of this equation?

$$3x^2 - 11 = 1$$

A. 2 and –2

B. 3 and –3

C. 4 and –4

D. 1 and –1

44. Solve the following inequality:

$$2(x + 1) \geq 3x - 2$$

A. $x \geq 2$

B. $x \geq 4$

C. $x \leq 2$

D. $x \leq 4$

45. Which equation could be used to solve the following problem?

"Three consecutive even numbers add up to 156. What are they?"

A. $x + (x + 2) + (x + 4) = 156$

B. $2x + 4x + 6x = 156$

C. $x + x + x = 156$

D. $x + (x + 1) + (x + 2) = 156$

Directions for the Open-Response Item Assignment

This section of the test consists of one open-response item assignment that appears on the following page. You will be asked to prepare a written response of approximately 150 to 300 words (1 to 2 pages) for this assignment.

For each assignment, read the topic and directions carefully before you begin to work. Think about how you will organize your response.

As a whole, your response to the assignment must demonstrate an understanding of the knowledge of the field. In your response to each assignment, you are expected to demonstrate the depth of your understanding of the subject area by applying your knowledge rather than by merely reciting factual information.

Your response to the assignment will be evaluated based on the following criteria:

- **PURPOSE:** the extent to which the response achieves the purpose of the assignment
- **SUBJECT KNOWLEDGE:** appropriateness and accuracy in the application of subject knowledge

- **SUPPORT:** quality and relevance of supporting evidence
- **RATIONALE:** soundness of argument and degree of understanding of the subject area

The open-response item assignment is intended to assess subject knowledge. Your response must be communicated clearly enough to permit valid judgment of the evaluation criteria by scorers. Your response should be written for an audience of educators in this field. The final version of your response should conform to the conventions of edited American English. Your responses should be your original work, written in your own words, and not copied or paraphrased from some other work.

Be sure to write about the assigned topics. Please write legibly. You may not use any reference materials during the test. Remember to review your work and make any changes you think will improve your response.

Open-Response Assignment

Use the information provided below to complete the exercise.

Carlos is planning to take the 8:45 a.m. train into the city. He wants to jog for $\frac{1}{2}$ hour, take a shower (15 minutes), stop and get coffee (10 minutes), and eat breakfast ($\frac{1}{3}$ hour). For what time should he set his alarm? It takes him 20 minutes to drive to the station.

Use your knowledge of math to create a response in which you analyze and solve this problem. In your response you should provide an alternative solution to the problem.

ANSWER KEY—PRACTICE TEST 2
MULTI-SUBJECT SUBTEST

Question	Answer	Objectives
1	B	01–05
2	A	01–05
3	D	01–05
4	B	01–05
5	C	01–05
6	C	01–05
7	D	01–05
8	B	01–05
9	D	01–05
10	A	01–05
11	B	01–05
12	D	01–05
13	C	01–05
14	A	01–05
15	B	01–05
16	B	01–05
17	B	01–05
18	D	01–05
19	D	01–05
20	D	06–09
21	B	06–09
22	D	06–09
23	B	06–09
24	A	06–09

Question	Answer	Objectives
25	B	06–09
26	C	06–09
27	D	06–09
28	A	06–09
29	D	06–09
30	D	06–09
31	C	06–09
32	A	06–09
33	C	06–09
34	B	06–09
35	C	06–09
36	D	06–09
37	A	06–09
38	B	06–09
39	D	10–14
40	A	10–14
41	B	10–14
42	D	10–14
43	A	10–14
44	C	10–14
45	B	10–14
46	C	10–14
47	A	10–14
48	D	10–14
49	C	10–14
50	B	10–14

Question	Answer	Objectives
51	C	10–14
52	B	10–14
53	A	10–14
54	D	10–14
55	C	10–14

PROGRESS CHART— PRACTICE TEST 2 MULTI-SUBJECT SUBTEST

Objectives 01–05: Language Arts —/19

1	2	3	4	5	6	7	8	9	10	11	12

13	14	15	16	17	18	19

Objectives 06–09: History and Social Science —/18

20	21	22	23	24	25	26	27	28	29	30	31

32	33	34	35	36	37	38

Objectives 10–14: Science and Technology/Engineering —/18

39	40	42	43	44	45	46	47	48	49	50

51	52	53	54	55

OPEN–RESPONSE QUESTION

Objective 015: Integration of Knowledge and Understanding

DETAILED EXPLANATIONS FOR PRACTICE TEST 2 MULTI-SUBJECT SUBTEST

1. **B.**

While the novel does contain some violent scenes, none of them is graphic enough to be considered unsuitable for young readers. The novel did challenge some attitudes toward race, however, because it portrayed a close fellowship between two people of different races and showed a young white man's willingness to take risks on behalf of a black man's freedom. It also frankly uses derogatory vocabulary considered offensive today.

2. **A.**

Haiku are by definition too short to contain elaborate descriptions. The haiku form does not emphasize logic or direct statements. Traditionally, haiku poems consist of three short lines and include references to nature.

3. **D.**

All of these themes have been emphasized in the works of Chinua Achebe, among other writers of world literature.

4. **B.**

Both *ante* and *pre* mean before, so B is correct.

5. **C.**

A metaphor is a comparison between two items without the use of *like* or *as*. In the proverb, death is called a black camel. A simile is a comparison that uses like or as. Alliteration is the repletion of a consonant sound, and hyperbole is an exaggeration.

6. **C.**

A phrase is often thought of as a small group of words; however, this is an incomplete definition. In fact, a phrase can be long. Independent clauses do contain complete thoughts, but dependent clauses do not—they depend on other parts of a sentence to express their full meaning. All clauses contain a subject and a predicate—phrases do not.

7. **D.**

Blank verse is unrhymed, but uses an iambic pentameter for its meter. Free verse does not use any specific meter and may be rhymed or unrhymed.

8. **B.**

A malapropism is a misuse (often humorous) of a word or the distortion of a word. A malapropism does not have anything to do with saying something inappropriate. If the misuse of a word results in an inappropriate comment, it is sometimes called a "Freudian slip."

9. **D.**

Fantasy can be very engaging and an effective teaching tool because it allows students to experiment with vivid language, exposes students to new situations, and encourages creative thinking.

10. **A.**

Editorializing is giving an opinion about an occurrence or an issue. Choices B and C are factual statements. Choice D is a straightforward question. Choice A's use of the words "extremely likable" and "well-deserved" illustrates editorializing because it provides the writer's opinion about Mr. McGee and his speech. Another author might not find Mr. McGee to be "extremely likable" and may conclude that the applause was perfunctory.

11. **B.**

Language is in a state of flux and always will be, no matter how much people try to impede its changes. Whether one views this state of flux as progress or as regression, language change is nonetheless a natural part of life and of history. Dictionaries reflect these fluctuations as they are constantly updated and revised.

12. **D.**

A period, a question mark, or an exclamation point can all be used to end sentences in formal writing. The exclamation mark, however, should not be overused. An ellipsis is often used in informal writing at the end of a sentence to show that a thought is trailing off or is incomplete, but in formal writing thoughts should not be incomplete or trail off.

13. **C.**

Item IV is the only correct answer. Jonathan Edwards was a preacher, but he used fiery language intended to frighten his parishioners into doing right by God. Walt Whitman was a very innovative poet who wrote on quotidian themes. The novelist William Faulkner is perhaps best known for his involved and rich descriptions of southern life.

14. **A.**

All four pairs are correct.

15. **B.**

The line "the black flower of civilized society, a prison" uses the negative connotations of *dark* to set up an ironical reading of the word "civilized." In such a reading, a society that builds prisons is not civilized. Thus, the imagery is used to point to our society's hypocrisy. Nature, symbolized by the odiferous red rose bush, is more capable of "pity" and is thus more civilized than society. Answers A and C, although possibly accurate statements about Hawthorne, are not examples of formalism because they focus on the author and not the text. Answer D is incorrect because allegory refers to a specific form of extended metaphor in which multiple aspects of a text work together to comment on something in the world of the author.

16. **B.**

Sandburg does not shy away from the fact that Chicago is dirty, dangerous, and even corrupt, but he still describes it in this passage as being strong, powerful, productive, and proud. As the "City of the Big Shoulders" it can carry the rest of the nation.

17. **B.**

A speechwriter should take all of these important rhetorical elements into consideration.

18. **D.**

Any activity that the writer does before writing the first draft is termed *prewriting*. Prewriting includes: thinking, brainstorming, jotting notes, talking with others, interviewing experts, researching in the library or online, gathering and assessing information, listing, mapping, charting, webbing, outlining, and organizing information. Rereading, marking-up, and annotating a text that is the focus of analysis is prewriting.

19. **D.**

A thesis statement should contain all of the listed elements.

20. **D.**

All three of answers are correct. Each answer speaks to one of the central tenets of the U.S. Constitution—power must be distributed to ensure a well functioning government.

21. **B.**

The period of time directly following the Civil War is known as reconstruction because the entire nation needed, in a sense, to be reconstructed. In the south, specifically, the economy needed to be redeveloped and the infrastructure needed to be improved. Moreover, the entire ethos of America needed to be reconstructed or put back together following the protracted and bloody dispute over the South's attempt at secession.

22. **D.**

The Amazon River Valley is the most biodiverse region in the world.

23. **B.**

Similar to "containment," the domino theory posited that if one country in a region fell to communism, surrounding countries would then topple like dominoes. This theory was used as justification for U.S. intervention in much of the world, including the Vietnam War (1964–1975).

24. **A.**

In England, Queen Elizabeth I (r. 1558–1603) valued political unity and stability over religious unity and harmony, imposing upon the Anglican Church a strictly controlled system. Elizabeth's rule was a success on both the domestic and foreign fronts.

25. **B.**

Massachusetts gets its nickname, the "Bay State," from the large number of bays that mark its coastline.

26. **C.**

There are numerous steps involved in enacting a law. Answer C does not list every step, but the steps listed are in the proper chronological order.

27. **D.**

The oceans cover approximately 71 percent of the Earth. The oceans are so vast that large areas, especially the deepest sections, have yet to be thoroughly explored.

28. **A.**

Geographic concepts can be separated into two categories: physical and social. Physical geography includes knowledge of place (capitals and countries), physical features (mountains and rivers), and climate (global warming and rainfall). Social geography involves considering how humans interact with their environment.

29. **D.**

Although migration westward eventually led to the signing of treatise with many native groups, Manifest Destiny directly lead to the settlement of westward territories.

30. **D.**

The president is most directly involved in the legislative process by signing bills into law or vetoing bills. The president is able to influence the writing of laws, but this is not his primary role as defined by the Constitution.

31. **C.**

Of pivotal importance in Western history is the rise of ancient Greek civilization, beginning with the conquest by Alexander the Great in the 4th century B.C.E. of much of the former territory of the previous Middle Eastern empires. This led to the spread of Greek culture and language. Ancient Greek culture and learning has had an enduring influence on western development in many areas: the sciences, philosophy, scholarship, political thought, games and sportsmanship, along with lasting literary contributions, notably the epic poems of Homer.

32. **A.**

Waterways have always provided a means of transportation, aided in commerce, and provided a food source for populations. For these reasons, people have tended to settle near waterways.

33. **C.**

Towns, not cities, in Massachusetts are governed by town meetings, a system that allows citizens direct participation in the democratic process, including ratification of local budgets and the enactment of local ordinances.

34. **B.**

Boycotts, sit-ins, and freedom rides are all forms of non-violent civil protest used during the civil rights movement.

35. **C.**

At the outbreak of the Civil War, both the Union and the Confederacy controlled desirable advantages. The Northern states had a larger population and greater control of factories, industries, and railroads. On the other hand, the Southern states were defending territory largely unfamiliar to Union forces.

36. **D.**

Between 1938 and 1941, America provided aid to the Allied forces as they fought against the advancing fascist armies of the Axis powers, but U.S. troops were not involved in either campaign because many Americans and politicians supported isolationism. Not until after the events of December 7, 1941, when Japanese fighter planes attacked Pearl Harbor, did President Roosevelt lead America directly into the war.

37. **A.**

The invention of the printing press is considered by many historians to be the single most influential social development in the history of the world. Once information could be printed quickly and cheaply, knowledge was no longer the possession of the privileged few.

38. **B.**

Sparked in large part by the assassination of the heir to the throne of Austria-Hungary, World War I soon claimed the lives of millions. In addition, in countries such as Great Britain and Germany, the immense scale of the war meant that for the first time, enlisted men from all walks of life—not only professional soldiers—became casualties of war.

39. **D.**

The Earth is composed of a 15 tectonic plates. These plates are constantly in motion, although they move very slowly. When two plates push against each other, mountains are often formed. When plates pull away from each other, the molten matter below the plates is able to bubble to the surface. It is in such area, also known as "hot spots," where volcanoes most often form.

40. **A.**

The ozone layer, which absorbs the Sun's damaging ultraviolet radiation, is found in the troposphere.

41. **B.**

Weather refers to atmospheric occurrences as they occur on a day-to-day basis. Climate refers to the atmospheric characteristics in a region. For example: the climate of America's southeast region is warm and dry whereas the climate of America's Northeast region is cool and damp.

42. **D.**

An empirical study is based on observation and tends to employ the scientific method.

43. **A.**

DNA carries (or stores) the genetic code for each organism. RNA has many functions in the cell: messenger RNA (mRNA) makes a temporary copy of genes that is used as a template for protein synthesis, transfer RNA (tRNA) decodes the genetic code, and ribosomal RNA (rRNA) catalyzes the synthesis of proteins.

44. **C.**

Organelles such as the nucleus, ribosomes, and the Golgi apparatus are located within a cell. Organelles such as cell walls and cell membranes provide a shape for the cell. Organelles are not organs like the heart, the stomach, or the liver, which are all complex multicellular structures.

45. **B.**

Primarily composed of the heart, blood vessels, and blood, the circulatory system transports gases such as oxygen, hormones such as insulin, nutrients such as sugar, and waste such as ammonia throughout the body, maintaining an internal balance called homeostasis. There is not a system called the transportation system.

46. **C.**

When bees land on a flower to collect nectar, pollen collects on the legs and body of the bee. When the bee moves to another flower, pollen (gametes) may transfer from its body to the flower's carpel (the structure with in which female gametes are stored), thus pollinating the flower. Less frequently, plant seeds are dispersed through the aid of animals, but a bee is most likely too small to participate in this process. Seeds can be transported by larger animals who eat a plant and then deposit the seeds through their feces.

47. **A.**

These invertebrates are all members of the animal kingdom, which is a member of the superkingdom Eukarya.

48. **D.**

Early doses of pesticide were strong enough to kill most of the insects; only a few survived that, perhaps because of some genetic trait, had a slightly higher tolerance to the poison. When these pesticide-tolerant insects reproduced, they passed the tolerance to their offspring. Higher doses of pesticide are initially effective, but again a few individuals survive with tolerance to that new level. Control of pest populations generally requires access to a variety of pesticides that work through different mechanisms, and which are applied in such a way as to minimize build-up of tolerance in the insect population.

49. **C.**

Genes are the sections of the DNA molecule that determine specific traits.

50. **B.**

Nuclear energy is nonrenewable. Nuclear energy has potential advantages in providing large quantities of energy from a small amount of source material, but the process of radioactive decay is nonreversible.

51. **C.**

The force of friction between the book and the table is the primary force that must be overcome to move the book. An experiment to study these frictional forces could keep all other variables (size and weight of the book, speed of travel) constant while measuring the force needed to move the book using a spring scale. Different experiments could change the surface of the book by covering the book with wax paper, construction paper, or sandpaper.

52. **B.**

The moon is much closer to the Earth than to any other planet or the Sun.

53. **A.**

Diseases caused by viruses, bacteria, fungi, or parasites that invade the body are called infectious diseases. These disease-causing organisms are collectively referred to as germs. Cancers and hereditary diseases are not infectious. For example, you cannot "catch" cancer or diabetes by being in close contact with a person who has one of these diseases.

54. **D.**

All are correctly matched.

55. **C.**

Metamorphosis is a biological process during which an animal, after birth, progresses through several distinctive changes in its body structure through cell growth and differentiation. A butterfly undergoes three metamorphic stages, changing from an egg into a caterpillar, a caterpillar into a pupa or chrysalis, and changing from a chrysalis into a butterfly.

A Strong Sample Response to the Open-Response Assignment

Every culture has myths. But before we describe the common elements of a particular type of myth, we first must define what a myth is. We can define a myth as a story embodying and declaring a pattern of relationships between humanity, some divine nature, other forms of life, and the environment. One type of myth common to just about all world cultures is the creation myth. Each culture's creation myth is a poetic and shared vision of how the world came into being and where humans came from.

We find creation myths among various Native American cultures, African cultures, south Asian cultures, Greco-Roman culture, as well as the cultures of the ancient Middle East in which the Sumerian, Babylonian, and Hebraic are the most popular. Just about all creation myths derive from the oral traditions of these cultures. If we compare different creation myths, we see that most use repetition for emphasis and ease of recall, the use of poetic devices such as alliteration, personification, metaphor and simile, symbolism, and a concern for numbers. It appears that creation myths share several common literary devices. The first choice has some divine being or beings creating order out of a preexisting nothingness or chaos. The second has the world created through some purposeful action by a creator or divine being. Unlike modern scientific thinking in which life occurs through random chemical processes, these ancient myths involve some creator with a plan. The third common theme is the creation of human beings who can mirror the nature of the creator. This is usually the implementation of the creator's plan. In other words, humans mirror the essence of the creator. In the Old Testament, the Hebrew god creates man in his image while in Hindu myths, when a man becomes perfect, he becomes part of the divine source. A final literary device in most creation myths is that the earth is usually created perfect, but something occurs that forces the divine being to make it a place where humans will have to toil so as to survive.

Using some of the themes and devices mentioned above, here is a simple creation myth: At the outskirts of the Milky Way Galaxy existed a small planet, going by the name of "Perfection." It was simple, a place envisioned by the gods that portrayed picturesque qualities. It was a true work of art that boasted immense beauty, a realistic fantasy. It accommodated all the needs of the dazzling creatures that walked upon it.

However, one significant piece of the puzzle was missing. People did not inhabit this planet, and the gods felt lonely because of this lacking aspect of life. To resolve this problem, the gods set up a contest to see who could create the perfect man. This would eventually be known as the greatest competition ever to face this planet.

The God of the Skies, Flufakus, tried to shape a person from his own clouds. But with one touch, the being would drift away. The first attempt was unsuccessful.

The God of Fire, Arsenigus, made a figure out of scorching flames, but Flufakus became overwhelmed with envy. The God of the Skies rained upon the God of Fire's living inferno.

It had come down to the final contestant, the God of Soil, to present his creation. He put together a man comprised of clay, but it remained motionless. The contest took place in the middle of the night; however, the sun, in pity of the God of Soil, ascended to the middle of the sky during nighttime. Suddenly, the clay's flesh somewhat hardened, and as a result, a phenomenal creation of man transpired.

There was a mutual relationship between the gods and their creations. The gods respected man, and man respected the gods. Furthermore, men had power over every creature in the world. They were above everything that surrounded them. The only things above them were the gods, and they accepted this because without gods, they would not be in existence. Now it was true that "Perfection" was absolutely perfect.

Analysis for the Strong Response to the Open-Response Item Assignment

Several important prerequisite skills are needed to accomplish the above task. One has to be able to compare and contrast different types of myths within the genre. One must understand that the creation myth is just one type of myth. Other myths explain natural phenomena as well as different types of human emotions and needs. Also, one needs to understand different types of literary forms when reading myths from different cultures, i.e., the elements of different poetic forms as well as other writing styles. In addition, one must have higher-level thinking skills so as to figure out the common themes among different myths and also how these myths truly represent the different cultures from which the myth derives. Finally, one must be able to apply this knowledge to create an independent piece of literature incorporating some of the common themes discussed in the creation of a myth.

ANSWER KEY—PRACTICE TEST 2 MATHEMATICS SUBTEST

Question	Answer	Objectives
1	C	16–19
2	D	16–19
3	C	16–19
4	A	16–19
5	D	16–19
6	B	16–19
7	C	16–19
8	A	16–19
9	D	16–19
10	A	16–19
11	B	16–19
12	A	16–19
13	C	16–19
14	A	16–19
15	D	20–22
16	B	16–19
17	D	20–22
18	C	20–22
19	B	20–22
20	A	20–22
21	B	20–22
22	D	20–22
23	B	23–24
24	C	23–24

Question	Answer	Objectives
25	D	20–22
26	A	23–24
27	B	23–24
28	D	23–24
29	C	25–26
30	A	25–26
31	B	16–19
32	D	16–19
33	C	16–19
34	C	16–19
35	B	23–24
36	A	23–24
37	B	23–24
38	C	25–26
39	C	25–26
40	A	16–19
41	B	16–19
42	C	20–22
43	A	20–22
44	D	20–22
45	A	20–22

PROGRESS CHART— PRACTICE TEST 2 MATHEMATICS SUBTEST

Objectives 16–19: Numbers and Operations —/21

1	2	3	4	5	6	7	8	9	10	11	12

13	14	15	16	31	32	33	34	40	41

Objectives 20–22: Functions and Algebra —/12

15	17	18	19	20	21	22	25	42	43	44	45

Objectives 23–24: Geometry and Measurement —/8

23	24	26	27	28	35	36	37

Objectives 25–26: Statistics and Probability —/4

29	30	38	39

DETAILED EXPLANATIONS FOR PRACTICE TEST 2 MATHEMATICS SUBTEST

1. **C.**

1.273×10^2. To express a number in scientific notation, move the decimal point to the place where there is one and only one digit to the left of the decimal point. In this case, that place is between the 1 and the 2. Then multiply the number by 10 raised to the power that is the same as the number of places you moved the decimal point. Remember, if you moved the decimal to the left, the power to which you raise the 10 will be positive, but if you moved it to the right, the power will be negative. In this case, we moved the decimal 2 places to the left, so the 10 is raised to the power of 2 (or 10^2). Therefore, the resulting answer is 1.273×10^2.

2. **D.**

4,359,000. When we round numbers to a certain place (in this case, the nearest thousand) we round the digit in that place, and change all the digits to the right of that place to zero. To round to the nearest thousand, we need to look at the digit to the right of the thousands place, which is the hundreds place. In this case, it is a 7. Because 7 is closer to ten than to zero, we round the 8 in the thousands place up to 9, and we change all the digits to the right to zero. The resulting number is 4,359,000.

3. **C.**

$\frac{5}{8}$. Here we know that Mom eats $\frac{1}{4}$ of the pie, and Emily eats $\frac{1}{8}$ of the pie. To find out how much of the pie is left, we need to convert the fractions so that they both have the same denominator. To do this we have to find the lowest common denominator (LCD). In this case, the LCD of 4 and 8 is 8. We can see that 4 and 8 can both go into 8 evenly. So, we convert the fraction of the pie that Mom ate by multiplying it by $\frac{2}{2}$ (which is equal to one). $\frac{1}{4} \times \frac{2}{2} = \frac{2}{8}$. We also need to change the fraction, which represents the original whole pie into eighths. The whole pie is represented as $\frac{8}{8}$. The amount eaten by Mom and Emily is $\frac{2}{8} + \frac{1}{8} = \frac{3}{8}$. We subtract $\frac{3}{8}$ from the whole pie to see how much is left for Dad. $\frac{8}{8} - \frac{3}{8} = \frac{5}{8}$. $\frac{5}{8}$ of the pie is left for Emily's Dad.

4. **A.**

8.25 pounds. This is a simple example of adding decimals together. If you don't have a calculator, the easiest way to do this is to write the numbers on top of each other, and the key is to make sure that the decimal points are all aligned in the amounts added and also in the answer. It is also helpful to write out all the amounts to the same number of decimal points.

$$\begin{array}{r} 3.50 \\ 2.25 \\ +2.50 \\ \hline 8.25 \end{array}$$

5. **D.**

312. In this problem we need to find out, what is 60% of 520? To figure out 60% we multiply .60 × 520. Thus, the answer is 312 people.

6. **B.**

$\frac{18}{25}$. To express 72% as a fraction, first think of "percent" as meaning out of 100. So, 72% can also be expressed as $\frac{72}{100}$. If $\frac{72}{100}$ were an option, it would be correct, however it is not. $\frac{72}{100}$0 can be reduced to its lowest terms by dividing both the numerator and denominator by 4. The resulting fraction is $\frac{18}{25}$.

7. **C.**

47%. To express the fraction $\frac{45}{95}$ as a percent, it's easiest to first convert the fraction into a decimal, and then from a decimal into a percent. To convert $\frac{45}{95}$ into a decimal, simply divide 45 by 95 ≈ .47. To convert .47 to a percent, we multiply by 100, and get 47%.

8. **A.**

15. Fifteen is not a prime number because it has factors other than 1 and itself. 3 × 5 = 15; therefore 15 is not prime.

9. **D.**

$3^2 \times 2^2$. To find the prime factorization of a number, we first split the number into any two factors that we know of. We know 9 × 4 = 36, so our first step is to break 36 into 9 × 4. Next we break down 9 and 4. We know that 3 × 3 = 9, and 2 × 2 = 4.

We have now broken down 36 into all prime numbers, and we have $3 \times 3 \times 2 \times 2$, which can also be expressed as $3^2 \times 2^2$.

10. **A.**

273. You can find this answer without using your calculator by using the math divisibility tricks. To see if a number is divisible by 9, add up all the digits in that number, and if the resulting number is more than one digit, add those digits together. Keep doing this until you have one single digit number. If that number is 9, then the original number is divisible by 9. In this case, you find that the other options (5,463, 6,021 and 72,045) are all divisible by 9, because if you add up the digits of the numbers, the sum is 9. However, if you add together the digits in 273, $2 + 7 + 3 = 12$. $1 + 2 = 3$. Because the single-digit number that you reach is 3, that tells you that 273 is divisible by 3, but not by 9.

11. **B.**

84. To find the least common multiple (LCM) of a set of numbers.

First, figure out the prime factorization of each number. 2 and 7 are both already prime. $12 = 3 \times 2 \times 2$.

Second, for each prime number listed, underline the most repeated occurrence of this number in any of the prime factorizations.

Here, the number 2 appears once in the factorization of 2, but twice in the factorization of 12, so underline the two 2's. The number 7 appears only once, so underline 7, and 3 appears only once, so underline 3. That leaves us with 7, 3, 2, and 2 underlined.

Third, multiply all the underlined numbers. $7 \times 3 \times 2 \times 2 = 84$. So the LCM of 2, 7, and 12 is 84.

12. **A.**

4. To find the greatest common factor (GCF) of a set of low numbers like we have here, the easiest way is to write out all the factors for each number in the set. The factors of 8 are 1, 2, 4 and 8. The factors of 36 are 1, 2, 3, 4, 6, 9, 12, 18 and 36. The factors of 48 are 1, 2, 3, 4, 6, 8, 12, 16, 24 and 48. The GCF is the highest factor that all 3 numbers have in common. In this case, the GCF is 4.

13. **C.**

9. To solve this problem, we need to remember that according to the rules of exponents, when a number raised to an exponent(1) is divided by itself raised to an exponent(2), it is the same as raising the number to the power of exponent(1) minus exponent(2). The rule in mathematical form is $\frac{a^m}{a^n} = a^{m-n}$. Applying the rule to solve this problem, we need to solve $3^{(7-5)} = 3^2 = 9$.

14. **A.**

48. To solve this problem we simply need to remember that absolute value means the distance from zero. So, the absolute value of -8 is 8. We then substitute 8 for $|-8|$ and the problem becomes $56 - 8 = 48$.

15. **D.**

$x = 4$. To solve this equation first we want to put like terms on the same sides of the equal signs. If we subtract $3x$ from both sides, we get $5x - 3x - 12 = -4$. If we then add 12 to both sides, we get $5x - 3x = -4 + 12$. We can simplify this by writing it as $2x = 8$. Then, we divide both sides of the equation by 2, and the result is $x = 4$.

16. **B.**

0, 6. The pattern in the sequence is to add 6 to each number. $-6 + 6$ gives us 0. $0 + 6$ gives us 6.

17. **D.**

4. To figure out the slope of the line, we have to convert the equation into slope-intercept form $y = mx + b$. When the equation is in slope-intercept form, the slope is represented by m. To convert $4y = 16x + 8$ into this form, we need to get the y by itself. To do this, we divide both sides of the equation by 4, giving us $y = 4x + 2$, which is the correct slope-intercept form. In this equation the m, or slope, is 4.

18. **C.**

$0.7p$. To solve this problem, we need to write an expression that means 30% off of p. In other words, the expression must mean 70% of p. We can express 70% as the decimal 0.7 and multiplied by p, we write is $0.7p$.

19. **B.**

$(0, -4)$. The easiest way to answer this question is by using trial and error. Try substituting the x coordinate and the y coordinate for x and y in the equation, and if the equation is true, then it is a point on the line. In this case, substitute 0 for x and -4 for y to get $3(-4) = 2(0) - 12$, or $-12 = -12$. Because this is true, we know that $(0, -4)$ is a point on the line.

20. **A.**

Go up. This is simply a question of vocabulary. If two variables vary *directly*, as one goes up, so will the other.

21. **B.**

4:1. First with this problem, we need to determine which information is relevant. To find the ratio of black cars to silver cars, we only need to know the number of black cars and the number of silver cars, and the rest of the information can be ignored. He counts 24 black cars and 6 silver cars, so the ratio of black cars to silver cars is 24:6. However, we have to reduce the ratio, the same as we would a fraction, so we divide both numbers by 6 to get a ratio of 4:1.

22. **D.**

1,760 yards. To convert 5,280 feet to yards, we need to divide 5,280 by 3, because there are 3 feet in a yard. 5,280 ÷ 3 = 1,760.

23. **B.**

32 inches. We know that a parallelogram is a 4-sided figure, with two sets of equal sides. The problem tells us that one side is 10 inches and one side is 6 inches. From this we can figure out that there must be two sides that are 10 inches, and two sides that are 6 inches. To find the perimeter we add up the lengths of all the sides, so we add 6 + 6 + 10 + 10 to reach the answer of 32 inches.

24. **C.**

72 cubic inches. To find the volume of a rectangular prism we multiply the height × width × depth, and because it's a 3-dimensional figure our answer will be in cubic units. 6 inches times 4 inches times 3 inches, or 6 × 4 × 3 = 72 cubic inches.

25. **D.**

10,080 minutes. To figure out how many minutes are in a week, first figure out how many minutes are in one day, and then multiply it by 7. We know there are 60 minutes in an hour, and 24 hours in a day. 60 × 24 = 1,440 minutes in one day. There are 7 days in a week, so 1,440 × 7 = 10,080 minutes in a week.

26. **A.**

Dilation. This is a question of vocabulary. *Dilation* is the enlargement or expansion of a figure.

27. **B.**

45 degrees. The 3 angles of a triangle always add up to 180 degrees. The two angles we are given, 90 degrees and 45 degrees, add up to 135 degrees. 180 – 135 = 45 degrees.

28. **D.**

87.2. To find the mean score, we add up all the scores and divide by the number of students who took the test. The sum of all the scores is 436. 436 divided by 5 (the number of students who took the test) gives us 87.2.

29. **C.**

1 out of 9.To solve this problem, list all the possible outcomes of throwing 2 dice. There are 36 of them because each die can come up one of six ways. The 36 possibilities are shown below.

Die 1	Die 2	Total
1	1	2
1	2	**3**
1	3	**4**
1	4	**5**
1	5	**6**
1	6	**7**
2	1	**3**
2	2	**4**
2	3	**5**
2	4	**6**
2	5	**7**
2	6	**8**

Die 1	Die 2	Total
3	1	**4**
3	2	**5**
3	3	**6**
3	4	**7**
3	5	**8**
3	6	**9**
4	1	**5**
4	2	**6**
4	3	**7**
4	4	**8**
4	5	**9**
4	6	**10**

Die 1	Die 2	Total
5	1	**6**
5	2	**7**
5	3	**8**
5	4	**9**
5	5	**10**
5	6	**11**
6	1	**7**
6	2	**8**
6	3	**9**
6	4	**10**
6	5	**11**
6	6	**12**

You can see that 4 of the 36 possibilities total 5. Therefore, the probability is $\frac{4}{36}$, which can be reduced to $\frac{1}{9}$, or 1 out of 9.

30. **A.**

1 out of 36. To solve this problem, you can also use the above list of possible outcomes. Of the 36 possible results of throwing 2 dice, only one of those is 1 and 1, or snake eyes, so the probability is 1 out of 36.

31. **B.**

The first step when dividing decimals is to make the divisor appear as a whole number by moving the decimal point to the right. In this problem, move the decimal point in the divisor two places to the right, to make the divisor read 5. Then, move the decimal point in the dividend two places to the right. The dividend now looks like 820. Move the decimal point straight up from the end of the 820 into the same spot in the quotient. Divide normally to reach the answer of 164.

32. **D.**

To solve this problem, you must set up an equation. The easiest way to do so is to write the equation as it is read: 14 = 22%n (with n being the unknown number). Rewrite the 22% as .22, and you have 14 = .22n. Divide both sides by .22 to isolate the unknown number. The result is 63.63, which is approximately 64, thus answer D.

33. **C.**

To solve this problem in scientific notation, simply multiply the first two digits inside each group of parentheses (2 × 6 = 12). To multiply the 10s notations, simply add the exponents ($10^3 \times 10^4$, add the 3 and 4, which results in 10^7). Thus far, the solution reads: 12×10^7. In scientific notation, however, the initial factor must be greater than one and less than ten. Therefore, we change the 12. 12 = 1.2 × 10. This gives us another power of ten, which changes the 10^7 to 10^8. The simplified answer to this problem, therefore, is 1.2×10^8.

34. **C.**

One way to solve this problem is to draw a chart that shows the growth of each rose bush.

Week	**1**	**2**	**3**	**4**	**5**	**6**	**7**	**8**	**9**
Red 39 in.	$39\frac{1}{2}$	40	$40\frac{1}{2}$	41	$41\frac{1}{2}$	42	$42\frac{1}{2}$	43	$43\frac{1}{2}$
Yellow $36\frac{3}{4}$ in.	$37\frac{1}{2}$	$38\frac{1}{4}$	39	$39\frac{3}{4}$	$40\frac{1}{2}$	$41\frac{1}{4}$	42	$42\frac{3}{4}$	$43\frac{1}{2}$

Track the rate of growth of the red rose bush by adding $\frac{1}{2}$ an inch for each week, and do the same for the yellow rose bush at the rate of $\frac{3}{4}$ of an inch per week. On the 9th week, both bushes are the same height, $-43\frac{1}{2}$ inches.

35. **B.**

If a square has a perimeter of 20 centimeters, that means that the length of each side is 5 centimeters. To find the area of a square, multiply the length (5) by the width (5) to reach the answer of 25 square centimeters.

36. **A.**

To find the volume of a cylinder, use the formula $\pi r^2 \times h$. Substitute 3.14 for pi, 4 for *r*, and 8 for *h*.

$3.14 \times 4^2 \times 8 = 3.14 \times 16 \times 8 = 401.92$ cubic inches

37. **B.**

There are two things one must know in order to answer the question. One is the meaning of the small square at the vertex of angle BXC. That symbol tells you that angle BXC is a right angle (which measures 90º). A straight line can be thought of as an angle that measures 180º. This is a straight angle.

In the figure in problem 37, therefore, the sum of the angles AXB, BXC, and CXD is 180°. That means the sum of the measures of angles AXB and CXD is 180° – 90° = 90°.

38 **C.**

To find the likelihood of drawing a white marble, set up a fraction that shows the number of desired outcomes (8 white marbles) over the total possibilities (24 marbles in all).

$\frac{8}{24} = \frac{1}{3}$ or 33%.

39. **C.**

The difference in gross income and profits in the year 2005 was 2,897 (4,459 – 1,562), which is the largest difference of all the years shown.

40. **A.**

To find the amount of tax, multiply the tax rate of 6.5% (.065 in decimal form) by \$31.99, the cost of the bracelet. (.065 × \$31.99 = 2.079, which rounds to \$2.08). Therefore, the total cost of the bracelet with tax is \$34.07. If she paid with \$35.00, subtracting \$34.07 from that amount will give the change she should receive (\$0.93, answer choice A).

41. **B.**

To determine the number of children in the entire sample of 415 that would watch TV for an hour or less, multiply 415 by the percentage in the survey who answered "one hour or less" (18.4%).

$415 \times .184 = 76.36$

Because we cannot have .36 of a person, round the answer to 76, thus answer B.

42. **C.**

To solve this equation for q, first you must isolate the term that contains q. In this example, add 9 to both sides.

$\frac{1}{4}q - 9 = 3$

$\frac{1}{4}q - 9 + 9 = 3 + 9$

Combine like terms: $\frac{1}{4}q = 12$

Multiply both sides by 4 to eliminate the fraction. $(4)\ \frac{1}{4}q = 12\ (4)$

Therefore, $q = 48$ (answer choice C).

43. **A.**

To solve this equation for x, first add 11 to each side, which gives $3x^2 = 12$.

Dividing both sides by 3 gives $x^2 = 4$.

Find the square roots of 4; 2 and –2.

The solutions can be checked by substituting them (one at a time) into the original question to see if they work. In this case, both 2 and –2 do work.

44. **D.**

To solve this inequality, treat it as a typical equation and solve it.

$2(x+1) \geq 3x - 2$

First, use the distributive property to simplify the left side.

$2x + 2 \geq 3x - 2$

To isolate the variable terms, subtract $2x$ from each side.

$2x + 2 - 2x \geq 3x - 2 - 2x$

Combine like terms: $2 \geq x - 2$

Add 2 to both sides to isolate the variable completely: $2+2 \geq x$

The answer currently reads $4 \geq x$. We typically read the expression with the variable first, in which case, we must "flip" the sign. The answer, then, is: $x \leq 4$.

45. **A.**

You know that the correct equation must show three consecutive even numbers being added to give 156. Even numbers are each two apart. Only the three values given in answer A are each two apart.

A Strong Sample Response to the Open-Response Assignment

Carlos needs to set his alarm for 7:10 A.M.

This problem requires us to work backwards from the departure time of 8:45 A.M. We have to be aware that two of the times are given as fractions of an hour ($\frac{1}{2}$ and $\frac{1}{3}$) rather than as a number of minutes. We need to convert these fractions to minutes to solve the problem. There are 60 minutes in an hour, so we divide 60 by 2 to find there are 30 minutes in a $\frac{1}{2}$ hour. We divide 60 by 3 to find that there are 20 minutes in a $\frac{1}{3}$ of an hour.

Now that we have all of the times listed in minutes, we can now figure out how much time Carlos needs to make the 8:45 A.M. train. We need to add the following: 30 + 15 + 10 + 20 + 20. The sum is 95 minutes. Carlos must set his alarm for 95 minutes before 8:45 A.M. We could look at a clock and count back 95 minutes to figure out what time Carlos needs to set. We would find that the time would be 7:10 A.M.

Another way to solve this problem would be break up the 95 minutes into easier chunks. We know that an hour is 60 minutes so that 95 minutes equals one hour + 35 minutes. We can go back an hour from the required time of 8:45 and get 7:45. Then we'd go back an additional 35 minutes to reach 7:10. To verify that we have the correct answer, we could add the various amounts of time to be sure that we arrive at the train time of 8:45 A.M.

Analysis for the Strong Response to the Open-Response Item Assignment

Purpose. The purpose of the assignment has been achieved. The problem has been solved correctly. The essay states how to solve the problem and doesn't omit any steps of the process.

Subject Matter Knowledge. The writer clearly knows how to solve the problem and is likely to be able to teach this concept to students.

Support. Specific calculations are detailed and explained.

Rationale. The answer is well organized and clear in its interpretation of both the problem in both the original solution as well as the alternative solution.

Index

D

N

O

P

Q

R

T

U

Installing REA's TestWare®

SYSTEM REQUIREMENTS

Pentium 75 MHz (300 MHz recommended) or a higher or compatible processor; Microsoft Windows 98 or later; 64 MB available RAM; Internet Explorer 5.5 or higher.

INSTALLATION

1. Insert the MTEL General Curriculum (03) CD-ROM into the CD-ROM drive.
2. If the installation doesn't begin automatically, from the Start Menu choose the RUN command. When the RUN dialog box appears, type d:\setup (where d is the letter of your CD-ROM drive) at the prompt and click OK.
3. The installation process will begin. A dialog box proposing the directory "C:\Program Files\REA\MTEL_Genl\" will appear. If the name and location are suitable, click OK. If you wish to specify a different name or location, type it in and click OK.
4. Start the MTEL General Curriculum TestWare® application by double-clicking on the icon.

REA's MTEL General Curriculum TestWare® is **EASY** to **LEARN AND USE**. To achieve maximum benefits, we recommend that you take a few minutes to go through the on-screen tutorial on your computer. The "screen buttons" are also explained here to familiarize you with the program.

TECHNICAL SUPPORT

REA's TestWare® is backed by customer and technical support. For questions about **installation or operation of your software**, contact us at:

Research & Education Association
Phone: (732) 819-8880 (9 a.m. to 5 p.m. ET, Monday–Friday)
Fax: (732) 819-8808
Website: *www.rea.com*
E-mail: info@rea.com

Note to Windows XP Users: In order for the TestWare® to function properly, please install and run the application under the same computer administrator-level user account. Installing the TestWare® as one user and running it as another could cause file-access path conflicts.